"Our Famous Guest"

"Our Famous Guest"

Mark Twain in Vienna

CARL DOLMETSCH

The University of Georgia Press   Athens and London

© 1992 by Carl Dolmetsch
All rights reserved
Published by the University of Georgia Press
Athens, Georgia 30602

Mark Twain's previously unpublished words quoted here are © 1992 by Edward J. Willi and Manufacturers Hanover Trust Company as Trustees of the Mark Twain Foundation, which reserves all reproduction and dramatization rights in every medium. Quotation is made with the permission of the University of California Press and Robert H. Hirst, General Editor of the Mark Twain Project. Each quotation is identified by a dagger (†).

The paper in this book meets the guidelines for permanence and durability of the Committee on Production Guidelines for Book Longevity of the Council on Library Resources.

Printed in the United States of America
96 95 94 93 92 C 5 4 3 2 1

Library of Congress Cataloging in Publication Data

Dolmetsch, Carl (Carl Richard), 1924–
"Our famous guest" : Mark Twain in Vienna / Carl Dolmetsch.
p. cm.
Includes bibliographical references and index.
ISBN 0-8203-1458-7 (alk. paper)
1. Twain, Mark, 1835–1910—Journeys—Austria—Vienna. 2. Americans—Austria—Vienna—History—19th century. 3. Authors, American—19th century—Biography. 4. Vienna (Austria)—Social life and customs. 5. Vienna (Austria) in literature. I. Title.
PS1334.D6   1992
818'.403—dc20
[B]
                                                                    91-45834
                                                                    CIP

British Library Cataloging in Publication Data available

Frontispiece: Portrait of Mark Twain by Imperial and Royal Court photographer Adele, Vienna, 1897 (Courtesy Mark Twain Project)

Contents

Preface *vii*

1. Mark Twain and Vienna *1*

2. Wanderjahre *19*

3. Zeitungskrieg! *31*

4. Witness to History *60*

5. "Leschy" *90*

6. "The Most Beautiful Theater in the World" *109*

7. "Choice People" *132*

8. Concerning the "Jew" Mark Twain *160*

9. "Lay Down Your Arms!" *181*

10. The Austrian Edison *198*

11. Home Thoughts *214*

12. Diogenes in Vienna *245*

13. City of Doctors, City of Dreams *261*

14. Auf Wiedersehen! *299*

Appendix A: Mark Twain's Concordia Speech *315*

Appendix B: "American Representation in Austria" *318*

Notes *323*

Bibliography *345*

Index *353*

Preface

nother Mark Twain book? After scores of dissertations, hundreds of books, thousands of articles, not only in English but in every other major and many a minor tongue, is there anything left to be written about America's most written-about author? Reviewing a recent monograph on Samuel L. Clemens's inventions, Doris Grumbach announced it was "time to close down the Mark Twain industry" in academia since everything knowable about Clemens and his literary alter-ego had already been published. Her myopia calls to mind the canard about a backwoods congressman who purportedly proposed closing the United States Patent Office in 1849 because everything discoverable had already been invented. The truth is there remain gaps in our knowledge of Samuel Langhorne Clemens and especially in the literary biography of "Mark Twain," and this book closes one of each. Yet more, it shows America's greatest humorist in a radically different light from any in which he has hitherto appeared.

Conventional wisdom holds that Mark Twain's last two decades (1890–1910) were years of inexorable decline into despair and desolation expressed in mostly inconsequential, unfinished works of inferior quality full of bitter pessimism. This condition, we are told, reflected cumulative incidents of financial reversals, unexpected bereavement, and family illness at a stage of life when most successful men anticipate retiring comfortably in the bosom of an expanding family. According to this assumption, Mark Twain's final phase can only be understood by what might be termed the "Bad Mood Theory," personal misfortune having turned this aging humorist into a misanthropic sour apple, a state of mind that halted his further literary development dead in its tracks.

The more I studied the volumes that began appearing in 1967 from the Mark Twain Papers at Berkeley in the continuing project sponsored by the Center for Editions of American Authors to bring to print Twain's previously unpublished manuscripts, notebooks, and letters, the less satisfied I became with conventional views of the author's last phase. The biographical facts were indisputable. So were his changes in outlook and style. Nevertheless, to infer causation, attributing these changes entirely to personal misfortune, seemed to me grossly oversimplified.

The weltschmerz that characterizes Twain's later writings is too much akin to that also pervading the works of many European authors and of such disparate American voices at the end of the nineteenth century as Ambrose Bierce and Henry Adams to have had an exclusively personal source. Mark Twain in his sixties was obviously responding to and reflecting his changing intellectual milieu to the same degree and in much the same way as he had throughout earlier phases of his uniquely diverse career. If one assumes that Hannibal and the Mighty Mississippi, the Comstock Lode and the Pacific Slope, the Quaker City excursion and Gilded Age Hartford provided Twain the bases for the sunnier major phase of his career, could not the experiences of his protracted hegira in the Old World from 1891 to 1900 have provided stimuli and formative influences on his supposedly uncharacteristic later, darker phase? I resolved to try to find out.

When I was awarded a research grant and sabbatical by the College of William and Mary in 1984 for a project then called "The German-Austrian Sources of the Later Writings of Samuel L. Clemens (Mark Twain)," I did not intend to write a book, let alone one that eventually took thrice as long to research and organize as the period it chronicles. I hoped only to cull enough new material from the Mark Twain Papers in Bancroft Library at the University of California at Berkeley and in Viennese repositories where I planned to work to yield one or two solid articles. This I have done in articles already published in the *Mark Twain Journal* and *Musical America*. But as soon as I started digging, I realized how ill-informed, superficial, and incomplete previous treatments of my subject had been. Here was a story that demanded to be told in full, and nothing less than a book would suffice for its telling. I was all the more convinced of this necessity by the reactions I kept getting from colleagues who were quite knowledgeable about Mark Twain and his works but who raised eyebrows at what I was doing. "Why, I never knew Mark Twain spent so much time in Vienna! Was that of any importance in his writing?" was the general thrust of remarks and queries I had from too many otherwise well-informed (dare I say?) Twainiacs.

Not that Samuel Clemens's Austrian sojourn was ever a secret. Most of his biographers, from Albert Bigelow Paine (1912) onward, have at least mentioned it, but all of them have also given it short shrift, lumping his twenty months in Vienna together with his shorter periods of residence in London, Paris, Berlin, Heidelberg, Florence, Weggis (Switzerland), and Sanna (Sweden) and with his globe-circling tour of the English-speaking southern hemisphere in generalized accounts of his years abroad from 1891 to 1900 as if these various episodes were all of a piece.

My first inkling that the Vienna years might somehow be different from the rest and at least as important to the final phase of Mark Twain's career as his 1895–96 tour through the British southern hemisphere came from Arthur L. Scott's *Mark Twain at Large* (1969), a particularized yet cohesive study of all the American writer's foreign travels and sojourns from the Holy Land excursion in 1867 that provided him the material for his first great success, *The Innocents Abroad* (1869), to his final winter in Bermuda in the weeks just prior to his death. Scott did not filch from other biographers, as most Twain scholars have done, but went directly to such original sources as Twain's unpublished notebooks and letters and to both American and foreign newspapers. His book piqued my curiosity about whether there might be even more such material to be disinterred if one concentrated on a single period or phase of Twain's experience abroad rather than on its whole sweep.

My conjecture was reinforced when I read Howard G. Baetzhold's *Mark Twain and John Bull* (1970), which dwells in detail on Twain's frequent, sporadic sojourns in Great Britain and is a model for anyone studying Twain's experiences outside the United States. If the author's British experiences and associations were formative in his writing of *The Prince and the Pauper* and *A Connecticut Yankee in King Arthur's Court*, among other things, why hadn't anyone studied closely the Austrian experiences of the writer of such works as "Stirring Times in Austria," "Concerning the Jews," and especially the two "Mysterious Stranger" manuscripts that have an Austrian setting?

Three other excellent monographs further persuaded me of the necessity to fill this last major gap in Mark Twain's literary biography. The first was Hamlin Hill's *Mark Twain: God's Fool* (1973), a concentrated biography of the last decade of the writer's life. Hill's book commences with Mark Twain's return to the United States in October 1900, greatly changed in both person and persona, suggesting at least an untold story behind those changes. The other two were critical studies: Sholom J. Kahn's *Mark Twain's "Mysterious Stranger": A Study of the Manuscript Texts* (1978), and William Macnaughton's *Mark Twain's Last Years as a Writer* (1979), both of which give tantalizing indications of the literary as well as biographical importance of Twain's Vienna sojourn without exploring his experiences there in detail.

Louis J. Budd's *Our Mark Twain: The Making of His Public Personality* (1983) gave me some of my first ideas about the direction an investigation of this subject should take. Samuel L. Clemens's true vocation as a writer began when he created a literary character, a pseudonymous mask, a persona, or in Budd's phrase, a "public personality" called "Mark Twain." For almost a half century, from 1863 until 1910, he had so skillfully maintained and so successfully marketed that character that "Mark Twain," not Clemens, remains for us today, in Everett Emerson's words, the "authentic" writer. Having read in Paine that the Viennese press paid an inordinate amount of attention to Mark Twain, a world-renowned celebrity when he lived there, I decided to see what image he presented to the journalists of Vienna and to find out, if I could, how he reacted to their image of him and how it may have affected what he wrote there. What I had in mind was a kind of study in literary cybernetics, so to speak. When I proposed this idea and described my plan separately to two friends and colleagues who had forgotten more about Mark Twain than I ever expected to know— the late Henry Nash Smith, of Berkeley, and Louis J. Budd, of Duke University—they both urged me to pursue it without delay.

Soon after I arrived in Vienna, Thomas A. Tenney, editor of the *Mark Twain Journal*, sent me a photocopy of a postcard in the files he inherited from his predecessor, Cyril Clemens. It had been sent to Mr. Clemens from Vienna in 1955 by a Dr. Karl Stiehl, proposing an article capsulizing a dissertation Stiehl had recently presented at the University of Vienna on Mark Twain's local press coverage during the Clemenses' sojourn there. No such article had ever been published in the *Mark Twain Journal* or elsewhere, as far as I knew, and I had never before seen any reference to this dissertation. Nevertheless, when I received Tenney's reproduction, I rushed to the telephone directory in the slender hope that Dr. Stiehl might yet be alive and still in Vienna. Sure enough, there was a Dr. Karl Stiehl, a secondary school teacher of English living in Vienna's third district. When I phoned he was just out of the hospital, recovering from a serious illness, so I did not meet him until some months later. He told me, however, that a copy of his unpublished 1953 dissertation could be found in the Austrian National Library as well as the university library.

Dr. Stiehl's dissertation was the key I needed to open the magic box. Had it been known and available to American scholars earlier, I am convinced this book (or one like it) would have been written long ago by someone else fluent in German. It propelled me literally years ahead in my research since, using it as a bibliography, I was able in a very short time to locate and photocopy a huge stack of hundreds of Viennese press reports of and numerous interviews with Mark Twain and, in due course, to find dozens more without great difficulty. Correlating these items with Mark Twain's letters and notebooks, both published and unpublished, I began to piece together a coherent and ever-clearer picture, both public and private, of Twain's experiences during his twenty-month stay in Vienna. Working with these three primary sources I could thus compile an almost day-by-day log or calendar of Samuel L. Clemens's life in Vienna from September 27, 1897, until May 26, 1899. This gave me the hitherto obscured biographical context I needed for elucidating the things he wrote in Vienna and Kaltenleutgeben.

The problem I then had to solve was how best to organize my findings to explain and illustrate the relevance, indeed importance, of Mark Twain's Vienna years to American readers who might know little about Vienna and less about the Habsburg Empire and that period of European intellectual and cultural history known by its French name, fin de siècle, roughly stretching from the late 1880s until the very early 1900s. Although I had often visited Vienna, sometimes for long periods, my own knowledge of the city's history, that of the Habsburg Empire, and of the fin de siècle in Central Europe itself, was mainly limited to what I had read in three indispensable books: William M. Johnston's *The Austrian Mind: An Intellectual and Social History, 1848–1938* (1972), Allan Janik and Stephen Toulmin's *Wittgenstein's Vienna* (1973), and Carl E. Schorske's collection of essays, *Fin-De-Siècle Vienna* (1980).

Although Johnston's extraordinarily enlightening analysis in *The Austrian Mind* gave me the theoretical apparatus I needed to categorize and describe the peculiarly Viennese elements I had noticed in Mark Twain's post-1897 writing, I still had to steep myself in local lore. I had to turn myself into a kind of Vienna antiquarian and spend a great deal of time studying the city and its inhabitants in 1897–99 in order to be able to understand the minutiae of Clemens's daily life in the city and to identify long-forgotten or obscure persons with whom he had associated. In effect, I had to try to relive his experiences in Vienna myself.

A straight chronological account, I could see right away, would not suffice. The organizational principle that seemed to work best was a topical one within a loose chronological framework. So, after a brief introductory chapter in which I laid out the map for the road ahead, I started with a summary chronicle of Clemens's travels from June 1891 until the summer of 1897 in Weggis and the arrival and settlement of the Clemens family in Vienna and proceeded to twelve topical chapters, each delineating in turn Mark Twain's involvements with the Viennese press, Austrian politics, Leschetizky and the musical life, Sigmund Schlesinger and the theater, the aristocracy and social (including diplomatic) life, anti-Semitism, Baroness von Suttner's peace movement, Jan Szczepanik's inventions, Kaltenleutgeben, Karl Kraus, Viennese medicine and Freud, and the meeting with the emperor and Twain's departure.

In each of these chapters I discuss one or more related works, both published and unpublished, which Mark Twain was writing or gestating at that time and which reflect the experiences I am describing. Although some of the works I discuss have received little or no previous commentary or exegesis, others, such as "The Man That Corrupted Hadleyburg" and the "Mysterious Stranger" manuscripts, already have an extensive bibliography of criticism. While I am aware of what others have said about the works I discuss, my purpose here has been neither to replicate nor to recapitulate existing scholarly interpretations or engage in critical argument aside from offering a few corrections here and there to prevalent errors of fact. Instead, my aim has been to provide some fresh perspectives to complement existing criticism and, where little or none exists, to provide a basis for further critical explorations.

I have tried consistently to keep the focus on Clemens's experiences and Mark Twain's writings even though, at times, I had to digress a bit to provide background information on persons or events that had a significant role in this story. The temptation to do more of that—to make this as much a book about fin-de-siècle Vienna as about Mark Twain *in* Vienna—was hard to resist. Much fascinating anecdotal material of the sort anyone who reads old newspapers cannot help acquiring simply had to be eliminated.

Another temptation I sidestepped was to write a final summary chapter following the old precept "Tell 'em what you're going to say, say it, then tell 'em what you've said." It seemed to me in this instance that would be overwriting, patronizing, and unnecessarily hortatory. The attentive reader will understand the meaning of the Vienna experience to Mark Twain's late phase without my having to restate the points I make along the way. Furthermore, the story has its own natural ending—the audience with Franz Josef and the Clemenses' departure for London. Anything else would have been superfluous.

Throughout this book I have followed the common practice among Mark Twain's biographers of using "Clemens" to refer to the private person and "Mark Twain" or "Twain," which I know is technically incorrect (since "Mark," in this pseudonym, is not a *first* name nor "Twain" a family name), to refer to the writer or public personality. It isn't always easy to make such a distinction, as I'm sure it wasn't at times for Clemens-Twain either. Nevertheless, I hope the context will make things clear enough to avoid confusing the patient reader.

In the end, I feel disappointment at not having been able to clear up all the ambiguities, problems, and mysteries surrounding Mark Twain's Vienna sojourn. For example, I have been unable to find a "smoking gun" in Mark Twain's relationship with either Sigmund Freud or Karl Kraus. Yet circumstantial evidence convinces me that at least Freud and Twain held converse even if Kraus and Twain may not have. The Twain–Theodor Herzl relationship is also one I have been unable to clarify. And I had hoped when I went to Vienna that I could locate Siegmund Schlesinger's papers and find among them the manuscript drafts of the two plays, *Der Gegenkandidat, oder die Frauen Politiker* (The Opposition Candidate, or Women Politicians) and *Die Goldgräberin* (The Lady Goldminer), on which Twain and Schlesinger collaborated. Schlesinger's papers, like those of many Jewish writers, may have been destroyed by the Nazis in 1938. The manuscripts of Mark Twain's translations of *Bartel Turaser* and *Im Fegefeuer* might one

day be discovered in some New York–area warehouse in the dusty files
of the last Broadway theatrical enterprise that handled them, but, alas,
they also have yet to turn up.

It is also unlikely that either Dr. Stiehl or I have located every item
about Mark Twain in every newspaper and magazine in Vienna between 1897 and 1899, but I doubt that we have missed many important pieces of this puzzle. Let this, nevertheless, serve as an invitation
to others to look for more. Meanwhile, I am content that there is
much more about Mark Twain's Vienna years in this book than either
Samuel L. Clemens or Mark Twain ever knew or that anyone else has
ever known.

The encouragement, expert advice, and help I received at the outset
from Henry Nash Smith, Lou Budd, and Tom Tenney were harbin-
gers of the support, assistance, and cooperation I have since received
from so many individuals and institutions that I almost despair of
being able to acknowledge them all properly or to express my gratitude
sufficiently.

First, I must thank the Committee on Faculty Research of the College of William and Mary in Virginia for a semester grant and two
travel-expense grants that enabled me to go to the fountainhead of all
Twain scholarship, the Mark Twain Papers in Berkeley, to begin my
research and then to Vienna to carry it forward.

My stay in Vienna would have been greatly foreshortened had not
my late lamented friend Harold Jantz and his dear wife, Eleanore,
now of Durham, North Carolina, provided me and my wife affordable
housing in the apartment they then leased in the Austrian metropolis. Their generosity has done as much as any person or institution to
make this book possible.

No researcher could wish for more cooperation and better assistance than I received in Berkeley from Robert Hirst, general editor of
the Mark Twain Project, and from the members of his staff, especially
Paul Machlis and Victor Fischer.

Dr. Peter Nics, of the staff of the Theater Collection in the Austrian
National Library and antiquarian par excellence of Kaltenleutgeben,

was enormously helpful in the early stages of my research in Vienna, thanks partly to the good offices of his former colleague, Stefanie Munsing Winkelbauer. Dr. Nics identified for me the Villa Paulhof (now Sonnenhof), so that I became the first American researcher to see and photograph the house where Mark Twain did so much important writing between May and October 1898.

Dr. Wolfgang Kraus and Frau Trudel Lisey, of the press department of the Vienna City Tourist Board, made helpful recommendations for expert contacts and repositories to investigate in their city, and Dr. Mag. Michael Draxlbauer, of the English and American Institute of the University of Vienna, provided some much-needed assistance with library research. Hilary Holliday, my last graduate assistant at the College of William and Mary, performed the same duties for me, adding her abilities also as a translator of German.

Of necessity, I use a great deal of German in telling this story, but I have tried to translate parenthetically all but the most familiar words and obvious cognates. In this I have had some expert help from my son, Dr. Christopher Dolmetsch, professor of German at Marshall University, whose abilities at rendering idiomatically the difficult, sometimes esoteric prose style of Karl Kraus I greatly appreciate.

Soon after I settled in Vienna in October 1984 I began a collegial correspondence with Prof. Sholom J. Kahn, of the Hebrew University in Jerusalem, the only other person who has made a comprehensive "on the spot" investigation of Mark Twain's Vienna years. Our exchange of letters developed into friendship and resulted in visits that have been tremendously stimulating and valuable to me, providing several critical insights I might otherwise not have had. I look forward eagerly to the published results of the work he now has in progress on Mark Twain in Vienna, extending and complementing this book with his own findings and viewpoints.

Prof. Dr. Johannes Pötzl, of the Vienna Technical University, and Frau Pötzl very kindly received me in their home and allowed me the privilege of examining and quoting from unpublished and previously unknown letters owned by them from Samuel and Olivia Clemens to

Professor Pötzl's grandfather, Eduard Pötzl, the newspaper humorist who was Mark Twain's closest acquaintance in the Viennese literary world.

Several of my German and Austrian colleagues in American literary studies helped me clarify my thinking by inviting me to present guest lectures on various aspects of my work in progress to their students. For such opportunities I am indeed grateful to Prof. Ursula Brumm of the John F. Kennedy Institute of North American Studies at the Free University of Berlin; Winfried Fluck, then of the University of Konstanz (now Berlin); Renate von Bardeleben, Hans Galinsky, and Winfried Herget, all of the University of Mainz; Jürgen Peper and Walter Grünzweig of the University of Graz; and Herbert Foltinek and Waldemar Zacharasiewicz of the University of Vienna. In the United States, Darryl Baskin at Elmira College's Center for Mark Twain Studies at Quarry Farm; Elaine Cheesman, former director of education at the Mark Twain Memorial in Hartford, Connecticut; and Brom Weber of the University of California at Davis deserve my thanks for performing the same service through their invitations to lecture on subjects related to my Vienna research.

To both George McMichael, of California State University at Hayward, whose ability to spot syntactical absurdity I envy, and to Louis J. Budd, of Duke University, Twain expert *sans pareil*, I owe gratitude for picking enough nits in my first draft to save me much embarrassment. My British friends in Vienna, Sue and Ian Murdoch, deserve special thanks for showing me how well-informed readers who are not Twainians might respond to some of this story. For generous advice, critical reactions, and the loan of books I am grateful to my William and Mary colleagues Scott Donaldson, Tom Heacox, Elsa Nettels, and Robert J. Scholnick.

Just as Sam Clemens had his Livy who, he said, "not only edited my works [but] edited me," so I have my patient partner, Joan, my goad and most candid critic who has suffered it all and in whose approval of the results of what at times must have seemed an endless project is my greatest reward and joy.

In sum, consciously or otherwise, many people have had a hand in developing this book, and I can only hope that what they will find in it now will be sufficiently gratifying to provide some recompense for the help they have given me. Yet more, I hope my readers will have as much pleasure from this book as I had in researching and writing it and will, like me, come away from the experience knowing a different Mark Twain from the one they thought they knew before.

"Our Famous Guest"

CHAPTER ONE

Mark Twain and Vienna

arly in September 1897, a good three weeks before his coming, Vienna was aflutter with the news that "the distinguished American humorist" Samuel L. Clemens ("Mark Twain") intended to spend several months in the city. Bookshops quickly sold out their stocks of both the English and German editions of his works, and in intellectual circles his impending visit was a prime topic of conversation. Candidates for certificates in English were advised to cram for examination questions like "What do you know about Mark Twain? Which of his works have you read? Give us an outline of . . . (the work mentioned)." For the moment, Byron, Milton, and even the Bard of Avon were put on a back shelf.

Hardly had he settled at the Hotel Metropole before newspaper interviewers swooped upon him like Stefansplatz pigeons on a dropped chestnut.[1] He had come to their city to study its people, seeking new subjects for stories, Mark Twain told them. That was not at all the reason why Samuel Clemens was in Vienna, but no matter. "Truth is the most valuable thing we have. Let us economize it," the author scrawled on postcards bearing his likeness for Viennese autograph hounds. Here was a case in point. He knew the true reason for his Vienna sojourn—so his daughter could study music there—might be less caressing to civic pride and less likely to ensure that his peregrinations in the Austrian capital would henceforth be fully reported in the press.

Incredible as it might seem to us—at times it must have seemed so to him, too—this former Mississippi steamboatman strolling the Corso amid hand-kissing boulevardiers and heel-clicking hussars, or taking the air on canal bridges traversed by lads in lederhosen, Galician Jews in kaftans, and Croatian housemaids in babushkas, was not merely a tourist but a temporary resident of the imperial city. Does literary history reveal a more incongruous pairing of person and place? Could one imagine, say, Johann Wolfgang von Goethe in Angel's Camp? Could that be more preposterous than the self-styled "Wild Humorist of the Pacific Slope" in the Danube city where what Karl Kraus called "The Last Days of Mankind" were unwittingly being played out at the very moment what this century calls "modern" was being created there? Yet, bizarre as it seems, Clemens and his inseparable literary twin, Mark Twain, lived in or near the Habsburg metropolis from September 1897 until the end of May 1899, a period of his life that has escaped close scrutiny by his numerous biographers.

This odd juxtaposition of Mark Twain and Vienna is best understood by considering, first, the man and his literary persona and, then, the setting wherein, by a set of curious chances, he found himself at the end of the nineteenth century. Clemens was in his sixty-second year when he came to Vienna, a place about as far removed spiritually as well as geographically as one could go from his Missouri origins. As "Mark Twain" for slightly more than half his life, he was already world renowned. Fourteen months earlier he ended a much-publicized globe-circling lecture tour across North America and the Pacific to Australia and New Zealand, Ceylon and India, Mauritius and South Africa, and thence to London to write *Following the Equator*, a book about those travels published soon after his arrival in Vienna.

The major phase of his enormously successful career had ended in 1889 with *A Connecticut Yankee in King Arthur's Court*. Some of his earlier works, notably "The Celebrated Jumping Frog of Calaveras County," *Innocents Abroad*, *The Adventures of Tom Sawyer*, and *The Prince and the Pauper*, were already "classics" in the English-speaking world and had been translated into every major tongue. (Although popular, *The Adventures of Huckleberry Finn* did not achieve "classic" status until

Caricature by Theodor Zasche, *Wiener Luft*, October 17, 1897

well into this century.) If other works, such as *Roughing It* and *Life on the Mississippi*, were somewhat less popular abroad than back home, they were known to a considerable European audience who could read the German editions of Robert Lutz (Stuttgart) if not the untranslated editions published by Bernhard Tauchnitz in Leipzig. *A Tramp Abroad*, describing his sojourn in Germany and Switzerland in 1878 and 1879, was a special favorite in central Europe. In short, wherever there were literate folk in 1897, at least in the Western world, Mark Twain was already a household name, perhaps the most famous American then alive.

The Hannibal lad who realized his ambition of becoming a paddle-wheeler pilot and who fled the Civil War to seek his fortune in the mining camps of the West had fallen almost accidentally into successful authorship by way of the printing trade and newspaper journalism. Early on he had found his métier as a humorist. But he was hardly the ingenuous provincial buffoon he projected in the character "Mark Twain," the homespun, wisecracking raconteur and horse-sense commentator on the passing scene who was unquestionably Sam Clemens's greatest literary creation. Having married into Eastern money and gentility, he joined the Eastern literary establishment, built himself an expensive house in Hartford, and became for nearly twenty years "an immovable fixture among the other rocks of New England."[2] Only figuratively "immovable" if one reflects that, by 1897, Clemens had seen more of his native land and more of the world beyond it than any major American writer before air travel.

By September 1897 he had already spent more than eight years of his life outside the United States and had crossed the Atlantic twenty-two times. For nearly a decade, from June 1891 until October 1900, he lived abroad, mostly in Europe, with only occasional trips home. He was close to fluent in German (though he often tried to conceal it), could read and haltingly speak some French and Italian, and read almost everything that came his way, from the local papers to belles lettres, wherever he happened to be. Although seldom acknowledged, the reality is that Samuel L. Clemens became perforce as much

Photo with facsimile of an autographed aphorism illustrating a brief notice of "Mark Twain in Vienna" by the editor, Vincenz Chiavacci, in *Wiener Bilder*, October 17, 1897 an international cosmopolite as his expatriate contemporary Henry James, whose urbanity is unquestioned.

In contrast to this reality, however, the image of Mark Twain his creator labored to promote and of which he was growing slightly weary by 1897 was anything but urbane. It was this image, however, that made him exotic to the Viennese, who have, at least since the time of Marcus Aurelius, been the most celebrity-mad society in history. The Mark Twain mask Clemens fashioned for himself in the *Territorial Enterprise* in 1863 of the foxy, folksy humorist had indeed been close to the flesh but, with age and increasing fame, unresolved tensions between the person and the persona created identity problems for him.[3] Austrians who caught rare glimpses behind the mask were startled, then charmed by the disparity between the public image and the private personality. Few, however, were permitted such peeks by this shrewd showman who preferred being the ringmaster at his own circus and who usually succeeded spectacularly at it.

His persona has been so successful, in fact, that the image of what one recent biographer calls "the authentic" Mark Twain has endured, even flourished, despite the demythologizing of scholars.[4] The picture we all enjoy of the garrulous, slightly palsied old codger in a rumpled white suit, bushy white locks flying, clutching his lighted havana, croaking irreverent jokes—an image lucratively perpetuated by dozens of impersonators, professional and amateur—would doubtless delight its creator. This despite the fact that Mark Twain adopted his white flannel look only in 1906 (four years before he died), generally wore formal evening suits for his public performances, and never smoked on the platform.

It would be less accurate to say that by 1897 Clemens had sloughed off his provincialisms, one after another—Southern, Western, even American—than that his intellectual horizons had constantly widened along with his geographical ones. Without losing his American moorings he had become a citizen of the world, and he was so ripe for what this place had to offer intellectually and artistically that the incongruity between Twain and fin de siècle Vienna is more apparent than real. This may become clearer by briefly examining the society of which, at a crucial time for both Vienna and Mark Twain, he was temporarily a member.

Had the world-weary Mark Twain spent the closing years of the nineteenth century in another of Europe's great cities—say, London, Paris, Rome, or even Berlin—the effect upon him and upon what he wrote during the last phase of his richly varied career could not have been near to what Vienna wrought upon his mind and, to a lesser degree, his art. Vienna at the end of the last century was a unique place at a unique moment of its history, a final flowering before what historians have called its *Lustige Apokalypse* (merry apocalypse) of August 1914. Physically much of the Vienna Mark Twain knew remains quite intact, carefully preserved in a city in which nostalgia is a major industry. Yet its great piles of historicist architecture along the Ringstrasse, its splendid palaces like the Hofburg, Schönbrunn, and Prince Eugene's Belvedere, and its Gothic and baroque churches on the old inner city's narrow streets only remind one of what Vienna has not been since the empire it ruled vanished without a trace in 1918.

In 1897, however, Vienna was not only Europe's third-largest city but also the political and commercial capital and cultural center of a vast polyglot domain sprawled across the map of central Europe, embracing lands and peoples who now compose all or large chunks of eight separate nations. It was a city of paradox, at once the most advanced and most backward of the great urban centers. The autumnal glow in which legend, the memoirs of its homesick émigrés, and the city tourist board have bathed fin de siècle Vienna is only half true. It was not all waltzes and whipped cream for the teeming proletariat from the empire's eastern and southern provinces who continued to swell Vienna's working-class suburbs throughout the last half of the nineteenth century. Behind the caryatids and curlicues adorning the facades of neo-baroque Ringstrasse apartments and fashionable villas in the garden districts of Hietzing and Doebling, the art of concealing squalor had reached new heights. The city itself was symbolic of a dynasty that had resided there six centuries and of the current state of affairs in their empire—a gleaming gold crown on a badly decayed tooth.

Clemens was neither unaware of nor insensitive to these paradoxes in his surroundings, but the rarified society in which he moved in Vienna and, during the summer of 1898, in nearby Kaltenleutgeben at the southern edge of the Vienna Woods was one of the most glittering and culturally influential to be found in any world capital at that time. He encountered little of the seamier sides of Viennese life. From address lists and anecdotes in his unpublished Vienna notebooks as well as in his letters and the local newspapers, one sees that the doors of Austria's grand salons were flung wide to him and that he hobnobbed at ease with aristocrats of the Habsburg court as well as with Vienna's foremost journalists, musicians, theater personalities, medical nabobs, and other leading intellectuals and artists. Since the days of Metternich Vienna had been Europe's diplomatic capital, and its large international community also lionized the famous American humorist in their midst.

In the year Clemens came to Vienna, the irascible and controversial Gustav Mahler succeeded Hans Richter as impresario of the k. k. Hofoper (Imperial–Royal Court Opera), and under the banner of "*Secession*," Gustav Klimt and his associates began setting rivers of modern art aflame. In the same year an obscure, untenured *Dozent* (assistant professor) in the University of Vienna's medical faculty, Dr. Sigmund Freud, was laboring to unveil the secrets of the unconscious even as one of his medical colleagues, Dr. Arthur Schnitzler, was unveiling the secrets of respectable bourgeois society on the Viennese stage and Prof. Dr. Ernst Mach was unveiling secrets of aerodynamics and founding a new philosophy of science. And with fiddle tucked under his chin, his bow as his scepter, the septuagenarian Johann Strauss, Jr., was still the undisputed Waltz King, not just of Vienna, but of the whole world.

Mark Twain knew most of these illuminati and many more of like stature in Vienna in this fiftieth year of the reign of Francis Joseph I, by Grace of God Emperor of Austria; Apostolic King of Hungary;

King of Bohemia, of Dalmatia, of Croatia, of Slavonia, of Galicia, of Lodomeria, of Ilyria, and of Jerusalem; Grand-Prince of Transylvania; Archduke of Austria; Grand Duke of Krakow; Duke of Lorraine, of Salzburg, of Styria, of Tyrol, of Carinthia, of Carniola, and so on. Even he, *Der Alte* (the Old One) as the Viennese affectionately dubbed their sovereign lord and kaiser (emperor), made Mark Twain's acquaintance before the American visitor the newspapers constantly referred to as "*unser berühmter Gast*" (our famous guest) quit the city in 1899.

By 1897 all the grandiloquent works of the historicist architects Semper, van der Null and Siccardsburg, Ferstel, Schmidt, and Hansen, flanking the spacious tree-lined boulevard that had replaced the old city walls, were in place. With its splendid neo-Renaissance Opera, museums of art history and natural history, Imperial–Royal Court Theater and university, its neoclassical imperial palace and parliament and neo-Gothic city hall, and the green expanses of the *Volksgarten* (people's garden) and *Stadtpark* (city park), Vienna was one of the handsomest of the world's great cities. Yet already a new generation of architects had rebelled against this stolid historicism, and in the pioneering works of Otto Wagner, Loos, Olbrich, and Josef Hoffmann, a new style was being developed in Vienna, called *Jugendstil*, that presaged what our century has called "modern" in decorative design.

Under the dynamic, demagogic Dr. Karl Lueger, whose election as mayor was ratified on April 10, 1897, Vienna had embarked on a program of urban social planning that would soon make it a model for cities throughout the world. Gas and electric services and indoor plumbing were being extended beyond the homes of the affluent city dwellers to those of the working-class suburbs, and an efficient public transportation system was being constructed with a street railway (part elevated, part subterranean) girdling the city and intersecting tramway lines radiating out to it from the city's central and commercial districts. All this construction, Mark Twain complained, made an inconvenient mess. Despite its antiquity, Vienna had an air of freshness and vitality not unlike what Twain had found in October 1891 in

Bismarck's bustling new Berlin which he perceptively nicknamed the German Chicago.

Across the Danube Canal in the Prater, the former imperial hunting preserve Joseph II granted his Viennese subjects in 1786 for a pleasure garden, the world's largest Ferris wheel was erected in 1897 as a sort of Viennese equivalent to Paris's Eiffel Tower. Beneath it one could glide by gondola through canals of *Venedig in Wien*, a Lilliputian Venice, or stroll tree-shaded avenues lined with wine taverns, *Würstel* kiosks, and tea salons where comely *Damenkapelle* (young lady musicians in white organdy) played Strauss waltzes and the latest operetta tunes. Even more than Paris with its can-can naughtiness, Gay Nineties Vienna seemed a city built for pleasure where new peaks of hedonism were scaled almost weekly. Each day the Viennese burgher could repair to his favorite *Kaffeehaus* and, come Saturday, to his favorite *Heuriger* in the wine villages flanking the city on the slopes below the Vienna Woods. The winters seemed endless rounds of balls and masquerades in this city where confectioners and pastry cooks were celebrities; where actors and actresses, musicians and opera singers, painters and *Feuilletonisten* (newspaper columnists) were demigods.[5]

Yet beneath the merriment and splendor were undercurrents of pessimism and a sense of fatalism that went well beyond the general weltschmerz gripping Europe at the century's end. The empire was beginning to come apart, to be pulled asunder by the unwillingness of its entrenched German-Austrian and Magyar bureaucracies to countenance the nationalistic yearnings of their Slavic constituencies. The murder of the crown prince (officially called suicide) eight years earlier had cast a dark shadow on the future of the dynasty, loyalty to which was the only bond between the disparate elements within the dual monarchy.[6] There was more than a little desperation, then, in Viennese self-indulgence symbolized by a refrain in act 1 of *Die Fledermaus* that could almost have been the city's motto: "*Glücklich ist, wer vergisst, / Was doch nicht zu ändern ist.*" (Happy is he who forgets what can't be changed.)

Nothing Vienna had to offer intellectually was lost upon Clemens, not its aestheticism and merrymaking, not its sharp contrasts between glittering aristocracy and servile masses, nor between brilliant intellectual striving and smug complacency (coupled with outright repression), nor above all between surface order and deep political instability. He was psychologically ready for the experiences he was to encounter there. Had he come a few years earlier, the effect upon him could not have been at all the same. After his bankruptcy in 1894 and numbing bereavement at the sudden death of his daughter, Susy, in August 1896, from both of which he was just beginning to recover, Vienna seemed a perfect place to seek solace, not only to lose oneself in momentary pleasures but also to regain one's intellectual bearings.

Moreover, by the time he came to Austria, his familiarity with its language and his knowledge of Germanic values, habits of mind, and ways of life gained during sojourns in Heidelberg, Bad Nauheim, Munich, Berlin, and German-speaking Switzerland were such that he could penetrate this alien culture to an extent achieved by few American writers. As sensitive as any good writer must be to stimuli provided him by strange, often exciting surrounds, Mark Twain breathed deeply the philosophical and aesthetic perfumes that pervaded Vienna's heady intellectual and literary atmosphere. The result was a surge of creative energy such as he had not known for a decade. He wrote more and in a greater variety of forms during his twenty months in Austria than during all but a very few comparable stretches of his career, and most of what he published or left unfinished thereafter was either commenced or conceived in Vienna or Kaltenleutgeben.

Not all of it is vintage Twain. Much of what he wrote in Vienna, especially his unfinished fiction, remained unpublished until recently, and some fragments have yet to see print. Hence many of the fruits of Twain's Viennese sojourn are obscure to all but the most avid scholars. They ought not to remain so. The best-known of these pieces, including the story "The Man That Corrupted Hadleyburg," two of the three versions of a novella popularly known as *The Mysterious Stranger*, the "Early Days" section of his autobiography, and the polemical essays "Stirring Times in Austria" and "Concerning the Jews," belong to the top category of his canon. Other works from the Vienna period, notably his Socratic dialogue *What Is Man?* and book 1 of *Christian Science*, while not obscure, have been neglected, underrated, or egregiously misunderstood.

The context in which Mark Twain wrote these works has never before been studied nor fully documented. In his three-volume official biography (1912), Albert Bigelow Paine devoted a scant 35 pages (out of 1,587, excluding appendixes) to the Vienna sojourn based exclusively upon the author's dictations, notebooks, and letters.[7] Later biographers have relied on Paine's account plus whatever might be gleaned from memoirs published by Clara Clemens, the author's daughter, and recounted by Katy Leary, the Clemens family's housekeeper who accompanied them to Vienna.[8] Until now, the evidence that has awaited scholars in Vienna itself has been ignored save for a brief survey article in the *Mark Twain Quarterly* in 1945 and an unpublished dissertation on the Viennese press coverage given Mark Twain's sojourn written (in German, of course) at the University of Vienna in 1953.[9]

In his letters from Vienna to Henry Huttleston Rogers, William Dean Howells, the Reverend Joseph H. Twichell, and others, Clemens carefully put the best face on his Austrian experiences. Here and elsewhere, especially in the material he provided Paine, the picture one sees is an unbroken series of social and literary triumphs. The truth seems to have been otherwise and far more interesting. Although never deliberately offensive or impolite, Mark Twain was not always a diplomatic guest, and when he unleashed his satiric wit, he sometimes came perilously close to wearing out his welcome among a thin-skinned folk who, if they might occasionally laugh at themselves or give local humorists that privilege, could also be indignant when foreigners lapsed from polite flattery. Before it was over, indeed before he was long into his Viennese sojourn, Twain was surprised to find himself under attack for candor he could have restrained had he sized up local prejudices more astutely. Thus Clemens may have wished Mark Twain's Vienna years to remain less than fully and frankly chronicled.

Another reason his Vienna episode has been neglected is that, until recently, Twain's late years and the works of his old age were of less interest to both scholars and the general reader than were his more colorful, adventurous early years and the popular works of his major phase. For a half century Mark Twain's pessimistic, misanthropic, even nihilistic late writings puzzled his admirers. Two theories were advanced to explain Mark Twain's so-called "pessimism," either or both of which made it easy to dismiss his late works as uncharacteristic and unworthy. First, Van Wyck Brooks portrayed the author in his declining years as a *poète manqué* who, in his later writings, released his frustrations at not having fulfilled his creative promise after a career bent upon easy fame and fortune as a literary clown. In his attempted rebuttal to this, Bernard DeVoto discussed what he called Twain's "despair" works as the vengeful rantings of a lonely old man embittered by financial reversals, devastating bereavements, and debilitating illnesses.

After the posthumously published *Letters from the Earth* made the best-seller lists in 1962, followed in the next two decades by a dozen more volumes edited from the vast cache of previously unpublished (or editorially botched) material in the Mark Twain Papers housed in the Bancroft Library of the University of California (Berkeley), interest in the final phase of Twain's career steadily increased. Those volumes made it obvious that the standard "explanations" of the writer's deepening pessimism were inadequate, and in the 1970s studies by Hamlin Hill, William Macnaughton, and Sholom J. Kahn, among others, greatly enhanced our understanding of the writer's last decade and the significance of the waning days of his career. Still the Vienna years awaited exploration, a missing piece in an almost completed jigsaw puzzle.

If Clemens himself did not wish to reveal more about his Vienna sojourn and if critics tended until quite recently to dismiss or undervalue most of his output after *A Connecticut Yankee* or, at the latest, *Pudd'nhead Wilson*, there remained yet another, perhaps more compelling reason why Mark Twain's Vienna years were neglected. That is the specious premise underlying most biographical criticism of Mark Twain that his intellectual growth and artistic development ceased rather early in his career. Although there is no critical consensus about the exact cessation point, there has been a tacit agreement that in his last two decades he was largely mining worked-out veins and repeating insights stored up many years before. The basis for this absurd assumption may be found in the view maintained by Albert Bigelow Paine and his successors as official "keepers of the flame" (that is, Twain's literary executors)—chiefly, Bernard DeVoto, Dixon Wecter, and Henry Nash Smith—that the paramount if not exclusive source of Mark Twain's ideas and artistry, along with his subject matter, was the life lived by Samuel Langhorne Clemens *before* he achieved literary fame—in Hannibal, on the Mississippi, in the Far West, and during his excursion in 1867 to Europe and the Holy Land recorded delightfully in his first great success, *The Innocents Abroad*.

This myopic view has been somewhat enlarged by more recent biographers who have also focused on Mark Twain's Hartford years, arguing that *A Connecticut Yankee*, written with what its author called "a pen warmed-up in hell" and rich in ideas, is the apogee of his creative development beyond which lay only repetition and stagnation. These commentators emphasized the writer's disillusion with late nineteenth-century industrialism and its concomitant liberal belief that moral advances follow upon technological progress, a disillusion resulting from the failure of James W. Paige's typesetting machine in which Clemens had invested heavily. As evidence that Twain's growth stopped in about 1889, these critics pointed to his succession of unabashed potboilers and his repeatedly flawed efforts to exploit what Smith called "the matter of Hannibal."

One must be puzzled at the general reluctance by critics and scholars to see Mark Twain's travels and contacts abroad as having had more than a merely cosmetic effect on his writing. Typical is one recent biographer's bald assertion that "Mark Twain's years abroad were valuable to him intellectually, no doubt, but they had little effect on *how* he wrote."[10] That view must seem unduly myopic in those who also readily acknowledge the influence foreign travel had on such other nineteenth-century American writers as Irving, Cooper, Emerson, Longfellow, Hawthorne, Melville, and Howells. Why should Mark Twain have been less impressionable, less educable than those writers? To assume he was is to pay high tribute to the success of his pose as an authentic provincial. In reality, Clemens was probably more receptive to stimuli from his foreign intellectual milieux than were those more highly educated Easterners (excepting perhaps Howells) precisely because he was self-conscious about his lack of formal schooling and determined to remedy it.

It is evident, for example, that he read voraciously if haphazardly and that his intellectual curiosity remained unflagging to the end. Hence it is fair to contend that the literary career he forged was of a piece with the education of Samuel Langhorne Clemens which ended only at the grave. The mind that informed the art of Mark Twain was no less responsive to what it encountered in Vienna than it had been decades before on the Mississippi, in the raw West, or in Hartford. "Training [i.e., education] is everything. Why training is all there is *to* a person," Hank Morgan remarks, an observation that applies as much to his creator as it does to the Yankee in Camelot himself.[11]

There was thus an unintended truth to Twain's proclaiming to Viennese interviewers that he had come to their city for new material. He not only found new subject matter, he found new ideas, new ways of looking at life. To be sure, much of what he expressed in what he wrote there and thereafter may also be found or foreshadowed in what he wrote earlier. After all, he carried to the Habsburg capital the accumulated insights and intellectual baggage of six decades of more richly varied experience than one might expect to chalk up in several ordinary lifetimes and after having tried virtually every trick then known to the literary trade. Yet he was very far from suffering intellectual or literary hardening of the arteries. He took to what fin de siècle Vienna offered with unusual gusto because much of it coincided with, confirmed, reinforced, or added new meaning to perceptions or vague, half-formed ideas he had harbored for some time.

What set Viennese intellectual and artistic life uniquely apart in that era was the confluence of what has been brilliantly categorized by the foremost historian of "the Austrian mind" as "impressionism," "Phaeacianism," and "therapeutic nihilism."[12] Although these key terms should become clear in later discussions where they will be illustrated or exemplified in Clemens's experience and Twain's writing in Vienna, some simple definitions may help to show their relevance here.

Impressionism is undoubtedly the most familiar of these categories of influence, and it therefore needs little definition. Generally it labels the aesthetic whereby artists and writers render perceived reality with a few deft strokes of brush or pen, suggesting rather than stating things literally. The literary impressionist relies upon the evocative power of a few words, the fewer the better, and his or her style depends heavily upon aphorism and wordplay. This style was pervasive among the journalists who were Mark Twain's closest Viennese associates, and, indeed, it is characteristic of almost every Austrian writer of the late nineteenth and early twentieth centuries from Ferdinand von Saar to Hugo von Hofmannsthal and Karl Kraus.

Phaeacianism, first applied to Viennese life by Schiller in a figurative analogy to the people in *The Odyssey* (books 5, 6) who were totally devoted to fun and games, feasting and leisure, is a somewhat recondite term. In the arts it was evidenced by lightness, frivolity, and entertainment rather than didacticism and "social relevance." It was aestheticism carried to excess, a Viennese version of *l'art pour l'art* attitudes that informed much Continental and English literature in the 1890s. In Vienna, however, this program was not merely self-conscious, like that of London's *Yellow Book* circle or of Jung Wien, led by Hermann Bahr, who copied Wilde's blue cornflower boutonniere, but one of values and a style of life that had prevailed in the Danube metropolis at least since Jan Sobieski raised the Turkish siege in 1683.

This Viennese variety of hedonism went hand in hand with therapeutic nihilism, a term drawn from mid-nineteenth-century Viennese medical practice and education wherein successful diagnostic procedures were more highly valued than successful treatments. Reduced to its elementals, this meant that an autopsy was preferable to a cure. Therapeutic nihilism was not, however, limited to medicine. It soon permeated the whole intellectual atmosphere of Vienna where, applied to nonmedical concerns, it became a quasi-philosophical form of skepticism about (if not outright rejection of) all customary efforts to find solutions to human dilemmas through religious practice, philosophical inquiry, or scientific investigation. Ergo: since life's great questions were unanswerable and society's problems insoluble, existence had only whatever meaning one wished to give it. This is solipsism in its purest form.

In virtually everything Mark Twain wrote after September 1897, one may discern attributes of impressionism or Phaeacianism or therapeutic nihilism or some combination of these. Are these the marks of Vienna or only coincidence? Was he influenced by what he read and saw in Vienna and by conversations he held there with such literary associates as Eduard Pötzl or Siegmund Schlesinger, among many others, or would he have written as he did without ever having set foot in the Habsburg capital? To answer these questions in a way that may elucidate works of Twain's final phase and thereby make them more accessible to a wider audience than they have yet had is the purpose and rationale of this book. There may be other reasons (simple curiosity, for instance) for wanting to know more than has elsewhere been written about Mark Twain's Viennese sojourn, but none more important than this.

In sum, wildly improbable though it seems, the spectacle of our Mark Twain in white tie and tails waltzing at a Viennese ball, sitting among the gilded caryatids of the *Musikvereinsaal* at a Johann and Eduard Strauss concert, or making a witty speech in German to the elite of Austrian journalism is not fiction. When he departed for London on May 27, 1899, he told reporters in the huge crowd who saw the Clemens family off at the Franz Josef Bahnhof: "Man kann nicht ein paar Jahre in Wien leben, ohne durch und durch dem Zauber der Stadt und der Leute zu verfallen. Mann gewöhnt sich bald ein in Wien, ist hier zufrieden und geht nie mehr ganz weg." (One can't live

a couple of years in Vienna without succumbing to the spell of the
city and its people. One quickly becomes accustomed to Vienna, feels
contented here, and never completely departs.) [13]

Safely in London a few weeks later, Twain candidly observed to
an American interviewer that "Vienna is the most politically corrupt
nest on the face of the earth." [14] Both his neatly turned compliment to
Viennese *Gemütlichkeit* and his harsh judgment of its political reali-
ties expressed firmly held convictions about what he had experienced
in the City of Dreams. In that paradox are some important implications for our understanding of the last phase of Mark Twain's literary
career.

CHAPTER TWO

Wanderjahre

"I have seen all the foreign countries I want to except heaven & hell," Clemens wrote to William Dean Howells before embarking for Le Havre on the *Gascogne* with his family on June 6, 1891, adding, "& I have only a vague curiosity about one of those."[1] What, then, had brought him to this strange, paradoxical city across the wild and wide Atlantic and a thousand miles into Europe's heartland? From Hannibal, from Hartford even, this place must have seemed as remote as the Gobi Desert or the other side of the moon. "Life is one long linked tape-worm of Accidents," the Old Man repines in a passage Mark Twain excised from *What Is Man?* It must indeed have seemed so to Clemens from the unforeseen chain of happenstance that led from his Farmington Avenue mansion to a hotel suite fronting the Danube Canal that became his home six years later.[2] So many sailings lay in between that it is scarcely a wonder that journeys and voyagings form the dominant motif or plot device in such a large body of Mark Twain's fiction.

His flippant valedictory to Howells was from a traveler who expected to return soon, unaware that circumstances would decree otherwise. In June 1891 it seemed a simple case of turning a neat profit from six travel articles for McClure's Syndicate and the New York *Sun* to pay for the "cure" Olivia Clemens and her husband sought at posh spas like Aix-les-Bains and Marienbad. Their trip was planned to last perhaps six months. By October, however, it was clear the family could live better at less expense abroad than in their Hartford house with its large retinue of servants. Ironically, it was this same reason that had held James Fenimore Cooper, whose "literary offenses" Mark Twain notoriously disparaged, in Europe for eight years in the 1820s and '30s. In Clemens's case, economies became imperative because of losses he had sustained (estimates run from $100,000 to $250,000) by investing in James W. Paige's unworkable typesetting machine at the same time income declined sharply from Charles L. Webster and Company, the publishing house he established in 1884 under the name of his nephew by marriage. Clemens settled his family in Berlin for the winter of 1891–92, and during the next three years, Paris, Florence, and then London became their temporary homes as the Wall Street crash of 1893, followed by the bankruptcy of his publishing enterprise, made their return to Hartford increasingly impractical.

Mark Twain slackened the pace of his writing after *A Connecticut Yankee* (1889) and might have quit his literary career entirely then but for his accelerating financial problems. At a time of life when most men who have been as successful at their trade as Twain certainly was during the 1870s and '80s are in sight of a comfortable retirement, Clemens had to put Mark Twain strenuously to work again to recoup his fallen fortunes. Not surprisingly, then, many of the works that issued from his pen in the mid-1890s were unabashed potboilers.

Early in 1894, Clemens put the management of his finances in the capable hands of Henry Huttleston Rogers, vice president of the Standard Oil Company, who negotiated a lucrative contract for Twain to make a lecture tour of the English-speaking southern hemisphere. The trip spanned an entire year, from mid-July 1895 until July 31, 1896, and the profits it brought, along with those from the book he wrote about it, eventually cleared Clemens of the debts he had assumed for the bankrupt Webster Company. Before the end of his Vienna sojourn, he could boast to Howells that he had "put away the potboiling pen" and thenceforth would write only what, when, and how he wished with little or no regard for publication.[3]

When their global tour ended in England in July 1896, the Clemenses settled first at Guilford, then in Chelsea, so Twain could write the travel book for which he already had contracts from both his London and Hartford publishers: *More Tramps Abroad* (British title) or *Following the Equator* (American). Word presently came that Olivia Susan (Susy) Clemens, the eldest daughter, who had stayed home with Jean, the youngest sibling, during the world tour, the two intending to join their family in England, was seriously ill. Olivia and Clara took the next steamer to New York, but they were less than halfway across when Susy died, on August 18, of meningitis.

The awful shock of this totally unexpected loss delayed his writing of the new travel book for two months, but working compulsively through a winter of secluded mourning, Twain finished it by the end of May 1897. The Clemenses remained in London two more months so Mark Twain could report for a New York newspaper on the celebrations of the Diamond Jubilee of Queen Victoria's accession. Then, remembering a peaceful, remote Swiss village he had first visited on his *Tramp Abroad* excursion nearly twenty years before, Clemens took his bereft family to the Continent, and on July 18, 1897, they began a two-month stay at the Villa Bühlegg, a pension in the village of Weggis, about an hour by paddlewheel steamer up the lake from the city of Lucerne.

It was a lucky find, this lakeside villa in a picture-postcard setting. Behind it was the verdant humpbacked Rigi, and from Bühlegg's front windows one saw the glistening bottle-green waters of Lake Lucerne (properly, Vierwaldstaettersee) beyond which, when the clouds lifted, loomed the Pilatus, one of the most imposing, if not one of the loftiest, of Swiss peaks. If ever nature's vaunted powers of rustic solitude, fresh alpine air, and a landscape combining serene, lush verdure and wild ruggedness could heal the heartache of Olivia and Samuel Clemens and their two remaining daughters, it was here in the sort of surroundings the English Lake Poets a century earlier had sought for their inspiration. Clemens wrote his financial advisor, Rogers: "I believe this place . . . is the loveliest in the world, and the most satisfactory. . . . The scenery is beyond comparison. . . . And Sunday in heaven is noisy compared to this quietness."[4] And his notebook for

that Weggis summer abounds with rhapsodic descriptive passages such
as this one:

> Sund, July 25. At 6 this am, for the first time in the week, sun & surface
> were just right for mirror-effects—so the lake was full of pictures. . . .
> The lake is glass, this morning, its surface richly painted with reflec-
> tions & as far away as the/your eye can detect the gliding spectre of a
> boat in the dreamy distances you can also make out its wake—not the
> usual disordered ruffle on the water, but a thin long white pencil mark
> as straight as a ray of light & sharply defined & intense.
> And of course with every little change in the position of the sun the
> colors of the water change & blend & dissolve, producing marvel after
> marvel, miracle after miracle, & these enchantments know no stay, no
> interruption, no limit while there is light for the magician to work with.
> This is a paradise, & the people who could enjoy it most shut themselves
> up in the world's suffocating cities & leave it to the undisputed possession
> of a handful of pious, ignorant, poor, good-hearted jabbering animals
> who are as happy in it as if they had in some way earned this distinction
> of being allowed to live in heaven before their earthly contract is up[†5]

Without visitors to entertain or other social obligations, their Weggis
idyl was punctuated only by boat trips to nearby Vitznau or shopping
excursions to Lucerne, on one of which Olivia encountered an old
Hartford friend and invited him to Weggis for a day. On August 12
a black American sextet, Fisk University's famed Jubilee Singers on
a European concert tour, arrived at the nearby *Gasthof "Zum Löwen"*
to give a performance of spirituals that Clemens thought "made all
other music cheap." A few days later he wrote to his Hartford pastor
and confidant, Joe Twichell: "I think in the Jubilees and their songs
America has produced the perfectest flower of the ages," adding ironically, "I wish it were a foreign product, so that she would worship it
and lavish money on it and go properly crazy over it."[6]

A few days after arriving in Weggis, the author engaged a room in
the Villa Tannen, about a quarter of a mile farther along the lake from
Bühlegg, to use as a studio. Normally, he did a good deal of writing
during summers when he was free of other distractions, but the Muse

absented herself, and none of the pieces he started in Weggis seemed to work or get finished there, though some found fruition later.

August 18, the anniversary of Susy's death, came and went, her mother spending the day in solitude at an inn across the lake, her father sitting under a lakeside tree to compose some rather maudlin memorial verses later published in *Harper's Monthly*. Meanwhile, Clara, the second Clemens daughter, who had just turned twenty-three, announced her hope of having a musical career. She had taken piano lessons off and on since childhood, and having heard that Prof. Theodor Leschetizky in Vienna was, if not the best, surely the most renowned keyboard pedagogue in Europe, Clara had formed a strong desire to study with him.

Neither of her parents seems to have been the least bit sanguine about Clara's musical ambitions, but neither would gainsay her. Moreover, the fresh memory of Susy's death outside the bosom of her caring family made the Clemenses tacitly resolve never again to be separated from Clara and Jean while they remained unmarried. Hence, if Clara wished to try her luck and uncertain talents in Vienna with Professor Leschetizky, why then her family must perforce accompany her there. There followed a flurry of letters—to the master himself, requesting an audition; to the American embassy in Vienna, asking about long-term accommodations; to Thomas Cook and Sons for travel arrangements.

Trunks and Clara's bicycle were packed and shipped, and on September 19, 1897, they bade farewell to Weggis and started their overnight train trip to Innsbruck by way of Lucerne and Zürich. They stopped at the Hotel Tirolerhof in Innsbruck for two days, then continued to Salzburg for a three-day stay. On the twenty-fourth, Clemens made this notebook entry about Mozart's city, venting his anticlerical spleen: "From the din of unpleasant church-bells it would seem that this village of 27,600 people is made up mainly of churches. Money represents labor, sweat, weariness. And that is what these useless churches have cost these people & are still costing them to support the useless priests & monks." Indeed, his impressions of the city on the Salzach and its imposing nine-hundred-year-old fortress castle were mostly negative, though he was amused by the frequency with which ubiquitous "Verboten" signs on the Getreidegasse, the Pferd-schwemme, and Salztor were ignored by the local citizens, noting, "There are prohibitions at every turn, but nobody obeys them. It is a very free town."†[7]

Monday, September 27, dawned dreary and gray, threatening rain. At noon, the Cook agent appeared punctually at the Clemenses' hotel to take them to the Salzburg railway station, and forty minutes later their train steamed slowly out of the Hauptbahnhof, heading east on the last 185 miles of their journey to the imperial city. By the time they reached the Kaiserin Elisabeth Westbahnhof, Vienna's western railway terminal, at seven that evening, *Niesel*, as the Viennese call a steady cold drizzle, had settled upon the city. In the early autumn dusk and the bustle of this strange metropolis, it was hard work finding two Droschkes to carry all five of them plus a pile of luggage.[8]

Worse still, they were without hotel reservations and had to engage the cabs until they could find suitable lodging. The new *Riesenrad* (giant Ferris wheel) and the newly opened entertainment "Venice in Vienna," in the Prater, had brought an unusually large influx of visitors, prolonging Vienna's tourist season. They were distressed when, as Clemens reported, "we found the town so nearly full that our coming filled it exactly to the brim."[9] Undaunted, they doggedly started down Mariahilferstrasse to make the rounds of the Imperial, the Grand, the Bristol, then Sacher's Hotel de l'Opéra, followed with flagging hopes by the Munsch and the Erzherzog Carl on the Kärntnerstrasse before alighting finally at the Hotel Müller at the very end of the Graben. Clara thought it "a dreadful little hotel . . . in a dreary, dirty street," but her father pronounced it tolerable considering the hour. Clara, for whose sake the family had trudged all this way, was dispirited. "No one could have believed, as we turned our lights out in our dingy rooms," she recalled, "that Vienna would ever come to seem a pleasant place."[10]

Early the next morning the party set out in search of more satisfactory quarters. The number of hotels they inspected is uncertain.

Clara Clemens, circa 1900 (Mark Twain Archives,
Elmira College, Elmira, N.Y.)

Clemens told one correspondent they had applied to nineteen and another seventeen throughout their arrival night and next day, but his notebook entry on September 28 gives it as fifteen.[11] Although Vienna's first district (inside the Ringstrasse) had twenty-one first-class hotels within reasonable proximity to each other, it would have been very difficult to visit as many as a dozen within one morning. Hence, the notebook entry seems the most likely. Whatever the number, it was to the huge, fashionable Metropole on Franz-Josefs-Kai that they moved that afternoon.

Despite their not having a reservation, the Clemenses' plans for sojourning in Vienna were not unheralded. Before leaving Weggis Clemens had advised the American embassy in Vienna of his wish to have a furnished flat or house in the city, and by September 30, Bailey Hurst, the American consul general, had located a capacious furnished house, the Villa Silling, in a section called the "Cottageviertel" in suburban Döbling.[12] Clemens had had a sudden attack of gout in his right foot that laid him up for a week, so he sent Olivia and Clara out in a fiaker the next day to inspect the villa. Whether, as he wrote Rogers, the offer from the hotel's manager, eager for the publicity a resident celebrity like Mark Twain might bring, to reduce their rent on a large suite by 40 percent made staying there cheaper than keeping house or, as he told Hurst, his daughters preferred to remain in the city (or both), the family decided to settle in at the Metropole for the next nine months.[13]

A huge, old-fashioned Viennese hostelry, its former elegance slightly faded, it lacked such newfangled amenities as lifts and private baths in most of its ninety-six suites. Nevertheless, its guest list included many bona fide aristocrats, such as the sister of the German emperor, partly because its *chef de cuisine*, Herold, was reputedly Vienna's finest. Whatever its other attractions for Clemens, the offer of seven spacious, high-ceilinged rooms, consisting of a parlor with balcony, a music room for Clara, a study for her father, and four bedrooms, all for $460 per month, including heat, attendants (both usually charged extra), and meals for five persons, was an irresistible bargain.[14] Baths, however, cost extra, so Clemens joked to Rogers when the family removed to the Krantz the following year: "The bathroom on our floor was 50 yards distant, and as I was often tired and they didn't allow bicycles in the hall, I didn't take any baths that year. I was never so healthy and warm in my life."[15]

Their Metropole suite, Number 62, was at a front corner of the top guest floor (servants' quarters were above)—the third in American parlance, second in European—overlooking the Donaukanal (Danube Canal) near its busiest bridge, the Ferdinandbruecke (now Schwedenbruecke). Front right their windows gave a distant prospect of Vienna's famed pleasure garden, the Prater, with its glittering brand-new landmark, the giant Ferris wheel, clearly in view. Passenger and barge traffic on the canal was heavy, with a landing at the Stefanibruecke close to the Morzinplatz fronting the hotel. The canal carried travelers and goods to and from the Danube River itself, while the *Kai* (quay) between the hotel and canal was a busy artery for horse-drawn trams (soon to be electrified), freight wagons, and the omnipresent fiakers. The tumult and din of a normal weekday must have made the recent bucolic tranquillity of Weggis seem all the more idyllic.

In light of what he was soon to experience of Viennese anti-Semitism, it is ironic that Mark Twain's first residence there should have been the Metropole. Neither he nor anyone else could have foretold that four decades later, when Adolf Hitler annexed his homeland to his Third Reich, the Metropole would become the Vienna headquarters of the Gestapo. A lucky bomb from a Ninth United States Army Air Force B-24 found its target there on March 12, 1945, and after the war, the Viennese demolished what remained of this hated Nazi landmark. Today, in Morzinplatz, a sculpted grey stone figure memorializes victims of the Holocaust near what the pedestal inscription says was for too many Austrians "the Door to Hell."

The Metropole's subsequent history lends an almost eerie prescience to a piece Mark Twain wrote within days of arriving there. Titled "Conversations with Satan," it is an unfinished, unpublished manuscript of twenty-nine typed pages. The plural, "Conversations," sug-

gests this may have been intended as the first in an abortive series
of such imaginary dialogues between Twain and the devil, a figure
that had long fascinated him. In Vienna, his interest in Satan would
become almost obsessive as he struggled inconclusively with two different versions of the novella popularly known as *The Mysterious Stranger*:
"The Chronicle of Young Satan" and "Schoolhouse Hill."

The Satan in "Conversations" is an adult Mephistopheles or Lucifer,
not the adolescent satan character variously called Philip Traum,
Quarante-quatre, and No. 44 in the three "Mysterious Stranger"
manuscripts. He is a dapper, distinctly aristocratic Austrian, "a slender
and shapely gentleman in black" whom the author hilariously mistakes
at first as perhaps "an Anglican bishop." The sketch begins promis-
ingly: "It was being whispered around that Satan was in Vienna incognito, and the thought came into my mind that it would be a great
happiness to me if I could have the privilege of interviewing him.
'When you think of the Devil' he appears, you know." Then Twain sets
the scene for their interview in a manner Edgar Allan Poe might have
envied:

> It was past midnight. I was standing at the window of my work-room
> high aloft on the third floor of the hotel, and was looking down upon
> a stage-setting which is always effective and impressive at that late hour:
> the great vacant stone-paved square of the Morzin Platz with its sleeping
> file of cab-horses and drivers counterfeiting the stillness and solemnity of
> death; and beyond the square a broad Milky Way of innumerable lamps
> bending around the far-reaching curve of the Donau Canal, with not a
> suggestion of life or motion visible anywhere under that glittering belt
> from end to end.

After a sudden "rush of wind, a crash of thunder and a glare of
lightning," Twain perceives Satan strolling leisurely across the platz
toward the Metropole, and then, in a twinkling, Satan appears beside
Twain in his study, like Mephistopheles to Faust in Gounod's opera.
The author is overawed and charmed by his visitor: "His carriage and
manners were enviably fine and courtly, and he was a handsome person, with delicate white hands and an intellectual face & that subtle air

Hotel Metropole, Vienna, 1890s. The Clemens family resided here
from September 1897 until May 1898.
(Picture Archives of the Austrian National Library)

of distinction which goes with ancient blood and high lineage, commanding position and habitual intercourse with the choicest society."

He addresses Satan in German, as *"Durchlauchtigst"* (most serene highness) and *"Ihre Maejestaet"* (your majesty), but his visitor disdains such ceremonial formalities. Familiarly taking chairs, the two fall to discussing the merits of the German (and Austrian) porcelain tile stove (*Kachelofen*). Twain agrees enthusiastically with Satan's praise of this stove as "the best in the universe" and is dismayed to learn that in Hell they use only American stoves.

Then the conversation shifts to pipe tobacco and peters out disappointingly in a monologue by the author on the relative merits of various types of cigars, though not before this rejoinder by Satan to Twain's complaint that he is unable to buy his favorite tobaccos in Vienna:

> You must be mistaken about that. You must remember that this is one of the most superb cities ever built; and it is very rich, and very fond of good things, and can command the best of everything that the world can furnish; and it also has the disposition to do it. *This is my favorite city. I was its patron saint in the early times before the reorganization of things, and I still have much influence here, and am greatly respected.* †16

Satan's remarks here could be dismissed as mere persiflage. On the other hand, Mark Twain seldom wasted such jibes, and one need not strain to discern serious meaning and a satirical motive behind this quip. Having sized up his new surroundings with acuity, it was already quite evident to Mark Twain that Vienna was more likely the fiefdom of the Prince of Darkness than anything resembling a putative *Civitas Dei* of his apostolic majesty, Franz Josef I. It would not be very long before Vienna's "famous guest" from America would have plenty to confirm that perception.

CHAPTER THREE

Zeitungskrieg!

No fewer than forty-five newspapers, including dailies, weeklies, and semiweeklies, plus a dozen humor magazines and some twenty journals of belles lettres and criticism were being published in Vienna at the time Mark Twain resided there.[1] In those far-off days before even cinema newsreels, let alone radio and television, began the irreversible erosion of newspaper reading, the daily paper was almost the only reliable source of information about anything outside one's four walls. Hence, each segment of Vienna's 1.7 million inhabitants, every social class, political faction, nationality, and ethnic minority had its newspaper. The news-hungry Viennese burgher generally read more than one paper a day, while, to compete for readers, the larger dailies published both morning and evening editions seven days a week.

Vienna had no home delivery or street vendors of newspapers, but kiosks where one might buy papers going to or from work dotted major intersections and tramway stops, and tobacconists sold newspapers and magazines as well as postage stamps and tram tickets. Special interest papers sometimes had only a few hundred subscribers, but even the largest, *Neues Wiener Tagblatt*, had no more than 65,000 in a single press run. This small number was because most Viennese papers could count on having several readers, sometimes dozens, per copy. Vienna's ubiquitous *Kaffeehäuser* (cafés) took all major dailies and often many lesser ones, and for a few kreuzer, the price of a cup of *Wiener Mélange* (coffee suffused with milk) or a glass of *Sprüdel* (mineral water), one might pass an entire day or evening at one's favorite café catching up on the news. Indeed, reading newspapers remains a major pastime in Viennese café life to this day, cable television and Sacher torte notwithstanding.

Freedom of the press as Clemens knew it back home had never existed in Austria-Hungary. Yet, by 1897, official censorship was sloppily enforced. Clemens was amused to observe a story suppressed by the censor in one newspaper, so that a white space with the word "*konfisziert*" (confiscated) appeared where the article might have been, appearing in another daily the censor had carelessly missed.[2] Nothing overtly critical of the regime, members of the royal family or high nobility (count or above), the military, or the Roman Catholic church was permitted in print, and the police routinely notified editors when breaking stories were to be disregarded, denied, or "interpreted" a certain way.[3]

With this plethora of papers and paucity of uncensored news, the scramble for the publishable and for scoops was fierce. The resulting *Zeitungskrieg* (newspaper circulation war), compared to which that between Hearst and Pulitzer in New York at the same period seems tame, knew no truce. Mark Twain's presence provided the city's press a fresh battlefield for at least a month before the mounting parliamentary crisis usurped their front pages. A veteran journalist himself, he knew exactly how to provide ammunition and even better how to manipulate its use. Eventually, his manipulations backfired with some unpleasant, even painful, results, but given his fondness for the limelight, the splash he made during his first six weeks in Vienna must have been indeed gratifying.

Newspapers in Vienna began trumpeting "the famous American humorist's presence inside our walls," as one daily put it, on the front pages of evening editions on September 30, 1897. First on line were the *Neues Wiener Tagblatt* and *Neue Freie Presse*, the two largest, the latter reporting that "the well-known American humorist, Samuel Langhorne Clemens, who is famous throughout the civilized world by his pen-name, Mark Twain, has been in the city for two days and has

an apartment in the Hotel Metropole," adding that he had been prevented by an unnamed infirmity (soon reported as gout) from leaving
his hotel despite the "splendid summer-like weather" which had set in
after the Clemenses' drizzly arrival. Within days almost every paper in
the metropolis contained a similar article, some offering biographical
sketches with inaccurate or downright fanciful details and several with
a drawing or photograph of the author. Before long, Twain's visage
became almost as familiar to the Viennese as that of their new mayor,
Dr. Karl Lueger, or the hotly controversial new opera director, Gustav
Mahler.

Two things resulted from this extensive coverage. The first was
a deluge of letters from sympathetic gout sufferers. Clemens wrote
Rogers that "The mail is made up of letters that are written in the
difficult German script. This blocks off all possible idleness and keeps
us all busy; for it takes us as long to spell out a German letter as it does
to answer it. All the good gouty people in Austria and Germany write
me and tell me what is good for gout, and some of the remedies are
good. I mean to try the whole (?darned) lot the next time I get the disease."[4] More important to Mark Twain than well-wishers' letters was
the swarm of reporters clamoring for interviews. *Figaro*, the leading
humor weekly, jested in its *Wiener Luft* supplement with hyperbole that
"all of Vienna's humorists want to interview their American colleague
these days. But because they are not being admitted there has been
such a crush that the police have had difficulty keeping the passage
[to his hotel] free."[5]

The detail about their "not being admitted" was not altogether true.
Although Olivia Clemens tried to discourage interviewers, her husband overruled her whenever he could. She returned from shopping
one afternoon a few days after their arrival to find him giving a bedside interview to a whole covey of reporters. Amelia Levetus, a British
correspondent new to Vienna, remembered the scene vividly: "No
fashionable lady desirous of creating the most favorable impression
could have taken more pains to make a striking entry into the world
of the representatives of the press, inland and foreign. He lay with his

head at the foot of the bed so that the light fell upon his finely marked
features and played with the glorious mass of his white hair, sending
whole symphonies of varying tones among its thicknesses. A nocturne
in white with the dark brown pipe as relief."[6] Having set his scene
with theatrical skill, Mark Twain, she noted with what seems almost
naive understatement, "did not seem to mind being interviewed in the
least. Rather, he seemed to enjoy it; he was at any rate accustomed to
cross-examination of this kind and he stood it well."[7]

Thus, within a fortnight of his arrival in Vienna, interviews prolif-
erated almost daily in *Neue Freie Presse*, *Wiener Tagblatt*, *Neues Wiener
Tagblatt*, *Neues Wiener Journal*, *Fremdenblatt*, *Illustrirtes Wiener Extrablatt*,
Neuigkeits-Weltblatt, *Wiener Bilder*, and *Salonblatt*. On what basis interviews were granted to these nine papers and not to others is unclear. It
may have been pure chance or because the reporters they sent out were
more aggressive or persistent than their competitors on such other
important dailies as *Die Presse*, *Reichspost*, *Deutsche Zeitung*, *Deutsches
Volksblatt*, *Oesterreichische Volkszeitung*, *Vaterland*, and semiofficial *Wiener
Zeitung* (with its *Wiener Abendpost*). Whatever the reason, most of those
granted interviews were Jewish, or the liberal papers they represented
were published by Jews, while those seemingly excluded were published by gentiles and, in some cases, were overtly anti-Semitic. To
those who were scooped this smacked of favoritism (*Beziehung*) of a
sort not at all uncommon in Viennese journalism, and repercussions
from this, as we shall see, could be quite unpleasant.

Although *Neue Freie Presse* gave front-page space to a brief visit with
Mark Twain as early as its evening edition on October 1, the first richly
detailed interview appeared in next day's *Neues Wiener Tagblatt*. This
one was a full-blown feuilleton, a peculiarly Viennese genre—forerun-
ner, perhaps, of the modern feature story—which occupied the lower
half of a front page and, in this instance, was continued inside the
paper. Entitled "A Quarter-hour with Mark Twain" (*Eine Viertelstunde
bei Mark Twain*), it was written by the paper's feature editor (*Feuilleton-
redakteur*), Siegmund Schlesinger, a writer with whom Twain was to
have a close if unproductive working relationship during his stay in

Vienna. This interview was very chatty and intimate, and it was clear that Twain was quite at ease with Schlesinger. At its conclusion, he accepted Schlesinger's invitation to write something at a later date for *Neues Wiener Tagblatt*, a commitment never fulfilled.

The following day (October 2), *Neues Wiener Tagblatt*'s most popular and probably best writer, Eduard Pötzl, devoted his Sunday feuilleton to a humorous sketch about "Herr Mark Twain." Titled *"Der Stille Beobachter"* (The Silent Observer), it narrates an imaginary incident in which Twain, standing on a city bridge to observe the passing scene, notebook in hand, is greeted by two typical city workmen who endeavor to converse with him in *Weanerisch* (Viennese dialect). The result is a hilarious series of misunderstandings and befuddlements.

Pötzl may have worked up this story from a remark of Twain's, quoted in the Schlesinger interview, about his observing the Viennese citizenry from his hotel balcony and hoping to have a chance to study their manners, speech, and character types more closely for use in his stories. In the interview, Twain had also mentioned his admiration for Pötzl's "gallery of pure Viennese types" from which he hoped to learn much. Most interesting is that the idea of comical misunderstandings arising from dialect is one that Twain himself often used, most notably perhaps in the colloquy in *Roughing It* between the western miner, Scotty Briggs, and the greenhorn preacher from the East.[8]

Even for literary-minded Austrians, Eduard Pötzl (1851–1914) is an obscure figure today, but during his lifetime, especially at the time of Mark Twain's stay in Vienna, he was immensely popular. Indeed, he was far better known to the reading public than such turn-of-the-century writers as Arthur Schnitzler, Hugo von Hofmannsthal, or Karl Kraus, who have achieved lasting fame. Like Clemens, he was a lawyer's son, but the biographical parallels end there. Although an *echt Wiener* (Viennese to the teeth), Pötzl grew up and attended school in Wiener Neustadt in Lower Austria. After dutifully trying legal studies for a while in Vienna, he took a clerical job on the southern railway and then, at twenty-three, joined the staff of *Neues Wiener Tagblatt* (*NWT*). He remained on its staff the rest of his life, rising from a lowly court reporter where, like Charles Dickens, he developed skill at sketching city low life and an ear for dialect, to become feature editor.

In March 1888, Pötzl was one of ten *NWT* journalists, most of them Jewish, mauled by a gang of German Nationals led by Georg von Schönerer who broke into the paper's office late one night to smash the presses of what they vilified as "this shameful Jewish rag." For this outrage the emperor nullified Schönerer's patent of nobility (*Ritter,* equivalent to English baronet) and banned him from holding public office for five years while he and his hooligans served jail terms. The incident nevertheless furnished a precedent for Schönerer's latter-day disciple, Adolf Hitler, to imitate more effectively a half-century later.

Pötzl himself was not Jewish but, although he was distinctly "philo-semitic," in other respects was a conservative satirist. His popularity came from dialect humor, from punning, and from his creation of a sort of Viennese Mr. Dooley character, a comic *alt Wiener Biz* (old Viennese stumblebum) named Herr Nigerl, who wryly comments on the foibles of his fellow townsmen and local politics. Every year or so Pötzl published collections of his feuilletons, and two of his volumes, *Hoch vom Kahlenberg* (1897) and *Landsleute* (1898), the latter including his Mark Twain sketch ("The Silent Observer"), he presented to Clemens with the flattering inscription *"an Seinen Verehrten Meister"* (to his esteemed master). Not surprisingly, a few of the *Landsleute* sketches, one of which is actually set in Chicago, evince traces of Twainian influence on this *echt* Viennese humorist.

A day or two after his "Silent Observer" feuilleton appeared, Pötzl came calling at the Metropole, and the two humorists hit it off immediately. Clemens was gratified that Pötzl could speak a little English, and, a gregarious and amusing raconteur, he soon became a frequent dinner guest of the Clemenses and companion on their outings. Clara's parents were delighted when she and Pötzl's son, later an eminent neurologist in Vienna, showed a more-than-casual interest in each other that they may have hoped would develop into something beyond mere flirtation. For their part, the Pötzls discouraged anything closer

Eduard Pötzl (1851–1914), journalist and dialect humorist who
was Mark Twain's closest Viennese friend
(Picture Archives of the Austrian National Library)

between the young people since their son had to finish his studies and establish his practice before he could even consider anything like courtship.[9]

Pötzl was not the only Viennese journalist with whom Mark Twain soon made friends. Siegmund Schlesinger, whose interview had evidently inspired Pötzl's "Silent Observer" feuilleton, was another. He was Clemens's elder by three years, born in a small Slovakian town then part of Hungary to a large family of assimilated Jews that produced several distinguished journalists, authors, and publishers. One cousin, Ferdinand Schlesinger, fled Hungary in 1849 after the defeat of Kossuth's rebel army in which he served, ending up eventually in San Francisco where he founded the city's first German-language newspaper at the time Mark Twain was a journalist there. Another, Max Schlesinger, was a popular feuilletonist for Moritz Szeps's *Wiener Tagblatt* and editor of the weekly *Salonblatt*. A third Schlesinger, Samuel, founded the Viennese weekly *Vororte-Correspondenz*, and in 1875, Josef Schlesinger, Siegmund's uncle, established the first Hebrew publishing house in Vienna.

Siegmund himself was drawn to the theater after serving a stretch as drama critic for *Neues Wiener Tagblatt*. For two decades before Mark Twain arrived in the city, he had enjoyed a string of popular successes on several Viennese stages, culminating in 1892 in a patriotic festival play with incidental music, *Vater Radetzky*, expensively produced at the k. k. Hofoper, followed the next year by an even more successful melodrama, *Die Taube der Messalina* (The Dove of Messalina), which premiered at the brand-new Deutsches Volkstheater. Thus it seems inevitable Schlesinger should have asked Twain in his first *Neues Wiener Tagblatt* interview: "Und das Theater? Hat es Sie nicht angelockt?" (And the theater? Hasn't it ever attracted you?) Twain's English reply, "I made some play, but it would not play," may have been slightly garbled by Schlesinger, whose English was not idiomatic but who, nevertheless, reported this as a *Wortspiel* (pun). Twain may actually have been obliquely referring to *Ah Sin*, the collaborative farce with which he and Bret Harte had failed spectacularly twenty years earlier. He added that someone else had done better adapting his *Gilded Age* as a successful comedy, *Colonel Sellers*, which Schlesinger misspelled "Colonel Salaries."

No doubt this exchange gave Schlesinger the idea he had two months later to propose to Twain that they collaborate on plays for the Imperial–Royal Court Theater (k. k. Hofburgtheater), then as now Vienna's most prestigious stage. If Twain would furnish plots and characters for two comedies with "Wild West" locales and subjects, Schlesinger would write the German dialogue. This frustratingly aborted collaboration will be discussed in a later chapter, but suffice it now that neither play was ever produced if, indeed, one was even entirely written. Had Clemens known of Schlesinger's reputation as a gay dilettante, a Viennese Oscar Wilde without Wilde's brilliance, he might not have committed himself so readily to the proffered collaboration.[10]

The most significant, certainly most penetrating, of the myriad interviews and articles about Mark Twain appearing in Viennese newspapers during the early days of his stay was a feuilleton in *Fremden-Blatt* on Sunday, October 10, 1897, by Ferdinand Gross, the paper's editor-in-chief, who was often called "Der Johann Strauss des Feuilletonisten" (the Johann Strauss of feuilletonists) in tribute to his popularity as a humorist writer. Gross's article showed greater familiarity than any other Viennese journalist with Twain's works. He made apt, illuminating references to *The Innocents Abroad* as well as to such lesser-known stories as "Cannibalism in the Cars," "The Stolen White Elephant," "Those Extraordinary Twins," and the burlesque "Encounter with an Interviewer," probably introducing some of these titles to Austrian readers for the first time.

Samuel Schlesinger (Siegmund's cousin), in *"Ein Plauderstündchen mit Mark Twain"* (A Chat with Mark Twain) in *Illustrirtes Wiener Extra-blatt* on the same day as Gross's interview (October 10), also referred to the burlesque "Encounter with an Interviewer" but, obviously less familiar than Gross with Twain's works, concentrated on the American

humorist's appearance and on anecdotes about Twain's early journalistic career:

> Mark Twain muss in seiner Jugend ein schoener Mann gewesen sein.
> Grosse, stahlgraue Augen erhellen das faltige Gesicht. Dichte Augen-
> brauen legen sich vor, den etwas breiten Mund ein weisser, borstig empor-
> gestraeubter Schnurrbart. Mark Twains Wesen ist sehr liebenswuerdig,
> er spricht ziemlich gut deutsch mit amerikanischem Akzente und unter-
> stuezt seine Rede durch eindringliche Geberden [*sic*]. (In his youth, Mark
> Twain must have been a handsome man. Large steel-grey eyes light up
> a furrowed face. Thick eyebrows protrude, and a white, bristly, unruly
> mustache droops over a somewhat broad mouth. Mark Twain is very
> affable. He speaks rather good German with an American accent and
> underscores his speech with emphatic gestures.)

The mention of his "rather good German," which other interviewers
corroborated, was something Twain often took pains to deny. He was
always unusually modest about his German proficiency. For example,
he wrote soon thereafter to Henry Harper, his New York publisher:
"You ought to see some of these newspaper interviews, wherein they
make me talk German—which I don't do. My German is bad, but not
that bad."†[11] Gross's article had an immediate and far-reaching result,
as this letter from Clemens, written that very day, indicates:

> What you have written of me in this morning's Fremden-Blatt has grati-
> fied me more than I can say, because of the friendly & hospitable feeling
> which pervades it, & because it penetrates to my literary inside with a
> sure instinct & reveals its secret springs & its carefully veiled system or
> procedure with a fine & happy accuracy, & puts the result on paper with
> felicitous clarity and precision. For this great pleasure which you have
> given me I hold myself your obliged debtor.
>
> When your kind letter came, ten days ago, we were in the turmoil &
> confusion of trying to get settled in new quarters, with the Gicht [gout]
> for uninvited helper, & I think I must have mis-read it, for I thought it
> only suggested a future invitation to meet the Concordia; but now that
> I examine it again I conceive it to be not a prelude to an invitation but
> the invitation itself. If I am right, I accept, with cordial thanks for the

honor offered me by my fellow-craftsmen of Vienna, & at the same time I beg to apologize for my mistakes; & if I am wrong I know you will be generous & forgive me.* 12

Eight months before Clemens came to Vienna, Ferdinand Gross had become president of Concordia, the older, larger, and more prestigious of Vienna's two press clubs. Within a day or two of the American humorist's arrival in the city, Gross invited him to address a meeting of the society. As this letter explains, Clemens had initially misconstrued his invitation as tentative rather than a firm commitment. As soon as he realized and rectified his error, he began preparations for what was one of the highest honors he received in his Viennese sojourn, an honor the Concordia only once before had granted a foreigner— Henrik Ibsen in 1891. It also proved to be one of the most memorable and colorful gatherings in the long history of the organization.

The meeting took place three weeks later, on Sunday night, October 31, beginning at eight o'clock in the great hall of the Merchant's Association (Kaufmännische Verein) in Johannesgasse, one of the most spacious of Vienna's many ballrooms. It was billed as a *Festkneipe,* a term that is now obsolete and for which there is no English equivalent but denoting a sort of stag party or festive evening of libations and conviviality rather than a banquet with formal after-dinner speeches. Founded in 1859, the Concordia had 348 members in 1897 (it has 337 today), and on such occasions members were permitted to bring guests, which many did to hear and even meet "unser berühmter Gast" (our famous guest).

Every paper represented in the Concordia—that is, those not in the rival, antiliberal, anti-Semitic "Deutschösterreichische Schriftsteller-Genossenschaft" (German-Austrian Writers' Association)—covered

---

"Die Mark Twain-Kneipe" at length. Their details vary slightly, some papers emphasizing one aspect, some another. Several of them printed Mark Twain's entire speech, some from reporters' notes, others from the official record of the *Referent* (club secretary). *Extrapost* scooped its rivals by running a lengthy report next morning (November 1), but it was *Neue Freie Presse* (*NFP*) that provided the fullest account, on November 2. The hall had been sumptuously decorated by Gilbert Lehner, holder of the impressive title "k.u.k. Decorations-Inspector und Maler" (imperial and royal inspector of decorations and painter), which meant he had veto power on all stage designs and the decor of public ceremonies and balls in Vienna. He garlanded the room with red-white-blue bunting. The back wall displayed the Stars and Stripes, the front a large portrait of the author by Lehner's son above a banner with the motto of the United States, "e pluribus unum." Beneath this the speakers' platform was bedecked with what *NFP* called "a grove of palms and flowers."[13]

Mark Twain had the seat of honor at center stage while on his right at the head table sat Concordia President Gross; Edgar von Spiegl, publisher-editor of *Illustrirtes Wiener Extrablatt*, who had organized the evening's program; the United States minister, Charlemagne Tower; General Consul Bailey Hurst; and representatives of both the imperial government and the city council.

Ranged on the honored guest's left were directors of Vienna's leading theaters including Gustav Mahler, director of the k. k. Hofoper; three legendary actors of the Viennese stage—Adolf von Sonnenthal, Joseph Lewinsky, and star comedian Alexander Girardi; leading tenor of the opera Ernest Van Dyck; piano virtuoso Alfred Grünfeld; Vienna's foremost cartoonist, Theo Zasche; and the director of the city library. Behind sat the foreign press corps, headed by William S. Lavino of the London *Times*.

At long tables perpendicular to the platform, each laden with bottles of *Sekt* (sparkling white wine) and *Gabelbissen* (small, open-face sandwiches) constantly replenished by watchful waiters, were the Concordia members and their guests. They included the leading liberal editors and publishers—Moritz Benedikt (*Neue Freie Presse*), Wilhelm Singer (*Neues Wiener Tagblatt*), Moritz Szeps (*Wiener Tagblatt*), and Friedrich Uhl (*Wiener Zeitung* and *Wiener Abendpost*), among others. There were also writers like Hermann Bahr and Richard Beer-Hoffmann, of the avant-garde Jung Wien (young Vienna) literati; Felix Salten, soon to be famous for his children's classic, *Bambi*; Viktor Léon, whose many successful operetta librettos include Franz Lehár's *Die Lustige Witwe* (The Merry Widow) and Kalman's *Czardasfürstin*; Theodor Herzl, father of the Zionist movement; utopian novelist Theodor Hertzka; and Eduard Hanslick, doyen of Vienna's music critics and immortalized by Wagner as Beckmesser in *Die Meistersinger*. In addition to Eduard Pötzl, of course, the city's foremost humorists were there: Vincenz Chiavacci ("Frau Sopherl von Naschmarkt"), Karl Weiss ("C. Karlweis"), Emil Kralik ("Habakuk"), and many more of lesser renown.

It would indeed be easier to say who was not present than to make an inclusive list of the members of the journalistic and literary establishment of the dual monarchy who were. One of those whose presence that evening cannot be irrefutably documented is Karl Kraus, Austria's peerless satirical essayist and prose stylist in the period between 1895 and his death in 1936 and one of her most influential writers in any age. Kraus was not a member of the Concordia, an organization he often criticized, but he was a close associate of many who were members, and what he later wrote about the affair seems to have come from first-hand experience, not from newspaper accounts or hearsay. Despite his sarcasms about the press club, he himself later accepted an invitation to address it, and it would have been completely in character for him to have availed himself of the opportunity to hear Mark Twain as a guest of a friend on this occasion.[14]

With or without Kraus, there cannot have been many such gatherings in the history of the Habsburg Empire that surpassed or even rivaled this for literary luster. Moreover, not even at Oxford, where he received an honorary doctorate a decade later, could Mark Twain have had a more distinguished audience than this.

The evening opened with the kind of lofty turgidity still fashionable in Germanic introductions. Herr Gross began with a florid speech in English welcoming "one of the greatest sons of America" and its official representatives, Ambassador Tower and Mr. Hurst. Then he switched to German, saying that Mark Twain was not just an American but one who, like Goethe, also belonged to every civilized nation, adding, "Dieser Abend ist ein bedeutsamer, denn er liefert wieder den Beweis, daß die als leichtsinnig verschrienen Phäaken an der Donau doch besser sind als ihr Ruf. . . ." (This evening is significant because it again brings evidence that the notorious lighthearted Phaeacians on the Danube are certainly better than their reputation. . . .), an allusion to Schiller's *Xenie* (1797), which first used "Phaeacian" to describe Vienna's special brand of *Gemütlichkeit*. He ended like a cheerleader, leading the assemblage three times in *"Hoch Amerika!"* (Long live America!). Ambassador Tower responded appropriately, expressing gratitude for the club's hospitality and the heartwarming token of Austro-American friendship.

Thirsts slaked, the company settled back for the evening's main event. As the famous guest arose many auditors surged toward the podium so as not to lose even a word. (This time was, remember, before electric amplification.) He began speaking softly, slowly, and very precisely in English to thank his hosts for this honor and privilege. Then, donning spectacles and pulling a sheaf of papers from his coat pocket, he commenced his speech "to the general astonishment" of his hearers (*NFP* reported) in German: "Entschuldigen Sie, daß ich verlese, was ich Ihnen sagen will." (Forgive me for reading what I want to say to you.) At this point, however, the *Referent* noted parenthetically, *"Er las aber nicht"* (but he did not read)! Apparently he had memorized the speech but held his written text against a memory lapse. The newspaper accounts agreed that he spoke "rather good" or "correct" German with an "English accent" or "American accents." At the outset he joked that he spoke German poorly but that experts had said he wrote it "like an angel." He disclaimed knowing this himself, however, because he had had no acquaintance with angels. "That comes later, when it pleases the dear Lord. I'm not in any hurry." Here Twain was punning on the words *Engel* (German for angel) and *englisch,* which can mean both English and "angel's speech." (See appendix A for the complete text.)

The main part of the speech itself, which Paine later titled *"Die Schrecken der deutschen Sprache"* (The Horrors of the German Language) when he published a garbled, misdated version of it (together with Twain's burlesque literal translation) in his posthumous collection of Mark Twain's speeches (1923), was given by most papers as *"Die Schwierigkeiten der deutschen Sprache"* (The Difficulties of the German Language), certainly a less offensive, perhaps more accurate labeling of its contents. Under Paine's title this piece is too easy to confuse with an earlier and lengthier essay, "The Awful German Language," appended to *A Tramp Abroad* (1879).

In its penultimate paragraph, Twain referred to Pötzl's recent "Silent Observer" sketch to "correct" the impression he said Pötzl had given the Viennese that his purpose in coming to their city was to stop traffic on the bridges. "My presence on the bridges has a quite innocent purpose," he explained: It was only there he had room enough to stretch out a German sentence, hanging the stem of a verb with separable prefix on one end of a bridge, its prefix on the other end and, by walking the bridge's length, at last making out the full meaning of the sentence.

Obliquely exculpating himself for any unintended affront to his hosts' linguistic sensitivities, he concluded, "Ich bin ein Fremder, aber hier unter Ihnen in der gastfreundlichen Atmosphaere Wiens habe ich es ganz vergessen." (I'm a foreigner, but here among you in the hospitable atmosphere of Vienna, I've completely forgotten it.) Even with pauses for frequent eruptions of laughter and applause, the entire speech took less than ten minutes, and at its end, according to the newspapers, a *"stürmische Beifall"* (tumultuous applause with cheers) resounded through the hall.

As the ovation subsided, Jakob von Winternitz, Concordia's past president, rose to offer a toast in English "to the Clemens ladies" sitting in the gallery with Bettina Wirth (who may have helped Twain draft his speech), Amelia S. Levetus, and other female journalists not then admitted to membership in this all-male club. The assemblage stood and raised glasses toward them with a resounding "*Hoch! Hoch! zum Ihr Wohl!*" (Hail! Hail! to their health!). The *kunstlerische Programm* (artistic program) thereupon commenced, consisting of a reading in German by the actor Lewinsky of Twain's "Niagara," a witty *Baenkel* (doggerel ballad) blending details of Twain's early life with topical jokes about present-day Vienna composed by Julius Bauer and sung by Girardi, who accompanied himself at the piano, and finally a performance by Alfred Grünfeld on the Bösendorfer of his famous potpourri of Strauss waltz paraphrases.

A group photograph session followed the formal end of the proceedings, the members eagerly crowding around their American guest to offer congratulations and express gratitude. Then, the ladies having politely exited this male bastion, came what *Extrapost* called the "*zwanglos Unterhaltung*" (informal entertainment), a euphemism for serious social drinking. How long into that part of the festivities the American guest of honor stayed was discreetly left unreported, but it was long after midnight—indeed, said *Neues Wiener Tagblatt*, "*Es war schon Morgen*" (it was already morning)—when the last guests staggered from Merchants' Hall.

Was his Concordia speech an unalloyed triumph? From the reception he had that bibulous evening, Mark Twain must have thought so, must have gone to bed happy and satisfied, must have been pleased with the press coverage in the days that followed. So he wrote in his notebook and to friends back home. If there were grumblings in the opposition press that his wisecracks about the local language were gauche or tasteless, his friends in the liberal papers, aware of his earlier jokes about German, brushed the subject aside diplomatically as being "a well-worn theme" with him, stressing the occasion itself and Twain's unique style.

He seems not to have been fully aware that those he was addressing were, after all, artisans of their language, as he was of English, and

Alfred Grünfeld, a piano virtuoso who performed on programs with
Mark Twain. He was a close friend of the Clemenses in Vienna.
(Picture Archives of the Austrian National Library)

just as he made of his mother tongue a fine-tuned instrument, so did many of these Viennese writers in their use of German, the language they instinctively cherished. His insensitivity on this occasion betrays a boorish streak he shared with too many of his compatriots then and now. Like most Americans, Mark Twain thought foreign languages, no matter how proficient he might be in them, hilariously funny, especially in their grammar and syntax. He often ridiculed French and Italian as well as German because to be idiomatic in those languages requires one to express things differently from the way one "naturally" speaks in English. For instance, when he saw a French translation of his Jumping Frog story in *Revue des Deux Mondes* (July 15, 1872), he made a burlesque literal translation of it into English, then capitalized on it by publishing the original, the French version, and his own retranslation, "clawed back into a civilized language once more."

Perhaps because German was the one foreign tongue in which he approached genuine fluency—sufficient at least for him to translate German works into English and some of his own into German with relative ease—it is the language he lampooned most often. His "Awful German Language" quickly became, as it remains today, the most quoted part of *A Tramp Abroad*. Less well known is his short farce "Meisterschaft," published in *The Century* in 1888 and later in his collected works, burlesquing a textbook he had used to learn German which startlingly anticipates by three-quarters of a century a main element of Eugene Ionesco's classic Absurdist one-acter, *La cantatrice chauve* (The Bald Soprano, 1950). Then there are the numerous passing jibes such as Hank Morgan's (in *A Connecticut Yankee*) describing Sandy's long sentences as coming from "the Mother of the German Language," adding, "Whenever the literary German dives into a sentence, that is the last you are going to see of him till he emerges on the other side of the Atlantic with his verb in his mouth."

Nor would Twain let go of the subject. In a segment of his autobiography, ironically called "Beauties of the German Language," written three months after his Concordia speech, he again has fun with the German habit of lengthily compounding old nouns to form new ones, blithely ignoring the same capability (which we often employ) in English. In the same month (February 1898), he inscribed the verso of a photo of himself autographed recto "To Ed. Pötzl with the love of S. L. Clemens" with an aphorism: "It is easier for a camel to enter the Kingdom of Heaven through the eye of a rich man's needle than it is for any other foreigner to read the terrible German script. Mark Twain."*[15] His Vienna notebooks contain other jottings for articles he (perhaps luckily) never got around to: a "Conversation between the Verbs, Adjectives, &c" containing the line "here comes old überhaupt, who is always intruding into the talk & never knows what he means," and another to "Write German Dictionary article & add some gout letters," meaning those he received from Austrian well-wishers when he was confined with gout during his first week in Vienna.†[16]

Such jokes embody a very, very "Amurican" cultural attitude: people who don't speak or spell English correctly are comical; people who don't speak English at all are weird. In colonial days and during later mass immigration, this kind of ridicule was a means of fostering linguistic conformity and hastening "Americanization." Now our ethnocentrism provides a rationalization of verbal laziness in a land where linguists and foreign language teachers are an underpaid academic proletariat. Although poking fun at the way people speak or misspell words is tabu today as being racist, ethnocentric, or xenophobic, such ridicule was a stock-in-trade of American humorists in the last century, from "phunny phellows" like Artemus Ward and Petroleum V. Nasby to Mark Twain himself.

To German-speakers, of course, there is nothing intrinsically comic about their language. German dialect humor, using city cockneys like "Ottakringer" (Viennese) and "Weddinger" (Berlinese) or the rural speech of Swabia and Bavaria, has been plentiful since the mid-nine-

---

*This previously unpublished inscription by Mark Twain is © 1992 by Manufacturers Hanover Trust Company as Trustee of the Mark Twain Foundation, which reserves all reproduction or dramatization rights in every medium. It is published with the permission of the University of California Press and Robert H. Hirst, General Editor, Mark Twain Project.

teenth century. In literary and popular entertainment, these social (that is, class) and regional dialects distinguish the yokel, the clown, or, as in the plays of Johann Nestroy, the wise fool. But *reines Hochdeutsch* (pure High German), the linguistic badge of an educated speaker, is a matter of pride, not a subject for ridicule. Unlike the French, whose chauvinism takes the opposite tack, German-speakers have ever been tolerant of foreigners' attempts to use their language, however imperfectly. Hence Mark Twain's complaints about its silly complexities were, at best, amusing as jokes about *his* problems, not those of his audience (or of cosmopolitan people generally) or anything inherent in their native tongue.

To anyone less prickly than Karl Kraus, who regarded his *Muttersprache* as almost sacred and held in contempt those who did not use it skillfully, Mark Twain's Concordia speech was not actually offensive. But it was hardly an unqualified triumph, nor did it endear him to the literati of Vienna. A serious speech would have been inappropriate and disappointing to his audience, that much he had correctly sensed. Yet another subject for his humor on that memorable evening, especially one that did not seem to be merely warmed over, might have rubbed less fur the wrong way.

Moreover, his timing could not have been worse. The Austrian government was at that hour embroiled in what one writer called a *"furor Teutonicus"* over a proposal to grant the Czech language parity with German in the administration of Bohemia and Moravia. The most severe crisis in a half-century was brewing over the language problem, and Mark Twain was soon to become more than merely a disinterested foreign observer of it. German-Austrian liberals and nationalists alike regarded their language as inextricable from their political and cultural hegemony which was under challenge from the Young Czechs. Thus to criticize German at this sensitive juncture even in jest was to touch a raw nerve and to allow one's motives to be called into question.

Mark Twain's popularity with the independent, liberal, and left-wing press in Vienna was not diminished by what its otherwise well-disposed journalists may have felt, on sober reflection, about his faux pas. He made good copy, so good, in fact, that it is possible to construct an almost diurnal account of his Viennese sojourn simply by reading the local papers from September 1897 until June 1899. Did the famous American take the evening air at the *Burgmusik*, an extravaganza of military bands at the twilight changing of the guard at the Hofburg? The reporters thought it merited at least a couple of paragraphs. Ditto a visit to the Börse (stock exchange) or a tour of the Burgtheater. If he went for a streetcar ride and had an altercation with the conductor because he had carelessly thrown his ticket out the window, a lucky reporter had a hot scoop. And at any ball, concert, theater premiere, or exhibition opening, the "among others present" listings seemed incomplete without "the distinguished American guest" who could often be depended on to provide a colorful anecdote.[17]

The circulation war continued unabated. No paper captured more than a corner of the field, but for a while the spoils seemed to go to that famous American guest who knew expertly how to turn the battle to his own advantage. On the other hand, Twain soon discovered there was a nasty side to this unholy war in which he was actually but a pawn. If he was the darling of the liberal *Neue Freie Presse, Neues Wiener Tagblatt*, and other papers that the *Reichspost* and *Deutsches Volksblatt* ceaselessly castigated as *"die Judenpresse,"* he was also a sitting duck for scurrilous barbs, slurs, and innuendos from the anti-Semites. That, too, sold newspapers in Old Vienna.

The sequel to Mark Twain's Concordia episode occurred some fifteen months later and 180 miles eastward in Budapest, the "other capital" of the Habsburg empire, when he addressed the Hungarian Journalists' Association on March 23 and 25, 1899. Like his Concordia speech, this also had a mixed reception but for quite different local reasons. The occasion for his invitation to Budapest was the fiftieth anniversary ("Jubilee") of the "emancipation" of the Hungarian press, an 1849 decree granting Magyars the right to publish in their own tongue. At the time of Twain's visit, there were nearly two hundred Magyar newspapers and periodicals being published in Budapest plus several dailies, such as Max Nordau's *Pester Lloyd*, in German, while

Front page of *Illustrirtes Wiener Extrablatt,* April 8, 1898, showing spectators (including Mark Twain) watching firemen rescue a Russian countess from a suicide attempt in the Hotel Metropole

Tagesneuigkeiten.

Eine Stunde bei Mark Twain.

"Kommen Sie Donnerstag um 4 Uhr," hatte Mark Twain "schreiben "ich bin jetzt so weit hergestellt, um einer solchen be-Pflicht zu Pflicht, ein Stündchen verplaudern zu können." —

Truth is the most valuable thing we have. Let us economise it.

Freilich übersetzt &c.:

Wir haben nichts die so werthvoll ist wie die Wahrheit. Also lasst uns davon sparsam sein Sie nicht verschwenden.

Truly Yours
Mark Twain

Wien, Oct. 8.

XI. österreichischer Aerztevereinstag.

A. D. G.

Otthon, the press club that was the Hungarian counterpart to Concordia, had nearly 1,200 members.[18]

Several of these Hungarian journalists were also stalwarts of Concordia, among them the venerable Mór Jokai (1825–1904), Hungary's premier writer in that era, who may have had something to do with the American humorist's invitation to Budapest. Author of nearly a hundred novels, one of which (*Saffi*, 1884) furnished the libretto for Johann Strauss's ever-popular *Der Zigeunerbaron* (The Gypsy Baron), Jokai had the same English publisher (Chatto and Windus) as Mark Twain. Although this septuagenarian doyen of Hungarian letters was ailing at the time of Twain's visit and unable to attend any of his American colleague's public appearances, Mark Twain paid a courtesy call on him which was lengthily reported the next day in the leading newspaper, *Magyar Hirlap*.[19]

His connection with Jokai aside, what prompted the Hungarian journalists to invite Mark Twain and what moved him to accept, apparently without honorarium, one may only conjecture. Perhaps the attention he continued almost daily to receive in the Viennese press had as much as anything to do with the invitation, and his unflagging appetite for self-promotion plus curiosity about "the Paris of the Danube" were sufficient motives for his acceptance. Although he had not then been as widely translated and read in Hungary as in the German-speaking countries, the Budapest daily *Pesti Napló* had printed his latest book, *Following the Equator*, in 101 translated installments in 1898–99, and his *Tom Sawyer*, *Huckleberry Finn*, and *The Prince and the Pauper* had already become children's classics in Magyar renderings. Nevertheless, a substantial number of the Hungarian literati, including those who wrote for the influential highbrow journal *A Hét*, took a decidedly dim view of this uncouth American humorist and his "intolerably vulgar taste."[20] If he knew this attitude, which is doubtful, Mark Twain would have had even more reason for a public-relations visit to Budapest.

The Clemens family entrained at Vienna's Nordbahnhof early on a chilly Thursday morning, March 23, 1899. Their route took them eastward through what is now Czechoslovakia—Pressburg/Pozsony (Bra-

tislava), Galánta, and Érsekújvár (Nové Zámky), Slovakian towns then
under Hungarian rule—to some surpassingly beautiful scenery from
the "Danube bend" (Duna-kanyar) opposite Visegrád and the Buda
hills south to the western (Nyugati) station in Pest. They arrived at the
Hotel Hungária in Pest at teatime. A note from a reporter for *Magyar
Hirlap*, offering a 1,000-forint note "for the pleasure of a few minute's
[*sic*] interview with Mr. Clemens" awaited them. The interview, published the next day, had been interrupted and foreshortened, however,
so Mark Twain could get to the journalists' association banquet at eight
o'clock.[21]

With its glut of newspapers, Budapest had a circulation war no less
intense than Vienna's, so *Magyar Hirlap* had already been scooped by
the rival *Pesti Napló*, Hungary's largest daily, which had sent a reporter
to board the Clemenses' train at Galánta. The lengthy interview he
obtained during the rest of the journey ran the next morning under a
banner headline, "Mark Twainnel Galántátó Budapestig" (With Mark
Twain from Galánta to Budapest).[22] Although he spoke no English,
the energetic young reporter had evidently done his homework well
on both the humorist's life and his works, and the interview, conducted
entirely in German (Twain yet again apologizing for his lack of fluency), is more accurate and more perceptive than most of the early
newspaper interviews Mark Twain had had in Vienna.

The banquet that evening was of a quite different sort from the Concordia "Festkneipe" honoring Mark Twain fifteen months earlier. This
was a ceremonial occasion to observe formally and with due solemnity
the anniversary of freedom of the press in Hungary. The American
guest was not expected to give an address or be the main attraction
but merely to make some appropriate remarks in response to the general speechifying. This he did with the utmost diplomacy, according
to Anna Katona, who notes that in the *Budapesti Hirlap* report the
next day, Mark Twain was quoted as making "a sharp distinction between liberty of press, which criticizes vice, and licentiousness, which
encourages it."[23]

In his pocket, however, he had another, quite different speech, a copy of which he had already given to a New York newspaper. He later confided to Howells: "Just as I was leaving here [Vienna] I got a telegram from London asking for the speech for a New York paper. I (*this is strictly private*) sent it. And then *I didn't make that speech,* but another of a quite different character—a speech born of something which the introducer said. If that speech got cabled and printed, you needn't let on that it was never uttered."[24] Maybe he had learned something from his ruffling of journalistic feathers in Vienna after all. The brief (about four-hundred-word) political burlesque, "German for the Hungarians," he had prepared (and discreetly pocketed) on the sensitive subject of the *Ausgleich,* treating it comically, would have been singularly inappropriate if not outrageously offensive. Nevertheless, it is printed in Paine's posthumous collection of Twain's speeches with a wholly erroneous identification as the "Address at the Jubilee Celebration of the Emancipation of the Hungarian Press, March 26, 1899" and with a fanciful headnote fallaciously stating "the Ministry and members of Parliament were present."[25]

Next morning the city lay buried under a late winter snowstorm when the Clemenses set out for some sightseeing. They went first to the visitors' gallery of the grandiose new Parliament (opened in 1896) on the Pest shore of the Duna (Danube) opposite the royal residence (Schloss) on the Buda hills. When they entered, according to *Magyar Hirlap,* "political debates were forgotten and all eyes turned to the celebrities."[26] After lunch, Olivia and her two daughters, who had apparently caught colds from the abrupt change of weather, returned to their hotel while Mark Twain continued to the Lipótvárosi Kaszinó (Leopoldtown Club) to check out the appurtenances and acoustic of its hall for his lecture the following evening.

Then he was escorted to the journalists' club, Otthon (which means "home" in Magyar), where he was introduced to members by the club's chairman, Jenö Rákosi, and offered cigars and a convivial glass of *Barack-Pálinka* (apricot schnapps), which he pronounced "too strong." This was followed by making an impromptu phonograph recording (apparently since lost) of Mark Twain giving his "Patent Adjustable

Speech," a parodistic all-purpose oration composed entirely of clichés that could be improvised on any occasion, no matter the topic.

Mark Twain's lecture at 8 P.M. on March 25 in the great hall of the Lipótvárosi Kaszino (now housing the Hungarian Ministry of Culture) was the high point of his week in Budapest, a reprise of his triumphant public lecture in Vienna on February 1, 1898. The newspaper accounts indicate tickets were in great demand among Budapest's English-speaking intelligentsia and that he held his audience "spellbound" for over an hour. His material was the same he had used in his Vienna readings: "The Lucerne Girl" and "The Stolen Watermelon" followed by an intermission and then "Encounter with an Interviewer" and "The Genuine Mexican Plug."[27] As he finished, the hall erupted in wild enthusiasm.

The press reaction was very much cooler. Ilona Györy, in the *Pesti Hirlap*, described the program's content as "thin" but praised Twain's "superb platform manner," as did *Pesti Napló*, which remarked upon his histrionics and effective sense of timing. Several newspapers, according to Katona, were quite skeptical, even sharply critical of the audience's celebrity madness, Twain's mangling of German, and his "lack of culture." Béla Tóth, a popular newspaper humorist who was perhaps the Magyar counterpart to Eduard Pötzl, asserted in *Pesti Napló* that Twain's peculiarly American brand of humor, not just his language, was alien to the Hungarian mentality. The leading literary weekly, *A Hét*, hostile as ever, went so far as to allege, apparently without basis, that the sponsors had hired an "interpreter" to stand behind Twain on the platform and give the audience laugh cues "by twirling his moustache."[28]

Basking in the warmth of his ovation, however induced, Twain seemed oblivious to his newspaper critics, telling Howells it had been "a darling night, & those Hungarians are lovely people." His lecture audience, he said, "understood me perfectly,—to judge by the effects." It seems an egoistic judgment in view of his also confiding that at the banquet the night before he had heard "a most graceful & easy & beautiful & delicious speech—I never heard one that enchanted me more—although I did not understand a word of it, since it was in Hungarian. But the art of it!—it was superlative."[29]

The Clemenses spent three more days in Budapest, mostly sightseeing, although Olivia's flu-like symptoms prevented her accompanying her husband and daughters on several excursions and forced cancellation of a farewell banquet planned for them at the Lipótvárosi Kaszino. They had much to see. Budapest had been formed in 1873 by joining twin cities, Buda and Pest, on opposite sides of the wide Duna (Danube) into a single municipality. By 1899 it was in many respects an even more "modern" city than Vienna. It had the first electrified streetcars (1889) in Europe, the first subterranean transit system (1896) of any city (it served as a model for New York's subway and for the Paris Metro), a sumptuous new opera house, world-famous mineral springs and thermal baths (modernized though dating from Roman times), and a splendidly beautiful boulevard (Andrássy Street) connecting Pest's thriving commercial center with the Városliget (city park) where a forum of public monuments and museums flanked a pleasure garden like Vienna's Prater. A quarter of the city's nearly 800,000 inhabitants were Jews who, even more assimilated and less discriminated against than the Jews of Vienna, helped give Budapest a cultural life the equal of almost any city of Europe.[30]

What amazed Clemens most about Budapest's "modernity," however, was not the city's new architecture or even its trams and subway, but that for a mere sixty cents per month, "the telephone reads the morning paper to you at home; gives you the stocks & markets at noon; gives you lessons in 3 foreign languages during 3 hours; gives you the afternoon telegrams [that is, latest news capsulized]; & at night the concerts & operas." Furthermore, he was impressed that "even the clerks & seamstresses & bootblacks & everybody else are subscribers" to this service.[31]

Olivia, on the other hand, was most impressed by the courtesy call they received at their hotel from Ferenc Kossuth (1841–1914), leader of the Independence Party in the Hungarian Parliament. Kossuth, who was but eight when he fled Hungary with his father after the abortive uprising Lajos Kossuth led in 1848, was educated in England (and married an Englishwoman) and had an illustrious career as a civil engineer in Italy before bringing his father's body back to Hungary for a hero's burial in 1894. Reluctantly, he remained to lead the opposition to the loyalist Tisza regimes. Clemens had heard Lajos Kossuth lecture in Saint Louis in the late 1850s on one of his barnstorming tours of the United States, and like most Americans, the Clemenses venerated this great "Champion of Liberty."

On their last afternoon, Mark Twain, along with Clara and Jean, attended a tea party where there was music and the girls were instructed in some Magyar dances. The Hungarian feminist author Clementina Katona Abrányi later recalled that Twain struck her on this occasion as "sensitive, reflective and introverted," and she was deeply impressed by his "erudition" and advanced opinions about the status of women. In her perceptions of the American humorist, she was, according to Anna Katona, "the first Hungarian to discover the serious Mark Twain behind the laughter."[32] One might add she was among the first to do so anywhere.

The Clemenses left Budapest at eight o'clock on the evening of March 29, 1899, from the city's eastern (Keleti) station, returning to Vienna in a wagon-lit carriage "put at their disposal by Hungarian Railroads," certainly a mark of unusual distinction. After examining all the newspaper reports and the literary journals, Anna Katona concluded that, although Mark Twain's Budapest sojourn was a popular success, it would have been an even greater one had his audience, especially the Hungarian journalists, been more fluent in English and if the latter had been less stuffy and pecksniffish.

CHAPTER FOUR

Witness to History

ext to religion, especially the Book of Genesis and the internal contradictions and conundrums of Calvinist theology, the subject most continuously fascinating to Mark Twain was politics. It was as a political journalist that Samuel Clemens first used this pen name, reporting proceedings of the Nevada legislature and state constitutional convention in 1863–64 for the Virginia City *Territorial Enterprise*. After that he did local political reporting in San Francisco, and in 1867 and early 1868, he worked in Washington as secretary to Sen. William Stewart of Nevada and then as a congressional reporter for the *New York Tribune* and several other newspapers. He was thus a close, skeptical, even cynical observer of political institutions and processes in his own country, and he was always tremendously curious about those in the foreign lands he visited.

Politics and politicians were often objects of Twain's satire in his belletristic writing from *Roughing It* onward. Excepting only what he regarded as their peurile religions, nothing in his view so exposed the hypocrisies, chicaneries, follies, and delusions of the "damned human race" quite as fully as their ridiculous political beliefs and postures. He referred, for example, to the Congress of the United States as "that grand old benevolent asylum for the mentally incompetent" and gave his Pudd'nhead Wilson the maxim that "it could probably be shown by facts and figures that there is no distinctly native criminal class in America except Congress." He was fond of taking verbal potshots at prominent politicians, domestic or foreign. For instance, at the height of Pres. Theodore Roosevelt's popularity, Twain pilloried him as "the Tom Sawyer of American politics."

Although John Marshall Clemens, the author's father, had held elective office as a justice of the peace in Hannibal, Samuel Clemens himself never sought or considered public office. He publicly endorsed the presidential candidacies of Ulysses S. Grant (the only one he seems unreservedly to have admired), Hayes, Garfield, and, after becoming a "Mugwump" in 1884, Grover Cleveland. His only active participation in politics, however, was in New York City soon after his return to America in 1900, when he spoke at political rallies and marched in parades for reform candidates who wrested the city government from the grip of Tammany Hall. In December 1906 he made a highly publicized appearance before Congress in his white flannel suit to lobby on behalf of a new copyright law.

Mark Twain nevertheless imagined himself an independent candidate for governor of New York in a feuilleton ironically titled "*Candidatenfreuden*" (The Joys of a Candidate) he contributed to the Viennese left-liberal weekly, *Die Volksstimme* (December 12, 1897, 1–3). This is evidently his own translation and slight revision of a sketch, "Running for Governor," he had written in 1870 detailing how his fictional opponents, John T. Smith and Blank J. Blank, carry on such a vile smear campaign in the press—accusing him of lying, stealing, and embezzling—that he is glad to "strike the flag" and withdraw early from the contest. Moral: politics is a messy, dishonest business of scoundrels that any person with integrity should avoid.

Twain's most sustained political statement is his novel *A Connecticut Yankee in King Arthur's Court* (1889). When Hank Morgan, the Yankee shop foreman of the title, gets knocked out and then regains consciousness in Arthurian England, he attempts to turn a backward, underdeveloped country by force majeure into a nineteenth-century industrial democracy. Although Hank succeeds by degrees in enlightening King Arthur and enlisting his aid, the results of his efforts, as he runs afoul of the church, entrenched feudalism, and most of all, the complacent ignorance of the masses, are futile, even apocalyptic. The work casts doubt on the view that progress is possible in politics or in any other sphere of human endeavor, implying that political idealism and revolutionary zeal are self-defeating delusions that destroy the values they seek to promote.

Beyond his vague commitment to Jeffersonian principles of democratic republicanism coupled with his own brand of Manchester liberalism, it would be hard to say exactly what constituted Mark Twain's political philosophy. In this as in all else, he was no ideologue, and even his well-known antimonarchist stance, epitomized by Hank's joke that Britain's royal family could be replaced by a family of cats that might function as well at less public expense, was not unswerving. He could mock Germany's Emperor Wilhelm II as a "cock-a-hoop sovereign," then flipflop to express his admiration for Austria-Hungary's Franz Josef I and intense outrage at the assassination of Empress Elisabeth. During his last decade he waxed increasingly antiimperialist in his public pronouncements, but, his Marxist apologists to the contrary, he never shared the socialist persuasions of his good friend William Dean Howells.

Given Twain's penchant for politics, it is not surprising that one of his first outings in Vienna after recovering from the gout was to attend a session of the Gemeinderat (city council) on Friday evening, October 15, 1897. His presence in the *Journalistenloge* (press box) created such a stir among councillors, spectators, and his colleagues of the local press that most of the latter made his visit the focus of their reports of the session.[1] It was an unusually raucous meeting even for this notoriously fractious, unwieldy body of 138 members. Mark Twain was asked by reporters to comment on what he had witnessed there, which he did with rather undiplomatic candor.[2]

The setting was splendidly theatrical. The neo-Gothic council chamber of the new town hall (Rathaus), with its frescoes of medieval history, Gobelins, and ornately carved chairs, looked more as if it were designed for the Minnesingers' contest in *Tannhäuser* than for debating such mundane matters as school levies and contracts for laying gas mains. The room was one of the masterstrokes of architect Friedrich von Schmidt, who copied the facade of his building from the fourteenth-century Hôtel de Ville on the Grand Place in Brussels. Completed in 1885, Schmidt's new Rathaus was the most expensive edifice erected in nineteenth-century Vienna and one of its most sumptuous.

On the dais, among the twenty-five-member *Stadtrat* (executive committee) at this meeting, sat the immensely popular new *Oberbürgermeister* (lord mayor), Dr. Karl Lueger, leader of the Christian Social Party in Austria.[3] *Der schöne Karl* (handsome Charles), as he was affectionately known to his huge following among the city's artisans and small shopkeepers, had been in office just six months. His three previous elections as mayor in 1895 and 1896 had been nullified by the emperor, who distrusted this rabble-rouser. By April 1897, however, Lueger's majority was so large the emperor considered it unwise if not dangerous to obstruct the public will longer, and Lueger began a tenure that, ending only with his death in 1910, made this *Herrgott in Wien* (Lord God of Vienna) one of the world's foremost pioneers of municipal socialism. Without doubt, Lueger was one of the most visionary administrators any city has ever had, and the stamp he left upon Vienna in public housing and welfare, health care, sanitation, and civic beautification remains indelible. His most enduring monument is the huge municipally financed home for the indigent aged in a lovely park-like setting in suburban Lainz to which he bequeathed his entire fortune.

Lueger was elected as a champion of the "little man" against the encroachments of finance capitalism and as a defender of the church against the secularization (*Los-von-Rom*) movement of Georg von Schönerer and his German Nationals in the Reichsrat. Though less vitriolic than *der Ritter von Rosenau* (the Knight of Rosenau), as Schönerer was called after his country seat in Lower Austria, Lueger and his party had stolen some of the German Nationals' fire in appropriating anti-Semitism as a propaganda tool for mobilizing the urban masses. Small wonder that Adolf Hitler, painting postcards in Lueger's Vienna in

1907, learned useful political lessons from *der schöne Karl,* praising him in *Mein Kampf* not only as "the last great German to be born in the ranks of the people" but also as "a statesman greater than all the so-called diplomats of the time."[4]

No resolutions or ordinances were passed at this council meeting, but two issues were hotly debated: the fear of the *Czechisierung* (Czechifying) of Vienna and of the *Verjudung des Richterstandes* (Jewifying of judgeships). The German Nationals were protesting the size of the Czech element in the city's population—every third Viennese was Czech by either birth or ancestry—and were trying to force some regulations to prevent further immigration into the city from Bohemia and Moravia. This occurrence was, of course, during the tension over the Badeni government's proposals to give the Czech language parity with German in the Bohemian civil service, and anti-Czech sentiment was already running so high in the city that many German restaurateurs were even refusing service to Czech customers!

The question of Jewish appointments to municipal judgeships had been raised by leaders of the city's Jewish community. They argued that although the Viennese legal profession had a large number of Jewish members—far out of proportion to the Jewish percentage in the city's population as a whole—few Jews were yet on the Austrian bench.

The pragmatic Dr. Lueger, who could turn his anti-Semitism on and off as the occasion demanded and was famed for his *"Wer a Jud is', bestimm' i'!"* (I decide who is a Jew!), took an unusually conciliatory stance on both issues at this session. Concerning the appointment of judges, he expressed the tolerant view that professional merit and experience alone, not *Konfession* (religious faith), should be the determining factor. This opinion was greeted with general uproar and howls of protest.

The following Sunday, October 17, 1897, a strange, enigmatic article about this session took up nearly half a page in the *Neue Freie Presse.*[5] Couched as a letter to the editor and signed "Mark Twain," the letter criticizes the noisiness of Vienna's traffic and the frequency of street barricades where gas pipes are being laid, then turns to the writer's visit to the Gemeinderat and his observations about the discussion he witnessed there on the *Judenfrage* (Jewish question). In America, he says, there are many false opinions about Vienna, one of which is that the city is anti-Semitic. Then he continues: "Und was hörte ich hier vom Bürgermeister ihm selbst? Er sagte: 'Ich werde nie dulden die Verunglimpfung irgend einer Confession, da der Glauben eines Jeden muß hochgehalten und hochgeschätzt werden.' " (And what did I hear right here from the mayor himself? "I won't tolerate disparagement of any faith because the believers of each must be held in high esteem.")

After listening to more such conciliatory views from the mayor, the writer says, he could no longer remain silent but sprang to his feet, waved his hat, and shouted: *"Hoch Lueger! Hoch die Juden! . . ."* (Long live Lueger! Long live the Jews!) At this point someone nearby landed him such a blow of the fist that he was knocked unconscious and had to be carried to his hotel in an ambulance. Regaining consciousness, he is thankful to have suffered only a few broken bones and a few knocked-out teeth, concluding with wonderful understatement: *"Ich werde die Sitzung ihres Gemeinderathes nicht so bald vergessen."* (I won't very soon forget the session of your city council.)

Below the "Mark Twain" signature is a postscript signed by "X.Y., Local-Reporter" explaining that after the letter was already in press, he had hurried to the Metropole to inquire about Twain's condition. The reporter concludes: *"Er ist wohlauf und meint, ein unbekannter Einsender müsse uns mystifizirt haben."* (He is quite well and believes an unknown contributor must have hoaxed us.)

Who hoaxed the proud *Neue Freie Presse*? Mark Twain himself? It was the sort of thing he had done several times when news was scarce in Virginia City and he could fill columns in the *Enterprise* with exaggerated or partly invented stories. Some of them, like his report of the discovery of a "petrified man" found thumbing his nose in a desert cave, were reprinted in a dozen western newspapers before being exposed as a "Washoe Joke."[6] Another indicator of Twain's possible authorship is that the writer is familiar with two of Clemens's private peeves about Vienna: the traffic noise that resulted because, in his opinion, too few wagons in Vienna used rubber tires on the cobblestone streets and the inconvenience of having to trudge around barricades and through mud where trenches were being dug in the streets to lay gas mains. Finally, the German prose here resembles the kind Mark Twain wrote on other occasions: carefully correct at the beginning, becoming less correct, less idiomatic later in the piece, from haste or impatience. So while Twain's authorship may be doubted, it is not completely implausible.

What does seem certain is that the incident is fictitious. No mention of it appears in any newspaper's coverage of the Gemeinderat meeting, and it would have been sufficiently sensational to have been reported fully had it really occurred. There remains, then, the question of motive. Why would anyone (including Twain) have made up such a story? To attack Lueger subtly? To embarrass *NFP*? To belittle Mark Twain?

If the latter two were intended, one possible suspect could be Karl Kraus, who made *NFP* one of his chief targets for many years and whose dislike of Twain was later openly expressed. But innuendos about the American writer's liberal leanings and his associations with Jews had already begun to appear in the anti-Semitic press in Vienna, and this letter might well be the work of a now-unidentifiable journalist from a rival paper targeting both Twain and the liberal *NFP* simultaneously.

In any case, it was by no means the last reverberation in the local press of Mark Twain's Gemeinderat visit. A week later, on October 23, the weekly humor magazine *Figaro* treated the readers of its *Wiener Luft* supplement to a superb cartoon by Theodor Zasche, one of the leading caricaturists of the day, showing Mark Twain dressed as Uncle Sam fishing in a bucket labelled "Wien." On the same page are three probably spurious brief passages purportedly *"Aus dem Tagebuche des amerikanischen Humoristen Mark Twain"* (From the diary of the American humorist Mark Twain) containing comments on the Gemeinderat proceedings. The first of the three, however, unerringly captures the ring of authentic Twainian humor:

Die israelitischen Gemeinderäthe der Stadt Wien sind der Meining,
daß es viel zuwenig jüdische Richter in Oesterreich gebe. Der Vizebürger-
meister Neumayer hingegen ist der Ansicht, es seien deren viel mehr
als genug.

Es ist sehr schwer zu erfahren, wer da im Recht sei. Lumpen kann
man die Beurtheilung nicht anheimstellen und die anständigen und
ehrenhaften Menschen sagen: Wir für unseren Theil brauchen gar keine
Richter.[7]

(The Israelite community councils of the city of Vienna are of the opinion that there are too few Jewish judges in Austria. Vice-mayor Neumayer
takes the opposite view that there are more than enough.

It's very hard to say who's right here. Riffraff can't be left to their own
judgment and decent, honorable people say: for our part we don't need
judges at all.)

When Clemens arrived in Vienna at the end of September 1897,
the talk of the town and the headline story in all the papers were
a duel with pistols that had been fought on September 15 between
Count Kasimir Badeni, the prime minister, and Karl Hermann Wolf,
a German Nationalist deputy in the Reichsrat (parliament) and editor of the scurrilously anti-Semitic *Wiener Volkszeitung*. Badeni was
slightly wounded, Wolf claimed vindication, and that normally would
have ended matters. But the affair continued to dominate the news
for weeks because duels, illegal in Austria-Hungary (though they occurred daily, and any officer who refused a challenge was dismissed
from the service), were also condemned by the church as a mortal sin.
Speculation was rife over whether these officials would be prosecuted,
excommunicated, or both.

In the end, nothing happened. Both claimed immunity from the
law as a privilege of office, and they escaped with but a "tush-tush"
admonition from the archbishop of Vienna. Reflecting on this affair some months later, Mark Twain was prompted to write a brief
article entitled "Dueling," posthumously published in Paine's collection, *Europe and Elsewhere*.[8] He begins with some invidious comparisons between the duel as practiced in France and in Austria: "Here

it is tragedy, in France it is comedy; here it is solemnity, there it is monkeyshines." He illustrates this by describing nine recent reports of duels he had collected from Viennese newspapers, beginning with the Badeni-Wolf duel.

The real principals in these and all other duels, he argues, are not the duelists themselves but their families who are the innocent victims of those who are slaves to custom: "The logic of it is admirable; a person has robbed me of a penny; I must beggar ten innocent persons to make good my loss. Surely nobody's 'honor' is worth all that." It would be easy, he concludes, to have an effective law to stop dueling by simply compelling duelists' families to be present at all duels.

Twain's essay waxes increasingly ironic until, near its end, he relates this chilling tale:

> In January a neighbor of ours who has a young son in the army was awakened by the youth at three o'clock one morning, and she sat up in bed and listened to his message:
>
> "I have come to tell you something, mother, which will distress you, but you must be good and brave and bear it. I have been affronted by a fellow officer and we fight at three this afternoon. Lie down and sleep now, and think no more about it."

Paralyzed with anxiety and fear, the mother spends the next twelve hours praying, after daybreak going from one church to another. At three that afternoon she goes home to await with dread the outcome of the duel.

> Presently she heard the clank of a saber—she had not known before what music was in the sound—and her son put his head in and said:
>
> "X was in the wrong and he apologized."
>
> So the incident was closed; and for the rest of her life the mother will always find something pleasant about the clank of a saber, no doubt.[9]

The story makes its skillful thrust at dueling with grim humor and what Freud, using another Twain story as his example, denominates "the economy of pity," rendered here effectively by the added "no doubt." Twain repeats this effect in the penultimate example in his essay, one about "a duel with cavalry sabers, between an editor and a lieutenant," which he summarizes succinctly: "The editor walked to the hospital; the lieutenant was carried." Then he deftly adds: "In Austria an editor who can write well is valuable, but he is not likely to remain so unless he can handle a saber with charm."

Is it mere coincidence that these same points about dueling are made in story after story, play after play with much the same aura of bitter irony during this period by Dr. Arthur Schnitzler, "the Austrian Chekhov," then practicing medicine just across the Ring in Grillparzerstrasse? The senseless Code Duello and the suffering it causes the innocent in fin de siècle bourgeois Austrian society are a major theme in Schnitzler's stream-of-consciousness novella *Leutenant Gustl* (translated as *None but the Brave*) and his domestic tragedy *Das weite Land* (translated as *The Undiscovered Country*), among others. If Twain and Schnitzler did not meet, and there is nothing to suggest they did, it may be because Schnitzler had by then withdrawn from the kind of literary socializing that went on at the Café Central and elsewhere.[10] Mark Twain apparently saw only one of Schnitzler's plays, *Liebelei* (Love Games), at the Burgtheater, and that one is not about dueling. But in 1898 both writers were breathing the same air, physically and intellectually, and both were reading the same newspapers.

The Badeni-Wolf duel was but one incident, albeit a dramatic one, in the political upheaval that commenced April 5, 1897 (three days before Lueger's fourth and final election as mayor), when Count Badeni submitted his language ordinances for Bohemia and Moravia to the Reichsrat. His doing so was the result of a deal he had made with Czech deputies (Young Czechs) for votes he needed to pass the stalemated decennial Ausgleich (Equalizer) defining the relationship within the dual monarchy between Austria and Hungary. First negotiated in 1867 and requiring parliamentary ratification every ten years, the Ausgleich united the two states in their conduct of foreign affairs, a common military and customs union, leaving both countries separate in internal affairs. Had the Ausgleich not been reaffirmed by December 1897, the two halves of the dual monarchy would have split automatically into independent nations under the same monarch. The Schönerianer (German Nationals) wanted the treaty renegotiated to increase Austrian authority rather than merely continuing the previous coequal arrangement.[11]

A rich Polish landowner and a political independent, Badeni had established a reputation as a strong man in seven years as *Statthalter* (governor) of Galicia. As prime minister, while also holding the post of interior minister, he had been politically astute. In this instance, however, he had not reckoned with the fury his proposal would unleash among the German Nationals who saw it as an intolerable affront to German hegemony in the Czech crown lands. By its end, Badeni would be ex-prime minister, parliamentary government would be suspended in Austria for a decade, and Mark Twain would have one of his finest, most enduring pieces of political journalism, "Stirring Times in Austria."

There was nothing unreasonable in Badeni's proposed Sprachverordnung. It was a much smaller concession than that granted to Magyar in 1867 as the sole language in the judicial and civil administration of Hungary. Badeni's proposal, however, would have meant that by 1901 all German-speaking judges, lawyers, and bureaucrats in Bohemia and Moravia would have to learn Czech or lose their jobs. Native Czech speakers in such positions, on the other hand, had always had to know German, so they would be unaffected. In retrospect, it seems a small sop to nationalistic sentiment and might have done much to placate the Czechs later on when their support was sorely needed and was withheld. Inevitably, the counterpoise to pan-Germanism was pan-Slavism which the German-Austrians, a minority in the empire, were too obtuse to understand and too politically inept to neutralize.

After deliberating upon Badeni's language bills for a month without result, the Reichsrat was prorogued in May 1897, not reconvening to take up the issue again until September. It was at this point that the exchange of insults between the prime minister and Deputy Wolf precipitated their duel. Nevertheless, a real crisis was not reached until late October when a series of filibusters was mounted to obstruct a vote on the Ausgleich renewal in order to force Badeni to withdraw his language bills. Unprecedented tactics were used, such as bringing in whistles, horns, drums, and bells to drown out opponents, and on October 28, a Czech deputy, Dr. Otto Lecher, president of the Brünn (Brno) Board of Trade, delivered a record-setting marathon speech lasting from 8:45 in the evening until 8:45 the next morning.

There had previously been longer speeches than Lecher's—for instance, in the United States Congress, by Irish members of the British Parliament, and in the Romanian parliament—but these were occasions in which a speaker could extemporize or read nonstop about whatever he pleased. The Reichsrat's rules, on the other hand, allowed a speaker the floor only so long as his remarks directly addressed the issue at hand. He could not indulge in irrelevancies to fill time. It was in this respect that Lecher's twelve-hour speech set a record. It made him the hero of the moment in Bohemia and Moravia and the subject of one of Sigmund Freud's self-analyzed dreams in *Traumdeutung* (The Interpretation of Dreams), the seminal work of psychoanalysis he was just then compiling.[12]

After several more cacophonous, chaotic sessions, one of the conservative deputies, Count Franz Falkenhayn, introduced (almost inaudibly) a measure on November 25 to permit the use of force to maintain order. Amid the din and uproar this so-called Lex Falkenhayn was railroaded through without most members being aware of it. When the Socialists, hitherto neutral in the debate, discovered what had happened, they mounted a noisy protest, and the next day they overpowered the presiding officer and seized the rostrum. At this action the government ordered police into the chamber to arrest and forcibly evict ten Socialist deputies.

On November 26 and 27 Vienna was awash in massive demonstrations by students, intellectuals, and workers on the Ringstrasse before the parliament, city hall, and interior ministry. Alarmed, the emperor dismissed Badeni, dissolved the parliament, and on November 28 invoked Article Fourteen of the *Grundgesetz* (basic law) empowering the new regime of Baron von Frankenthurm to rule by decree. Parliamentary government, at least in the Austrian half of the dual monarchy, never completely recovered from this debacle, and the judgment of historian Joseph Redlich that "from this moment the Habsburg realm was doomed" does not seem excessive.[13]

The fall of Badeni's regime and the effective defeat of his language bills, though they were not officially withdrawn until a year later, provoked in Prague, Brno, and Pilsen as well as in Vienna, Graz, and Salzburg widespread rioting of a more violent nature than any seen in the dual monarchy since 1848. As a result of carefully orchestrated efforts by Schönerer and his followers who whipped up anti-Semitic hysteria at a monstrous "Pan-Germania" rally in Vienna in early December, it was ironically the Jews rather than either German-Austrians or Czechs who became targets of some of the ugliest violence.

These events form the background of "Stirring Times in Austria," which Mark Twain completed December 9, 1897, published in the March 1898 *Harper's Monthly*, and included in his volume of mainly Viennese pieces, *The Man That Corrupted Hadleyburg, ETC.* (1900). Most of the essay is drawn from first-hand observation with a few details filled in from local newspaper accounts. Through the kindness of Bettina Wirth, a local novelist, Vienna correspondent for the London *Daily News*, and translator of Bret Harte (among other English and American authors), Clemens obtained a gallery ticket, though not a press seat, for the Reichsrat sessions. On October 28–29 he witnessed at least some if not all of Dr. Lecher's record-breaking twelve-hour speech, and he attended several sessions between November 3 and the fateful *Krawall* (uproar) on November 26 when the police invaded the chamber.[14]

Written for American readers who could know little about the events he was reporting and less about Austrian governmental institutions and politics, "Stirring Times" is a tour de force of political reportage, informing without patronizing his readers and rendering vividly dramatic, even gripping, events about which he could presume scant natural interest from Americans.[15] Twain divides his essay into four subtitled sections. The first and briefest, "The Government in the

Frying-Pan," economically provides all the history and background information one needs for understanding the events Twain is about to
relate. Instead of making his readers feel provincial or ill informed,
he piques curiosity, introducing his subject by pretending that "no one
really understands this political situation, or can tell you what is going
to be the outcome of it." 16

His second section, "A Memorable Sitting," recounts the thirty-three-
hour session of October 28–29 during which Dr. Lecher delivered his
marathon speech. Here Twain hits his stride, setting the scene with
the skill of a good dramatist:

> The gallery guests are fashionably dressed, and the finery of the women
> makes a bright and pretty show under the strong electric light. But down
> on the floor there is no costumery.
>
> The deputies are dressed in day clothes; some of the clothes neat and
> trim, others not; there may be three members in evening dress, but not
> more. There are several Catholic priests in their long black gowns, and
> with crucifixes hanging from their necks. No member wears his hat. . . .
>
> In his high place sits the President, Abrahamowicz, object of the Oppo-
> sition's hatred. He is sunk back in the depths of his arm-chair, and has
> his chin down. He brings the ends of his spread fingers together in front
> of his breast, and reflectively taps them together, with the air of one who
> would like to begin business, but must wait, and be as patient as he can.
> It makes you think of Richelieu.

Twain then employs a roving "camera-eye" technique to let the
reader see, though not hear, Dr. Lecher's speech which, he says, is delivered in "pantomime" because the deafening clamor set up by other
deputies renders it inaudible in the galleries. Mark Twain nevertheless
reproduces in dialogue form the snatches of traded invective one could
catch amid the din. Here and indeed throughout the entire "Stirring
Times," Twain's technique is impressionistic. The reader gains a sense
of the whole not through inclusive description saturated with naturalistic detail but by a series of highly selected, vividly rendered vignettes.
In contrast to "bull-voiced" Schönerer and the obscenities (the worst
being left untranslated) hurled by other deputies, Lecher is made to

appear handsome, appealing, and admirable: "He is a young man of thirty-seven . . . tall and well-proportioned, and has cultivated and fortified his muscle by mountain-climbing." As for his extemporized speech, Twain puts the reader in awe with this almost rapturous description: "he had his facts in his head; his heart was in his work; and for twelve hours he stood there, undisturbed by the clamor around him, and with grace and ease and confidence poured out the riches of his mind, in closely reasoned arguments, clothed in eloquent and faultless phrasing." Twain's obvious sympathy for Lecher may have been the result of their meeting in the Reichsrat restaurant during a break in the November 3 sitting. They then had, so *NFP* reported in its November 5 evening edition, a lengthy convivial chat during which Twain promised to be present "from beginning to end" the next time Dr. Lecher made a twelve-hour speech, to which Lecher replied "*auf Englisch mit ernster Miene, nächste Woche bei der zweiten oder dritten Lesung werde er seine Leistung wiederholen oder verbessern*" (in English, looking sternly, that at next week's second or third reading he will repeat or improve upon his performance).

The third section, "Curious Parliamentary Etiquette," is a small gem of journalistic compression. Noting that a high percentage of Reichsrat members are men of learning who legitimately hold the title of "Doctor" (still more meaningful in Austria than its debased ad libitum counterpart in the United States today), he then constructs a scenario compounded of several sessions both before and after Lecher's October 28–29 speech in which these "learned gentlemen" players engage in exchanges using the cheapest kind of gutter language. He gives, for example, a remark flung at Schönerer, "*Die Grossmutter auf dem Misthaufen erzeugt worden!*" (Your grandmother was bred on a dung heap!), then adds: "It will be judicious not to translate that. Its flavor is pretty high, in any case, but it becomes particularly gamey when you remember that the first gallery was well stocked with ladies."

Later, he reproduces this colloquy:

Dr. Lueger (replying to Schönerer): "The Honorless Party would better keep still here!"

Gregorig (the echo swelling out his shirt-front): "Yes, keep quiet, pimp!"
Schönerer (to Lueger): "Political mountebank!"
Prochazka (to Schönerer): "Drunken clown!"

And then, without giving the speakers' names, he simply lists these "many happy phrases . . . distributed through the proceedings":

"Blatherskite!
Blackguard!
Scoundrel!
Brothel-daddy!
Polish Dog!"

In truth, however, many of the epithets and expletives Twain jotted in his notebook at the November 3 and 24 sittings that were evidently a main source for this section of "Stirring Times" are far stronger, more obscene, more anti-Semitic than these. Rather than pile on more examples, he concludes by noting that even the "easy-going, pleasure-loving" Viennese are aggrieved by the level to which parliamentary debate has sunk, so much so that perhaps "some day there will be a Minister of Etiquette and a sergeant-at-arms, and then things will go better," to which he adds ominously: "I mean if parliament and the Constitution survive the present storm."

"The Historic Climax" is the fitting title of the final section describing succinctly the violence in the Reichsrat on November 24, the passage on November 25 of the infamous Lex Falkenhayn, and the momentous events of the following day's session.

Thursday, November 25, 1897, was Thanksgiving Day in the United States, and the Clemens family had been invited to a huge dinner party beginning at three o'clock in the afternoon in the American embassy, given for the American community by Ambassador and Mrs. Tower. Earlier in the day, however, Mark Twain was again in the parliament, and his notebook contains this almost laconic summary: "*Nov. 25.* Thanksgiving. Attended Reichsrath, 1 p.m. Saw a *viva voce* vote taken on changing Rules of the House so as to do away with roll-call on motions. Was told that the President declared the measure carried—

a high-handed thing, if true. One could hear nothing, it was such
a stormy time."†[17] The provision for suspending roll calls was only
one part of Count Falkenhayn's rule-changing resolution that also
empowered the presiding officer "to use whatever force he thought
necessary to maintain order," including calling in police.

The next day Twain was in his seat in the gallery of the chamber at
noon. At 1:30 P.M., following the takeover of the rostrum by a phalanx
of Socialists, he witnessed what he calls "an odious spectacle" and "a
thing beyond all credibility"—the entrance of sixty armed, helmeted
police and the seizure and bodily eviction of ten duly elected legisla-
tors—"a free parliament profaned by an invasion of brute force." He
continues: "It was a tremendous episode. The memory of it will outlast
all the thrones that exist to-day. In the whole history of free parlia-
ments the like of it had been seen but three times before. . . . I think
that in my lifetime I have not twice seen abiding history made before
my eyes, but I know that I have seen it once."[18] Twain thus under-
scores perceptively but without hyperbole the historical significance
and importance of the episode.

The newspapers reported that the spectators' galleries were ordered
to be cleared at this point and that, in the words of the *Oesterreichische
Volks-Zeitung:* "*auch der amerikanische Humorist Mark Twain gehört zu den
'aufgeräumten'*" (also the American humorist, Mark Twain, was among
those removed).[19] In a letter to Twichell, on the other hand, Twain
explained that as he was leaving he met William Lavino of the London *Times* who escorted him into the press gallery "and I lost none
of the show."[20] Whatever the case, Twain ends "Stirring Times" with
two ironic paragraphs about the fall of the Badeni government and
the ensuing riots, concluding, "public opinion believes that parliamentary government and the Constitution are actually threatened with
extinction, and that the permanency of the monarchy itself is a not
absolutely certain thing!"[21]

A master stroke, this rhetorical imputing to "public opinion" what
was, in fact, Mark Twain's own prescient assessment of the consequences of the history he had witnessed. Did he hope it might stir

Austrian Parliament, where Mark Twain witnessed riotous sessions
described in his "Stirring Times in Austria"

some of his Austrian colleagues to reflect upon the seriousness of their political predicament? He surely knew that, though published in the States, his piece would be read in Austria. And, indeed, several Viennese papers reported lengthily on "Stirring Times" when it appeared in *Harper's*.[22]

In the early days of December, however, when Twain was writing his article, the local press gave no hint that "public opinion" held anything except feelings of either joy or frustration at the defeat of Badeni and his language bills. When Article Fourteen was invoked, when rioting ceased, and when the Ausgleich was made fiat, Vienna and those in the lands it ruled breathed a collective sigh of relief and turned their minds to the coming Christmas and the winter ball season ahead. Things continued to muddle along as they always had and, at least as long as *Der Alte* was at his desk in the Hofburg, seemingly always would. In politics, as in everything else, *Schlamperei* (muddling through) could be counted on to prevail. Why worry?

In February 1898 Twain wrote a little-known, quite brief sequel to "Stirring Times," using one of his favorite devices to frame such an essay—an elaborated response to a supposed question. In this case, the question is about Austrian parliamentary system from someone (real or fictitious) who had read his *Harper's* article. Entitled "The 'Austrian Parliamentary System'? Government by Article 14," it comprises a dozen manuscript pages with numerous insertions and emendations in which Twain tries to elucidate the Austrian electoral system and the composition of the Reichsrat by its five "curias," or privileged bodies, each of the first four representing a discrete class or segment of the voters while the fifth is allotted to the general suffrage, which also includes the previous four.[23] He ridicules this system as an "antique" patchwork of blatantly undemocratic, unrepresentative privilege, acknowledging nevertheless that

> If you ask the citizen why the suffrage is in this shape, and how the nation's voters came to be boxed off in the nation's hold in five non-communicating water-tight compartments, he will say something like this:
> "The obvious intention of the authors of the Constitution was to give the

people as limited a share in their own affairs as possible, and to preserve the far-reaching prerogatives of the Crown as nearly as possible intact; the working of the Constitution has proved that they succeeded in their object."

The main problem with the system—that which makes it unworkable—Twain correctly perceives to be that of nationality. In addition to the tags Reichsrat deputies wear of curia and party, they "have also an extra tag, and a very important one—the tag of *nationality*." He likens this situation to that in the British House of Commons with its recalcitrant Irish members and their obstructionist tactics, then notes, "Well, nine nationalities are represented in the Reichsrath; it makes nine Irish parties, so to speak, with all that that means, of difficulty, when there is need to solidify the representation upon a life-and-death national issue." By implication, he asks, Great Britain might endure one Ireland successfully, but can a great power long survive comprising nothing but Irelands?

Since, under these conditions, parliamentary government had evidently broken down for good, Article Fourteen of the Constitution, which he ridicules as "the political Seventh Commandment," seemed the only viable way to keep Austria-Hungary from falling apart. Under it, the executive acts as the legislature without being accountable to anyone but itself, things go along smoothly, and Austria, Twain observes, can "continue business at the old stand." He concludes bitingly, "You asked me about the Parliamentary system only, and I have confined myself to that. There used to be one."

His letters to Rogers, Twichell, and others as well as his notebooks during the remainder of his stay in Austria repeatedly show that Clemens felt uneasy in this political climate, fearing revolution or civil war could be imminent.[24] In light of the subsequent history of the dissolution of the Austro-Hungarian Empire and of the wobbly states that emerged from it, Twain's fears were well founded, even prescient, and his writings about what he experienced display remarkable political acumen for a foreigner. Few of the Viennese writers and intellectuals he knew shared his sense of impending doom, at least not publicly, and if one may trust such accounts as Stefan Zweig's moving memoir, *The World of Yesterday*, neither did very many others who lived in Austria all their lives. Or, perhaps more accurately, they refused to consider such a thing seriously. "Happy is he who forgets (ignores?) what cannot be changed."

History, it has often been said, has "many cunning, contrived corridors" of "what ifs" and "might have beens." But it seems likely that had the Habsburg Empire survived World War I or been reconstituted as a federation of the Danube nationalities (such as Dr. Otto von Habsburg urged during World War II) with or without a monarch, the Third Reich could never have happened. What endless possibilities that thought opens—no Holocaust, no World War II, no Iron Curtain or Cold War!

In "Government by Article 14" Mark Twain indicated that the nationality problems threatening the empire, of which the crisis he had witnessed was a foretaste of coming events, were not yet insoluble if promises could be kept and reason and good faith allowed to prevail. Did he also sense what the poet, Kürnberger, meant by *"Unseres Oesterreich ist eine kleine Welt / Woran die Grosse ihre Probe hält"* (Our Austria is a little world in which the big one holds its rehearsals)? Could he possibly for a split second have caught a fleeting glimpse that nationalism, evil legacy of the French Revolution, might one day in another epoch—one possessing cobalt bombs and missiles to deliver them efficiently—cause the destruction not merely of a tottering, anachronistic monarchy but of life on earth?

Hardly. Whatever else he may have been, Mark Twain should not be counted a soothsayer. One of his best aphorisms, in fact, written just weeks before he reached Vienna, holds that "unfortunately none of us can see far ahead; prophecy is not for us. Hence the paucity of suicides."[25]

Any doubts about his prophetic powers may quickly be dispelled by his report of another episode in his Viennese sojourn, one that he confidently predicted would "still be talked of and described and painted a thousand years from now" but which today gets scant attention when it is mentioned at all. Although the event seems less significant to us than it did at the time, history nevertheless did not leave Samuel L. Clemens alone for long in Austria. At about 6 P.M. on September 10, 1898, as he and his family were preparing for their evening meal at the Villa Paulhof in Kaltenleutgeben, a neighbor, the Countess Misa Wydenbruck-Esterházy, brought them the shocking news that the Empress Elisabeth had been assassinated shortly after noon that day in Geneva.[26] Clemens wrote Twichell he was "living in the midst of world-history again," mentioning Queen Victoria's Jubilee, then

> the invasion of the Reichsrath by the police, and now this murder, which will still be talked of and described and painted a thousand years from now. To have a personal friend of the wearer of the crown burst in at the gate in the deep dusk of the evening and say in a voice broken with tears, "My God the Empress is murdered," and fly toward her home before we can utter a question—why, it brings the giant event home to you, makes you a part of it and personally interested: it is as if your neighbor Antony should come flying and say "Caesar is butchered—the head of the world is fallen!"[27]

Next to the four-month Spanish-American War, which had ended barely a fortnight before, the empress's assassination was by long odds the most momentous event of worldwide interest, certainly the most shocking, to occur during his Austrian residence. Sixteen years later at Sarajevo the sequel to this assassination precipitated a world war, and under slightly altered circumstances, this murder might have had similar consequences. That it occurred in neutral Switzerland, not in a country whose relations with Austria-Hungary were already strained, and that the assassin, Luigi Lucheni, was a demented Italian anarchist without nationalistic motives made this a dynastic tragedy instead of an international crisis.

The state obsequies and burial of the beloved empress a week later, on September 17, 1899, furnished one of the most extravagant displays of funereal pomp ever seen in the history of European royalty. Three days before the funeral, Clemens told Rogers: "The Austrian Empire is hung in black. The lamentings (particularly in Hungary) are deep and universal. I have not seen anything like it since General Grant died."[28] The day of the burial, the Clemenses had a ringside seat, having been invited by Josef Krantz, owner of the new hotel where they had already engaged a suite for the following season, to occupy for the day a room with balcony overlooking the Neuer Markt directly opposite the Capuchin Church containing the Habsburg crypt. Many spectators paid fancy sums to merchants, office tenants, and apartment dwellers around the Neuer Markt for such a vantage point, and there was no window, balcony, ledge, or roof not thickly populated for a view of what Clemens told Twichell, with gross understatement, would be "a spectacle."

The procession into the square and the elaborate ceremonial of entering the crypt lasted nearly five hours during which Twain made almost moment-by-moment, highly impressionistic notes, some of which he worked into an article intended as a sequel to "Stirring Times in Austria" but which was rejected by Edward Bok at *The Ladies' Home Journal,* then in turn by Henry Alden at *Harper's* and R. W. Gilder at *The Century.* Although vividly descriptive, it lacks the cutting edge and drama of "Stirring Times," expressing, instead, deeper personal feelings and philosophical musings which may account for its rejections. Paine included "The Memorable Assassination" in his posthumous collection with *What Is Man?* in 1917.[29]

Many of Twain's notes and almost half the article vent his rage at the senselessness of this act by someone "at the bottom of the human ladder . . . without gifts, without talents, without education, without morals, without character, without any born charm or any acquired one, without a single grace of mind or heart or hand; . . . a mangy, offensive, empty, unwashed, vulgar, gross, mephitic, timid, sneaking, human polecat . . . a sarcasm upon the human race"—a heaping figure rarely equaled in his works for vituperation if not magnitude.[30] Since the real motives of Luccheni, an unemployed construction worker and lonely drifter, remained obscure, especially after he committed suicide in prison, Twain surmised the murderer did it out of "hunger for notoriety"—to gain a kind of infamous immortality—and, a curious turn for a journalist, Twain assails "the friendly help of the insane newspapers" for giving "this animal" the publicity he sought. In his notebook Twain was even harsher: "He has made money in every village & city in the world for his enemy the press."†31

Twain first insists "it was militarism" that brought about the empress's murder, adding, "Better do as Nicolas [sic] desires" (a reference to Czar Nicholas II's call for a conference on peace and disarmament) and then asking, "Who is ~~guilty?~~ the principal? This man? No—militarism which burdens & impoverishes & maddens. Royalty is itself the E's murderer before the fact.†32 But a week later, writing his article, he reversed himself: "Some think this murder a frenzied revolt against the criminal militarism which is impoverishing Europe and driving the starving poor mad. That has many crimes to answer for, but not this one, I think."33 The most ridiculous explanation, he continues, was the German emperor's—that the assassination was an act of God "ordained from above."

Wilhelm II's pronouncement brings Twain squarely to the enigma with which he wrestled repeatedly in his imaginative writing in Vienna: free will versus determinism. Musing in his notebook, he says Wilhelm's statement "is no compliment to God" because

> the remark acquits the prisoner. No different meaning can be given it. It was always a fool remark—for if God does a thing His agent is guiltless & by no logic can be *made* responsible. . . .
>
> If it is a crime, "ordaining it from on high" *leaves* it a crime. It is God's crime. The agent is secondary. When people lay it on God they should forbear to call it a crime. But W^m. calls it "a deed unparalleled for ruthlessness. Queer!"†34

In a postscript to his letter to Twichell before the funeral, he had already written:

> Among the inadequate attempts to account for the assassination we must concede high rank to the German Emperor's. . . .
>
> I think this verdict will not be popular "above." A man is either a free agent or he isn't. If a man is a free agent, this prisoner is responsible

for what he has done; but if a man is not a free agent, if the deed was ordained from above, there is no rational way of making this prisoner even partially responsible for it, and the Geneva court cannot condemn him without manifestly committing a crime. Logic is logic; and by disregarding its laws even Emperors as capable and acute as William II can be beguiled into making charges which should not be ventured upon except in the shelter of plenty of lightning-rods.[35]

He transferred these paragraphs verbatim to "The Memorable Assassination" except for tactfully excising all references to the German emperor, attributing Wilhelm's illogic instead to "the many" and its beguilement to "even the most pious and showy theologian."[36]

In addition to posing the free will–determinism conundrum in his article, Twain also postulates the dark view that "in one way or another all men are mad. . . . There are no healthy minds, and nothing saves any man but accident—the accident of not having his malady put to the supreme test."[37] Hardly a proposition to amuse genteel readers of American magazines or their editors in 1898, its original notebook formulation was yet more astringent: "But we are all insane, anyway. . . . The suicides seem to be the only sane people."[†38]

A detailed report of the funeral procession both fleshed out and condensed from his eyewitness notes comprises the latter half of "The Memorable Assassination." The Clemens family had come by train from Kaltenleutgeben at mid-morning the day of the funeral, and, sending Olivia, Clara, and Jean ahead in a cab, Twain walked the two miles from the Sudbahnhof, noting the black flags on the houses along the way, the hushed pedestrian crowds clad in black, and the closed shops with their black-draped windows containing pictures of the empress.

At noon on the Hotel Krantz balcony with his binoculars, Mark Twain began verbally painting the scene before him in the way a radio or television reporter would today—the silent, empty square cordoned noiselessly by "a double-ranked human fence" of soldiers, the "severely plain" little church, adding this poignant detail:

In a doorstep sat a figure in the uttermost raggedness of poverty, the feet bare, the head bent humbly down; a youth of eighteen or twenty, he was, and through the field-glass one could see that he was tearing apart and munching riffraff that he had gathered somewhere. Blazing uniforms flashed by him, making a sparkling contrast with his drooping ruin of moldy rags, but he took no notice; he was not there to grieve for a nation's disaster; he had his own cares, and deeper.[39]

Twain almost revels then in the awesome panoply as it unfolds, with the various components of the procession passing through the square to enter the church—the honor guards of Hungarian Hussars, the Knights of Malta and of the Golden Fleece, the Deutsch Ritter Ordnung (Teutonic Knights), the ranks of clergy and low and high prelates of the realm in their red and purple cassocks and richly embroidered albs and surplices, the lancers in their plumed gilt helmets. "It was a sea of flashing color all about," he says, heightened by the black evening clothes of the official mourners.

At precisely 4:12 P.M., Twain notes, the cortège itself entered the square, following the lancers. First, the three six-horse mourning coaches bearing the imperial family with their bewigged coachmen and footmen; next, troops "in splendid uniforms, red, gold, and white, exceedingly showy"; and finally, "the sumptuous great hearse . . . drawn at a walk by eight black horses plumed with black bunches of nodding ostrich feathers."

Had he been closer he would have heard a touching ritual colloquy between the sacristan and the imperial chaplain before the closed doors of the Capuchin Church thus: The chaplain knocks and is asked by the sacristan, "*Wer begehrt Einlass?*" (Who seeks entrance?) The answer: "Her Majesty Elisabeth, Empress of Austria and Queen of Hungary" (with all of her twenty-odd other titles). To which the sacristan responds: "*Kenne ich nicht*" (I know not such a one). Then a second knock with the same question, answered: "Elisabeth, Her Majesty, the Empress and Queen," with the reply, "*Wir kennen Sie nicht*" (We do not know her). A third knock with the same question is answered,

"*Unsere Schwester Elisabeth, ein sterblicher, sündiger Mensch*" (Our sister Elisabeth, a deceased sinner). This time the sacristan says, "*So komme Sie herein*" (So let her enter), and the church doors slowly swing open to admit the waiting bearers with their coffin. Then, after a brief ceremony, the sarcophagus is borne to its place among the sumptuous sepulchers of six centuries of Habsburg monarchs, their consorts, and their children.

Unable to hear this dialogue, Mark Twain ends his description by saying merely, "the coffin is borne into the church, the doors are closed," and as the great crowd slowly melts away, he notices that "in the turn of a wrist the three dirtiest and raggedest and cheerfulest little slum-girls in Austria were capering about in the spacious vacancy."[40] In truth, his disjointed notes, still unpublished, are far more vivid and precise in detail than the connected narrative he made of them. Even more interesting are the asides in the notebook, such as: "Essentially, nobilities are foolishnesses, but if I were a citizen where they prevailed I would do my best to get a title for the ~~inexpensive~~ consideration it furnishes—that is what we want. In Republics we strive for it with the surest means we have—money."[†41] Was he, as the saying goes, "going native" just a bit here?

The somber pageantry he had witnessed and described so fully was a quintessential exhibition of the Austrians' preoccupation with death, the most elemental expression of their therapeutic nihilism. Even more than in Victorian England, the Austrians then and now have made a fetish of *Trauerfeier* (funerals)—festivals in black where the *schöne Leich* (beautiful corpse) is the centerpiece of a magnificently staged procession to an interment where everyone has a turn at the ceremonial silver spade, a hallowed burial tradition in the Germanic world. As Stefan Zweig pointed out, every Viennese burgher's ego is soothed by the certainty that he, too, will one day be the star of such a show after a lifetime of quiet, well-ordered desperation. The excessive aestheticism attached to funerary rituals is part of Viennese "theatromania" and the point in the Austrian soul where Phaeacianism and therapeutic nihilism join.[42]

Moreover, when the "beautiful corpse" was none other than the empress of Austria and queen of Hungary, the spectacle had to be even more extraordinary. "Sisi," a Wittelsbach princess who came to Schönbrunn looking rather like a pretty Bavarian milkmaid of seventeen to wed her twenty-three-year-old first cousin, had captured the hearts of the Viennese. After bearing Franz Josef three children, including a crown prince, Elisabeth blossomed into one of the most strikingly beautiful matrons ever to grace a throne, but she was bored and restless by being merely decorative, unable to use her abilities in meaningful ways and for decades overshadowed by a domineering mother-in-law. Hating court life, she withdrew from it completely after Rudolf's death in 1889, preferring the Hungarian countryside, Korfu, and shopping trips abroad. It was on one of these excursions, as she was boarding a steamer on Geneva's lakeside, that Luccheni's knife, almost by accident (since she was not his specific target), ended her unhappy life.

If Twain errs in "The Memorable Assassination," it is in the encomiums he heaps upon Elisabeth, whom he lauds as "blameless" and "so beautiful, in mind and heart, in person and spirit." He concludes a two-paragraph paean to this paragon of feminine, maternal, queenly virtue: "Crowns have adorned others, but she adorned her crowns."[43] One discerns here his well-known worship of women and senses that had a male member of the House of Habsburg-Lothringen been the victim, even including the emperor himself, Twain might not have been so indignant at the murder nor so generous in his praise. In actuality, Elisabeth had grown haughty and imperious after the death of the Archduchess Sophie, imposing a rigid, stifling protocol upon her courtiers. What few opportunities she might have had for statecraft she shirked, the sole exception being to persuade Franz Josef to the compromise with Hungary that saved his realm in 1866.[44] But to Mark Twain the martyred empress was like the tragic Joan of Arc and like his dear, dead Susy. He closes his eulogy with some saccharine lines (in his own translation) about her from Alfred von Berger's *Habsburg*, a festival play he had enjoyed at the Burgtheater the previous season.

On the other hand, there may be a saving grace in Twain's excessive praise of the empress's presumed virtues if an anecdote by Henry W. Fisher, a correspondent in Vienna for several American newspapers at that time, can be trusted. He recalls Twain's admitting to "several friends in Vienna," after reading them his article:

> I know it is full of exaggerations. . . . I did gown her with virtues she never thought of possessing and I have denied all her frailties. As I learn now, she was just an ordinary woman, and her surpassing vanity was the only extraordinary thing about her. But think how much she suffered and think of the man she was married to. Re-read, too, that story about the murdered Rudolph. When Count Something approached her to break the news, she ran to him wringing her hands and cried: "My Rudy is dead. Oh, my Rudy!" What told this Niobe among royal women that her son had been destroyed—killed in a low debauch? When I reflect how she maintained her self-respect in a life of constant disappointment and tragedy, I think I did well making her out a noble soul.[45]

Ninety-one years later, on April 1, 1989, the identical scene he witnessed, minus a few military details, was repeated, this time with millions enjoying via television a better view of the proceedings than Twain had had. No historic reenactment, this was an actual burial in the Habsburg crypt of a real empress of Austria and queen of Hungary—Zita von Habsburg-Lothringen (née di Bourbon-Parma), the ninety-six-year-old widow of the last monarch of Austria-Hungary, Karl I, who succeeded his great-uncle, Franz Josef, in 1916 and abdicated in 1918. The *schöne Leich* of this ancient lady who survived seventy years in exile, sixty-seven in widow's weeds, and died (*ecce!*) in Switzerland, was returned to the capital of a modern republic to lie in state five days, viewed by thousands who had not been alive and, in many cases, whose parents had not even been alive when she briefly reigned, and then be interred with the same pomp and splendor afforded her predecessor in 1898. This spectacle drew nearly 100,000 to Vienna from all parts of the old empire and abroad, including even the United States! Was it mere nostalgic hankering after a long-vanished world order, or were Austrians as much in love with death and its panoply at the end of this century as they had been at the end of the last? And did the ghost of Mark Twain, one hoped, surveying the awesome spectacle from a balcony of the Hotel Krantz (now Hotel Ambassador), sardonically mutter in the language he said was spoken in Hell: *"plus ca change, plus c'est le même SHOWS"*?

CHAPTER FIVE

"Leschy"

Every third Viennese in 1897 was Czech, by ancestry if not by birth, and nearly one in five was Polish, mainly from the empire's easternmost provinces, Galicia and Bukovina. A prime example of such mixtures was Theodor Leschetizky (Teodor Leszetycki, in Polish), a "Wiener" to the fingertips but also a native of Galicia whose father was Czech and mother Polish. "Professor" Leschetizky, as he was respectfully known to the Viennese, was almost a living legend by 1897. But Clemens had trouble wrapping his tongue around that many sibilants and dentals in the same word or spelling their consonantal sequence correctly, so in private discourse he settled for "Leschy." The gregarious little pedagogue didn't seem to mind. Perhaps he thought it an amusing instance of American egalitarian disregard of titles and surnames and the notorious American penchant for immediate first-name or nickname intimacy.

Leschy was, of course, the reason the Clemens family was in Vienna, at least until Clara left his tutelage in June 1898. Even afterward he was the linchpin of their cultural and much of their social life in the city. Had he remained in St. Petersburg, where he spent twenty-seven years of his earlier professional life, mostly on the faculty of its conservatory as a colleague of Davidoff, Auer, and Anton Rubinstein, Clara presumably would have dragged her family all the way to Russia. Since 1878, however, he had been one of the most puissant patriarchs of Vienna's musical life. Being members of his circle, as the Clemenses were, meant being at an epicenter of the fin de siècle musical world.

The hegemony Vienna had enjoyed since about 1750 as Europe's musical capital was already drawing to its close. Under Josef II and his immediate successors, the city had been a magnet of opportunity for great musical talents from far and near—Haydn and Mozart, Beethoven and Brahms, Bruckner and Mahler, and others. But under a monarch whose tastes were mostly for ballroom music and military bands, Vienna had increasingly little to offer to anyone save composers of waltzes, marches, and operettas. A generation later, Austria's best composers—such as Korngold, Krenek, Schönberg, Webern, and Wellesz—would be driven into exile or compelled to seek opportunities elsewhere. Vienna's stately opera house and its gilded concert halls are musical museums today and, like other Ringstrasse architecture, sad reminders of an illustrious past. Although outstanding musical events still do occur there occasionally, it is as if the Muse had packed all her bags save those labeled PERFORMANCE and fled the city with the Habsburgs, leaving a few stragglers for the exodus of 1938 when the Nazis took over.

Nevertheless, in 1897 Vienna was musically still a quite exciting and stimulating place, especially for study. One of those who made it so was Professor Leschetizky, a one-man institution who attracted aspiring pianists from across the map of Europe, Great Britain, and North America. This time was, of course, before Asia discovered western music and overflowed the academies of Vienna and Salzburg with aspiring virtuosi.

Leschetizky was born in 1830 in the Galician village of Lancut, near Lemberg (Lwów), later annexed by the Soviet Union, where his father was music master in the household of the local count. Taught by his father from the age of five, Leschy made his concert debut at nine in Lemberg as soloist in Carl Czerny's concertino under the baton of Wolfgang Amadeus Mozart, Jr. A year later, he came to Vienna to study with the great Czerny himself, a protégé of Ludwig van Beethoven and by then the leading piano teacher of Europe, one who numbered Franz Liszt among his pupils.[1]

After a series of successful concert tours, Leschetizky settled in St.

Petersburg, where he headed the piano department of the conservatory from its founding in 1862 until he returned to Vienna as the self-appointed successor to Czerny and Beethoven—thus, through his pupils, their pupils, and their pupils' pupils, establishing a kind of keyboard apostolic succession from Beethoven to the present. In Russia, Leschetizky combined teaching, concertizing, and composing, writing a couple of now-forgotten operas and nearly fifty piano pieces, but in Vienna he stuck strictly to pedagogy, performing only privately. The roster of his *Schuler* in Vienna, though incomplete, includes more than twelve hundred names. In addition to such celebrated pianists as Ignace Jan Paderewski, Artur Schnabel, and Ossip Gabrilowitsch (whom Clara Clemens married in 1909), the list also includes Fannie Bloomfield-Zeisler, Alexander Brailowsky, Ignaz Friedman, Mark Hambourg, Mieczyslaw Horszowski, Frank La Farge, Benno Moiseiwitsch, Elly Ney, John Powell, Wassily Safanoff, Franz Schmidt, Paul Wittgenstein, and many more of only slightly lesser renown.

Just how and when Clara Clemens first heard of the legendary pedagogue and conceived her ardent desire to study with him is unclear. Her friendship in London in June 1897 with Evelyn Suart (later Lady Hárcourt), a pupil of Leschetizky, may have had something to do with it. Her memoirs are circumspect on the subject, however, merely observing that "Stories of all sorts, both good and bad, were told of him by friends, pupils, enemies, but in the end one always kept the impression Leschetitzky [*sic*] must be a fine man and a unique personality. . . . In spite of the highly colored pictures drawn of this remarkable man, my heart was set on ascertaining what his panacea might be for weak fingers and stiff arms."[2] Were the "stories of all sorts" and "highly colored pictures" that intrigued Clara perhaps of Leschy's notorious womanizing? Katy Leary remembered that "almost all the women fell for him. He made wives of most of his pupils."[3] "Most" is a gross exaggeration, of course, though he did marry four of his pupils, his first three marriages ending in divorce because of his alleged peccadillos.

Being a bon vivant with an eye for a pretty face and a well-turned ankle was certainly an important aspect of Leschy's personality. The

Theodor Leschetizky, Clara Clemens's piano teacher, in his studio, circa
1900 (Picture Archives of the Austrian National Library)

story of his death, though possibly apocryphal, suggests much about the man. He was in Dresden on November 14, 1915, to visit his gravely ailing son and staying at a hotel with his Czech housekeeper, Pepi. Feeling suddenly ill himself, he announced, *"Heute Nacht werde ich sterben"* (Tonight I'm going to die) and asked the frightened girl to fetch him a bottle of *Sekt* (German champagne) from the concierge. When she did, he commanded, *"Nun betet!"* (Now pray!). While Pepi was on her knees, he downed the bubbly and expired. His remains were carted home to Vienna for interment in an *Ehrengrab* (grave of honor) near his mentor, Czerny, in a section of the Zentral Friedhof reserved by the city for its most famous burghers.[4]

Whatever her reasons, Clara had to audition with Leschy before the Clemenses could settle in at the Metropole, so on their very first day in Vienna, their trunks and gladstones delivered by Cook but still unpacked, she and her father went out to Döbling in a fiaker for the appointment. Almost overcome by nervousness, Clara "stammered through" her interview in German and then "stumbled into a piece on the piano." There followed a lengthy disquisition by the master on the preparatory study Clara needed before he could teach her himself, punctuated by her impatient father with *"Ich verstehe, ich verstehe."* The only thing Clemens really wanted to know was whether they were to remain in Vienna. When Leschy responded *"Aber sicher!"* (but, of course!), they hastened home to unpack.[5]

Mark Twain regarded "old Leschy" with awe and, in due course, something like affection. What he thought of his daughter's musical ambitions is enigmatic. Neither he nor Olivia openly opposed her efforts, and at odd times he even displayed paternal pride in her achievements. When she suddenly switched from piano to singing, he uncomplainingly subsidized her fruitless attempts to establish herself on the concert stage. But he avoided her public performances whenever possible, perhaps in deference to her insistence that she not be publicized as "Mark Twain's daughter" with the unreasonable expectations that appellation might arouse or the excuses it might offer.

Then again, he may have wished to dissociate himself from a talent he secretly or subconsciously regarded as mediocre.[6]

His initial response to Clara's decision to study with Leschy evoked this rough draft of an undeveloped sketch obviously intended as a platform piece, a burlesque monologue to be punctuated or underscored with passages he might play on the piano:

> That's it. (Music. Pupil of Letchitizky [sic]. It's in the family. I can play myself. Let me see—what is that great thing—that grand concerto of Bach, no not Bach, Mendellsohn [sic]—no, Wagner—the Wedding March in Saul—re do re mi do la sol—(put in a false note here) beautiful thing—sublime—but I am out of practice. I was a pupil of L's grandfather—1815—same year that I first met Napoleon—met him on the battlefield. When you meet people, you, well, you *can't meet* a man ~~unless he is~~ if you are both going in the same direction. It was on the battlefield. He—well, one of us was going into battle, & the other was, I think the other, was going out back to see what time it was—I don't remember which one it was, but that isn't any matter—just a detail, you know. A great man, N—a wonderful man, & had a passion for music. (Play) Oh, he had a most delicate & sensitive enjoyment of music & yet the fact of (play)—I have known him to ~~faint~~ swoon when I played that.†[7]

Despite somehow having taught himself to play the piano by ear, Mark Twain's musical proclivities were, to say the least, unexceptional. In music, as in all other areas of artistic and intellectual endeavor, he was innocent of any formal schooling, and although it was not entirely peripheral, music was seldom one of his central concerns. He occasionally entertained family and close friends by accompanying himself at the keyboard while singing spirituals like "Swing Low, Sweet Chariot" and "Go Chain the Lion Down" with expressive fervor. "He had a curious way of playing," Clara remembered, "with his fingers stretched straight over the keys, so that each time he played a chord it seemed as if a miracle had happened. He always cleared his throat many times before he began, and then sang quite loudly with his head thrown back and his eyes fixed on the ceiling. . . . He interrupted himself constantly to correct wrong chords, but usually in vain, for he could not find the right ones."[8]

Small wonder, then, that musical allusions and figures of speech are sparse in Twain's fiction. When they do occur, it is usually with devastatingly satirical effect, as in Huck Finn's deadpan description of the Grangerford girls' "beautiful" rendition on their out-of-tune piano of "The Battle of Prague," the Capello twins charming the Dawson's Landing yokelry with their slam-bang four-hand piano recital, the townsfolk of Hadleyburg jeering at their leaders with a parodied chorus from *The Mikado*, or Hank Morgan's narrative of a banquet entertainment in Camelot: "In a gallery a band of cymbals, horns, harps, and other horrors opened the proceedings with what seemed to be the crude first draft or original agony of the wail known to later centuries as 'In the Sweet Bye and Bye.' It was new, and ought to have been rehearsed a little more. For some reason or other the queen had the composer hanged, after dinner."[9]

During his San Francisco days, according to one of his autobiographical dictations, he "infested the opera" as a fledgling reviewer, and his notebook for that period contains a marvelous burlesque, first published in 1967, of Verdi's *Il Trovatore*.[10] In *A Tramp Abroad*, he describes his first encounters, at performances of *Lohengrin* in Mannheim and Munich, with Richard Wagner's "music of the future" as being akin to having one's teeth drilled by the dentist. In the latter city he also saw Francois-Adrien Boieldieu's *La Dame Blanche* (given in German as *Die Weisse Frau*), which he enjoyed, he wrote in his notebook, because it was "real music," not like Wagner's.[11]

In late July 1891, Mark Twain took his family to the Wagner Festival in Bayreuth about which he wrote perceptively in an article in the New York *Sun* aptly titled "At the Shrine of St. Wagner" which he thought good enough to include in his collected works. Although he enjoyed the *Tannhäuser* he saw performed there ("One of the most engaging spectacles in the world is a Wagner opera force marching on the stage, with its music braying and its banners flying," he wrote in Vienna), he sent Olivia and their daughters up the "Green Hill" to the Festspielhaus for the Ring Tetralogy while he remained at the Hotel Anker to read the memoirs of the Margravine Wilhelmina of Bayreuth, the precocious sister of Frederick the Great. A pity that *Die Meistersinger von Nürnberg*, Wagner's comic masterpiece which Twain should certainly have found appealing, he seems not to have known at all. On the whole, while his musical horizons constantly widened, his tastes remained plebeian if not downright philistine, and he valued the antebellum blackface minstrel show, he said, above all the operas in the European repertory.

During his twenty months in Vienna, Samuel Clemens probably experienced more highbrow music willy-nilly than he had in the previous six decades of his life combined. Then, as now, the Court Opera (now State Opera) was one of the two leading musical institutions of the city, the other being the Vienna Philharmonic, which furnished the pit orchestra for the Opera. Leschy had a box at the k. k. Hofoper in which Clemens and his family were frequent guests for performances, and they were also often invited by other boxholders among their acquaintances, though Clara said her father rarely stayed through to the final curtain. In 1897–98, Mahler's first season as *Hofoperndirektor*, forty-seven works were in the repertory, with forty-eight the following season. Among these offerings, Clemens saw at least *Die Walküre* (on December 8, 1897, after which he noted, "W. music is better than it sounds"), *Cavalleria Rusticana* (its intermezzo became his favorite opera tune), *Carmen*, *Die Zauberflöte*, *La Traviata*, *Fidelio*, and Smetana's *Dalibor*, except for the last, a selection identical to what he might see were he to return to Vienna today.[12]

At the end of his first November in Vienna, on Sunday, the twenty-eighth, Mark Twain made the acquaintance of the Waltz King himself, the seventy-three-year-old Johann Strauss, Jr., at a concert in the sumptuously gilded *Grosser Saal* (great hall) of the Musikverein. Two world premieres were on the program performed by the Eduard Strauss-Kapelle (the orchestra of Johann's younger brother): a new waltz, "An der Elbe," by Johann, and a new polka, "Für Alle Welt," by Eduard Strauss. Johann conducted the first half of the program, containing his new waltz among other works of his own, then retired to a loge (box) for the remainder of the program his brother conducted. When someone pointed out during the interval that "the famous Mark Twain and his daughters" were present, Strauss invited them to join him in his box for the rest of the concert.[13]

Mark Twain attended at least two other concerts at which the Waltz King conducted one or more of his own works, and two days before the Clemenses were to leave Vienna in May 1899, Strauss asked Twain to inscribe a book (probably *Following the Equator*) for him. Twain said he would gladly do so if the book were sent around to his hotel, but when it had not arrived on the day before his scheduled departure, Twain sent Strauss a note with his London address, suggesting Strauss simply write him the title of the work he wanted autographed so that Twain could have Chatto and Windus (his London publisher) send a new inscribed copy directly.[14] Soon after the Clemenses reached London, however, they were shocked by the news of Johann Strauss's unexpected death on June 3, 1899, prompting this note of condolence to Strauss's widow, Adele:

> Dear Madame Strauss:
>
> I am deeply pained and shocked to learn from the newspapers of the passing from this life of Your great & gifted husband. When I talked & smoked with him in your house only twelve days ago, he seemed in all ways his old natural self—alert, quick, brilliant in speech, and wearing all the graces of his indestructible youth; & now—why it seems impossible that he is gone! I am grateful that I was privileged to have that pleasant meeting with him, & it will remain a gracious memory with me.
>
> I beg to offer to you and to all the bereaved household & kinship the heartfelt sympathy & condolence of my daughter & myself.
>
> > With the profoundest respect
> > I am, dear Madame,
> > Sincerely Yours
> > S. L. Clemens.[15]

A few nights before the Clemenses' first Strauss concert, the *NFP* reviewer spotted Mark Twain in a box at the Theater an der Wien for yet another world premiere. This one was of the now-forgotten operetta *Blumen Mary* (Mary's Flower Shop), set in New York, with music by Charles Weinberger and book and lyrics by Leo Stein and Alexander Landesberg. In the *Hofloge* (court box) next to Twain's sat the Archduke Franz Ferdinand, heir to the Habsburg throne whose assassination at Sarajevo plunged the world into war, and Archduke Otto, whose son, Karl, became the last Austrian emperor. The performance was a great success with both the critics and the public, but Mark Twain, asked for a comment on the operetta's depiction of American life, smiled and diplomatically said nothing.[16]

Several musical performances Twain experienced in Vienna were connected with his public readings, many of which ended with what seemed to him anticlimactic musical programs. At his first reading, for example, on February 1, 1898, in the old Bösendorfer-Saal in the Herrengasse, a much larger auditorium than the present concert hall of that name, Twain shared the platform with two American divas of the Hofoper, Frances Saville and Edyth Walker; concert singer Eduard Gärtner; the violin virtuoso Fritz Kreisler; and the sixteen-year-old piano prodigy, Artur Schnabel.[17] On at least two other occasions (one of them his Concordia speech), the musical portion of the evening was supplied by the celebrated pianist Alfred Grünfeld, whose performances as soloist with the Vienna Philharmonic under the baton of Hans Richter the Clemens family also enjoyed.[18]

This was not the first contact Clemens had with Hans Richter, the Hungarian former director of the Hofoper and *Chefdirigent* (chief conductor) of the Vienna Philharmonic, whose residence at Sternwartestrasse 56 in the same neighborhood as Leschy's is in Mark Twain's Vienna address list. How they first met, whether through Leschetizky or earlier, in London, where Richter conducted a renowned concert series annually from 1879 until 1910, is unclear, but the maestro and his wife were in the Clemenses' Viennese social circle, and Mark Twain inscribed a copy of *More Tramps Abroad* (the English edition of *Following the Equator*) to Richter. Vienna's musical life was then bitterly polarized between the partisans of this esteemed figure whom Richard

Wagner had chosen to conduct the world premiere of *Der Ring des Nibelungen* (1876) as well as other works at Bayreuth and those of the "upstart" Gustav Mahler, who replaced him in 1897 as *Hofoperndirektor* and briefly (1898–1901) as chief conductor of the philharmonic, but it seems the Clemenses, no doubt because of their association with Leschetizky, had a foot in both camps.

One of the most glittering of the many musical events attended by Clemens and his daughters in the company of the Leschetizkys came near the end of their Vienna sojourn, on Karsamstag (Easter Saturday), April 8, 1899. It was a concert by the philharmonic in which Lorenzo Perosi, music director of the Sistine Chapel in the Vatican, conducted his newest oratorio, *La risurrezione di Cristo* (The Resurrection of Christ, text adapted from Saint Matthew), with soloists imported from Rome. Perosi, now almost forgotten, was a protégé of Pope Leo XIII and then widely regarded as one of world's foremost composers of religious music.[19] A few weeks earlier, Gustav Mahler had had a fiasco with both the critics and the Viennese public conducting a philharmonic performance of another new Perosi oratorio, *La risurrezione di Lazzaro* (The Resurrection of Lazarus, with a text adapted from Saint John). However, the appearance on the podium of the dashing young abbot (Perosi was twenty-six but looked younger) under papal sponsorship brought to the Golden Hall of the Musikverein nearly everyone of importance in musical and social circles in the capital.

The press gave almost as much space to those who attended and the ladies' couture as to the concert itself, and, indeed, *NFP* gave the event double coverage: a critique by the venerable Eduard Hanslick of the premiere itself, which he thought *"nichts besonders"* (nothing special), coupled with a detailed report (unsigned) on who was who and who wore what in the audience. In addition to numerous princes of the church and lesser prelates, the entire diplomatic corps, dozens of the highest nobility of the realm, and such musical denizens as the Strauss brothers (Johann and Eduard), Karl Goldmark, Mahler, and Leschetizky, the *NFP* did not neglect to mention that *"Auch Mark Twain war mit beiden Töchtern anwesend*" (also Mark Twain was present with both daughters).[20]

What Mark Twain may have thought of Perosi's music or of most of the other concerts and opera performances he experienced in Vienna is anyone's guess. Nowhere does he comment upon them. On the other hand he is unstinting in his notebooks with praise for Leschy's musical prowess. Most of Twain's musical experiences in Vienna occurred in the regular biweekly "classes" the pedagogue held from September through May in his Döbling villa which the Clemens family, sometimes also including Katy Leary, attended faithfully. In reality, these evenings were not classes in the instructional sense but instead salon recitals. Leschy's pupils were expected to volunteer to perform for an audience of their families or friends and the professor's invited guests, always including some of the leading lights of the Viennese musical and social worlds. Sometimes nearly a hundred would be jammed into a studio that would have seemed overcrowded with more than thirty.

One such musicale, on January 19, 1898, Twain vividly described in his notebook thus:

> Tonight, drove out to Lestchetitzky's [*sic*] house (wife & Clara along) to attend one of the fortnightly meetings of his piano-class. . . . The master sat at one piano, & each of 7 pupils in turn sat at the other. It was a wonderful performance. Young Voss, a handsome American, carried off the honors, by a little. Now & then the master would let fly a rebuke, & play a passage as a pupil had played it, then play it as it *ought* to have been played. Beautiful as the pupil's work had been, the superior splendor of the master's touch was immediately recognizable. . . . What life, energy, fire, in a man past 70!—& how he does play! He is easily the greatest pianist in the world.[21]

In an undated notebook entry of a few weeks earlier, Twain expressed similar sentiments after hearing Leschy in another setting: "At Madame von Dutschka's. Choice people there. Leschetitzky [*sic*] played. A marvelous performance. He never plays except in that house (she says). He sacrificed himself for his first wife—believed she wd. be the greatest pianist of all time—& now they have been many years separated. If he developed himself instead of her, he would have been the world's wonder himself. ~~without a doubt~~"[22]

The author's excessive judgment of Leschetizky's keyboard prowess ("the greatest . . . in the world") was doubtless somewhat colored by his admiration for the master's skill as a musical entrepreneur. What Leschy actually managed in Vienna was something on the order of a factory for keyboard instruction or, more politely, a private conservatory. At any one time he might have as many as a hundred pupils with whom he used a kind of assembly-line system, employing his more gifted (and often penurious) pupils to tutor his less prepared or less talented charges. As he did with Clara Clemens, he customarily assigned newcomers to study with an assistant for weeks, even months, before they could fully enter his temple. Even afterward, he would sometimes require a pupil to continue with the assistant for practice sessions between lessons.

The system worked admirably, providing him an enormous fiefdom. Leschy knew realistically that only a few who came to him could ever be concert stars although many more could become good, even outstanding, teachers. What's more, he could thereby take from one pocket and put in the other, subsidizing his few gifted *Schüler* (pupils) through his many inferior ones, a system not altogether unknown in American graduate education.

Leschy's soirées were often scenes of dramatic confrontations and the verbal fireworks he loosed whenever a pupil displeased him by failing to volunteer to perform or, having been chosen after volunteering, being poorly prepared. Mark Twain noted on one occasion, "He gave one young lady a devastating dressing-down—poured out wrath, criticism, sarcasm and humor upon her in a flood for . . . as much as 12 minutes."[23] Clara recalled that "if one of his *pupils* aroused his ire, he wasted no time with gentlemanly sarcasm. He picked up the music, threw it on the floor, and helped the culprit to remove himself as quickly as possible."[24] And Katy Leary, who confessed she "never really liked him [because] he used to grin and show his teeth, like a gorilla," perhaps exaggerated only slightly that "he almost killed Mark Hambourg for playing bad at a concert."[25]

The fact is, Theodor Leschetizky was a volatile martinet with a sharp, sarcastic tongue, more Prussian than gemütlich Austrian in temperament, who demanded total devotion from his charges, tyrannizing his domain by instilling fear and awe. Pupils and fellow-musicians either worshiped or despised him, and the latter types kept their distance from the circle whose members had only to give the approving echo he desired. To those who did obeisance and of whose abilities he thought well, he could be kindly, generous, even paternal. It was known, for instance, that gifted but impoverished pupils, like the young Bohemian Jew Artur Schnabel, he willingly taught gratis.

Whatever her shortcomings of "weak fingers and stiff arms" or, as Katy Leary perhaps exaggeratedly observed, hands that were "so small she didn't have any stretch—couldn't reach an octave," Clara received only kindly treatment from the master. It was not long before Leschy and his third wife, Donnimirska Benislava (known professionally as Mme. Leschetizka), became more than mere polite acquaintances of Olivia and Samuel Clemens.

In the depths of the Clemenses' first winter in Vienna (February 1898), the two families plus two American medical students and some of Leschy's pupils, including Ethel and Mary Newcomb and Jane Olmsted, went tobogganing in the mountains of the Semmering, about fifty miles southwest of Vienna. At Mürzzuschlag they rented six sleighs with drivers for the four-hour ascent to the top of the highest mountain. After the horses were unhitched, the group ate a hearty lunch and then made a ten-minute high-speed descent over the steep course they had just taken four hours to travel. Their evening suppers while at the Semmering were made memorable for Ethel Newcomb because "Mark Twain and Leschetizky vied with each other as after dinner speakers. Mr. Clemens used jokingly to complain that Leschetizky made the best speeches he had ever heard."[26]

Indeed, Twain remarked more than once in his notebook that

Leschetizky was "a most capable & felicitous talker—was born for an orator, I think," and the admiration of one skilled raconteur for another was clear when both Leschy and Eduard Pötzl came to dinner with the Clemenses at the Metropole on January 16, 1898, about which Twain wrote:

> Last Sunday night, at dinner with us, he [Leschetizky] did all the talking for 3 hours, & everybody was glad to let him. He told his experiences as a revolutionist 50 years ago in the '48; & his battle-pictures were magnificently worded. Pötzl had never met him before. He is a talker himself & a good one—but he merely sat silent & gazed across the table at this inspired man, & drank in his words, & let his eyes fill & the blood come & go in his face & never said a word.[27]

Like a great many Viennese musicians and composers, Leschetizky had a *Ferienhäuserl* (summer vacation cottage) in the Salzkammergut, and he invited the Clemens family to visit him there in August 1898. There was a saying then current that "in summer Vienna moves to Bad Ischl," a resort in the Alpine lake district known as the Salzkammergut, about 180 miles west of the capital, where the emperor had a hunting lodge to which he repaired in July and August each year and where his mistress, the Court Theater actress Katharina Schratt, had a nearby villa. Brahms and Bruckner (both very recently dead) had summered in Ischl and so, too, had Johann Strauss and Franz Lehar, among many others of the musical world. Leschy's tiny house was not in Ischl itself but on a lake in nearby Hallstatt, and it was in that direction the Clemens family set out from their summer villa in Kaltenleutgeben on August 16, stopping for six days at the Hotel Post in Bad Ischl, a resort famed for its mineral springs and "milk cure."

Leschy met them there on the twenty-second, arriving from Vienna at noon to escort them to Hallstatt. They expected Martinus Sieveking, one of Leschy's advanced pupils who had tutored Clara, to join them, but when he failed to appear, Mme. Leschetizka went to inquire of his whereabouts and learned he had been arrested for failing to remove his hat while a priest was passing in the street with the viaticum en route to a deathbed. At this news, Twain noted, "Professor, Jean & Clara rushed away to see him in jail," though they made it back in time to catch the 2:43 P.M. train for Hallstatt, where they remained until the twenty-seventh.†28

The railway trip from Kaltenleutgeben and Vienna to Ischl had been hot and dusty, and Clemens found their accommodations "in this hot town in a hot hotel . . . primitive and depressing," with no baths to be had in the hotel and no lights save candles. "We have dropped back into the dark ages," he fumed. Yet worse, a cinder had become imbedded in Olivia's eye on the journey and had to be removed by a local doctor at Ischl, her husband noting sarcastically that "a cinder in your eye can improve any pleasure trip."29

At Hallstatt, with a lake breeze cooling them, things went more smoothly, although on the first day there Clemens snapped the metal rim of his spectacles and had to hunt up a *Spängler* (tinsmith) whose chubby apprentice soldered it with impressive efficiency in just thirty-five minutes. He was pleased that the "Whole bill for mending my glasses & restoring my sight" was only ten kreuzer, about five American cents. The Hallstattersee, he noted, was a "Beautiful lake in a cup of precipices" but its "surface [was] littered with refuse & sewer-contributions [despite which] men . . . swim in it." He was also impressed that "Pre-historic remains are found here," referring to the excavations of one of the earliest Celtic civilizations in Central Europe, predating the Roman settlements there by several centuries.†30

En route home to Kaltenleutgeben on the twenty-seventh, the Clemenses stopped off in Vienna to look over the new Hotel Krantz and engage rooms there for the coming winter. They discovered there that Sieveking's Bad Ischl adventure—forty-eight hours in the *Karzer* and a heavy fine for "disrespect to the Eucharist"—had been widely publicized in European newspapers, becoming a cause célèbre for the anticlericals. "People call him a 'made man,'" Twain noted, adding skeptically: "No—this is merely notoriety; it won't last; it is but a temporary advertisement."31

Back in Kaltenleutgeben, the summer lazily winding down, Clara surprised her parents with the announcement that she had decided to forego further piano studies and take voice lessons instead. To a friend back in Hartford, Olivia confided: "Her father and I are both glad & sorry."[32] She had apparently been persuaded to this switch by Alice Barbi, an American singer with whom she became friends. Barbi had heard Clara sing that summer at a soirée at the home of one of the aristocrats in Leschetizky's circle who had summer houses near the Clemenses' in Dr. Winternitz's hydrotherapy resort.[33]

Barbi was a protégé of a retired *Kammersängerin* (privileged diva) of the Court Opera, Marianne Brandt (stage name of Marie Bischoff), one of the most acclaimed contraltos of the late nineteenth century, and Barbi somehow persuaded Frau Brandt to take Clara as a pupil during the following winter (1898–99). Brandt had sung in every major opera house in the world from Vienna to Covent Garden to the Metropolitan (where she was the leading Wagnerian contralto, 1884–88), and she had created several important roles in Bayreuth at the world premieres in 1876 of *Siegfried* (Erda) and *Götterdämmerung* (Waltraute) and in 1882 of *Parsifal* (Kundry). Her standing as a voice teacher was thus roughly equivalent to that of Leschetizky as a piano pedagogue.[34]

By all accounts, Clara Clemens had a pleasant contralto voice and, in due course, a well-schooled one. But whether she had greater talent for a professional career in singing than she did as a pianist is questionable. In any case, she stuck with her vocal studies in Vienna and, later, London (with Blanche Marchesi) and Florence, and she made a rather expensive attempt at a concert career in the United States which she abandoned only after her marriage to Ossip Gabrilowitsch.

Leschetizky, according to Katy Leary, "felt terrible bad to lose [Clara] for a pupil, because he thought she was very talented musically."[35] Perhaps. Nevertheless, her Leschy relationships did not cease when she started studying with Frau Brandt. During the following season she was occasionally asked to perform at one of his classes as a singer so that a pupil could demonstrate his or her abilities as a piano accompanist, and she remained devoted to her former teacher until she and Gabrilowitsch, then living in Munich, were forced by the outbreak of World War I to immigrate to the United States a year before the master died.

Considering how closely Mark Twain was involved with Leschetizky and his circle, and indeed the whole Viennese musical world, for two entire seasons, his failure to make more of it literarily is puzzling. "I don't much care for music myself," he told a *New York World* interviewer in London who was summarizing the Vienna sojourn for American readers.[36] The aphorism he wrote on one of Dagobert Wlaschim's photo postcards that he autographed for Clara's fellow piano pupil Stefan Czapka, "All of us contain Music & Truth, but most of us can't get it out," seems closer to the reality.[†37] He shunned few opportunities in Vienna for musical experiences that someone who didn't "care much for music" could easily have escaped.

That he did, in fact, greatly enjoy music and was a capable judge of its performance is obvious from his comments on Leschetizky and others, even in such a casually perspicacious note as this on the entertainment at a Viennese dinner party: "The new baritone from Bayreuth (von Rooy) sang—a wonderful voice. He is but 26 & has a future before him."[†38] The Dutch bass-baritone Anton van (not von) Rooy (1870–1932) did indeed enjoy an illustrious career following his stage debut as Wotan in 1897 in Bayreuth. A year later he joined the Metropolitan Opera roster for a decade, singing Amfortas there in the first *Parsifal* outside Bayreuth (1903) and Jokanaan in New York's first *Salome* (1907).

That Mark Twain also knew how to write discerningly and appreciatively, not just satirically, about music and musicians is evident in an episode he wrote in November 1897 in "The Chronicle of Young Satan" in which Philip Traum (Young Satan) completely enthralls the three boys and their friends by accompanying himself on an old spinet (which he has magically put in tune) while singing a romantic ballad. "I was in raptures to see him show off so," Theodor, the narrator, says: "For this was no music such as they had ever heard before. It was not one instrument talking, it was a whole vague, dreamy, far-off orchestra—flutes, and violins, and silver horns, and drums, and cymbals, and all manner of other instruments, blending their soft tones in one rich stream of harmony."[39] What follows is a kind of imaginative paradigm of a performance at a *Liederabend* (song recital) such as Twain heard more than once in Vienna. And throughout the "Chronicle" and the later "No. 44, The Mysterious Stranger" are many such passages in which music is used thematically and as a catharsis.

Mark Twain's seeming reluctance to write as directly about his Viennese musical experiences as he did about political events there may betray a sense of insecurity about his lack of musical training amid such high falutin' company as he encountered at Leschy's soirées. Although modesty and humility were not among his virtues, it would have been unnatural for him not to have felt somewhat intimidated in the midst of luminaries like Johann Strauss, Hans Richter, Gustav Mahler, Karl Goldmark, Eduard Hanslick, Alexander von Zemlinsky, and Antonin Dvorák.

Whatever the explanation for Twain's taciturnity concerning his musical experiences, his Vienna notebooks contain one superb unpublished musical aphorism which one might read as a too-subtle, hence suppressed, comment on his daughter's capricious switch from piano to singing: "She played the medulla oblongota with feeling, deftly changing in the 3rd bar from an Asia minor to a major maxillary."[40]

CHAPTER SIX

"The Most Beautiful Theater in the World"

𝔄 mong the few common denominators of Mark Twain and Henry James, other than the close relationship each independently enjoyed with another great literary contemporary, William Dean Howells, was the infatuation both writers had with the theater and the passionate desire they shared to succeed as dramatists. Both failed abysmally. James spent a small fortune and nearly a decade of his creative energy in the futile attempt to write a hit play. Twain made sporadic forays onto the stage with badly flawed efforts, always with disastrous results, for about a quarter-century before finally giving up. Ironically, both writers lived to see others' highly successful stage adaptations of their novels and stories.[1]

Hence it was no coincidence that the playwright-journalist Siegmund Schlesinger, interviewing Mark Twain on his arrival in Vienna and obviously knowing something of Twain's penchant for the theater as well as perhaps of his failed dramatic efforts, should have tried to draw him out with:

"Und das Theater? Hat es Sie nicht angelockt?" warf ich hin, um seinen Bekenntnissen über diesen Punkt die Wege zu ebnen. Er schmunzelte, strich seinen Schnurrbart und erwiderte mit einem Wortspiel: "I made some play but it would not play," das heißt er versucht sich wohl, aber es war nicht spielbar; dagegen sind manche seiner Arbeiten in Amerika dramatisirt worden, nicht von ihm, sondern von Anderen.[2]

("And the theater? Hasn't it ever attracted you?" I threw in to smooth the way for his confessions on this point. He grinned, stroked his mustache and replied with a pun: "I made some play, but it would not play," which means he tried but it wasn't playable; despite this many of his works have been dramatized in America, not by him but by others.)

The disagreement of "some" and "it" here suggests that his interlocutor either misunderstood or mistranscribed what Twain actually said. In any case, he may have been referring to *Ah Sin*, his collaborative attempt with Bret Harte in 1877 to dramatize the latter's immensely popular ballad "Plain Talk from Truthful James," which folded after some weeks in Washington and New York, as well as to Twain's own *Simon Wheeler*, also written in 1877, which he could not even get produced. He boasted to Schlesinger, however, of earning $75,000 in royalties from John T. Raymond's stage adaptation of Twain's novel *The Gilded Age*, called *Colonel Sellers*, which Schlesinger hilariously mistranscribed as *Colonel Salaries*.

Even before he came to Vienna, Twain was doubtless aware of the imperial city as a theatergoer's paradise, that theatrically it was to the German-speaking world what London was (and is) to the English-speaking. But he probably never dreamed he could become involved in writing for the Viennese stage, which was where Schlesinger's disingenuous question was leading. In the end, his involvement with the theater in Vienna bore no more immediate fruit than it had elsewhere, although it influenced and affected him in other, perhaps more interesting, ways.

Vienna's preeminence since the eighteenth century as a theatrical center was not owing to its large number of theaters, particularly in comparison, say, with London's West End or New York's Broadway-cum-Off-Broadway in recent decades. There have rarely been more than a dozen major "legitimate" houses alight in Vienna at any one time. But with a few exceptions, Viennese theaters have traditionally housed resident repertory ensembles that alternated a dozen or so productions per *Spielzeit* (season), so that in any given ten-month season (September through June) one might have the opportunity to see as many as seventy-five different works performed. Add to this quantity a higher standard of performance and of sumptuous production, no expense spared, than one could encounter in most cities of the world, and it is easy to understand why, in Stefan Zweig's words, "the first glance of the average Viennese into his morning paper was not at the events in parliament, or world affairs, but at the repertoire of the theater, which assumed so important a role in public life as hardly was possible in any other city."[3]

Although all of Vienna's theaters received some form of government subvention in order to keep them under the thumb of the imperial censor, two kinds of theaters existed in the city. In one elite category were the k. k. Hofoper, which was devoted chiefly, though not exclusively, to musical drama (opera), and the k. k. Hofburgtheater, known colloquially as the "Burgtheater," which was the leading legitimate theater of the realm. These institutions belonged to the crown as appendages to the imperial court, like the k. k. Hofkapelle (the boys' choir of the imperial chapel and the musicians in the opera orchestra). Those who administered, directed, and performed in them were salaried servants of the imperial household, and the imperial purse bore the entire operating expenses of these institutions. The emperor's subjects and foreign visitors were permitted to purchase tickets or even to subscribe seats by the season for performances in the Hofoper and Burgtheater except on those infrequent occasions when the emperor or a member of his family or (with his permission) a courtier commanded a *geschlossene Vorstellung* (closed performance).

The other theaters were, like the theaters of Britain and America, privately owned and operated as commercial enterprises, called in Vienna k. k. Privilegierte (imperially royally licensed) theaters. The major houses in this category included the two oldest theaters in the city, the Theater in der Josefstadt, built in 1788, and the Theater an der Wien, built by the actor-impresario Schikaneder (Mozart's *Zauberflöte* librettist) in 1801, plus the mid-nineteenth-century Carltheater in Leopoldstadt, the newer Deutsches Volkstheater (opened in 1889), and the newest of all, the Raimundtheater, built in 1893. In summers there was also the open-air Wiener Volkstheater in the Prater and, in the winter, Ronacher's Établissement, a variety theater that mainly booked touring entertainers (troupes and solo performers) doing vaudeville and other light theatrical and musical fare.

While the Clemenses were living in Vienna, on December 14, 1898, another new theater was inaugurated. Later renamed the Volksoper (People's Opera) and devoted largely to operettas, it was originally the Kaiser-Jubiläum-Stadttheater, a gift to the city of Vienna from a group of its wealthiest burghers to commemorate the fiftieth anniversary of the accession of Emperor Franz Josef I. Since there is no record of Mark Twain's attending a performance there, it was evidently the only major Viennese theater he seems not to have frequented with some regularity. Furthermore, he made it his business to become acquainted as rapidly as possible with the managers, directors, and principal actors of the leading theaters, and it is doubtful that he ever had to buy a ticket to the many performances he attended in Vienna.

What the Viennese were still calling the "new" Burgtheater in 1897 was his favorite. Built in monumental neo-baroque style by Gottfried von Semper and Carl Hasenauer on the Ringstrasse in the so-called Rathaus Quarter, opposite the town hall, and magnificently decorated by the brothers Ernst and Gustav Klimt and Franz Matsch, it opened on October 14, 1888. The old Burgtheater it replaced (to the dismay of many patrons), the auditorium of which Semper and Hasenauer copied as faithfully as possible, had been built in 1776 by Emperor Josef II to provide his capital with a "German national theater." It was at the old Burg that Mozart's *Die Entführung aus dem Serail* and *Le nozze di Figaro*, among other important operas and spoken dramas, had been premiered, and for 120 years before Mark Twain's arrival the Imperial–Royal Court Theater, old or new, had been, as Zweig observed, "for the Viennese . . . more than a stage upon which actors enacted parts; it was the microcosm that mirrored the macrocosm, the brightly colored reflection in which the city saw itself, the only true *cortigiano* of good taste.[4]

One of Twain's first sightseeing excursions in the city after recovering from the gout was a private tour of the Burgtheater given him on the afternoon of October 19, 1897, by its general manager, Dr. Max Burckhardt. For his visit all the new electric lights were turned up throughout the house, an unusual favor for anyone less than royalty or for a special festive occasion, and Vienna's famous guest was permitted to peer into every nook and cranny of the grand staircases, foyers, *Pausesäle* (bars and lounges), *Zuschauerraum* (auditorium), stage, dressing rooms, and backstage storage areas. For his special pleasure the stage crew demonstrated its machinery for special effects, reputedly the most advanced in Europe, by simulating a sea storm, including thunder and lightning. He closely scrutinized many details of the lush decor, lingering before portraits of the legendary tragedienne Charlotte Wolter, recently dead, and of the celebrated Adolf von Sonnenthal, whose acting he was often to admire in the months ahead. At the tour's conclusion, the *begeistert* (enraptured) visitor pronounced the theater's furnishing and decorations *unvergleichbar* (incomparable) and asserted unequivocally that the Burgtheater was *das schönste Theater der Welt* (the most beautiful theater in the world) and the tour itself "worth the trouble of a trip to Vienna."[5]

Then as now, the "Burg's" repertory was largely drawn from playwrights memorialized in gilded cartouches on its facade: Goethe, Schiller, Lessing, Grillparzer, Hebbel, Halm, Calderon, Shakespeare, and Molière. During the two seasons Mark Twain attended Burg performances, for example, he could choose from among such German classics as Schiller's *Maid of Orleans*, which he very likely saw, Goethe's *Faust, Part I*, Franz Grillparzer's *The Jewess of Toledo*, or Gustav von Freytag's comedy *The Journalists*. Had he a penchant (doubtful) for Shakespeare in the much-admired Schlegel translations, there was *Richard II* or *A Midsummer Night's Dream*. There was also Scribe's *Adrienne Lecouvreur* and the brand-new hit from Paris, Rostand's *Cyrano de Bergerac*.

As the Rostand offering suggests, the Burg might also, providing the imperial censor concurred, bestow the honor of a production upon a contemporary playwright. Thus, during his Vienna sojourn, Twain could see the premiere of Gerhart Hauptmann's *Die versunkene Glocke*

(The Sunken Bell) on December 7, 1897, Schnitzler's two-year-old *Liebelei* (Games of Love), and Adolf von Wilbrandt's *Der Meister von Palmyra* (The Master of Palmyra), which had its world premiere in Munich in 1889 and entered the Burgtheater repertory in 1892. By Wilbrandt's ponderous five-act *Dramatische Dichtung* (dramatic poem), he was totally captivated.

How often Mark Twain attended performances of *The Master of Palmyra* is hard to determine precisely. It was performed five times during the 1897–98 season and four during 1898–99, and although it is unlikely he saw all nine of those performances, he did see the play at least two or three times during the first season, the first occasion quite likely being the evening before his private tour of the theater, and he saw it again at least once (December 29, 1898) during the second.[6] Undoubtedly what impressed Twain most and brought him back into the theater again and again to enjoy what he called this "remarkable play" was the excellence of the old-fashioned declamatory acting of Sonnenthal (in the title role); of Stella Hohenfels, whose portrayal of all five of the *ewige Weibliche* roles Twain praised as a histrionic tour de force; and of Robert Emmerich, as Pausanius, the Spirit of Death. In lesser hands *The Master of Palmyra* might have struck him as tedious, overblown, and jejune, as it must today almost anyone who reads the play. The great Adolf (Ritter) von Sonnenthal's acting, however, reminded Twain of Edwin Booth's Hamlet thirty years earlier—a style that by 1897 had gone quite out of fashion in the English-speaking theater, though Mark Twain seems not to have realized it—and the play deeply stirred and affected him.

The theme of the play, that "life without end can be regret without end," that life is meaningless without death, that those like the Struldbrugs in *Gulliver's Travels*, who can live forever, are doomed to endless suffering, appealed to him mightily. Although Wilbrandt was a North German, the anti-Faust theme of his play is quintessentially Viennese. It perfectly suited a society that was fascinated with death, that then had the highest suicide rate in the world, and in which, even more than Victorian England, what the King in *Huckleberry Finn* called

Imperial Royal Court Theatre (Burgtheater), from the city hall tower, 1898
(Picture Archives of the Austrian National Library)

funeral "orgies" surrounding the *schöne Leich* (beautiful corpse) had reached the level of a fine art.

Set in the ancient Roman capital of Syria, the plot of *Der Meister von Palmyra* recounts the trials and tribulations of a handsome victorious young general, Apelles, who is granted his wish for a deathless life. (How, one wonders, did the sixty-three-year-old Sonnenthal project this character?) He realizes his mistake almost at once, but it takes five acts (with a playing time of over four hours) of miseries and misfortunes before he is able to get Death to release him from his bad bargain, to which the expiring Apelles says simply: "Ich danke dir" (I thank thee). "Nothing," Mark Twain averred, "could be more moving, more beautiful, than this close. This piece is just one long, soulful, sardonic laugh at human life."[7]

The Viennese cultural value that Wilbrandt dramatized so cogently and, at least in Twain's judgment, so artfully, was the logical extension of Phaeacianism—the "Baroque vision of death as the fulfillment of life."[8] In the City of Dreams it was at least as old as W. A. Mozart's famous letter to his father (April 4, 1787) in which he confesses, "As death, when we consider it closely, is the true goal of our existence, I have formed during the last few years such close relations with this best and truest friend of mankind, that his image is not only no longer terrifying to me, but is indeed very soothing and consoling!"[9] And this sentiment was as recent as Hermann Bahr's, one of the leaders of the "Jung Wien" literati when Mark Twain was in Vienna (and whom he knew), who wrote at the turn of the century: "I am fond of death. Not as a saviour, for I do not suffer from life, but as a consummator. It will bring me everything which I still lack."[10]

It would be hard to overestimate the influence *The Master of Palmyra* exerted on Twain's thinking and writing. Its immediate effect was to stimulate him to begin a new novel embodying his own variations on the play's theme. In late October or early November 1897, within weeks of his first encounter with Wilbrandt's play, he commenced "The Chronicle of Young Satan," the first of three versions of the "Mysterious Stranger" narratives on which he worked sporadically for two months before setting it aside, returning to the idea the following summer in Kaltenleutgeben in the briefer, second "Schoolhouse Hill" version.[11] In 1902 he again encapsulated the theme precisely in a brief fable, "The Five Boons of Life."

A second effect of his enthusiasm for Wilbrandt's play was to rekindle Twain's own interest in playwriting with results to be explored shortly. The third, and most tangible, was a critical essay, written in late May and early June 1898, on Wilbrandt's play itself. Entitled "About Play-Acting," it was first published in the *Forum* magazine in October 1898 and subsequently included in *The Man That Corrupted Hadleyburg and Other Stories and Sketches* (1900).

In his article, Twain gives a synopsis of this "deeply fascinating" play, calling it "a great and stately metaphysical poem," and describing the Viennese reaction to it: "the audience sat four hours and five minutes without thrice breaking into applause, except at the close of each act; sat rapt and silent—fascinated. . . . I know people who have seen it ten times; they know most of it by heart; they do not tire of it; and they shall still be quite willing to go and sit under its spell whenever they get the opportunity."[12]

Then, after some laudatory comments about the Vienna cast's acting and a disquisition on the play's philosophical import, he comes to the point of his essay: that *The Master of Palmyra* is vastly superior to anything then playing in New York and should forthwith be imported. As proof of this he reprints the theater list from a New York newspaper for Saturday, May 7, 1898, and, commenting on the "lightsome feast" in Broadway's plethora of farces and melodramas, he admonishes his countrymen: "You are trying to make yourself believe that life is a comedy, that its sole business is fun, that there is nothing serious in it. You are ignoring the skeleton in your closet. . . . You are eating too much mental sugar; you will bring on Bright's Disease of the intellect."[13] The remedy for this is to "have a Burg in New York, and Burg scenery, and a great company like the Burg company. Then, with a tragedy tonic once or twice a month, we shall enjoy the comedies all the better." Hardly was the ink dry on the article before some enterprising

Broadway producer took Twain at his word, commissioned a translation of *The Master of Palmyra*, and brought it to the New York stage, where it closed after a few performances amid loud critical guffaws.

Since Adolf von Wilbrandt and his wife, the famous Austrian actress Auguste Baudius, frequented the salons of the Countess Misa Wydenbruck-Esterházy and other members of the Leschetizky circle, the Clemenses became acquainted with the Wilbrandts during their first winter in Vienna. The following season, on March 8, 1899, Mark Twain shared a platform with Frau Wilbrandt-Baudius when he did a benefit reading for a charity hospital, in the Festsaal of the Kaufmännische Verein where, sixteen months earlier, he had given his Concordia speech.[14]

Having informed the grande dame she could have but thirty minutes of the program to read some poems of her husband's and others so that he might have forty for his reading plus five for a speech in German, he was infuriated, as he confided in his notebook, when "She occupied the stage just an hour, & then I came before a perishing audience that had the death-rattle in its throat. I only saved their lives by cutting the M.[exican] Plug out of my program. Frau W. had privately *added* a long (written) speech glorifying me. I will never accept of help, musical or otherwise, on the platform again."†[15] Two days later, however, he had sufficiently recovered his composure to write her with the utmost tongue-in-cheek diplomacy:

> Dear Frau Wilbrandt:
>
> I am rested-up again, & am young again; & as my first pleasure I wish to thank you in the best & heartiest words for taking half my burden off my shoulders, & for so stirring the hearts of those people with the beauty & pathos of your reading & for saying those gracious things of *me*. And won't you send those lines to me, that I may keep them, in memory of that pleasant day & you?
> Sincerely Yours,
> S. L. Clemens*[16]

The chance to sit almost nightly, if he so wished, in the "most beautiful" or in another of Vienna's theaters at spectacles like Friedrich Halm's *Wildfeuer* (Wildfire), Baron Alfred von Berger's popular historic drama *Habsburg*, and especially Wilbrandt's play fired Twain's ambition to write plays once more.[17] Soon after New Year's 1898, which he said was a "fine sunny day," his notebook begins to overflow with jottings for plays—titles, characters, plot situations—such as these random excerpts:

> The ~~English~~ Duke. Farce in 2 acts. Duke a monkey. . . . Make plays—with a German for Principal character (Dutchy) an Irishman, a Scotchman, a Chinaman a Japanese, a negro (George) Uncle John Quarles who was very like the Yankee farmer in Old Homestead. Write an Old Homestead of the *South*. . . . Play denouement. Girl to recognize disguised sweetheart by a false note in a song which they had formerly used as a signal. . . . Spanish-barber. Duke Grande of Spain, for a play. . . . *Play*—the *Comedy* side of hypnotism—hypnotic suggestion—the hypnotic or sonnambulic [*sic*] memory &c.†[18]

Repeated reference to Denman Thompson's tremendously popular melodrama *The Old Homestead* (1886), one of the greatest American box-office successes of all time, along with other notations in this passage, clearly show the direction Twain's playwriting bent was taking. His preachments in "About Play-Acting" notwithstanding, it was comedy and melodrama, the genres he knew would fetch the public, that really stirred Mark Twain into action. On January 14, 1898, he noted: "Began to write comedy 'Is He Dead?' (Francois Millet)."[19] In it, he used several of the ideas he had jotted in these excerpts, including the "Play denouement" and several of the character types and names (such as "Dutchy"), but it is no *Old Homestead* of the South.

Instead, *Is He Dead?*, the two-act comedy he finished within twenty-four days—unusual speed for him—is a farcical fantasia set in France

---

reproduction or dramatization rights in every medium. It is published with the permission of the University of California Press and Robert H. Hirst, General Editor, Mark Twain Project.

in the 1840s about the painter Jean François Millet, adapted from a satirical story ("Is He Living or Is He Dead?") that Twain had published in *Cosmopolitan Magazine* in 1894.[20] Although he exuberantly felt he had at last written "a play that would *play*," *Is He Dead?* was never published or produced, and it marks his final completed effort at an original piece for the stage.[21] He sent it to Bram Stoker (the author of *Dracula*) in London, with high hope that Stoker, acting as his agent for 15 percent of the gross profits, would find a willing West End producer, at least, and that Rogers, to whom he later sent a copy, might do the same in New York.[22] By late summer, however, after several discouragements from Stoker and others, he dejectedly told Rogers: "*Put 'Is He Dead?' in the fire.* God will bless you. I too. I started in to convince myself that I could write a play or couldn't. I'm convinced. Nothing can disturb that conviction."[23]

Fortunately, Henry Rogers did not carry out this injunction, and the surviving manuscript in the Mark Twain Papers holds more than passing interest. *Is He Dead?*, like Twain's earlier unsuccessful spoof on whodunit plays, *Simon Wheeler*, is quite possibly stageworthy today as a museum piece and curiosity for a university or other noncommercial theater. But its large, theatrically unwieldy cast of stock characters in which the central figure, the young Millet, is the only historic personage holds little intrinsic interest and almost no dimension. The characters include a group of young artists of various (and obvious) nationalities with names like Agamemnon Buckner (known as "Chicago"), Hans von Bismarck (called "Dutchy"), Sandy Ferguson and Phelin O'Shaughnessy, a French "picture-dealer & usurer," three rich tycoons (one English, one American, one Australian), Millet's pupils (a Turk, a "Hindoo," a Spaniard, a Chinese), and assorted pretty girls, their widowed mothers, and one doddering Papa, plus the usual servants.

Moreover, the central plot situation in which the painter fakes his own death in order to extricate himself and his prospective father-in-law from debt by thus driving up the price of his paintings, although novel and interesting, is too slight to sustain two acts. The point of the play—that collectors are less interested in artistic merit than in an artist's celebrity—is insufficient to compensate for its slightness of incident and thinness of character. Despite the comic inventions in Twain's play, it is based on historical fact. The prices of Millet's paintings did escalate dramatically following his death in 1875, and in an incident Twain used in his comedy, taking "the pardonable liberty to highly antedate" it (he noted on the script), the *Angelus*, one of Millet's two most famous paintings (the other being the *Gleaners*), was bought at a Paris auction by an American for five hundred thousand francs and repurchased "on the spot" by the French government (for the Louvre) for fifty thousand more. So Twain was doubtless counting on his play to have a topical interest it has entirely lost for us today.

At about the same time he began writing *Is He Dead?*, Twain entered negotiations with Siegmund Schlesinger to collaborate in the writing of plays to be produced in Vienna. Two plays at least were contemplated, but whether either was finished remains a mystery. In any event, neither reached the stage nor publication, and there are no known extant manuscripts of either play. Still, we know a good deal about the progress (or lack of it) of the collaboration and something of the intended content of the two projected plays.

The same day Twain told Rogers that "work is become a pleasure again—it is not labor, any longer. I am up to my ears, these last 3 or 4 weeks—and all *dramatic*" and referring to his "play that would *play*" (*Is He Dead?*), he added: "And there's another one—a joint production. An Austrian playwright is plotting it out, and we are going to write it together."[24] This was a comedy to be called *Der Gegenkandidat, oder die Frauen Politiker* (The Opposing Candidate, or Women Politicians).

The collaboration moved swiftly at first, and already in early February, Twain indicated *Der Gegenkandidat* "is about finished—it won't take many more days."[25] By February 1, Schlesinger had evidently sketched out enough of the plot that Twain could send him a "gemixt pickles" postcard with "Gut! Also werde ich Sie am 3tn Februar expect. Es freut mich sehr daß Sie unseres heiliges Werkes schon so weit gebracht habe. [Dies ist mein eigenes Grammatik—kommt nicht aus des Buches.]"*[26] (Good! Thus I will expect you on February 3rd. I'm glad you've brought our holy work so far. [This is my own grammar—it doesn't come from a book.]) And on February 24, the "holy work" became the object of a contract executed between S. L. Clemens and Siegmund Schlesinger, whose signatures were witnessed by their wives, Olivia L. Clemens and Marie Schlesinger, authorizing Clemens to negotiate productions in the United States and Great Britain, Schlesinger to do likewise in Austria and Germany, with the profits from productions wherever they might be performed and regardless of the negotiator to be divided equally between the collaborators.[27]

The subject of *Der Gegenkandidat* was timely and topical. There was much discussion in the 1890s in Austria, as in Britain and America, of extending the suffrage to women and, indeed, in the debates on the electoral reforms proposed by the Badeni regime and sanctioned by the emperor in June 1896, there had been some agitation for granting women at least a limited franchise. Rosa Mayreder, the Viennese counterpart of Susan B. Anthony (in the United States) and Emmeline Pankhurst (in England), had founded the Allgemeiner Oesterreichischer Frauenverein (General Austrian Women's Association) in 1893, giving impetus to the movement for women's political rights. Mark Twain publicly supported Mayreder while he was in Vienna and gave a reading for her Frauenverein.

Nevertheless, what stance the collaborators intended taking on the "woman question" and whether the political implications of their comedy prevented it from coming to fruition—if, indeed, it ever got as far as being submitted to the official censor—must remain part of the riddle of what happened to *Der Gegenkandidat*. From the available correspondence between Twain and Schlesinger, it seems a reasonable guess that this first play was written in English, the plot being sup-

Siegmund Schlesinger (1842–1918), who collaborated with Mark Twain on
two plays intended for the Burgtheater that were never produced or
published (Picture Archives of the Austrian National Library)

plied by Schlesinger, the dialogue by Twain, with the former doing a German translation for the Viennese stage. A second collaboration, which apparently never got very far off the ground, was to have been a comedy called *Die Goldgräberin* (The Lady Goldminer) in which the writing tasks were to be reversed: Twain developing the plot, Schlesinger writing German dialogue for Twain to translate for London and New York performing.

This play, too, would have topical appeal and immediacy. The discovery of gold on Klondike Creek in the Yukon territory of northwest Canada in 1897 had occasioned a kind of replay of the California gold rush of almost fifty years earlier, luring scores of young Austrians and firing the imaginations of countless others through tales filtering back to the Viennese newspapers. Mark Twain, furthermore, was inextricably associated in the European mind with his days, few though they really had been, as a prospector in the mining camps of the Far West— a region and an era that fascinated Europeans—and he did everything he could to perpetuate his frontiersman image abroad.

Small wonder, then, that Dr. Paul Schlenther, who had come from Berlin in February 1898 to succeed Burckhardt as the new general manager of the k. k. Hofburgtheater, wanted to capitalize on Twain's celebrity in the city and the timely appeal of *Die Goldgräberin* to score a hit during his first full season (1898–99) at the Burg.[28] Could it be that Mark Twain would get the chance to see a play of his on the stage of "the most beautiful theater in the world"? Yet more, it was to be a vehicle for the Burg's leading comedienne, the emperor's mistress, Katharina Schratt.

What eventually became of *Die Goldgräberin* is, like the fate of *Der Gegenkandidat*, shrouded in uncertainties. Henry W. Fisher, an American newspaperman whom Twain had known for two decades in the States and on various assignments in Europe, wrote a memoir of an incident connected with the play that, if true, might serve to explain why *Die Goldgräberin* went unfinished. According to Fisher's anecdote, he and Twain went to call on Frau Schratt when the play was well along so that the playwright could gather some first-hand impressions of the actress for whom he was writing the title role:

Well, we went, saw, and—wondered at Francis Joseph's taste. In speech and manner, though, the Schratt was a fine old girl. Showed us a big houseful of presents, all gifts from his Majesty, and elaborately so marked.

We had duly admired the silver bed, the silver folding stool and the ditto cabinet, likewise other chamber paraphernalia of white metal, when the Schratt said: "There is one thing more the like of which you haven't in America."

"You don't say so!" ejaculated Mark, in blasphemous German.

The Schratt pushed a button, a wall panel shot sideways, and the handsomest silver-gilt bathtub ever came waltzing in, or rather roller-skated in.

In our homeward bound fiacre, Mark remained silent for fully ten minutes; then he delivered himself sadly but firmly:

"No, it's all off with that mellerdrammer. For if I let Schratt ride down to the footlights in that golden tub, people will want to see the Empress in it, too; next they will holler for Kaiser Bill, Sarah Bernhardt, Loie Fuller, and William Jennings Bryan. It won't work—people are such hogs!"

And the drama was never proceeded with.[29]

Colorful, tempting, even plausible as Fisher's story might seem, a more likely reason why *Die Goldgräberin* may never have been finished, if it ever actually got beyond the talking stage, is Siegmund Schlesinger's interminable delays and procrastinations. To glimpse what probably happened, one must read between the lines of extant correspondence consisting entirely of notes from Twain to Schlesinger, replying to letters Twain evidently did not see fit to keep.

When Twain finished the dialogue for *Der Gegenkandidat* and sent the script to his collaborator, Schlesinger appears to have been unwell and unable to commence translating at once. On May 20, 1898, Twain told Schlesinger of his coming move to Villa Paulhof in Kaltenleutgeben.[30] Ten days later, evidently responding to a request for more time because of lingering illness, Twain felt generous: "Certainly! Take another month—and don't hurry; hurrying doesn't help a sick man to get well."[†31]

It would seem, however, that Schlesinger's English may not have been even as good as Mark Twain's German, especially for translating the kind of idiomatic American English Twain was so completely

habituated to writing, and Schlesinger may have found his task compounded by the difficulty of reading Twain's handwriting. That, at
least, would seem the point of Twain's apologetic letter of July 28,
1898, consoling Schlesinger that "a manuscript written in an unfamiliar hand is at a heavy disadvantage. It loses *points*. Please send it to Miss
Marion v. Kendler to be type-written, & let me pay the cost. . . ."†32

Thereafter Twain's notes become even more terse and almost testy
as, preoccupied with other writing himself, he seems to have sensed
that Schlesinger would never produce anything they had originally
agreed to in the collaboration. For instance, there is this enigmatic
postcard from Twain to Schlesinger, postmarked October 20, 1898,
with "November 1. Schon gut. Daß ist wie ich's verstanden habe."*33
(November 1. Okay. That's the way I understood it.) Was this to set a
meeting date or another postponed deadline for Schlesinger? Finally,
on New Year's 1899, Twain writes in his notebook:

> Note from Schlesinger, asking another month's delay. Answered "If
> you can. Delay it till April or May—that will be still more convenient for
> me; for I am now deep in work which I cannot very well interrupt before
> that time."
>
> ~~He would like me to promise the use of my name in advance, I think,
> & unconditonally.~~
>
> It will be a marvel if he produces a play which I can work into a shape
> which will satisfy me, after all his delays. I shan't allow my name to be
> used in connection with it unless it shall in all ways warrant the risk.†34

Thus the collaboration, if it can really be called that, ended in disappointment. Schlesinger never fulfilled his end of the bargain on
Der Gegenkandidat, and his irresponsible dilly-dallying completely ob-
structed progress on their second projected play.

Mark Twain was doubtless unaware of Schlesinger's reputation for

Dilettantismus and what the Austrians call *Schlamperei* (sloppiness), or he might have been chary of Schlesinger's proposals.[35] What he did know was that the sixty-six-year-old feuilletonist-playwright had had a string of more or less successful Viennese stage productions and that he was well connected. Malicious gossip in Vienna, however, attributed his success to the fact that Schlesinger's brother-in-law was Moritz Szeps, one of Austria's most influential publishers. Whatever the reason for the fruitless ending to the Twain-Schlesinger collaboration, it was certainly not the one A. B. Paine assumed: "they good-naturedly agreed that it would be necessary to wait until they understood each other's language more perfectly before they could go on with the project."[36] There is little "good nature" evident in Twain's "it will be a marvel if he produces a play. . . ."

When Siegmund Schlesinger died in 1918 at the ripe age of eighty-six, he was already forgotten, and today he is unknown even among historians of Austrian literature and drama, his published works gathering dust in but a few of his country's libraries. A pity, then, that he missed his chance to have his name linked with one of the half-dozen American writers of undeniable world stature.

Twain's many theater-going opportunities in Vienna amid his surge of interest in playwriting led him during his first season there to try his hand at translating some of the local hits in hopes of peddling them in New York or London. In the same January 20 letter in which he informed Rogers about writing his own play (*Is He Dead?*) and his "joint production" with Schlesinger, he added: "Thirdly, I've (been) [*sic*] acquired the American and English rights in a new and powerful and successful Austrian drama, and have nearly finished translating it. The author and I share the American and English profits half and half."[37] The play referred to, the first of two he was to translate within the next two months, is *Bartel Turaser*, a three-act naturalistic tragedy by Philipp Langmann, a thirty-five-year-old Czech-born industrial chemist who had begun writing fiction and drama avocationally and was enjoying his first stage success. *Bartel Turaser* premiered at the Deutsches Volkstheater on December 11, 1897, to almost unanimous critical acclaim, and it had been a box-office hit as well. It was very much in the vein of the "worker" dramas of Gerhart Hauptmann, such as *Die Weber* (The Weavers), then in vogue in the German theater.

Although Twain told Rogers it was a "dismal but interesting piece" that "doesn't much resemble a play," he noted that "it crowds the house every time it is billed" and thought it should attract producers because its simple, single set with "old clothes" costuming "costs nothing to 'stage.'" Moreover, its theme—the corrupting power of money—is one that always strongly appealed to him and one he used repeatedly in some of his best stories. In order to feed his family, a starving worker (Bartel) accepts a bribe to perjure himself when a female fellow-worker accuses their boss of sexual assault. Ostracized by the community for his betrayal, Bartel's children die, and he is hounded by his conscience, in the form of hallucinatory accusing voices of his dead children, to a deathbed confession of his perjury.

In early March 1898 Twain was attracted by yet another new Viennese hit, this one a *Schwank* (farce) closer to his natural talents. On March 11, *NFP* advised its readers that "Mark Twain is doing a brisk business in the export of our native literature." Having already prepared the proletarian play *Bartel Turaser* for the English stage, the paper reported, he had commenced translating Ernst Gettke's and Alexander Engel's farce, *Im Fegefeuer*, and had made a contract with the coauthors for it.[38] This occurred less than a week after the premiere of *Im Fegefeuer* at the Raimund-Theater on March 5, 1898, to rave reviews and a healthy box office. This translation, however, went more slowly than that for Langmann's play, and Twain soon began to weary of the undertaking. In late April, summer plans beginning to preoccupy him, he was still at it but confided to Rogers: "Translation is dull and stupid work, and I'll do no more of it. For the present anyway."[39]

Nevertheless, he finished *In Purgatory*, as the English version was called, a few weeks later, and sent it off to Charles Frohman in London. Frohman rejected it for West End production as "all jabber and no play," which Twain thought curious since "it tears these Austrians to pieces with laughter." Still he admitted it did not read well: "When I read it, now, it seems entirely silly; but when I see it on the stage it is exceedingly funny."[40] A clever variation on the time-honored plot of young lovers circumventing parental disapproval, differences in social status, and prearranged engagements to clear their path to the altar, its coauthors were the Raimund-Theater's director (Gettke) and a popular writer of light comedies and operettas (Engel). The secret of the play's popularity in Vienna, despite its hackneyed theme, was doubtless its many inside jokes about the foibles of the nouveaux riches of the city. Hence it was probably not really exportable.

Despite his complaints about translating, he did not keep his resolve to make an end of it with *In Purgatory*. In late July he was busying himself "at odd intervals" with yet another dramatic translation. This was Theodor Herzl's *Das neue Ghetto* (The New Ghetto), which he had seen at its premiere in the Carl-Theater on January 5, 1898, and had actually commenced work on in early April when a visit from Charles and Jervis Langdon, Olivia's brother and nephew, from Elmira, interrupted his writing for a fortnight. He laid it aside thereafter to finish *In Purgatory*; then the impending move to Kaltenleutgeben and other tasks preempted his attention. On April 24 the United States went to war with Spain over Cuba, and by the time he returned to the idea of translating Herzl's social problem play in late June, he had discouraging advice from New York that only "war-plays are all the go there, these days."[†41] So *The New Ghetto* was shelved.

Written in 1894 when the "Father of Zionism" was covering the first Dreyfus trial in Paris (where he met Mark Twain) for *NFP*, Herzl's was by far the most significant of the three Austrian plays to engage Twain's translating interest. Like Schnitzler's *Professor Bernhardi* some years later, it deals directly and powerfully with the burgeoning issue of anti-Semitism in Austrian life. Since this was a subject of increasing importance to Mark Twain, it is regrettable he never got around to completing a translation of the piece. Whether it would have fared better with his London and New York agents than did his *Bartel Turaser* and *In Purgatory* scripts, one may only speculate.

The central character in Herzl's play, whose surname, interestingly, is Samuel, is an assimilated Jew who discovers through several plot episodes that, although he has been freed from the ancient walled ghetto, he now (in 1893) lives in a new, psychological one of complex, invisible barriers. The climax occurs when Samuel's best friend, a Christian, snubs him rather than risk compromising his own political ambitions amid the rising tide of anti-Semitism in Vienna. Samuel dies in a duel with a Jew-baiter who has insulted him but not before a melodramatic deathbed reconciliation with his Christian friend who has been made to realize that the walls of the "new ghetto" must be breached for everyone. Is it, one is tempted to ask, mere coincidence that Mark Twain saw this play only weeks before he wrote his essay on dueling and while the polemic on anti-Semitism he completed six months later, "Concerning the Jews," was gestating?

Little more came of these three translating projects than had issued from the Schlesinger collaboration. What became of the two manuscripts that resulted—*In Purgatory* and *Bartel Turaser*—remains a mystery. They passed through many hands—those of Bram Stoker, Charles Frohman, Henry Rogers, Dr. Clarence Rice (Clemens's physician who acted briefly as his agent), William K. Harris (a Broadway producer)—and when last seen were in the office of the Klaw and Erlanger Managers' Exchange in Manhattan. If they still exist they may be in some dusty boxes of the Erlanger organization's files in a forgotten New York warehouse.[42]

A sidelight to Mark Twain's theatrical involvements in Vienna was a stage portrayal of him as a character in an entertainment presented March 14, 1898, at Ronacher's vaudeville theater. It was the annual benefit show of the Austrian Touring Club, an association of wealthy and aristocratic Viennese cyclists and, not many years later, motorcar enthusiasts. *Die Velodramatische Revue des Jahres 1897*, as it was called, was a series of satirical vignettes dramatizing major local news stories of the previous year by Wilhelm Anders, Bernhard Buchbinder, and Twain's collaborator, Siegmund Schlesinger. In one sketch, "Mark Twain," played by Josef Schildkraut, the prominent actor who also had the male lead in Engel and Gettke's *Im Fegefeuer*, then running at the Raimund-Theater, goes about Vienna "constantly taking notes and suffering humorous misunderstandings"—an obvious burlesque of Pötzl's "Silent Observer" story in *NWT*.[43] Played before a glittering audience that included the American humorist, himself a cycling enthusiast, the *Revue* raised enough money to pave the bicycle paths still in use along the inner side of the Ringstrasse.

In the end Mark Twain's flirtations with the Viennese theater proved no more overtly fruitful than had his theatrical enterprises in his native land. Neither of his collaborative efforts reached their intended stage in that "most beautiful theater in the world," and neither of his completed translations nor his one original piece was ever produced in an English-speaking theater. Nevertheless, the experiences and ideas that informed these abortive efforts bore fruit elsewhere in his nondramatic writings—in "The Chronicle of Young Satan," the essays "Dueling" and "Concerning the Jews," and especially "The Man That Corrupted Hadleyburg," with its insistent theme, *Radix Malorum est Cupiditas* (the root of evil is greed), so bitterly embodied. A form of literary economy in which little that Samuel L. Clemens experienced in life or read in a book or newspaper was ever actually lost or discarded by Mark Twain was one of this artist's greatest gifts.

CHAPTER SEVEN

"Choice People"

*T*o Countess Misa Wydenbruck-Esterházy, with the homage of her friend and admirer, S. L. Clemens," was the way Mark Twain inscribed her copy of *More Tramps Abroad* (British title of *Following the Equator*). "Homage" is not a word the author used indiscriminately, but Gräfin (Countess) Misa was accustomed to homage as one of the most beautiful women—some said *the* most beautiful woman—in Austria in 1897. Such judgments naturally depend upon one's standards of feminine beauty in a competition limited by money and class privilege. The countess, moreover, had numerous competitors for such distinction in an empire renowned for the beauty of its haut monde. Vienna's salons, ballrooms, and Ringstrasse "Corso" thronged with languid beauties whose delicate features, high cheekbones, and wistful dark eyes captured in Gustav Klimt's gilt paintings betokened centuries of mixing Alemannic with Slavic, Magyar, Ottoman, and Italian blood. The couture of these stunning *Hochwohlgeborene Damen* was seldom less than the latest Paris fashion. In such surroundings, Clemens, with undimmed eye for comely matrons or their "angelfish" daughters, was in his glory.

His initiation into Viennese high society came two months after his arrival. Although the German princess royal, a fellow guest at the Metropole, had invited the author to tea soon after he settled there, in his first sixty days he consorted mainly with journalists and perforce with the musical circle of Professor Leschetizky of which Clara had immediately become a member. The Clemenses had also been feted by the American ambassador, Charlemagne Tower, and taken up by the diplomatic community at large. On December 1, 1897, Clemens recorded in his notebook: "Night before last Madame Letschtishki [*sic*] came & took Clara & me to Ritter von Dutschka's to dine. Twenty persons at dinner: Count von Eulenberg (German Ambassador) & others came in after dinner. A remarkable gathering—no commonplace people present, no leatherheads. Princes & other titled people there, but not *because* of their titles, but for their distinction in achievement. It was like a salon of old-time Paris."†1 What charmed this usually cynical and intrepid democrat into naively believing this "remarkable gathering" had assembled "not *because* of their titles, but for their distinction in achievement" was not the rarefied intellectual atmosphere at the dinner table. Although this was the evening after Graf Badeni's regime had collapsed and Austria-Hungary was still deep in crisis, if anything as serious as politics was discussed or if bon mots were aired, Twain makes no mention of it. Instead, he describes only musical entertainment.

What else he found noteworthy about the party was the attractiveness of his Russian-born hostess and of some of his other table companions. "Madame Dutschka is large & stately & beautiful; cordial, & full of all kinds of charms of manner, ways & speech." She was fifty-two and had a twenty-eight-year-old son, but Clemens noted incredulously that she "appears to be about 30." Among the guests he met "a young countess there, whom I took to be a girl of 18; she has a daughter who is 13." This was the Countess Wydenbruck-Esterházy, who soon became the Clemens family's cicerone in Viennese society and their closest friend outside musical and literary circles. Her influence on what happened to them in Austria and upon Clara's musical plans was almost as great as that of Leschetizky himself.

Despite Clemens's impression of her as girlish, this thirty-eight-year-old widow was one of the reigning grandes dames of Vienna's social and cultural life. She was indeed strikingly pretty and graceful, as well as myopic, according to her niece, the British actress Nora Wydenbruck, who thought "her short-sightedness added to her charm" since, like most ladies of fashion then, she disdained eyeglasses.[2] Her social status was owed in no small degree to having been born an Esterházy, among the richest, most powerful families of the Austro-Hungarian nobility. One of her ancestors had assured himself a footnote in musical history as patron of the great Franz Josef Haydn, and Misa's grandfather had employed Franz Schubert as his children's music master for a time.

As this history suggests, children in Esterházy households received a sound musical education, and Misa's talents were clear at an early age. In her teens she was already an accomplished pianist and a promising singer. "Aunt Misa had a small but lovely voice and was a true musician," Nora Wydenbruck recalled. A concert career, however, was unthinkable for one of her class, so the countess, widowed at an early age with only an infant daughter to rear, joined the circle around the eccentric Pauline Fürstin von Metternich, and for three decades the countess's name graced almost every committee list for charity benefit concerts, exhibitions, theatrical performances, and readings Princess Metternich organized. The lovely countess became patroness, friend, even confidante of such leading musicians as Gustav Mahler, Marie Guttheil-Schoder, Erich Korngold, the young Bruno Walter, and members of the famed Rosé Quartet.

In her salon they performed for aristocrats and mingled with *Sezession* painters, Jung Wien poets and visiting foreign luminaries like the Swedish dramatist Strindberg (then married to a Viennese actress), and, of course, Mark Twain. "Poor Misa likes to surround herself with 'jugglers,'" her late husband's relatives sniffed, indicating how sadly the Viennese aristocracy had changed in their outlook and values since the time of Beethoven.[3] Her "jugglers" were, in fact, some of the most illustrious figures of fin de siècle artistic and intellectual life, not only in Vienna but in the world.

For the Clemens family the countess did two important favors. She introduced them to Dr. Wilhelm Winternitz, whose *Kaltwasserkur* (hydrotherapy) was then all the rage among the Austrian aristocracy as a cure for anything from lumbago to cancer, and found them a house, the Villa Paulhof, to rent near hers at Winternitz's *Kuranstalt* in Kaltenleutgeben from late May until mid-October 1898. The summer there was one of Twain's most productive in years, and it was considerably enlivened by the rounds of entertaining in which the countess invited the Clemenses into a circle at the resort that also included luminaries like Count Richard Coudenhove, Countess Bardi, Princess Khevenhüller, and "Carmen Sylva," Queen of Romania.

More important, she also provided her own daughter, Clementine, as a companion for Jean Clemens throughout the family's stay in the imperial city as well as at the resort, thus alleviating constant fears and worries Jean's parents had for her well-being. Jane Lampton Clemens (called Jean), the youngest Clemens daughter, had been even more devastated by the death of Susy, her oldest sister, than had Clara, the middle daughter. In London not long after Susy died Jean began having fainting spells with vomiting in violent seizures that were finally diagnosed as epilepsy, a disease about which little was then known. Her parents decided Jean must never be left alone lest she have a convulsion when no one could keep her from swallowing her tongue and choking to death or seriously injuring herself in a fall. Clara's studies precluded her being a constant companion, and neither Olivia Clemens nor Katy Leary could forego other obligations to watch over Jean every waking hour. She was too old for a governess, and to have hired a nurse would have alarmed the girl at a time when her frantic parents still wished to conceal the seriousness of her disorder.

Clementine was a godsend. Although four years younger than Jean, she was in some ways more mature than the high-strung, capricious Clemens girl. She recalled as an octogenarian in 1967 that she had been "on call constantly [and] had to drop whatever I was doing and go immediately whenever Jean wanted to play."[4] Her mother told her Jean was ill but never revealed the nature of the illness. Clementine never saw Jean have a "fit," but she was often mystified by the girl's moodiness and unpredictable behavior, recalling occasions in Kaltenleutgeben when Jean, on sudden impulse, would jump out of the window and be otherwise hyperactive. What most impressed her as a fatherless girl herself was "Mr. Clemens's great tenderness" toward his afflicted daughter and "his many acts and expressions of gratitude to my mother and me."

Quid pro quo, it was to benefit a favorite charity hospital of the countess's and Princess Metternich's that Mark Twain was induced to give his first, and in many respects most important, public reading in Vienna. It occurred the evening of February 1, 1898, in the old Bösendorfer Saal at Herrengasse 6. Although he accepted two more invitations to read in Vienna at the countess's behest and then gave two impromptu readings and one more in Budapest within the next fourteen months, he vowed to Rogers this "will be my last final permanent appearance on the platform—I hope."[5] The eight-hundred-seat house, he noted with evident pride, was packed to capacity plus numerous *Stehplätze* (standees): "Several rows of seats were $4 apiece. Still, there was far from room enough in the hall for all that applied for tickets."[†6] The *Neue Freie Presse* reporter observed that "the hall was much too small because the demand for tickets had not been sufficiently taken into account."[7] By seven o'clock, a half-hour before the reading was to begin, the Herrengasse was already choked with carriages and fiakers that brought the glittering, preponderantly female, audience.

Besides Princess Metternich, Prince Alois Liechtenstein, Countess Wydenbruck-Esterházy, other patrons of the charity and members of the American community, the Viennese journalistic, literary, and medical professions were well represented, including Dr. Sigmund Freud, playing truant from a lecture that evening by Prince Bismarck's personal physician.[8] What's more, Twain bragged to Rogers, "Six members of the Imperial family [were] present and four princes of lesser degree, and I taught the whole of them how to steal watermelons."[9] This refers to his opening selection, his "Morals Lecture," which Freud, recalling the evening almost three decades later, used to illustrate a principle in his *Civilization and Its Discontents* (to be discussed in chapter 13).

The performance opened and closed with music. Arthur Schnabel, referred to by *NFP* as "the young piano virtuoso," led off the program with several concert pieces played "with bravura," and at the conclusion of Mark Twain's reading, Frances Saville and Edyth Walker, American stars in the Court Opera, plus concert baritone Eduard Gärtner, violinist Fritz Kreisler, and pianist Sigmund Grünfeld provided several selections and encores. The whole program lasted well over two hours, and Mark Twain was detained in the hall almost an hour longer by well-wishers and the crush of those wanting to meet him.

Twain, in *Festtoilette* (white tie and tails), was introduced by Ambassador Tower and greeted with tumultuous applause. He began, as was his custom on such occasions in Vienna, in German: "Es ist über meine Kraft das grosse Vergnügen welche mir dies so freundlich Empfangen gibt, in Worte fassen zu können—I could not adequately do it in my own tongue—ich kann nur sagen daß ob ich er verdient habe oder nicht, ich bin Ihnen nichtsdestoweniger aufrichtig dankbar dafür—It is not good German, but the intention is good—better than the clothes it wears."[10] (It is beyond my power to put into words the great delight this very friendly reception gives me— . . . —I can only say that, whether it is deserved or not, I am nevertheless sincerely grateful for it—. . . .) Unlike his Concordia address three months earlier, this audience had no difficulty hearing him since the hall, a former riding academy remodeled for concert use with wood paneling, had, Stefan Zweig observed, "the resonance of an old violin" that floated Twain's every syllable easily, the *Neue Freie Presse* reporter noted, "to the farthest corners of the Saal."

Although he was aware, Twain continued, that his German wasn't very good, until yesterday he had spoken perfect High German—in fact, the "Highest." Last night, however, he had had a dream in which, though it had lasted barely fifteen minutes, he had lived through seven years during which he resided in Heaven with angels who spoke such miserable German that his beautiful facility in the language had declined, and he had now to start in and learn it all over again correctly. Dreams, he added, can have such potency that one may live five thousand years in five minutes in such a state quite *"kostenlos"* (free of charge)—this to an audience that included the writer then in the final stages of preparing *The Interpretation of Dreams.*

The upshot, he said apologetically, was that he had now to continue in English, which he did with some prefatory explanations for his opening "Stolen Watermelon" story. This was followed by two other standbys—"The Story of Grandfather's Old Ram" and his Negro ghost story, "The Golden Arm." He concluded with his five-quatrain comic doggerel, "Ornithorhyncus." What impressed reporters most was his "reading" from memory without books or notes, using "eye contact" with his audience to heighten dramatic effect. Vienna was experiencing for its first time the platform artistry of Mark Twain, the great American raconteur, an artistry that some would argue has not since been equaled, and this audience, like others around the globe, was mesmerized. He had scored an unqualified triumph.

Twain was delighted. "We like Vienna immensely," he glowingly wrote Rogers afterward, adding, "and by and by if we can persuade Mrs. Clemens to go out a little and mingle with people more, we shall like it better still."[11] No doubt his gregariousness was heightened by the fact that at no other time in his life and in no other place—not in his homeland, nor in England, France, or Germany, nor yet in his travels in the Southern Hemisphere—had he such entrée to the very highest reaches of society. Back home he had hobnobbed with the likes of President Grant (whose memoirs he edited and published) and with industrial tycoons and Wall Street moguls such as Carnegie, J. P. Morgan, and Henry Rogers; he was invited to exclusive London clubs and some of England's great country houses, and in Berlin in 1891–92, thanks partly to a distant cousin, Mollie (Clemens) von Versen, wife of an officer on the Imperial German General Staff, he got a few whiffs of royalty at state banquets and even private dinners. Yet nowhere were the doors of a country's entire social establishment flung so wide to him as in Austria-Hungary. He reveled in it. There is perhaps less exaggeration than envy in the report young Stephen Crane, passing through the city on his way to cover the last shots in the Greek-

Oesterreichische

Illustrirte Zeitung

VI. Jahrgang.

Nummer 36.   Erscheint jeden Sonntag.   Wien, IX., Frankgasse 10.   Erscheint jeden Sonntag.   5. December 1897.

Ein Siegeszug des Humors.

(Text innstehend.)

Mark Twain hält eine humoristische Vorlesung im Goldgräber-Lager.

Cover of *Oesterreichische Illustrirte Zeitung,* December 5, 1897

Turkish War, sent to his newspaper that in Vienna Mark Twain had degenerated into a "society clown."[12]

One of that era's many archaic social rituals which the Clemenses assiduously observed, especially abroad, was that of leaving visiting cards at the homes of people of fashion at appointed times. The telephone not yet being in common use for social intercourse, one sent cards by hired courier or, if a member of a rich or noble family, by liveried footman. Vienna had a regular pecking order for this ritual. Persons of high rank did not leave cards on those of lower. Persons of lesser rank, commoners, or foreigners like the Clemenses did not leave cards on those of rank to whom they had not yet been formally introduced, though their cards could be presented by someone else of rank who had already met them. Thus, Clemens's Viennese address book brims not only with the names and addresses of those he regarded as "choice people" but, for many of them, notations of their "at home" days, the times they "receive," and by whom cards might be sent:

Princess Khevenhüller
Türkenstrasse 19. (Before 2 P.M.

Count de Busirei
Wohllebengasse 11. (3 P.M. Weds.)

Princess Metternich
Rennweg 27—The Palace 6 P.M.

Countess M. Wydenbruck-Esterházy
Rennweg 1a. Monday, Wed. & Friday

Count Lanckoronski   )Cards to be left by Count
& Her Excellency his wife)Coudenhove. They have no
Jaquingasse 8[†13]   )day.

And so on. After leaving or sending a card, one waited, usually not many days, to receive an invitation to call in person, perhaps to take tea. If one was found socially acceptable and reciprocated the invitation, a dinner party or soirée and further acquaintance might follow.

The etiquette and protocol of card-leaving and visiting customs were responsible for one of the most awkward and amusing episodes in Twain's Viennese sojourn—one that he described in detail in his notebook and in a memorable letter to his old Hartford friend Twichell.[14]

The episode had its origin in the Bösendorfer Saal reading when Countess De Laszowska presented the Clemenses to Her Royal Highness Adelgonde do Bourbon y do Braganca, Countess von Bardi, daughter of the King of Portugal, and her sister, the recently widowed Archduchess Maria Theresa (1855–1944), stepmother of the ill-fated Franz Ferdinand (then heir-apparent to the Habsburg throne). Noting that the countess was "very cordial" as well as "very beautiful, too, both in body & spirit," Clemens decided it would be "proper etiquette" to drive to her palace and "write our names in her visitors' book," a variant of the card-leaving custom.

When they arrived at the palace about noon three days later, they were surprised to be told: "You are expected. Her Royal Highness is out, but she will be in in a minute." They hesitated, saying there must be a mistake, but the footman insisted if they were Americans, they were indeed "expected," and he forthwith began escorting them up the entrance stairs. "The sentinels were close by, with their guns," Twain observed, concluding: "I am a prudent man. I said we would obey."

Olivia, still convinced this was a terrible mistake, asked the servant to go within and inquire for particulars in order to save them embarrassment. "But I was not troubled," Twain continues in his notebook,

> I was charmed by the situation, charmed with the fine literary flavor of it, & with the story-book completeness of it. I believed there was a mistake—I was sure of it—but I wouldn't have missed it for anything. I was full of eager curiosity to see how it would turn out, & I could hardly enjoy a beautiful oil-painted lake-scene which fascinated me, my mind was so luxuriously busy *imagining* what was going to happen. And I had one deep deep regret—that Howells was not there—there to fill the occasion with colossal blunders, & make it too funny for this world! Howells, or Rev. Twichell—or both. However, with three born blunder-makers together, perhaps that would have been too much.

Before he could get deep into his imaginary scenario of faux pas, however, the princess entered with her sister, the archduchess, and immediately put them at their ease for "a charming twenty minutes." When they returned to the Metropole after their impromptu visit, they found a tardily delivered invitation waiting for them which indicated "we *were* the Americans who were expected, after all—but at 2 o'clock, not 12:30." Twain then muses upon the event, asserting he is not sorry they went at the wrong hour because he learned from this exhibition of noblesse oblige that "these are princes which are cast in the echte [pure] princely mould, & they make me regret—again—that I am not a prince myself. It isn't a new regret, but a very old one. I have never been properly & humbly satisfied with my condition. I am a democrat only on principle, but not by instinct—nobody is *that*. Doubtless some people *say* they are, but this world is grievously given to lying."†[15]

Two factors in Viennese society made it easier for Mark Twain to enter the halls of the mighty there than elsewhere. One was the immense curiosity central Europeans had about America and Americans in the last century. To the English, Americans were declassé Britons, miscreant colonials, inferior by definition. In the Habsburg lands that, before the 1890s, had sent fewer emigrants to people the wilderness across the wide Atlantic than had Britain, Germany, or Scandinavia, Americans were still exotic creatures, and an educated Amerikaner of distinction—a writer, say, or an artist or musician—was the most exotic of all, a fascinating anomaly rather like a talking chimpanzee or a dancing Lipizzaner. When such a wonder breached their walls, they vied with one another to get a closer look. Mark Twain, the most famous American writer of his day, was a trophy for any au courant Viennese hostess.

The Austro-Hungarian aristocracy, moreover, was a charmed circle, even more closely knit than its German or English counterparts. It was really three tiered, the highest nobility in 1897 comprising some eighty living descendants of the sixteen children of Empress Maria Theresia and of the seventeen of her son, Leopold II, bearing the titles *Fürst* (prince), *Graf* (count) or, if immediate members of the royal family, *Erzherzog* (archduke), with the distaff forms *Fürstin, Gräfin,* and *Erzherzogin*. With some exceptions, such as Esterházy, Batthány-Strattmann, or Thurn und Taxis, hereditary titles from other parts of the realm, forming the second tier, were usually no higher than *Graf* (or *Gräfin*), a large majority of them Hungarian. A lower stratum of *Dienstadler* (those ennobled for services to the crown) were the *Freiherr, Ritter,* and *Edler* or simply *von*, all but the last colloquially called "Baron."[16] In actuality, the eighty families in the top tier were so intermarried they constituted a single extended family who used the familiar *du* with each other even in public—a practice that gave rise to the common currency of that pronoun among casual friends in Austria today in contrast to the formality of *Sie* that still exists in Germany.

Having been taken up by one hostess, someone like Mark Twain would find himself besieged with invitations, even competed for by the others unless he committed some unspeakable faux pas or proved maladroit at table talk. His self-characterization as a stumblebum notwithstanding, by 1897 Twain was too cosmopolitan, too polished to be indiscreet, intemperate, or ungallant. Very far from being Huck Finn in the drawing room, he was, in fact, quite adept at playing the social lion.

Only Olivia's continued demurrals prevented their being overwhelmed with hospitality during their first Vienna winter. She was a punctilious hostess, always ready to receive visitors graciously and avoiding no opportunity to entertain at dinner or at tea (according to Katy Leary, almost daily) or to reciprocate their invitations, yet she seldom accompanied her husband to public or even to purely social events in Vienna. Nevertheless, her reluctance "to go out a little and mingle with people more," which began with their mourning for Susy and intensified with her growing worries about Jean and her own neurasthenia, did not inhibit her husband's social life. There were indeed some temporary suspensions in his activity, as in the fortnight following the news of his brother's death in December 1897 and during the cancellation of all social events, including the long-planned

Jubilee celebrations of Franz Josef's accession, after the empress's assassination in September 1898, but these were merely pauses. Most of the time, he refused no invitation to a ball, a dinner, a reception, or a soirée.

As Vienna's winter *Ball Saison* commenced in earnest after New Year's Day 1898, not even Olivia's continual reclusiveness held the gregarious Clemens at home. On Valentine's Day, he was guest of honor at the annual Concordia Ball in the Sophiensäle, then as now one of the most glittering events of any Viennese social season. This time Olivia accompanied him so they could waltz to music conducted by the illustrious Eduard Strauss, *Hofballdirektor* (court ball director) and youngest of the Strauss dynasty.[17] Three weeks later, Clara was on his arm when he attended the ball of the Artists' Benevolent Guild at the Kunstlerhaus to enjoy a convivial evening with Eduard Pötzl and other friends in artistic and literary circles.[18]

As this activity suggests, having a very beautiful, marriageable daughter like Clara was a distinct asset to Clemens's social life in Vienna. Poor Jean, on the other hand, at an age when many Viennese girls were already debutantes, was gangly, plain, and afflicted. Not that her Viennese peers were all beauty queens, but the danger of an epileptic seizure sadly limited her social activities then and thereafter. Nor did it make life easier for her that sister Clara at twenty-three was the belle of the ball in every sense, though the mores of that era required her to be chaperoned by an older person in all private encounters with men at least until she became engaged to be married. In later years, this custom would become an issue of contention between Clara and her parents, but in Vienna she was not rebellious, although in late March 1898 she chafed when Olivia vetoed a moonlight ride in the Prater with an unchaperoned mixed company of friends.[19]

Katy Leary, self-described as the Clemenses' "faithful and devoted servant for thirty years," who occasionally had to substitute as a daytime chaperone at the Metropole, left a charming if somewhat erratic, highly colored memoir of "Delirium Clemens," as Clara's father jokingly called the constant swarm of swains around her in Vienna:

Miss Clara had lots of officers for beaux that Winter. They used to call every day for tea and was musical. I don't remember who they was, but some of them was Royalty, though not very deep in the Royal blood. . . .

It was a wonderful sight to see them coming up the hall. You'd think it was a whole regiment, the way they walked and clicked their swords against their heels—and oh, the wonderful uniforms they wore! They'd come in the room with such style. They was very fond of music and Miss Clara would always play for them. Oh, my! They'd make such a low bow, such a wonderful bow, and click their heels together when they come into the room. It was so different from anything we ever seen in this country.[20]

Lending credence to Leary's anecdote is a report by the *New York World*'s unnamed Vienna correspondent that "Vienna's gossips" (for Vienna has ever been an unusually gossipy city) were whispering at one point that Clara's marriage to an impecunious Austrian count who hoped to catch a rich American heiress was "as good as arranged" until the prospective bride-groom discovered the true state of the Clemenses' fortune and discreetly withdrew his suit after arranging for his army unit to be ordered to the provinces.[21] There were, however, plenty of eligible compatriots of Clara's among Vienna's two hundred American medical students, and Clemens recorded one pleasant social evening when ten of them came calling.[22] The attentions of one American medical student, George Cole, son of California's Sen. Cornelius Cole, the Clemenses seemed for a while rather inclined to encourage.

Not all his social life revolved around balls, dinners, or Clara's gentlemen callers. Mark Twain was not known for any passionate interest in sports—he liked, in fact, to joke about never having "taken any exercise, except sleeping and resting"—but when Sir Horace Rumbold, the English ambassador, brought a football (soccer) team from Oxford for a series of three exhibition matches with a handpicked Austrian team, the envoy made certain Mark Twain was among the invited celebrity spectators, knowing the newspapers would duly report the American humorist's attendance.[23] Incredible as it seems, *Fussball*, as soccer is called in German, a sport that now rivals skiing as Austria's most popular, was then still exotic on the Continent, requiring strenuous promotional efforts to draw a crowd. This series was aborted, however, after the second game because the scores were too embarrassingly lopsided in Oxford's favor.

During late March 1898 Twain was prompted to two more public readings, both quite unplanned and gratuitous. The English-French Conversation Club held a meeting on March 21 at which a certain Miss Alice Potter (not otherwise identified) was scheduled to read two Mark Twain selections—"The Californian's Tale" and "Adam's Diary"—followed by Jerome K. Jerome's "A Story from Novel Notes." Politely invited to attend as guest of honor, though apparently not asked to read, Twain nevertheless volunteered to present his two selections himself much to the delight of the assemblage. How Miss Potter felt about it, however, the newspapers neglected to report.[24] A week later, on the twenty-eighth, he visited Miss Baillie's Home for English Governesses where a midnight benefit fete was in progress. Asked to speak, he obliged with a rendition of his "Genuine Mexican Plug" story. Afterwards, he recorded in his notebook, he was approached with a request for his autograph:

> "The Princess Hohenlohe wishes you to write on her fan."
> "With pleasure—where is she?"
> "At your elbow."
> I turned & took the fan & said "Your Highness's place is in a fairy tale; & by & by I mean to write that tale." Whereat she laughed a happy girlish laugh, & we moved through the crowd to get to a writing table—& to get to a stronger light, so I could see her better. Beautiful little creature, with the dearest friendly ways, & sincerities, & simplicities, & sweetnesses— the ideal princess of the fairy tales. She is 16 or 17, I judge.†[25]

Between these engagements and throughout the spring there were luncheons, dinners, and receptions at the American and British embassies, at the Metropole, and at the city palaces and suburban villas of their widening circle of acquaintance. On April 10, Olivia's brother, Charles Langdon, arrived from Elmira with his son for a fortnight's visit, occasioning another round of entertaining to introduce the Langdons to Viennese friends. Clara was delighted she could invite her latest beau, George Cole, the medical student from Los Angeles whose father was a senator, to an "informal supper on Friday (April 15) to meet the Grand Mogul Leschetitzky [*sic*] and my cousin Jervis Langdon," hastening off a second note by *Rohrpost* (pneumatic tube) to clarify: "J. Langdon is a boy."[26] At this dinner Clara met for the first time her future husband, Ossip Gabrilowitsch, a Leschetízky protégé then beginning a stellar concert career. The social whirl that seemed to engulf them that spring may be glimpsed from Twain's entry for May 9, 1898: "Visitors yesterday, Countess Wydenbruck-Esterházy, Austrian; Nansen & his wife, Norwegians; Freiherr de Laszowski, Pole; his niece, Hungarian; Madame XXX, Hollander; 5 Americans & 3 other nationalities (French, German, English). Certainly *there is plenty of variety in Vienna*. Today, the Nansens to luncheon."†[27] Fridtjof Nansen, the Norwegian arctic explorer and statesman, staying at the Metropole on a goodwill tour of Austria-Hungary with his wife and small daughter, formed a friendship with the Clemenses. Although the papers represented it rather grandly as a *diner* (in Austria, a formal dinner party), the Clemenses hosted a farewell luncheon the day before the Nansens departed for Budapest.[28]

The Pole, De Laszowski, whom Twain mistakenly refers to here as "Freiherr" instead of "Graf" (count), was a diplomat with whose wife Mark Twain developed an intriguingly ambiguous relationship. Scottish by birth (née Emily Gerard), the countess had grown up in Romania unable to speak English until she was school age, but she had become a writer in English and German, though of distinctly limited talent, who had already produced two novels and a nonfiction work about Transylvania. Socially as well as literarily ambitious, the Laszowskis frequented the circles of Princess Metternich and Countess Wydenbruck-Esterházy and took one of Dr. Winternitz's villas near the Clemenses' in Kaltenleutgeben for the summer of 1898. Three years later, when "E. Gerard" published a two-volume novel, *The Extermination of Love, A Fragmentary Study in Erotics*, it had this bizarre verse dedication that reads as if it were written by Emmeline Grangerford:

To thee whose mark twain hemispheres attest,
Wherever thou hast cast thy pilot log,
That German speech with humour can invest,
And make a classic of a jumping frog,
A grateful muse inscribes her modest tome.
Warmed at thy genial hearth to life anew,
While flourished here the innocent at home,
Where all was cultured, yet was nothing "blue."
Though winter reigned, yet found I sunshine there,
No need to venture on a tramp abroad,
Spurred on afresh another flight to dare,
A frozen spirit from its torpor thawed.
And though again the ocean roll between,
Be sure no malice of ungracious fate
Can dim the memory of what has been,
Nor "love" for thee and thine "exterminate."[29]

What, if any, sub-rosa meaning lurks in these very tantalizing sixteen lines? Their allusions to Twain and his works, with some wordplay thereon, are mostly obvious and innocent looking, but there are lines hinting at an arcane subtext. Why, for instance, does the author refer to herself as "a grateful muse" (his?) who was "warmed . . . to life anew" and "a frozen spirit" who has been "from its torpor thawed" ostensibly by Twain? What significance should one attach to the quoted "blue," "love," and "exterminate"? Do they contain some esoteric meaning to be derived from an undisclosed context?

Unfortunately, the novel itself offers no clues to any particular reading of this dedicatory poem. If *The Extermination of Love* is, as one is tempted to suspect from its dedication, a roman à clef, there is no character or episode in it that one could even in wildest fancy associate with Samuel Clemens or to any known social situation he experienced in Austria. The central plot concerns a provincial Austrian physician who, trapped in a loveless marriage, deludes himself into believing he has discovered a serum that will "exterminate" one's "amatory emotions" (a Victorian euphemism for sexual desires) only to be "awakened" to the true nature of those "emotions" when he is aroused to jealousy by another man's flirtation with the wife he has believed he did not love. Aside from the author's heavy use of dream imagery—the first part of the novel is called "The Dream Life," the second volume, "The Awakening"—motifs that informed much of Twain's own work that summer in Kaltenleutgeben—what her enigmatic dedicatory verse or the narrative itself suggests about Emily Gerard-De Laszowska's personal relations with Mark Twain can only be guessed.

On the other hand, if one avoids fatuously pursuing literal parallels and instead considers metaphoric meanings, it might be possible to read this novel and its dedication on a different level as a kind of allegory of Clemens's own "awakening" in Vienna, sloughing off his "torpor" as he eagerly embraced the Phaeacianism of Viennese social life. Surrounded by seductively beautiful aristocratic ladies in this City of Dreams that seemed to move around him in three-quarter time, Clemens and his alter ego were revitalized and rejuvenated after months of deep depression over the loss of Susy and the years of anxiety over declining fortunes which had at last turned upward. No longer does one find him complaining of ailments, impotence, and the encroachments of age but senses instead a joie de vivre and new vigor in his work and his business plans. He is plainly having the time of his life. This metaphor may be the covert meaning, if there is any, to the ironic title the lovely Scottish countess gave the novel she so oddly dedicated to Mark Twain.

Furthermore, there may be more than a merely coincidental connection between the "dream life" motif of the countess's novel and a story Twain himself dashed off in the last week of July 1898. Entitled "My Platonic Sweetheart," it was rejected by three magazines and only posthumously published in abridged form in *Harper's Monthly* in December 1912. The seeds of what he first called "The Lost Sweetheart" appear in an undated jotting that summer:

I was 22 when I met her, & she 16. It was in a dream.

Go on with the story. Meetings extending over years. Both are as young

as ever, always. First time, she ~~crosses~~ jumps across a brook ahead, &
when I am about to follow, a steamboat rushes along & when it gets by
she has vanished & the brook is a mile wide. Put in such things.†30

The story he finished on August 2 or 3 omits the steamboat episode,
but in the various "meetings extending over years" he recounts of the
lad (variously called George and Robert) and his sweetheart (called
Alice, Helen, and Agnes) while "both are as young as ever"—in a Missouri log cabin, in an antebellum Natchez plantation house, in the Iao
Valley on the Hawaiian island of Maui, in Periclean Athens, in Bom-
bay, at Windsor Castle—it is an unusually exotic tale for Mark Twain
and at once both erotic and reticent. In the finished version he makes
the lovers even younger—seventeen and fifteen, respectively—and in
their first dream encounter on a rural Missouri footbridge, he sweeps
her wordlessly into an embrace and they kiss.

But not passionately. It is not the kiss portrayed so sensuously by
Gustav Klimt or the Russian sculptress Theresa Fedorowna Ries whose
work Twain knew in Vienna: "There was no ecstasy in that tranquil
kiss, but it was freighted with a deep charm and a serene joy, and
it had a dignity about it not known to those other sorts of kisses. It was
not cold, it was not hot; it was warm, tender, gracious, softly and suf-
fusingly enchanting. It was a sweetheart-kiss cleansed of its grossness,
its earthiness, its slag and its dross, and spiritualized."†31

Five years pass before they again meet in Dreamland. Her hair and
eyes have changed from "flossy gold" and blue to, respectively, black
and dark brown, and her name has changed, but to her lover "she was
the same girl she was before, absolutely," because, he explains, "We
were living in a simple and rational and beautiful world where everything that happened was natural and right, and was not perplexed
with the unexpected, or with any forms of surprise. . . ."32

Their third meeting, some four years later in chronological (but not
dream) time, is in a lush Hawaiian setting and abounds with sensu-
ous imagery that becomes surrealistic: "A man-of-war bird lit on her
shoulder; I put out my hand and caught it. Its feathers began to fall
out, and it turned into a kitten; then the kitten's body began to con-

tract itself to a ball and put out hairy long legs, and soon it was a tarantula; I was going to keep it, but it turned into a star-fish and I threw it away."[33] This foreshadows a dark episode in which a 130-year-old Kanaka leper "accidentally" shoots the girl with an arrow and she "dies" in her despairing lover's arms, only to reappear quite alive at his side in another dream sequence a short while later. Her hair and eyes have meanwhile changed color again, but she is still fifteen and he seventeen.

Here the narrative breaks off abruptly, and the story ends in a long disquisition on the nature of reality. Evidently Twain could not forego a chance to philosophize, so he concludes the tale:

> For everything in a dream is more deep and strong and sharp and real than is ever its pale imitation in the unreal life which is ours when we go about awake and clothed-on with our artificial selves in this vague and dull-tinted artificial world. When we die we shall slough off this cheap intellect perhaps, and go abroad into Dreamland clothed in our real selves and aggrandised and enriched by command over the mysterious mental magician who is here not our slave but only our guest.[34]

This anticlimax no doubt explains why "My Platonic Sweetheart" was initially rejected. Paine amputated it in the published version, ending with the couple's final meeting. Nevertheless these ideas deeply concerned Twain at the time, and he returned to them and to the technique of dream adventures again at greater length in "The Chronicle of Young Satan" and other works that occupied him in Vienna and Kaltenleutgeben. Although there is no novelty in the Platonism he expresses in these works—not in European nor yet in American belles lettres—the particular thrust of his ideas and the kinds of fictional schemes into which he wove them have a distinctly Viennese flavor. It is Goethe's *"Ewige Weibliche"* (eternal feminine) symbolized in his dream girl whose several incarnations reflect the beautiful aristocratic young women who surrounded Mark Twain at this time—Countess Emily De Laszowska, Countess Misa Wydenbruck-Esterházy, perhaps especially, and the "fairy tale" Princess Hohenlohe. This is not to suggest he was having or even contemplating having affairs with any of these temptresses who, as a matter of fact, might not have rejected his advances.

On the contrary, "My Platonic Sweetheart" evinces a writer who had found a way to sublimate and fantasize whatever yearnings the belles of Vienna may have aroused. To do so, however, he had also to shed forty-six years imaginatively and make himself, like Hofmannsthal's Graf Rofrano (Octavian), an ardent lover of seventeen, though a curiously chaste one. In short, it is unnecessary and irrelevant to hark back, as some scholars have, to young Sam Clemens's Hannibal days and his adolescent crush on Laura Wright, the putative original of Becky Thatcher in *Tom Sawyer*, in order to find his dream sweetheart.[35] She was everywhere he looked in Vienna!

If ballroom and salon did not surfeit this Phaeacian convert's appetites for pleasure, there were always the gustatory delights of the famed Viennese *Kaffeehaus* (or café) and the *Beisl*, the inexpensive, unpretentious, intimate restaurant that is the Viennese equivalent of the French bistro. Twain discovered these pleasures early on and could easily be lured by Pötzl or another journalist friend to linger at the Café Central in the Herrengasse, which had recently supplanted the demolished (now restored) Griensteidl as the hangout of the literati, or Landtmann's by the Burgtheater, or Gerstner's, overlooking passers-by in busy Kärntnerstrasse, for a cup of what he called "that unapproachable luxury—that sumptuous coffeehouse coffee, compared with which all other European coffee and all American hotel coffee is mere fluid poverty."[36] It was not just the enormous varieties of coffee these and dozens upon dozens of other cafés in every neighborhood of the city offered, from *kleiner Brauner* (espresso) to *Wiener Mélange* (half milk, half coffee) to *Einspänner* (coffee with shaved chocolate and whipped cream) among others, but also counters brimming with awesome arrays of torten and mountains of whipped cream enough to tempt even the most jaded palate.

It is uncertain whether he frequented the *Heurigen*, those peculiarly gemütlich wine taverns operated by the vintners themselves in suburban villages dotting the edge of the Wienerwald, but the beer in

Reichenberger's "Griechenbeisl" he pronounced "incomparable; there is nothing like it elsewhere in the world." It was the original pilsener (Pilsneske Prázdroj, or Pilsener Urquell), brewed in Bohemia, and it is still served on draft in this historic restaurant today. Twain waxed ecstatic about his favorite *Beisl*. "It is always Sunday there," he remarked, alluding to the lack of bustle or traffic noise in the secluded Fleischmarkt. "One may live in Vienna many months and not hear of this place, but having once heard of it and sampled it, the sampler will afterward infest it."[37]

His paean to Pilsener Urquell and the "Griechenbeisl" introduces the whimsical sketch, "At the Appetite Cure," that he finished on May 30, 1898, and sent immediately to *Cosmopolitan Magazine*.[38] It describes an imaginary Bohemian health resort named "Hochberghaus" (house on a high mountain) whose director, "Professor Haimberger," restores Twain's flagging appetite by locking him up until he is starved enough to order from a menu of revolting dishes "calculated to insult a cannibal" like "tough, underdone, overdue tripe, garnished with garlic" (a travesty on the popular Viennese *Beuschel*) and "sailor-boots, softened with tallow—served raw." He is pronounced permanently cured by the fictional doctor when he is sufficiently famished to wolf down "soft-boiled spring chicken—in the egg; six dozen, hot and fragrant!" With humorous anecdotes this sketch burlesquing the ubiquitous Austrian spa or *Kurort* ("the empire is made up of health resorts") makes a simple point: as Poor Richard says, "Hunger is the best pickle." To the extent that this obviously fictional trifle has been noticed by critics or scholars at all, it has been unaccountably read as serious journalism, as though it were a factual report of an actual cure![39]

In part, there was an altruistic, one might even say patriotic, motive behind some of Mark Twain's socializing in Vienna. "During 8 years, now, I have filled the post—with some credit, I trust—of self-appointed Ambassador at Large of the U. S. of America—without salary," he groused before leaving the city for his summer in Kaltenleutgeben.[†40] American newspaper correspondents had, in fact, cabled reports that his suite at the Metropole was "like a second embassy"

in the Habsburg capital, and he unquestionably felt his celebrity con-
ferred upon him a quasi-official status as his country's representative and took the responsibilities that attended this quite seriously.
Although he never actively sought a diplomatic post, he would have
accepted an offer with alacrity, and he could barely disguise his envy
when Bret Harte received a consular post in Germany. In his many
foreign sojourns he had had to deal with numerous American diplomats for most of whose capabilities he had a low opinion. "I wonder
where our Government fishes for its average foreign-service officials,"
he asked rhetorically.[41]

For Charlemagne Tower, Envoy Extraordinary and Minister Plenipotentiary of the United States of America to His Apostolic Majesty,
Franz Josef I, Emperor of Austria, King of Hungary, et al. he had
only admiration. In fact, Ambassador Tower was his beau ideal of an
American diplomat. A wealthy Philadelphia lawyer who had studied
history at Harvard under Henry Adams and, afterward, languages
and regional politics in Europe and the Middle East for four years, who
had enjoyed business success in the Midwest and, as a writer, had published a well-received biography, *The Marquis de Lafayette in the American
Revolution*, Tower was the kind of cosmopolitan, dedicated public servant Mark Twain could respect. Appointed to the Habsburg court by
President McKinley in March 1897, he remained there two years until
he was sent to Russia for the next three. From 1902 until 1908, he was
American envoy to Germany before returning to private business life.
In all three posts, Tower negotiated important treaties and favorable
trade agreements, helped settle some thorny disputes, and ingratiated
himself and his government with local regimes through a lavish social
life financed mainly from his own private fortune.[42]

Tower recognized the social value of having Mark Twain in Vienna
and capitalized on it. He saw to it that the Clemenses were quickly
made "at home" in the American community, then numbering almost
a thousand, some two hundred of them medical students at the university and almost that many more studying music or voice privately (like

Clara) or at a conservatory, and the Clemenses soon had close personal ties to the ambassador's wife and five children. On the Fourth of July 1897 and 1898 Tower gave elegant receptions for Austrian officialdom and Vienna's enormous diplomatic community, and on Thanksgiving and Christmas he held open house for Americans in the city, always making sure Mark Twain was a well-publicized guest of honor.[43] For Tower, the famous writer was an ornament for embassy dinners, such as the one Mark Twain registered in this February 10, 1898, entry: "Dinner at the Embassy. Present, the German Ambassador [Count von Eulenberg]; Marquis [Count] Hoyos; Nigra, Italian Minister; Paraty, Portugese Minister; Löwenhaupt, Swedish Minister; Ghika, Roumanian Minister, Secretaries &c from the various Embassies—& ladies. 30 guests."†[44]

Even from this barebones listing one senses Twain's pleasure at being in such company at what he felt was a noteworthy evening. Tower was being called upon to display extraordinary diplomatic skill. American involvement with Cuba had created a tense international crisis by February 1898. A few days after this dinner, the battleship *Maine* went to the bottom of Havana harbor, precipitating a war with Spain which lasted from April until August that year. Austria-Hungary was even more sympathetic than most of Europe to the Spanish cause, and Tower was able to neutralize some of the anti-American sentiment in the country by getting Secretary of State John Hay to lobby a bill through Congress exempting Austrians who had become naturalized Americans from military service.

No wonder that at the farewell banquet given Ambassador and Mrs. Tower at the Hotel Bristol by the American colony on February 28, 1899, Mark Twain, delivering the main after-dinner encomium, spared no superlatives, calling Tower "the best ambassador the American nation has ever sent forth," and particularizing: "Mr. Tower did not arrive here in political sunshine. The close relationship between Spain and Austria and the clouds of war then gathering made his mission in Austria especially delicate, the most delicate in these

times, demanding unusual and special qualities of mind and character. The success he has had gives evidence that, as the old saying goes,
'he was the right man in the right place.'"[45]

Charlemagne Tower's successor, arriving a month later, was defi-
nitely the wrong man at the wrong place as far as Mark Twain was
concerned. He was Addison Clay Harris, a fifty-nine-year-old Indianapolis lawyer and leader in Hoosier Republican politics. Bred in the
Quaker faith, he was a farmer's son and a man of plain speech and
plain living who, until his appointment, had scarcely traveled beyond
his native prairies. He was, in sum, as provincial as Tower was urbane.
Manifestly unqualified and pitifully unprepared for his duties, he was
a shining example of the kind of inept political appointment that has
hobbled American foreign relations for two centuries. Fortunately,
Ambassador Harris had no crisis nor great problems to cope with
during his three blessedly uneventful years in Vienna, after which he
retired to his Indianapolis law practice and well-earned obscurity.[46]

Lacking private means for the sort of posh Stadtpalais that Tower
had rented for his ambassadorial residence in fashionable Schwind-
gasse, just off Karlsplatz, Harris engaged rooms in the Hotel Krantz,
where the Clemenses were spending their second winter, while he
scouted affordable quarters. Mark Twain thus found himself living
in a temporary, makeshift American embassy, and after his first encounters with Harris, he vented his chagrin and embarrassment over
the man's inadequacies in what is probably the most scathing, vitriolic
essay of his career. Where or even whether he intended to publish
this seven-page diatribe called "American Representation in Austria"
cannot now be known. It is not on his lists of the writings he was then
trying to market. Nor is it likely that any American editor would have
touched this damning exposé during Harris's (or his staff's) tenure in
Vienna, and since its topicality, which is its main interest, faded rapidly
thereafter, it has remained unpublished. Still, it is such vintage Mark
Twain in its biting wit, and it touches so closely the writer's personal
concerns as an American abroad that it deserves inclusion here in its
entirety. (See Appendix B.)

"The American Diogenes," cover of *Der Floh*, December 1897

Part of poor Harris's problem, Twain recognized, was that he was not a man of means, and his government was too stingy in paying its diplomats' salaries and expenses to enable them to represent their country properly without spending their own money. Why, he indignantly asks in "Diplomatic Pay and Clothes," an article penned in January 1899, should they have to subsidize their work?[47] Noting with approval a report that the United States paid its peace commissioners $100,000 each for six weeks' work of negotiating the treaty ending the war with Spain (signed December 10, 1898), he argues that our government should show such munificence to all its foreign representatives, supporting his contention with invidious comparisons between what the British then paid their ambassadors and what their American counterparts received. In Vienna, for example, Sir Horace Rumbold's salary was $40,000 while Mr. Tower's was a mere $12,000, and in addition, the British government owned its embassies abroad so its ambassadors did not have to rent quarters, as the Americans did out of their own salaries.

Twain's concern in this essay is twofold. If our diplomats are so underpaid, they are unable to live as they should and can only entertain in a manner "unworthy of the flag"; the clothes they are officially required to wear are even more disgraceful. Referring to the colorful dress uniforms of European diplomats, most of them members of the nobility holding military rank, he observes: "At a public function in a European court all foreign representatives except ours wear clothes which in some way distinguish them from the unofficial throng, and mark them as standing for their *countries*. But our representative appears in a plain black swallow-tail, which stands for neither country nor people." He attributes this to a perverse reverence for the "Republican simplicity" precedent set by Franklin at Versailles. Whatever the occasion, this "humbug" of Republican simplicity, which is by no means characteristic of the nation that has "the gaudiest flag the world has ever seen," requires our ambassador to appear in an "undertaker-outfit . . . in the midst of the butterfly splendors of a Continental court."

The remedy he suggests is "that, whenever we appoint an ambassador or a minister, we ought to confer upon him the temporary rank of admiral or general, and allow him to wear the corresponding uniform at public functions in foreign countries." Above all, he concludes, for a nation as rich as ours to pay its diplomats so inadequately and to put them in such drab attire as to make "the very cab-horses laugh" constitutes "the most inconsistent and incongruous spectacle contrivable by even the most diseased imagination. It is a billionaire in a paper-collar, a king in a breechclout, an archangel in a tin halo."

Since Mark Twain wrote that, the "butterfly splendor" of the diplomatic circuit has gone the way of the cab-horse, and "Republican simplicity" has swept the stage even in the few remaining monarchies. The United States now owns most of its embassies around the globe and compensates its foreign service personnel at least comparably to those of other world powers. It would be fatuous to suggest that Twain's polemic had anything to do with these developments. On the other hand, it may not have been entirely disregarded. Charlemagne Tower, when he reached his new post at the czar's court in 1899, according to *The Dictionary of American Diplomatic History*, "strove to elevate the U.S. embassy [there] to equal status with those of the European powers in display as well as diplomacy, *most obviously by ordering uniforms for the embassy staff, thus marking a sharp departure from U.S. diplomatic tradition*" (italics added).[48]

CHAPTER EIGHT

Concerning the "Jew" Mark Twain

he cluster of prejudices subsumed by *Antisemitismus,* a German euphemism coined in 1879 by Wilhelm Marr to dignify the more blunt *Judenhass* (hatred of Jews) and swiftly adapted in other tongues as the English "anti-Semitism," did not originate in Austria-Hungary. This bigotry was imported as a concomitant of Christianity by the Romans who lived in the Danube region they called Noricum and Pannonia in the fourth century A.D. Nevertheless, the specific character of *Antisemitismus* in political thought and action in the half century preceding the attempted genocide of European Jewry by Hitler's minions was chiefly a Viennese invention. One must not underrate the conspicuous contributions of the Russians, Poles, Germans, French, and British to anti-Semitism in the twilight of the last century and the dawn of this, but to the people of the Habsburg lands and especially to the Viennese goes the dubious distinction of bringing to first flower the means of expressing the social mentality that distinguishes anti-Semitism as a political force in our time.

It is no coincidence that Adolf Hitler, premier anti-Semite of this or any century, obtained in Vienna in the decade before 1914 what he called "foundations for a philosophy in general and a political view in particular which later I needed to supplement in detail, but which never left me."[1] To those of Hitler's mentality it seemed that the way to their own artistic or commercial, if not political, advancement in fin de siècle Vienna was blocked by a Jewish hegemony which they preferred for many reasons to see as a conspiracy.

When Samuel L. Clemens arrived there, anti-Semitism had long been a paramount political force in the city, though he seems to have had no foreknowledge or preparation for what he immediately encountered of it. In this ignorance he was indeed an "innocent abroad" who paid a bitter price for the lessons in bigotry and nastiness he quickly received. Mark Twain embodied his reactions in "Concerning the Jews," an article he finished in Kaltenleutgeben during the last week of July 1898, published in *Harper's Monthly* in September 1899, and included the following year in his collected works.[2] Factually flawed and myopic, it is nevertheless one of his best-written, most cogently argued polemical essays, and although it evoked a significant response on first publication and three decades later was the basis for Sigmund Freud's "A Comment on Anti-Semitism" (November 1938), it has been grossly underrated or altogether neglected by scholars because its origins and purpose have not been clearly perceived.[3]

To correct this neglect and permit "Concerning the Jews" its rightful place in the Twain canon, one must understand the social context of this essay. It is important to know, for instance, that Vienna then was—as it remains, two generations after Baldur von Schirach jubilantly cabled his führer the news that *"Wien ist Judenrein"* (Vienna is purified of Jews)—the most anti-Semitic metropolis in Europe and to understand how and why it became that way.

To summarize briefly, the rise of anti-Semitism as a political force in Vienna followed upon the rapid growth of the city's Jewish population in the last quarter of the nineteenth century. Other cities of the empire, notably Budapest and Prague, had larger proportions of Jews among their inhabitants, but the gentile lower and middle classes there did not feel as threatened by increasing Jewish immigration from the East as did their Viennese counterparts. Between 1860 and 1897 the percentage of Jews in Vienna's population more than quadrupled, from barely 2 percent to nearly 9 percent. During Mark Twain's residence there about 147,000 of the city's 1.7 million residents (that is, those having *Heimatrecht,* not transients) acknowledged themselves Jewish, half of whom had migrated to the city after 1880 from the rural *shtetl* of Bukovina and Galicia or the long-established urban ghettos of Cernowitz, Krakow, Lemberg (Lwów), Brünn (Brno), or Pressburg/Pozsony (Bratislava).[4]

Numerous Jewish families who settled in Vienna before the great influx, some as far back as the early eighteenth century, entered the haute bourgeoisie to find a secure if circumscribed place in the city's social structure. Liberal Vienna had been an oasis of tolerance, and such subtle or occasionally overt anti-Semitism as existed before about 1890, the city's assimilated Jews ignored or dismissed as they did other "harmless" boorishness by the ruder sorts of the city's *Untertan.*[5] These Jews prospered and advanced socially, entering the learned professions and rising in banking or publishing to the extent that a few, like the Rothschilds, Wertheimsteins, and Frydmann-Prawys, became petty nobility, so-called *"Hofjuden"* (court Jews), as baron (*Freiherr* or *Ritter*) or *Edler* (plain *von*). In the liberalism that dominated Austrian political life between 1867 and 1891, these affluent Jews had a prominent part. The high aristocracy was not overtly anti-Semitic because the emperor frowned upon public expressions of racism even while refusing to promote Jews beyond *Oberst* (colonel) in his army and limiting their patents of nobility to *Freiherr*. Contrary to its rising tide of anti-Semitism, Vienna, a polyglot metropolis with multiethnic citizenry, was justly proud of its tolerant cosmopolitanism.

This atmosphere, as much as economic opportunity, made Vienna a magnet in the 1870s and '80s for Jews fleeing Ukrainian pogroms or dissatisfied with life in the Polish provinces. Many of them, however, did not prosper as they had hoped, and, crowding into the ghetto-like *Mazzesinsel* (matzoh island) of the city's second district, Leopoldstadt, between the Danube Canal and the river, they took to sweatshop work, an ever-increasing urban Jewish proletariat in their odd-looking kaftans, yarmulkes, and sidelocks. To the assimilated middle- and upper-class Jews of Vienna, these orthodox newcomers were an embarrassment, and when they competed toe to toe with the gentile proletariat for the few available jobs, usually winning, they exacerbated the prejudices and tensions that such massive immigration brings to any society.

For all Jews in Vienna, not just the newly arrived, the situation changed drastically in the 1890s after a series of liberal defeats at the polls and the rise to prominence of two demagogic politicians for whom "*Ausländerfeindlichkeit*" (xenophobia), including rabid anti-Semitism, was an essential tactical weapon: Georg von Schönerer, leader of the German Nationals (popularly called *Schönerianer*) in the parliament, and Dr. Karl Lueger, chief figure in the Christian Social Party who became mayor of Vienna in 1897 and held that office until his death in 1910. Although Lueger and Schönerer differed on most other issues, Schönerer attacked the Jews, the only ethnic element in the empire (other than gypsies) without nationality, as subverters of his Pan-Germanism, while Lueger made them scapegoats for the economic woes of Vienna's artisans and small merchants who composed his power base. Both of these politicians were idolized by the young Adolf Hitler, who called Lueger "the greatest German mayor of all times" and imitated Schönerer's methods of using thugs and fomenting violent anti-Jewish demonstrations.[6]

At the same time, several Viennese academicians and writers attempted to provide a theoretical basis for anti-Semitism by advocating pseudoscientific theories about racial purity and the superiority of so-called *Arier* (Aryans), misapplying Social Darwinism mixed with ideas filched from Nietzsche, Kant, Count de Gobineau, and Richard Wagner. Foremost among them were Adolf Josef Lanz (1874–1954), whose crackpot ideas exerted a formative influence on another Adolf, the future Nazi führer, and his generation; Houston Stewart Chamberlain (1855–1927), a renegade English Germanophile who divorced his Viennese Jewish wife and married Richard Wagner's daughter; and in the political sphere, Karl Baron von Vogelsang (1818–90), Lueger's mentor and founder of the anti-Semitic newspaper *Vaterland*.

This state of affairs—that is, the activities of the *Schönerianer*, the Luegerites, and their intellectual camp followers and the Jewish response to them—is what Mark Twain refers to when he writes to

Twichell on October 23, 1897, that "there is much politics agoing, and it would be interesting if a body could get the hang of it." Then he particularizes:

> It is Christian and Jew by the horns—the advantage with the superior man, as usual—the superior man being the Jew every time and in all countries. Land, Joe, what chance would the Christian have in a country where there were 3 Jews to 10 Christians! Oh, not the shade of a shadow of a chance. The difference between the brain of the average Christian and that of the average Jew—certainly in Europe—is about the difference between a tadpole's and an Archbishop's. It's a marvelous race—by long odds the most marvelous the world has produced, I suppose.[7]

It was not the first time Mark Twain had encountered and responded to expressions of anti-Semitism. In his posthumously published manuscripts are two versions, written sometime in 1897 and 1898, of a story recounting an incident Clemens heard narrated by a fellow pilot during his Mississippi steamboat days in which a beneficent Jew rescues a Negro slave girl from a notorious professional cardsharp after her foolhardy owner has lost her in a riverboat poker game. In both "Newhouse's Jew Story" and the fuller, later version, "Randall's Jew Story," the unnamed Jew becomes a hero when, in contrast to the moral cowardice of his fellow passengers, he challenges the unscrupulous gambler to a duel and kills him.[8]

In March 1890, Clemens (this time oddly eschewing his nom de plume) wrote a brief essay in reply to four questions sent him by the editor of *The American Hebrew* for a symposium by prominent intellectuals and clergymen on causes and suggested cures for anti-Semitism. For some unknown reason, his contribution was omitted when the compiled replies were published, but he reworked some of his ideas in it for "Concerning the Jews."[9]

The implication, in his letter to Twichell, that Austria was "a country where there were 3 Jews to 10 Christians," was, like Twain's later exaggeration of the Jewish population of the empire in "Concerning the Jews" (misremembered from an old *Encyclopaedia Britannica* article), probably because most of his Viennese acquaintances were Jews and a large proportion of the rest were "philosemites," gentiles who openly associated with Jews and publicly deplored anti-Semitism. Among these latter were persons like the Princess Metternich, sneered at in the anti-Semitic press as "Notre Dame de Zion" for her sponsorship of Jewish artists and intellectuals, and the author Marie Ebner-Eschenbach, who publicly proclaimed she would patronize *only* Jewish merchants to protest anti-Semitic demands to cease doing business with Jews.[10] In such surroundings, it was easy for Mark Twain to form an exaggerated impression of the numbers of Jews in Austria.

Nor was it unusual for any visiting foreign writer to find his collegial acquaintanceship in fin de siècle Vienna to be preponderantly Jewish, given the disproportionate representation of Jews in the arts and journalism in the city. Stefan Zweig did not overstate when he observed that "nine-tenths of what the world celebrated as Viennese culture in the nineteenth century was promoted, nourished, or even created by Viennese Jewry."[11] One need only recall a few names like Goldmark, Mahler, and Schönberg in serious music; Oskar Straus, Leo Fall, and Imre Kalmán in operetta; Hofmannsthal, Schnitzler, Richard Beer-Hofmann, Peter Altenberg, and Karl Kraus in belles lettres; Freud and Breuer in medicine; Hans Kelsen in jurisprudence; Ludwig Wittgenstein in philosophy; among many others, to corroborate Zweig's generalization.

Moreover, with a few exceptions, many of the city's leading newspapers had either Jewish publishers like Moritz Benedikt (*Neue Freie Presse*) and Moritz Szeps (*Wiener Tagblatt*) or editors like Ferdinand Gross (*Fremdenblatt*) and Friedrich Uhl (*Wiener Abendpost*) or a preponderance of Jewish writers on their staffs. Of 348 members of the Austrian press club, Concordia, in 1897, about 150 were Jewish. As a result, anti-Semitic journalists on the *Deutsche Zeitung, Deutsches Volksblatt, Reichspost, Vaterland,* and other newspapers withdrew to form a club of their own.[12] The press of Vienna was thus polarized between a dominant liberal group branded *"Judenpresse"* by anti-Semites and a lesser, though quite influential, number of newspapers that were

overtly, even blatantly, anti-Semitic in their policies and, not confin-
ing their opinions to the editorial columns, did not scruple to report
so-called "straight" news with undisguised bias.

Whether or not Jewish reporters and feuilletonists of the liberal
press were more aggressive or shrewder than their rivals in circumventing Olivia Clemens's efforts to keep interviewers from her husband while he was laid up with gout during his first week in Vienna,
the fact is the earliest interviews Mark Twain granted at the Metropole were to Jewish journalists like Max and Siegmund Schlesinger,
Adolf Gelber, and Ferdinand Gross. The anti-Semites lost out in the
scramble to exploit the city's "famous guest" as circulation bait, and
they thought they knew why. It was either the author's philosemitism
(which was accurate) or, since no Austrian gentile is ever christened
Samuel (or few other Old Testament names not in the Calendar of
Saints), that he was himself a Jew. The latter explanation suited them
better.

Attacks on "*der Jude Mark Twain*" began in the anti-Semitic press even
while the initial interviews with him were appearing in other papers
in early October 1897. Mild at first, these attacks built in intensity and
venom in the succeeding months. A good example of their direction
may be observed by contrasting two cartoons that appeared almost
simultaneously in response to Mark Twain's often-quoted statement
in his interviews that his reason for being in Vienna was to study the
city and its citizenry in the hope of finding new material for stories.
The first is a cartoon by Theodor Zasche (1862–1922), Austria's foremost caricaturist of that era, in the weekly *Wiener Luft* (Vienna Air)
supplement of the humor magazine *Figaro*. It portrays Twain as Uncle
Sam with an oversized quill pen as a rod, fishing in a tub labeled
"Wien" (with the spire of Saint Stephen's sticking out of it), and with
a pail labeled "*Novellen Material*" (story material) behind him for his
catches. The likeness is good, the idea and composition apt, clever,
and amusing, and the cartoon's obvious statement cordial or at least
neutral.[13]

The other cartoon appeared within a matter of days in *Kikeriki!*

(Cock-a-doodle-doo!), a semiweekly that flaunted the candid subtitle *Antisemitische Humorblatt* and engaged in bigoted journalism and racial slanders vicious enough to make a Nazi wince. The unsigned drawing, attributed in the next issue obliquely to a lady staffer (*Collega*) named Horn, is titled *"Mark Twain sucht in Wien Stoff zu neuen Erzählungen"* (Mark Twain seeks in Vienna material for new stories), and it depicts the writer, hat, walking stick and notebook in hand, surrounded by eight stereotypic caricatures of supposed Jewish merchants with names like "S. Cohn" and "P. Lowenstein" (in background shop signs) who are trying to sell him clothes and bolts of cloth (playing on the word *Stoff*). Beneath is the caption "—*Da muß er aber Acht geben, daß er keine Pofelwaare erwischt"* (—but he must be alert that he doesn't pick up shoddy goods). The likeness is farfetched (Twain is drawn to look rather Semitic), the composition is satiric, and the statement is obviously malevolent.[14]

Kikeriki!'s next issue contained *"Ein Interview mit Mark Twain (von unserem Leibberichterstatter)"* (An Interview with Mark Twain [by our Body Reporter]), burlesquing his interviews in the liberal press as well as Pötzl's recent feuilleton ("The Silent Observer").[15] The fake interview is strained and sophomoric in its humor, and though not specifically anti-Semitic, its clear intent is to ridicule Twain for his obtuseness about Viennese ways. Both cartoon and "interview" in *Kikeriki!* were shots across the bow, warning Twain of the unfavorable consequences of his continued Jewish associations and candidly philosemitic pronouncements. They might actually have triggered the hoax letter in *Neue Freie Presse* (see chapter 4) reporting a fictitious incident in the city council meeting in which "Mark Twain" was physically assaulted by an anti-Semite.[16] One plausible way of reading that enigmatic letter is as a counterattack by Twain on his anti-Semitic critics.

Whatever the case, it may be more than coincidence that during the week these first anti-Semitic attacks on Twain appeared, Adolf Gelber, interviewing him for the *Neues Wiener Journal*, found him reading a German translation of the drama *Le Juif polonais* (The Polish Jew) by a team of Alsatian Jewish playwrights, Émile Erckmann and Louis Gratien Charles Alexandre Chatrian, who collaborated on several popular successes in the late nineteenth century under the joint nom de plume "Erckmann-Chatrian." [17] Since the piece was almost thirty years old and was not then being performed in Vienna or under current discussion, the only explanation for Twain's interest in reading it at that time would seem to be its pertinent subject matter. It is a creaky melodrama with scant literary merit. Some of its motifs, however, were of immediate use to Mark Twain when he wrote "The Chronicle of Young Satan" and, a bit later, "The Man That Corrupted Hadleyburg."

The scene of *Le Juif polonais* (or *Der polnische Jude* in the version Clemens read) is an Alsatian village in the early nineteenth century. In a howling blizzard on Christmas Eve 1808, Mathis, the local miller and tavernkeeper, has murdered Baruch Kosweski, an itinerant Jewish grain dealer, and robbed him of his bag of thirty thousand gold livres. Although the crime weighs heavily upon Mathis, it goes undetected. Years later, as the prosperous village mayor, he and his wife are celebrating the engagement of their daughter to the local police sergeant on another such snowy Christmas Eve. Amidst the conviviality the tavern door opens and another Polish Jew, identical in dress to the murdered man, stands at the threshold with the greeting Kosweski had used: "Peace be with you!" Mathis, inexplicably to the others, faints from shock.

Recovered the next day, he shrugs off the "apparition" but decides to hasten the wedding so that, as the gendarme's father-in-law, he might have greater protection from exposure. He offers the sergeant a dowry of thirty thousand louis d'ors and, when the marriage contract is signed, retires contented. His sleep is disturbed, however, by a dream in which he is tried and hanged for the murder he committed years ago. His dream is so realistic that he dies of fright. The next morning the doctor pronounces that "white wine has been his death," and a neighbor comments ironically: "The easiest death—no suffering." [18] In the same *Neues Wiener Journal* interview in which *Der polnische Jude* is mentioned in Twain's reading together with *Die wundersamen Erlebnisse des Freiherrn v. Trenck in Spielberg* (The Wondrous Experiences of

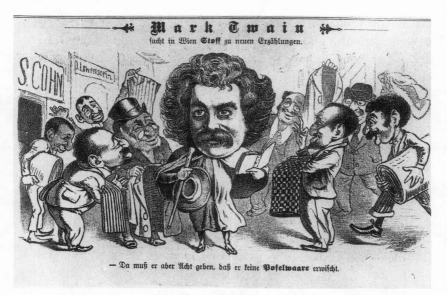

Anti-Semitic cartoon, "Mark Twain seeks material in Vienna for new stories," *Kikeriki!* October 10, 1897

Baron von Trenck in Speilberg), the interviewer (Gelber) asked Twain
to write something in German for his paper. Whereupon the humorist "put on horn-rimmed spectacles, took up a book for support, took
out pen and ink" and wrote in English one of his latest aphorisms:
"Truth is the most valuable thing we have. Let us economize it." Then
he added a labored, somewhat inept translation: "Freilich übersetzt:
Wir haben nichts die so werthvolle ist wie die Wahrheit. Also lasst
uns [crossed through]—(davon sparen seien) sie nicht verschwenden/
Truly Yours/Mark Twain/Wien, Oct. 8." This handwritten aphorism
and its translation were photographically reproduced to illustrate the
interview, along with a pen portrait of the author.[19]

The anti-Semitic *Reichspost* was quick to seize on this, quoting the
aphorism two days later (October 12, 1897) with: "Mark Twain, with
[those] words, so to speak, gave the 'Motto' of the whole of Jewish
journalism: 'Let us not squander the truth, let us economize it!' One
cannot better characterize the Jewish lying-press. That could be done
only by a charming Jewish humorist!"[20] *Reichspost* had stopped short
of calling Mark Twain a Jew, but it soon got around to that and kept
piling on such epithets throughout his stay in Austria.

The attraction for Mark Twain during his first winter in Vienna of
yet another play with Jewish themes, Theodor Herzl's *Das neue Ghetto*,
has been discussed in chapter 6 (see also chapter 13). This was perhaps less a consequence of his having met Herzl, feuilleton editor of
Neue Freie Presse, in Paris in 1895 when Herzl was covering the Dreyfus
affair for his paper, than because he was intrigued by Herzl's writings and activities on behalf of what the Hungarian-born Jew himself
called "a modern solution to the Jewish question," the subtitle of his
epoch-making *Der Judenstaat* (*The Jewish State*, 1896). *Zionismus* (Zionism), which Herzl founded as a political movement with this proposal
for a Jewish state in Palestine, then part of the Ottoman Empire, and
with his first Zionist Congress in Basel in August 1897, was one of
the most extreme of several Jewish responses to the rise of Viennese
anti-Semitism.

Another extreme was radical socialism—to rid the world of anti-

Semitism by destroying the root cause of this cancer, capitalism itself. This route was taken by Viktor Adler, who founded the Austrian Social Democratic party in 1888; Max Adler, the leading theorist of Austro-Marxism; and Otto Bauer, who became Austria's first foreign minister after World War I. Despite the specious claims of Twain scholars in the Soviet Union and of the late Maxwell Geismar, socialism (Marxist or otherwise) held little appeal for Mark Twain then or later. In Vienna, he seems to have had no contact whatever with either Viktor or Max Adler or with any of the other socialist leaders, Jewish or gentile.

A third extreme response to anti-Semitism among Jews was typified by the young Karl Kraus, the satirical essayist and pundit whose periodical, *Die Fackel* (The Torch), founded during Twain's last year in Vienna, quickly became the bible of the rebellious young intellectuals of Austria in the first three decades of this century. Although born and reared in a wealthy Jewish family, Kraus renounced Judaism, becoming by turns a Catholic and a socialist but, above all, a vehement anti-Semite. Kraus's variety of anti-Semitism expressed what was called "*Jüdische Selbsthass*" (Jewish self-hatred), which he shared with numerous gifted Jewish intellectuals in Vienna who internalized the norms of their dominant society and, whether they converted to Christianity or not, tried to out-gentile the gentiles. Such a one, for example, was the tragic Otto Weininger, whose book *Geschlecht und Charakter* (Race and Character, 1903), published only a few months before this brilliant Jew's self-hatred drove him to suicide, became one of the chief intellectual bulwarks of modern anti-Semitism. If Twain was aware of this Jewish anti-Semitism at all, he does not mention it.

Most Viennese Jews responded to anti-Semitism by ignoring discrimination and even persecution as best they could, clinging to the orthodoxy of their fathers and to Jewish folkways with a steadfastness that, however admirable, would one day be their undoing. A small number joined the Union for Defense Against Anti-Semitism and later the B'nai B'rith. Additionally, a significant proportion, perhaps even a majority of middle-class Jews, were assimilationists. Whether, like Gustav Mahler, Moritz Benedikt (publisher of *Neue Freie Presse*),

and Karl Wittgenstein, they converted at least nominally to Catholicism or (more often) Protestantism, or like Sigmund Freud, Arthur
Schnitzler, and Stefan Zweig, they were simply, unaffectedly nonprac-
ticing Germanized Jews, these assimilationists sought an accommodation with and within the dominant element of their society by overtly
denying their Jewishness while covertly, even subconsciously, maintaining it. Most of the Clemens family's Jewish friends and acquaintances in Vienna were assimilationists, and it is their views Mark Twain
seems to have accepted and espoused, with some reservations, when he
came to write "Concerning the Jews." That the accommodation they
sought was never granted was their ultimate tragedy and, indeed, the
tragedy of modern European history. Less than a half century later,
they went to bitter exile or to the gas chamber for their naive trust in
the viability of social and political liberalism. As the late Bruno Bettel-
heim said, too many died for naively refusing to believe they could be
"legally" killed simply *because* their only "crime" was being Jewish.

    That trust received its first severe jolt in December 1894 when a
French military court convicted Captain Alfred Dreyfus, an Alsatian
Jew, of high treason for offering military secrets to the Germans on
evidence so circumstantial and flimsy that the verdict could only be
explained as blatant official anti-Semitism. The Dreyfus affair, as it is
known, lasted through several episodes and various permutations for
the remainder of the decade. As a staple item of almost daily news, it
polarized opinion in Europe. On the one hand were those who were
outraged by the gross injustice of Dreyfus's sentence to life impris-
onment and its reimposition after a retrial in 1899 when it became
obvious the evidence against him was forged. On the other side were
the "anti-Dreyfusards" who doggedly insisted Dreyfus could not be
absolved of suspicion, whatever the facts, because, as a Jew, he could
never be loyal to France or any other nation. This prolonged, festering
case exacerbated anti-Semitic sentiment in Austria at least as much as
did the Tisza-Eszlár case in Hungary in 1882 or the Polna case in Bohemia in 1899 in which Jews were absurdly accused of ritual murders of
Christians to obtain blood for matzohs.

Although by no means ignored, the Dreyfus trials and their ramifications did not receive the constant attention in the United States that they did elsewhere, but living in Europe throughout most of the affair, Mark Twain took the keenest interest in every aspect of the several trials of Dreyfus and others implicated in the case. Of greatest concern to Twain was the arrest and conviction of the renowned writer Émile Zola (1840–1902) for libeling the French government in January 1898 in his letter "*J'accuse*" (I Accuse) to *L'Aurore*, in which the novelist flayed the French authorities for framing Dreyfus. Along with what Twain considered France's betrayal of Joan of Arc, it became Exhibit A in his constant indictment of the French as uncivilized, even subhuman. In mid-January 1898 Mark Twain wrote to Percy Mitchell in Paris, seeking a copy of *Aurore* "containing Zola's grand letter" ("*J'accuse*"), which elicited the reply: "I hasten gladly to send you Zola's letter. I had put it away among my archives under 'Clean French Literature.' The compartment is empty now."†21 After reading it, Twain drafted a laudatory note to Zola: "J̶[oan] ~~saved F~~[rance]~~'s life, you will save/are saving~~ ~~F.~~[rance's]~~honor. Hold your head high.~~ Accept the homage of a stranger. Ecclesiastical & military courts made up of cowards, hypocrites & time-servers can be bred at the rate of a million a year & have material left over;/to spare; but it takes 5 centuries to breed a Joan of Arc & a Zola."†22 Twain evidently never sent this, probably because Zola fled to England to escape sentencing and his exact whereabouts were unknown for a while.

References to the Dreyfus affair permeate almost everything Mark Twain wrote in Vienna. The outcome of the second trial, in which Dreyfus was again found guilty even though the court judged the original evidence against him to have been forged, provided the denouement of Mark Twain's short story "From the 'London Times' of 1904," and the Dreyfus affair is an important key to understanding "Concerning the Jews."

Twain's outspoken defense of Dreyfus and Zola and his attendance at a February 22, 1898, meeting of Baroness von Suttner's pacifist group, the Austrian Friends of Peace, at which Zola's views received a ringing endorsement, were widely noticed in the Viennese press. The liberal papers reported them without comment, but, predictably, the anti-Semitic *Reichspost* editorialized that "the unavoidable Mark Twain, who seems to have no idea of how he is being mishandled by the Jews in Vienna," was expressing opinions about things of which "he is really ignorant." The reporter continued with heavy irony that even as Twain boasted "the idea of peace is making great progress in America," his country was "grabbing Spain by the throat over the blowing up of a warship," a reference to the sinking of the *Maine* a few days earlier.[23]

Meanwhile, the appearance of Twain's article "Stirring Times in Austria" in *Harper's* did not escape notice in the Vienna newspapers, adding more fuel to the anti-Semites' fire. Even his friends on the *Neue Freie Presse*, lengthily reviewing "Stirring Times" in two separate articles and generally sympathetic to his views, were surprised at his "brutally frank" report of the stormy scenes he had witnessed in the Reichsrat in November 1897 and at his being so "shaken" by the events. They were, moreover, offended by his quoting a Viennese friend's remark, whether true or not, that "there is not a single Austrian who has made a name for himself that would be known around the entire globe."[24] Mark Twain's "friend," the anti-Semitic press observed, "was another Jewish lie," and *Kikeriki!* found it a good excuse for yet another burlesque interview, *"Mark Twain und die Antisemiten,"* in which it depicted Twain mistaking Jews for anti-Semites and vice-versa, with the heavily Jewish Concordia supposedly being described by him as an exclusively gentile anti-Semitic press club (*judenreiner Journalisten-Verein*).[25]

At what point that spring or early summer, perhaps soon after the move to Kaltenleutgeben, Twain began the notebook jottings he used in "Concerning the Jews" is uncertain, but the notes indicate the article had some lengthy gestation and is its author's considered riposte to slanders laid upon him in the anti-Semitic Viennese press, not an impromptu reply to questions in a letter from an American lawyer who had read "Stirring Times." These undated sententiae and extended aphorisms were incorporated almost verbatim in the published article:

I can stand any society. All that I care to know is, that a man is a human being—that is enough for me; ~~he can't be any worse~~ [In the notebook but omitted in the essay: "I can get right down & grovel with him."]

A person [Satan] who for untold centuries has maintained the imposing position of spiritual head of ⅕ of the human race, & political head of the whole of it must be granted the possession of executive abilities of the loftiest order. In his large presence the other popes & politicians shrink to midges for the microscope. . . . [Written in the margin of the notebook but omitted from the essay: "He hasn't a single salaried helper, The Opposition employ a million."]

The Jew has been staged in many uncomplimentary forms, but so far as I know no dramatist has done him the injustice to stage him as a beggar. . . .

If the horses knew their strength we should not ride any more. . . .

Some men worship rank, some worship heroes, some worship power, some worship God, & over these ideals they dispute & cannot unite—but they all worship money. . . .

We have all noticed that when the average man mentions the name of a multi-millionaire he does it with that mixture in his voice of reverence & lust which burns in a Frenchman's eye when it falls on another man's centime. . . . †26

Altogether omitted in the finished essay is this notebook aphorism: "There is nothing lower than the human race except the French." In its place he substituted a lengthier observation about the condemnation of Satan by all religions without hearing "*his*" side" of the case: "To my mind, this is irregular. It is un-English; it is un-American; it is French. Without this precedent Dreyfus could not have been condemned."27

Four questions and two general comments in the unnamed lawyer's letter, whether genuine or contrived, provide Twain the means for organizing an inquiry into the roots, history, and possible remedies for anti-Semitism. He eschews that euphemism in the essay, however, preferring instead what he forthrightly calls "prejudice against the Jew." First exculpating himself of all prejudices "bar one" (another obvious dig at the French), he proceeds with a burlesqued academic flourish to define his key term: "In the present paper I shall allow myself to use the word Jew as if it stood for both religion and race. It is handy; and besides, that is what the term means to the general world."

After these preliminaries, he elaborates with several illustrations upon his fictional lawyer's point that "the Jew is a well-behaved citizen." Emphatically agreeing, he concludes that "the merits and demerits being fairly weighed and measured on both sides, the Christian can claim no superiority over the Jew in the matter of good citizenship."

The central section of the article deals at length with the "lawyer's" question: "Can ignorance and fanaticism *alone* account for his [that is, the Jew's] unjust treatment?" Twain argues that anti-Semitism antedates Christianity, tracing it back to ancient Egypt, and that whatever religious complexion it acquired from medieval Christian doctrine about Jewish guilt for the Crucifixion was specious to begin with and is now only vestigial. This point he had made earlier in his unpublished letter to the *American Hebrew*, but here he gives it an economic spin: "I am persuaded that in Russia, Austria, and Germany nine-tenths of the hostility to the Jew comes from the average Christian's inability to compete successfully with the average Jew in business—in either straight business or the questionable sort. . . . The Jew is a money-getter; and in getting his money he is a very serious obstruction to less capable neighbors who are on the same quest."

His thesis thus stated, he turns to the question of remedies. There is none. "Race prejudice cannot be removed." It is rooted in our instinctive dislike of those who are different from ourselves. "Even the angels dislike a foreigner," he asserts, adding: "I am using the word foreigner in the German sense—*stranger*. Nearly all of us have an antipathy to a stranger, even of our own nationality. We pile gripsacks in a vacant seat to keep him from getting it; and a dog goes further, and does as a savage would—challenges him on the spot." This is unavoidably an argument for assimilation. In direct transactional discourse, he bluntly tells Jews, "You will always be by *ways and habits and predilections* [italics added] substantially strangers—foreigners—wherever you are, and that will probably keep the race prejudice against you alive." In other words, only Jews who give up distinctive "ways and habits and predilections" can expect acceptance by the non-Jewish world.

As a further way of ameliorating their condition, he advises Jews to develop political power by organizing, bloc voting, lobbying, and other means of gaining representation and influence in parliamentary governments, emulating the recent example of the Irish immigrants to America. Here, he concedes, concentration of population is of great value, a point that brings him to a comment on Zionism: "Dr. Herzl has a clear insight into the value of [concentration]. . . . He wishes to gather the Jews of the world together in Palestine, with a government of their own—under the suzerainty of the Sultan, I suppose. . . . I am not the Sultan, and I am not objecting; but if that concentration of the cunningest brains in the world was going to be made in a free country (bar Scotland), I think it would be politic to stop it."

The final section of the essay is lighter. In response to his imaginary lawyer's question "What has become of the golden rule?" Mark Twain adopts a mocking, sarcastic tone: "It exists, it continues to sparkle, and is well taken care of. It is Exhibit A in the Church's assets, and we pull it out every Sunday and give it an airing. But you are not permitted to try to smuggle it into this discussion, where it is irrelevant and would not feel at home. It is strictly religious furniture, like an acolyte, or a contribution-plate, or any of those things." This is the authentic voice of Mark Twain once again laying the lash on the hypocrisy of the pious Christian anti-Semite.

That "Concerning the Jews" was finished in Kaltenleutgeben on or before July 26, 1898, is obvious from Twain's mention in its penultimate section of a hailstorm that damaged Vienna's Central Cemetery shortly before midnight on July 19 as having occurred "last week." The tornado-like storm cut a swath through the Christian part of the cemetery, leaving the Jewish section untouched, to which Twain remarks jocosely: "Such nepotism makes me tired." On July 26 he wrote Rogers about having just completed three magazine articles, one of which, "The Jew article," he called

> my gem of the ocean. I have taken a world of pleasure in writing it and doctoring it and polishing it and fussing at it. Neither Jew nor Christian will approve it, but people who are neither Jews *nor* Christians will, for

they are in a condition to know the truth when they see it. I really believe I am the only man in the world who is equipped to write upon the subject without prejudice. For I *am* without prejudice. It is my hope that both the Christians *and* the Jews will be damned; and to that end I am working all my influence. Help me pray. . . .

If I have any leaning it is toward the Jew, not the Christian. (There is one thing I'd like to say, but I dasn't: Christianity has deluged the world with blood and tears—Judaism has caused neither for religion's sake.) I've had hard luck with *them*.[28]

His prediction that "neither Jew nor Christian will approve of" his article was only partly accurate. When the piece appeared in the September 1899 *Harper's*, Twain had already left Vienna for London, and although there were predictable sneers in the Viennese anti-Semitic press, there were no adverse comments from other Christians there or elsewhere. Although one American rabbi took swift umbrage at Twain's criticism that Jews have "an unpatriotic disinclination to stand by the flag as a soldier—like the Christian Quaker," publishing a sharp rejoinder listing Jewish patriots and their contributions to American freedom from Gouverneur Morris onward, and *The Jewish World* (London) found it "well-intentioned" but "weakened by sundry jokes" and "wrong statistics," a typically moderate response was Cyrus L. Sulzberger's, in *The American Hebrew*, that "in a spirit of absolute fairness and clearly without prejudice, Mark Twain makes some interesting suggestions regarding the Jewish question."[29]

Curiously, in the 1930s the Nazis attempted to make propaganda use of "Concerning the Jews" by wrenching portions of it from context to show Mark Twain to have been a sympathizer to their racist poison! Robert Edward Edmondson, an American Nazi, pulled out Twain's unflattering comments about Jews having "some discreditable ways" to make a distorted pastiche titled "Jewish Persecution—A Business Passion, by Mark Twain." His "vile and dishonest misrepresentation" was quickly exposed by Bernard DeVoto. On the other side of the coin, in the same year, the aged Sigmund Freud, living in London exile, published a précis of Twain's article (whose author and title he was then unable to recall precisely) in *Die Zukunft*, in Paris, in the vain hope of diminishing prejudice against displaced Jews like himself.[30]

During Mark Twain's second year in Vienna, sneers at him in the anti-Semitic press slackened, probably because there were fewer interviews and stories about him in other newspapers. Nevertheless, references to *"der jüdische amerikanische Humorist"* continued from time to time. In early May 1899, the anti-Semitic dailies had a field day with Karl Kraus's combined assault on Twain and *Neue Freie Presse* in the third number of his new journal, *Die Fackel*. *Reichspost* and other anti-Semitic papers published gleeful summaries of it, quoting Kraus with evident *Schadenfreude* (gloating). Typically, *Reichspost* told its readers the *Judenpresse* (Jewish press) in Vienna had been exposed by Kraus as the only reason why in *Juda-Wien* (Jewish Vienna) *"der jüdische amerikanische Humorist Mark Twain"* was once again *"ein berühmter Mann"* (a famous man) long after his importance as a humorist in America had faded.[31]

Some final salvos during his sojourn were fired at Twain by *Deutsches Volksblatt* and *Reichspost* in response to a report that while in Vienna Twain had commenced memoirs he would not allow to be published until a century after his death. In an article headlined *"Die Judenpresse und Wien,"* *Deutsches Volksblatt* accused Mark Twain of abusing Vienna's hospitality by constantly seeking publicity, by using every occasion for "self-advertisement," and by inconsiderately ridiculing and insulting the majority of the citizenry *"unter dem Beifalle der Judenbuben von der 'Concordia'"* (with the applause of the Jew-boys of the "Concordia").[32]

The most intemperate attack during his entire stay came, ironically, on the very day of his departure in an article in *Reichspost* headlined *"Mark Twain—und die Judenreclame"* (Mark Twain—and the Jewish Advertisements). The lead paragraph began: *"Mark Twain—der Jude Mark Twain—sonst wäre er ja nicht der 'weltbekannte Schriftstellerr' . . ."* (Mark Twain—the Jew Mark Twain—otherwise he would certainly not be the "world-famous author" . . .). Noting that he said his memoirs to be withheld from publication for a hundred years were "about various personalities whose acquaintance he had made during the course of his life" and that his "portrait gallery undoubtedly includes Viennese characters," the writer impugns Twain's motives. When publication finally occurred, no one would be alive to refute "his lies and misinformation" and his flattery of his Jewish and philosemitic friends in Vienna—"Alexander Scharf, [Moritz] Szeps, Emil Frischauer, Dr. [Moritz] Benedikt, Dr. Philippovich, Edgar von Spiegel, Lucian Brunner, Hermann Bahr, Oscar Friedmann, etc." (not one of whom, incidentally, appears in Twain's published or still-unpublished reminiscences). The *Reichspost* editorialist infers this from Twain's statement that delaying publication for a hundred years "gives me freedom I can't get in any other way to write without fear of offense."[33]

One may easily imagine Mark Twain's vexation at the way his innocent and candid revelations could be so maliciously twisted and assigned such nefarious ulterior motives. For nearly two years he had lived among intelligent, liberal, fair-minded people who had been a delight to know and also among some bigoted, unthinking, mean-spirited ones whose company he had been lucky enough to avoid. Despite all he had witnessed and learned in Vienna, it was still beyond his comprehension that such evil creatures might one day get the upper hand, that the worst was yet to come. Nor, despite some penetrating insights and realistic assessments in his flawed apologia "Concerning the Jews," could he foresee that, ere another half-century passed, the prayer in which he asked Rogers to join, "that both Jews and Christians will be damned," would be horribly answered.

In a moment of petulance in Vienna he predicted bitterly, "Christianity will doubtless still survive in the earth ten centuries hence— stuffed & in a museum."†[34] Then, in mellower yuletide mood, he whimsically quipped: "I hold in just as much reverence that little Jew baby that was born in Bethlehem nineteen centuries ago as if it had been a Christian baby."†[35] Paradoxically, both sentiments express the Jew-Christian nihilist who was the essential Mark Twain. Being the "Jew Mark Twain" for almost two years, however painful and baffling, had been a valuable chapter in his education.

CHAPTER NINE

"Lay Down Your Arms!"

uring the Vietnam War there was a largely successful effort in academia to portray Mark Twain as having been a "dove," a "peacenik," an ardent pacifist. Some of his sharpest thrusts at militarism and imperialism which give credence to this view were first published in the 1960s and early '70s, and it is a rare survey anthology of American literature edited since 1968 that does not include either "The War Prayer" or "To the Person Sitting in Darkness" among its Twain offerings. These pieces were penned in the white heat of his indignation at the ruthless "pacification" of the Philippines and crushing of the Boxer Uprising in China in 1901, and both suggest parallels to American involvement in Vietnam. Capitalizing on anti–Vietnam War sentiment, Hal Holbrook, the popular Twain impersonator, titillated audiences on and off campuses with antiwar passages culled from the posthumously published 1896 essay "Man's Place in the Animal World," which Twain himself never used on the platform.[1] What Holbrook and the anthologists presented was a distinctly partial, perhaps distorted view of the author's often ambivalent opinions on the subjects of war and peace.

Certainly there is no mistaking the meaning of these lines excerpted by Holbrook:

Man is the only animal that deals in that atrocity of atrocities, War. He is the only one that gathers his brethren about him and goes forth in cold blood . . . to exterminate his kind. He is the only animal that for sordid wages will march out . . . and help to slaughter strangers of his own species who have done him no harm and with whom he has no quarrel. . . . And in the intervals between campaigns he washes the blood off his hands and works for "the universal brotherhood of man"—with his mouth.[2]

How, when, and why he came to view war as "the atrocity of atrocities," which may or may not be pacifism, and in what ways this opinion was influenced, strengthened, or ameliorated by his experiences in Vienna must be closely examined. No one has noticed Mark Twain's association in Vienna in 1898 and early 1899 with Freifrau Bertha Kinsky von Suttner (1843–1914), Austria's premier pacifist, and her Oesterreichische Gesellschaft der Friedensfreunde (Austrian Society of Friends of Peace). Yet this friendship provided a number of colorful and bizarre experiences during his Vienna sojourn.

By all accounts Baroness von Suttner was an extraordinary person. Touched with brilliance, if not genius, and with rhetorical and organizational skills of a high order, she was the kind of obdurate, single-minded visionary fired with evangelical fervor who, by *force majeure*, has often changed the course of history. Her personal tragedy was that, despite being the only Austrian woman ever to win a Nobel Peace Prize (1905), she did not succeed in changing anything. Her life's work was in ashes even before she had the good luck to die just one week before the assassinations at Sarajevo exploded the world she had so ardently but vainly striven to save from itself.

How and when Mark Twain gravitated into her orbit is uncertain. It was probably at one of the dinners or soirées he enjoyed among the high born during December 1897 and January 1898. Among his aristocratic friends were many who altruistically devoted themselves to philanthropy in the original sense, not just by donating money or lending their names to letterheads but through active humanitarian service. In 1878, the ill-fated Crown Prince Rudolf in an anonymous pamphlet excoriated his noble confrères for their wastrel lives devoted to hunting parties, lavish balls, and "intimes Soupers" at the Hotel Sacher instead of participation in public affairs. Yet there were plenty of exceptions to the general truth of his indictment.

Freifrau Bertha Kinsky von Suttner, a novelist and founder of the Austrian
Friends of Peace, who was awarded the Nobel Peace Prize in 1905
(Picture Archives of the Austrian National Library)

Among Twain's social acquaintances, for instance, was Prince Ladis-laus Batthyány-Strattmann (1870–1931), who, after taking doctorates in both philosophy and medicine, erected two hospitals in the Hungarian borderland and Slovakia at his own expense and performed there gratis some three thousand cataract operations for the elderly poor. To his notebook, Mark Twain candidly confessed his "splendid pleasure" at being in the company of this prince and his wife, "who assists her husband in his noble work of affording relief to people whose eyes have suffered from disease," adding: "To relieve pain—that is an exalted office; & when a prince does it, & doesn't *need* to do it, it makes the princely dignity ideal."†3

Undoubtedly it was Prince Batthyány-Strattmann's example and the sense of noblesse oblige Clemens encountered among the Austrian nobility that prompted his botched attempt at an essay, "A Defence of Royalty & Nobility," only the beginning of which he sketched. A muddled, disjointed draft, it gets only to the suggestion "That an aristocracy is a valuable adjunct to society is confessed by the fact that even in our republic we have laid the foundation of one" in the dollar aristocracy of New York's Four Hundred.†4 It was clear his social education in Vienna was challenging the old verities of this staunch democrat.

In the same circle of Clemens's friends as the Countess Wydenbruck-Esterházy and Princess Metternich, whose eleemosynary activities were endless, was Count Richard Coudenhove. (He should not be confused with his namesake nephew who founded the Paneuropa Movement after World War I.) Count Coudenhove had links with Baroness von Suttner in the Friedensfreunde and with her husband, one of the gentile founders (along with Johann Strauss, Marie von Ebner-Eschenbach, and Dr. Theodor Billroth) of the Verein zu Abwehr des Antisemitismus (Union for Defense Against Anti-Semitism). Twain's frequent notebook references suggest the count may have been the one who introduced Mark Twain to the baroness.5

Mark Twain's first appearance with the Friedensfreunde was at a *Kundgebung* (rally) in the great hall of the Scientific Club the evening of February 22, 1898, one week after the sinking of the *Maine* made war between the United States and Spain seem likely. He was invited to the rally by Baroness von Suttner, to whom he replied candidly on February 17:

> Dear Madam:
>
> It is going to be difficult for me to get a day off from my work, still I mean to go to the meeting if I can—not to help smoke the pipe of peace, but to meet *you*.
>
> I am indeed in *sympathy* with the movement, but my head is not with my heart in the matter. I cannot see how the movement can strongly appeal to the selfishness of governments. It can appeal to the selfishness of nations, possibly, but nations have no command over their governments, & in fact no influence over them, except of a fleeting & rather ineffectual sort.
>
> If you could persuade the Powers to agree to settle their disputes by arbitration you would uncover their nakedness. You would never persuade them to reduce their vast armaments, & so, even the ignorant & the simple would then discover that the armaments were not created chiefly for the protection of the nations but for their enslavement.
>
> Sincerely Yours,
>
> S.L. Clemens*6

It was not the international tension created by the Cuban crisis that formed the agenda of this meeting but a general resolution supporting world peace initiatives and expressing solidarity with Émile Zola, "a fellow-Friend of Peace" (and, by inference, Alfred Dreyfus), enjoining kindred "friends of peace" throughout the world to shun the planned Paris Exposition (1900) if the French persisted in their disregard of justice. That and another motion expressing pleasure at the formation of an International League of Journalists in the Interest of Peace were adopted, the first by a good majority, the latter unanimously. Twain did not speak at the rally, but his presence was duly noted in the press, which was doubtless his main reason for being there.[7]

Had he thought this might be his only contact with the Friedens-freunde, he would have been less astute than usual as a judge of char-acter. The baroness was not the sort who let an exploitable celebrity like Mark Twain get away easily once he had entered her orbit. Born in Prague into a noble family of ancient Bohemian lineage a few weeks after her father died, Countess Bertha Kinsky (she "demoted" herself by marriage) might have led a life of aristocratic indolence had her father's death not put the Kinskys in straitened circumstances. Having studied music, she became *Musiklehrerin* in the Suttner household in Vienna, where she fell in love with her employer's son. When both families opposed their marriage because he was seven years her junior, she fled to Paris where she became Alfred Nobel's private secretary.

The following year (1876), she and Arthur Suttner eloped to Tiflis (Tbilisi), in Russian Georgia, where he eked out a living as an archi-tectural draftsman and business translator. When he was engaged by *Neue Freie Presse* to report on the Russo-Turkish War (1877–78), the couple saw first-hand the horrible suffering of both soldiers and civil-ians in war, whereupon Bertha resolved to spend the rest of her life in the cause of peace. This cause she served with compulsive vigor and, for a time, significant results.

The Suttners returned to Vienna in 1885 to claim his rather con-siderable patrimony. This enabled them to divide their time thereafter between the city and a handsome country estate, Schloss Hermanns-dorf, in Lower Austria. Financially secure, the couple then entered productive parallel careers as novelists, using their Caucasian experi-ences in naturalistic narratives. In 1889 Bertha von Suttner published *Die Waffen Nieder! Eine Lebensgeschichte* (Lay Down Your Arms! A Life Story), a searing pacifist novel describing the mutilations she had wit-nessed on the battlefield at Tiflis and the suffering of bereaved wives and mothers. It immediately became and remained for many years a best-seller in the German-speaking world.

Throughout the 1890s she coedited, with Alfred Hermann Fried (1864–1921), a prominent Jewish bookseller who later received a Nobel Peace Prize himself (1911), the monthly pacifist magazine with the same title (*Die Waffen Nieder!*). This became the official journal of the Friedensfreunde, founded by her in 1892 and over which she presided until her death. Until his death in 1902, Baron von Suttner assisted his wife unselfishly in her peace endeavors. The two carefully studied each new development of weapons technology proliferating during the massive arms race of the 1890s and early 1900s, and she correctly foresaw that future wars would be total and indiscriminate in their slaughter and devastation and that nothing less than the survival of humanity was at stake.[8]

For Mark Twain to have associated himself publicly with Baroness von Suttner's movement at this juncture was a shrewd maneuver. The "Remember the *Maine!*" hysteria that pushed a reluctant President McKinley to ask Congress to declare war on April 24, 1898, *despite* Spanish capitulation on almost every demand was emphasized in the European press in which Americans were painted as maniacal warmongers. In Austria, whose monarch was related by blood to the queen-regent of Spain, Americans were especially vulnerable. Hence attending meetings of the Friedensfreunde was not a bad palliative for the "warmonger" image. Nevertheless, it would be unfair to say Mark Twain's ulterior motive of using the baroness and the Friedensfreunde for image-making belied his sincere interest in and sympathy with her ideas and objectives.

Privately, Clemens waxed jingoistic as he contemplated the Cubans' struggle against Old World imperialism. Echoing the official Washington line, though perhaps unwittingly, he wrote Twichell, whose son had enlisted: "It is a worthy thing to fight for one's freedom; it is another sight finer to fight for another man's." In February 1898, however, he had still thought European fears about the threat of war nonsensical, and he sought unsuccessfully to lampoon them with a jejune burlesque, "The New War-Scare," wasting fifteen typed pages to portray the minuscule Principality of Monaco as having imperial ambitions that were threatening the Great Powers and endangering the peace of Europe. Wisely, he decided against publication.[9]

After the Americans landed in Cuba, he followed the war reports with keenest interest, recording "our glorious" naval victories at Manila (May 1) and Santiago de Cuba (July 3) in his notebook with undisguised jingoism. To Austrian critics he grew increasingly defensive about American conduct of the war, writing to Bettina Wirth on June 19: "I see that the mutilation of our soldiers killed on picket is denied in Madrid. I wish the denial might be true, but as an American Admiral made the charge, that ends the matter. The mutilations were probably done by guerrillas—it's a part of their trade; but as Spain recognizes the guerrillas, their acts are Spanish acts, and official."†[10]

His myopic view of America's holy war against imperialism began to waver only after a letter in early August in which Howells fumed indignantly that "our war for humanity [has been turned] into a war for coaling stations."[11] When the armistice of August 12 made it obvious that, however it might be disguised, the United States intended merely to usurp Spain's position as a colonial power in the Caribbean and Far East, acquiring a far-flung empire of possessions from Puerto Rico to the Philippines and Guam, Clemens's disillusion began in earnest. It would deepen during the next five years with the bloody suppression of Aguinaldo's uprising, the intensifying of the Boer War, and the bludgeoning of China by the European Concert and the United States.

Although he soft-pedaled his patriotic sentiments for public display, his press colleagues obviously got wind of them. Thus the *Humoristische Blätter* on April 17 gave its readers some jocular *Unverbürgte Nachricht* (unconfirmed news): "It has been reported that Mark Twain will be called back to America to command an army against Spain. The battle plan is for him to read his humorous sketches to the enemy at which they will laugh themselves to death."[12] Except for the anti-Semitic *Reichspost* which predictably accused him of hypocrisy in attending a Friedensfreunde rally while his country was "grabbing Spain by the throat," no adverse reactions to Twain's stance on the war appeared in Viennese newspapers. It is undoubtedly just as well he did not publish his brief "A Word to Our Blushing Exiles," originally intended for the Paris *Herald*, during this time. In this apologia for American policies, he made invidious comparisons with recent colonial atrocities by European governments, notably France and the French mockery of justice in the Dreyfus affair, advising Americans abroad to hold their heads up and not to shrink from arguing their country's cause.

While Spanish and American emissaries were negotiating in Paris, the Friedensfreunde held another rally on October 18, 1898. Its purpose was to endorse a manifesto from His Imperial Majesty Nicholas II, Czar of All the Russias, calling upon all governments to send representatives to an international conference within six months at The Hague to discuss ways to achieve world peace and general disarmament. Because of its size, Etablissement Ronacher (a vaudeville theater and ballroom) was chosen for this rally which was thrown open to the general public free of charge, not restricted to the society's members. An hour beforehand the *NFP* reporter found it *"ganz dicht im Parterre und auf der Galerie besetzt war"* (quite thickly occupied from main floor to gallery).[13] It was Bertha von Suttner's hour of triumph, not least because she had snagged Mark Twain as one of her speakers for this glorious occasion.

The principal address was by Lt.-Col. Manfred von Egidy, who had been cashiered from the Prussian army for his antiwar pamphlet *Ernste Gedanken* (Serious Thoughts) and was making the rounds of peace groups in the Germanic world. When he stepped forward after the baroness's introduction, she remembered, "his words rang out like bell tones . . . bronze in his voice, gold in his words, consecration in the room." He explained the czar's proposal "in clear, occasionally witty language, and always with logical conciseness. And the audience vibrated with him. Every satirical point was punctuated with a laugh, at every allusion a murmur of appreciation ran through the assembly."[14] He ended to *stürmischer Beifall* (a storm of applause) that no one should

worry about negative results from the proposed conference—"We will
battle shoulder to shoulder with the Czar and cry out: Away with
official and public sham! The soul of the people demands peace!"[15]

   This florid rhetoric was a hard act to follow, but Mark Twain rose to
the challenge. He excused himself for using English in his talk, pointing out that, as the czar's manifesto had been issued in Russian and
had been understood by people of every culture, he had no fears he
would not likewise be perfectly understood. He noted thankfully that
the war between his homeland and Spain was over, that it had cost
much in money and human suffering on both sides and had achieved
nothing that could not have been done without a war. Although he
personally had had doubts about the idea of world peace, thinking it
was just so many words, the fact that the czar of Russia was issuing
such a call and was ready to disarm was now enough for him. He had
only a penknife with him, but he was ready to disarm, too![16]

   An even more colorful and dramatic finale awaited when an eccentric painter, Herr Diefenbach, garbed in the sackcloth and rope of a
penitent pilgrim (in which he was apparently often seen around town),
gained the podium to deliver a philippic against the church and its tradition of blessing weapons and saying mass on battlefields, then turned
to animal rights and a string of other grievances. When he got to a call
for lifting the death penalty, the official representative of the government, who had to be at all such gatherings to give them legality, rose
and took his leave. Amid the general uproar Colonel Egidy stepped
forward to shout peremptorily: "Disarmament, yes! Our hearts unbur-
den themselves of fury and resentment against the past!" This rather
upstaged Herr Diefenbach and ended the meeting.[17]

   Afterward the baroness gave a gala supper at the Hotel Sacher for
her committee, the speakers, and other guests. During the table conversation, Herr von Gniewicz, a member of the Reichsrat who had
been an officer in the imperial army during the Austro-Prussian war
in 1866, discovered that he and Egidy had been face to face as enemies at Königgrätz (July 3, 1866), where Prussia decisively defeated

Austria, and might then have killed one another. "And now here they were," the baroness beamed, "both adherents and champions of the peace cause, united in joyous festal mood." Overhearing this colloquy, Mark Twain, she remembered, "used the Egidy-Gniewicz incident for a brilliant improvisation, full of wit and feeling."[18] Evidently he regaled the company with a tale he often used on the platform about a chance post–Civil War meeting in friendly circumstances between a Union and a Confederate officer who had similarly faced each other at Bull Run (the first Battle of Manassas in 1861).

A fortnight after this festivity, William T. Stead, founder of the influential London *Review of Reviews* and one of England's most indefatigable pacifists, came to Vienna to meet Baroness von Suttner and renew an acquaintanceship with Mark Twain begun on a transatlantic liner in 1894.[19] Stead, whose life ended on another ocean liner, the *Titanic*, in 1912, was then traversing Europe to gather material for articles urging Britons to support the czar's world peace initiative. He was enchanted by the Baroness von Suttner and she with him, so they agreed to link forces thereafter in their work for world disarmament. Mark Twain's conversations with Stead and others at this time may form the background for his inquiry of November 17, 1898, to the eccentric Croatian-born inventor, Nikola Tesla:

Dear Mr. Tesla –

Have you Austrian & English patents on that destructive terror which you are inventing?—& if so, won't you set a price upon them & commission me to sell them? I know cabinet ministers of both countries—& of Germany, too; likewise William II.

I shall be in Europe a year, yet.

Here in the hotel the other night when some interested men were discussing means to persuade the nations to join with the Czar & disarm, I advised them to seek something more sure than disarmament by perishable paper-contract—invite the great inventors to contrive something against which fleets & armies would be helpless, & thus make war thenceforth impossible. I did not suspect that you were already attending to

that, & getting ready to introduce into the earth permanent peace &
disarmament in a practical & mandatory way.

I know you are a very busy man, but will you steal time to drop me
a line?

Sincerely Yours,

Mark Twain [20]

A few months earlier, at the first Electrical Exhibition in New York,
Tesla had demonstrated what his biographer calls "the common an-
cestor of modern guided weapons" in the vain hope of interesting the
American navy in its possible uses. Born in 1856 in what was then
an Austro-Hungarian province, Tesla had immigrated to the United
States in 1884 and had worked for Edison and, later, George Westinghouse before striking out on his own. Although he died in almost
penniless obscurity at the Hotel New Yorker in 1943, scientists have
recently acknowledged his numerous important discoveries and pioneering achievements in electronics—including much of what is now
called "Star Wars" weaponry—which have undeservedly been credited
to others.

Mark Twain first made Tesla's acquaintance at The Players' Club
during a business trip back home in 1894, and they occasionally met
after Twain settled in Manhattan in 1900, but Tesla's response to this
letter from Vienna (if there was one) is not extant. In his deathbed
delirium in January 1943, however, Tesla, hallucinating that Twain
had visited him the previous evening, recalled the writer had been in
financial straits when they first met and, refusing to believe Samuel L.
Clemens dead (some thirty-three years before!), repeatedly sent a mes-
senger out into a fierce snowstorm to deliver some cash to Clemens at
his old Fifth Avenue address.[21]

Twain's letter to Tesla evinces his enormous interest in gadgetry and
inventions to be discussed in the next chapter, his consummate greed
(he called it "genuine business sense"), and by implication his convictions about disarmament. More trusting of technology than of human
nature, he sees treaties and declarations ("paper contracts") as futile.
Only an ultimate weapon against which there is no defense might com-

pel peace. The problem is not the gun but the finger on the trigger. On this theme he later played several variations, and it is but one more datum of his growing disenchantment with human solutions and his embrace of therapeutic nihilism.

By January 1899 enough governments had ratified the czar's call that the First International Peace Conference at The Hague could be scheduled to open May 18. It was not, of course, the "first," but three preceding ones in 1843, 1851, and 1878 had produced nothing. William T. Stead, founding *The Peace Apostle,* a new weekly devoted to the issues and proposals to come before the conference, asked Mark Twain to contribute. Twain cabled him on January 9: "Dear Mr. Stead,—The Czar is ready to disarm, *I* am ready to disarm. Collect the *others,* it should not be much of a task now. Mark Twain." Then, thinking it better not to appear blatantly cynical in print about so serious an issue, he sent Stead a short, 750-word article in letter form. In it he reiterated the basic assumption of his Tesla letter: "Peace by compulsion. That seems a better idea than the other. Peace by persuasion has a pleasant sound, but I think we should not be able to work it. We should have to tame the human race first, and history seems to show that that cannot be done." After tangling himself in unreliable statistics to show the enormous increase in firepower per soldier since Waterloo, he concluded: "Perpetual peace we cannot have on any terms, I suppose; but I hope we can gradually reduce the war strength of Europe till we get it down to where it ought to be—20,000 men, properly armed. Then we can have all the peace that is worth while, and when we want a war anybody can afford it."[22]

Reporting on this letter to Stead synoptically, *NFP* pointed out errors in Twain's statistics but made no comment on his argument.[23] His obvious disillusion or impatience with the peace movement implied in this piece evidently escaped Baroness von Suttner's notice, and she solicited him again in March to speak or read at a Friedensfreunde benefit to raise money to send deputations to The Hague. While in Budapest to address the Hungarian Press Club, he responded with elaborate courtesy on March 27, 1899:

Dear Madam:

It is with grief that I decline but I feel obliged to do it. I am booked for one little engagement in April, & after that, for the rest of the season I am promising myself a holiday from reading & talking. You are good, & you will forgive me. I know it! For you will have charity for age & indolence.

With thanks to you for the compliment of your invitation, & with homage to yourself & your husband, I am

Sincerely Yours,
Mark Twain*[24]

In early May she sent him an invitation on behalf of the new Comité für Kundgebungen zur Friedenskonferenz (Committee for Rallies at the Peace Conference) to attend a rally at the departure of the Austrian delegates for The Hague, but he replied that he was now too busy with his own preparations to depart from Vienna.[25]

When the time for his departure came, the conference was already under way. It sat until July 29 and produced little except high-flown rhetoric and the establishment of the so-called "Hague Tribunal" (Permanent Court of Arbitration) to settle international disputes, thus rendering wars unnecessary. The day before the Clemenses left Vienna, Mark Twain had his private audience with the emperor at which, he told his friend Pötzl, he had suggested the emperor could immediately establish world peace if he would have his subject Jan Szczepanik ("the Austrian Edison") invent a device for suddenly withdrawing the oxygen from the earth's atmosphere, thus destroying all life on the planet. The mere threat of its use by the government owning it would compel world peace![26]

A year later, in London, Twain received from Baroness von Suttner an invitation to a Friedensfreunde rally in Vienna to celebrate the first anniversary of the conference at The Hague. Only the rough draft of his reply, dated May 7, [1900], on a Chatto & Windus letterhead, survives:

Dear Baroness von Suttner:

It is ever so kind of you to remember me, & I thank you for it. I wish I believed the Czar, now, as before the Finland episode: in wh case I should hold it a pleasure & a privilege to be allowed to come & hear him praised. I wish you every (happiness in your difficult sorely embarrassed situation) success—for *you* are in earnest, I know *that*.

I am not as young as I was. I realize it when I put the Finland tragedy & the Hague Comedy together, & find that I want to cry when I ought to laugh.

Sincerely yours,
SLC*27

How poignant that note of disillusion in the final paragraph! In the interval between the conference and this letter, czarist troops had fired upon a crowd of peaceful demonstrators protesting the "February Manifesto" abrogating autonomy in what was then the Russian Grand Duchy of Finland, and there had been many casualties. Twain was not alone in his outrage at the hypocrisy of Nicholas II, "the Apostle of Peace," ordering or at least condoning such violently repressive measures. In due course, Nicholas II became one of Mark Twain's arch-villains and, in "The Czar's Soliloquy" (1905), the target of one of his most scathingly brilliant political satires.

For him the czar's behavior was sad corroboration of what he had written to Stead: "Perpetual peace we cannot have on any terms, I suppose." After all, what could conclaves of idealistic speechifying do to bring peace and disarmament as long as there were cynic kings capable of tyrannizing the masses who, in Bertrand Russell's phrase in

1949, were "always ready to rush into the street to cheer the news the government has decided to have them all killed"? Twain plumbed the depths of his distrust of what he considered merely cosmetic means for solving basic human problems of war and peace in an episode for "The Chronicle of Young Satan" written at about the time he drafted this last regretful letter to the baroness. In it, Satan tells Theodor and his friends there has never been a "just" or "honorable" war and this will not change in a million years. In every crisis,

> the loud little handful—as usual—will shout for the war. The pulpit will—warily and cautiously—object—at first; the great big dull bulk of the nation will rub its sleepy eyes and try to make out why there should be a war, and will say, earnestly and indignantly, "It is unjust and dishonorable, and there is no necessity for it." Then the handful will shout louder. A few fair men on the other side will argue and reason against the war with speech and pen, and at first will have a hearing and be applauded; but it will not last long; those others will out-shout them, and presently the anti-war audiences will thin out and lose popularity. Before long you will see a curious thing: the speakers stoned from the platform and free speech strangled, by hordes of furious men who in their secret hearts are still at one with those stoned speakers,—as earlier,—but do not dare to say so! And now the whole nation—pulpit and all—will take up the war-cry, and shout itself hoarse, and mob any honest man who ventures to open his mouth, and presently such mouths will cease to open. Next the statesmen will invent cheap lies, putting the blame on the nation that is attacked, and every man will be glad of those conscience-soothing falsities, and will diligently study them, and refuse to examine any refutations of them; and thus he will by and by convince himself that the war is just, and will thank God for the better sleep he enjoys after this process of grotesque self-deception.[28]

There are many such passages in Twain's writing in Vienna and thereafter that may be labeled "therapeutic nihilism"—a deep distrust of all human remedies for human problems that nonetheless clarifies them sharply—but none more deserving that label than this.

What is clear from this passage is that, however much he hated war, Mark Twain was not a postulant for the pacifist movement in

Austria or elsewhere and that, in his view, Baroness von Suttner and her admirably enlightened, well-intentioned, idealistic colleagues were swimming against an irreversible tide of darkness in which (though Twain did not forecast it) ere long they were doomed to drown. In the last year of the nineteenth century, prospects for lasting peace and world disarmament, for settling disputes by international tribunals such as the czar proposed never looked rosier, yet within two decades Europe would destroy itself. Mark Twain certainly did not foresee World War I, but he clearly understood the elements in human nature and in the *Realpolitik* of the age that made it likely, if not inevitable, and he doubted they could ever be altered.

CHAPTER TEN

The Austrian Edison

One afternoon in mid-March 1898, Amelia S. Levetus, Vienna correspondent for several London and New York newspapers, came to tea with the Clemenses at the Metropole. She was received with the usual graciousness of Olivia Clemens whose husband, called away on a pressing errand, returned too late to share in a fateful tea-table chat Miss Levetus had with her hostess. The Englishwoman had recently interviewed a young electrical engineer, Jan Szczepanik (pronounced "Shta-pan´-nick"), and she recalled her *Plauderstündchen* (social chat) with Olivia, thus: "One day during a visit to Mrs. Clemens I happened to tell her of a young man named Stepanik [*sic*], an Austrian Pole who had invented a telectroscope which was to revolutionise the world and a machine which was to revolutionise weaving. All Vienna was brimful of excitement about the matter, the newspapers were full of the famous invention, cablegrams were sent to America, the journalists interviewed the inventor."[1]

Upon her husband's return, Olivia recounted this to him, and that evening he urgently dispatched a note to Miss Levetus saying, "I am sorry I didn't hear that talk about the wonderful invention, for I would like to have the opportunity to raise the capital and introduce it in America. I am acquainted with a lot of enterprising New York millionaires & I should have as little trouble as anyone in quickly & advantageously placing such a thing. Is it too late? Will you ask (for) me?"[2]

The "wonderful invention" Clemens referred to was not the *Fernse-*

her (distance-seer) or telectroscope, a primitive form of what is now called closed-circuit television—though Mark Twain would soon find literary use for that, too—but a laborsaving device Szczepanik had developed for the carpet and textile industries. The *Raster,* as it was known, was a machine for electrically copying graphic images directly into woven fabric without stenciling or other ways of patterning the weaving, and Clemens thought its patent rights would be a bonanza to anyone who shared in them. When word came from Miss Levetus that Szczepanik had not yet sold the American rights to this device, Clemens asked her to arrange an interview with the inventor and his business manager without delay.

Their first meeting occurred in the Clemenses' parlor at the Metropole the following night (March 16), lasting from nine o'clock until midnight. Clemens had spent the entire day feverishly boning up on the British and American textile industries and the potential marketing opportunities for Szczepanik's inventions in the United States and Great Britain from reference books in the U.S. consulate (the newest of which, he noted disgustedly, was 18 years old!) and from material supplied by William Lavino, Vienna correspondent of the London *Times.* He boasted he had "ciphered on the data, & wrote 11 pages of questions; & when the inventor and his capitalist (Mr. Ludwig Kleinberg) arrived at 9 with Miss Levetus & Dr. Winternitz, I was ready for business, & rich with my new learning. My extraordinary familiarity with the subject paralyzed the banker [i.e., Kleinberg] for a while, for he was merely expecting to find a humorist, not a commercial cyclopedia— but he recovered presently."†3

Whether he was impressed or not, Kleinberg was eager to sell and suggested a price of $1.5 million. Clemens said he would "sleep on it" and meet the banker again at four the next afternoon, but by breakfast time on the seventeenth, he had convinced himself sufficiently to send for Kleinberg immediately to enter into an agreement. Clemens was to have a two-month option at $1.5 million payable in several installments and extendable upon request. If he sold the American rights to the *Raster* at that price, he would receive a 12 percent commission, payable out of each installment reaching Kleinberg. Szczepanik was then at work on two more advanced design machines, one nearing completion, one still on the drawing board. To sweeten the deal Clemens could have the rights to the second machine at 10 percent less than "the best offer by anyone else" and first refusal of the American rights to "No. 3" (a machine for weaving cloth from peat moss) when it was patented.

On the seventeenth a Mr. William M. Wood, representing an unnamed American carpet manufacturer, arrived from Paris in hot pursuit of the rights to Szczepanik's invention. "He is a very charming man," Clemens gloated, "but he is exactly one day too late—which seems to show that I am a more charming man than he is." They chatted "very pleasantly" for two hours, but Clemens demurred and abruptly changed the subject when Wood asked him to name a price for his option. "I was afraid he would offer me half a million dollars for it. I should have ~~felt~~ been obliged to take it," he explained, adding: "But I was born with the speculative instinct & I did not want that temptation put in my way." [†4] The contract on which Clemens and Kleinberg had shaken hands still needed to be written and signed before a notary. With Wood "nibbling" at his option, Clemens had "three days of mute discomfort—during which I chewed my bowels."[5]

His fears were groundless. Kleinberg remained steadfast and circumspect, referring all of Wood's inquiries to Clemens. Clemens described their colloquy to Rogers with what is known in German as *Schadenfreude* (glee at another's discomfiture):

> So he (Wood) came to me at once. Was there a machine which he could see? I said I didn't know. What—hadn't I seen it? No, I hadn't. Was I actually taking an option on a thing which I had never seen? Yes, that was what I was doing. Would I mind explaining why I was acting in this way? Yes; because *my* evidence wouldn't be worth anything; my men were business men; they would value none but evidence furnished by experts— experts of their own selection. He thought it strange. Surely I must tell my men *something* to proceed upon; would I mind saying what it was? I said I was quite willing—I was merely proceeding upon *circumstantial* evidence.[6]

Whereupon Clemens launched into a wearisome disquisition on the details of his "circumstantial" evidence before delivering his coup de grace: "A week ago you seemed to be kind of indifferent: no time to fool away. . . . *But here you are yet.* . . . And without knowing the terms of my option, you are asking me to name the *cash* profit at which I will sell. . . . Don't you notice that you are furnishing me some circumstantial evidence yourself? And don't you begin to believe that as between sworn testimony and circumstantial evidence the advantage is quite likely to be with the latter?" Clemens concludes this account with a "generous" offer to make an appointment for the two of them to view the *Raster* together at Szczepanik's laboratory the following Friday (March 25), savoring his victory by noting Wood's "parting flattery" that "You don't seem to be as much of a fool as you look."[7]

Ironically, this was no victory at all. Although he could not foresee it, not negotiating immediate sale of his option to his competitor was another huge error in Clemens's business judgment, if one that cost nothing save the loss of a profitable deal. It was not to be a reprise of disastrous investments like those he had made a decade earlier in James D. Paige's unworkable typesetting machine. It was more like his allegedly spurning a chance to be one of the first investors in Alexander Graham Bell's "crazy" invention in 1877. Lacking capital of his own with which to speculate, Clemens had gambled this time on Henry Rogers's backing to obtain and profitably sell the rights to Szczepanik's machines, and he was headed for disappointment.

Between March 17 and the end of May 1898, Clemens wrote Rogers almost weekly, passionately but vainly arguing his case for the American patent rights to the *Raster*. The letter recounting his "victory" tactics over Wood is the cleverest, most subtle of his attempts to persuade Rogers to this investment. Other letters are loaded with statistics on the machine, of figures on the investments being made in it in Germany, Britain, and elsewhere in Europe, and glowing accounts of advances Szczepanik was making in auxiliary machines. He frantically urged Rogers to come to Vienna immediately to see the prototypes himself, offering free room and board (hardly an enticement to a multimillionaire!), or "if there is a war here" to meet him in Germany

Szczepanik's *Raster* photo device (from *Herstellung von Jacquard-Patronen auf photographischen Weg*, 1899)

Szczepanik's *Raster* card looming device (from *Herstellung von Jacquard-Patronen auf photographischen Weg*, 1899)

to see the *Raster* already in use there. Rogers's replies are not extant, but it is not difficult to discern his stance and tactics from Clemens's increasingly crestfallen responses. At first, Rogers stalled for time to make a thorough investigation of the market prospects in the United States. Then he began sending discouraging reports of his findings, suggesting the machine would be a poor investment risk in the American weaving industries as they were then constituted. Finally, the onset of war with Spain made such an investment seem even riskier. In May, Clemens's option expired, and having meanwhile picked up some negative information on his own, he decided against extending it.[8]

By then, however, Clemens had become firm friends with the inventor himself. Born and reared in a remote rural village (Krosno) in eastern Galicia, then a Polish province of the Austro-Hungarian Empire, Jan Szczepanik was twenty-five years old when Mark Twain described him as a man of great personal charm and magnetism who had "black hair, very striking face, mobile & alert, splendid eyes."[†9] Educated at a teachers' seminary in Krakow, Szczepanik was virtually an autodidact in mechanics and electrical engineering. He was teaching school in rural Galicia and dabbling at various electrical inventions when the banker Ludwig Kleinberg heard of him and brought him to the imperial capital in 1895 to exploit and market his inventions, setting him up in commodious quarters at Ungargasse 12 in Vienna's third district and engaging a staff of trained assistants. Kleinberg obviously hoped to reap a huge fortune as Szczepanik's capitalist.

Mark Twain was tremendously impressed with both the Polish inventor and his Viennese backer. On April 2, 1898, he wrote Richard Watson Gilder, editor of the *Century*, that Szczepanik was "an interesting young creature" who "comes and drinks beer with me every now and then, and talks till midnight. Is well born, educated, dresses nicely, and is an echte [*sic*] gentleman. He was a village school teacher in the provinces a few years ago, with a salary in proportion; but he is comfortable, now, and has a laboratory 3 or 4 stories high, in the centre of Vienna, and has inventions enough in his head to fill it to the roof."[10] During his summer in Kaltenleutgeben, Twain made several lengthy bicycling excursions with Szczepanik and his partner.

In his notebook he described the "fine laboratory" as also containing a "nicely furnished bedroom, parlor, bathroom, etc. for [Szczepanik] himself." Then, reflecting on the symbiotic relationship between inventor and patron, he mused:

These two men belong together. They are necessary to each other; both are honorable gentlemen; each appreciates the other's value.

The whole of the vast modern material civilization is the creation of a combination of Inventor & Fool. The Fool has been exactly as necessary as the Inventor. It was he that furnished the money to develop the inventions & prove their value—then the Wise Man came forward & occupied the stately Mansion prepared by the Inventor & the Fool, & transferred these latter to the Almshouse.

There have always been Inventors; abundance of them; in all countries, in all the centuries—but in all the centuries, in all the countries, the Fool was lacking. That lack made inventive genius absolutely worthless, hence the material world stood still, advanced hardly a step in a thousand years.

It was America that produced the Fool; that stupendous credit is wholly hers. The Car of Progress had stood motionless & waiting since Adam's time. Am[erica] hitched the Fool to it—behold the result!—a century of inventive miracles! †11

America's contribution of "the Fool" he sees as the direct consequence of the first United States Patent Act in 1794 which gave inventors rights they could sell to "the Fool" investor. Some eighty years later, he notes, Europe imitated America with its own patent laws. The "Wise Man" is the johnny-come-lately who "steps in & makes a vast fortune out of their work" after both Fool and Inventor have exhausted their resources establishing the practical value of an invention. He is, in a way, a kind of dull, unimaginative parasite that Twain calls "a mere mercantile ass."

It was Szczepanik's "extraordinary luck" at the outset of his career to have found a man like Kleinberg who combined the traits of both Fool and Wise Man, and this good luck, Clemens thinks, "has saved the two from the customary fate—the poorhouse." He concludes with an unusually candid assessment of his own perspicacity: "Szczepanik is not a Paige, but a gentleman; his backer, Mr. Kleinberg is a gentleman, too, yet is *not* a Clemens—that is to say, he is not an Ass."†[12]

In actuality, Kleinberg was much less astute than Twain judged him in his handling of Szczepanik's inventions. The *Fernseher*, or telectroscope, might have had significance for the development of telecommunications in tandem with the achievements of Guglielmo Marconi, who first transmitted long-wave radio signals in 1895, and Lee De Forest, whose vacuum tube made television practicable. Kleinberg, however, sequestered the invention too long by selling exclusive rights to a French syndicate to exhibit it first at the Paris Exposition of 1900. That important event passed without the *Fernseher* being exhibited. Whether its French concessionaires had meanwhile developed doubts about its viability or were intentionally sidetracking it to protect some other investment, they effectively killed it. By 1901 Marconi transmitted radio signals across the Atlantic, and rapid developments thereafter in wireless telegraphy preempted interest in Szczepanik's telectroscope, in effect rendering it obsolete. Amelia Levetus commented ruefully in 1912, "After a time excitement cooled down with regard to the 'distance-seer' and it has long sunk into oblivion and will remain dark till some other man strikes the same path when he will want it for reference."[13] Szczepanik's *Raster* (design machine) sold well enough when put into production, but its market was soon exhausted, and neither he nor Kleinberg made any great fortune from this enterprise. Eventually he returned to his native Poland, resumed his teaching career, and died there in obscurity in 1926.

One of Ludwig Kleinberg's cleverer publicity stunts in his efforts to market Szczepanik's *Raster* was to have another Pole, the painter Heinrich Rauchinger, do a chalk portrait of Mark Twain which, with the author's signature on it, was copied by the design machine onto a piece of cloth "the size of a large handkerchief" in cream and black silk threads.[14] Twain was so taken with Rauchinger's portrait that he had it reproduced on postcards by Dagobert Wlaschim, who supplied the author with gratis copies in return for exclusive rights to market the cards in Austria-Hungary.

Although Samuel L. Clemens, would-be tycoon, lost a chance to make money on Jan Szczepanik's inventions, Mark Twain did not squander his chance to make literary capital of the man he called "the Austrian Edison" (though actually a Pole, Szczepanik was then an Austrian citizen) and his ill-fated *Fernseher*. In the October and November 1898 issues of the *Century* magazine, he published two pieces on these subjects written early in his stay at the Villa Paulhof. The first, a brief article entitled "The Austrian Edison Keeping School Again," dashed off in mid-June, is a subtle satire masquerading as reportage. The second, "From the 'London Times' of 1904," is a short story in the genre known today as science fiction. Both pieces were later included in the collected edition of Twain's works.

"The Austrian Edison" is an amusing impressionistic trifle about a quite typically Austrian bureaucratic ruse whereby Szczepanik avoided compulsory service in the *k. u. k. Armee*. As a schoolteacher, Szczepanik had an occupational exemption from military duty. Under the Austro-Hungarian conscription law, teaching was considered "alternative service," and had he remained at his school post continuously a year or so longer, he would have fulfilled his military obligation. When he went to Vienna to work, however, he lost his exemption and was in immediate danger of being called up. Loath to take the inventor from his laboratory and put him to bayonet practice in peacetime, the authorities, as Twain put it, "labored at it until they found a forgotten law somewhere which furnished a loophole."

The solution was to reinstate Szczepanik as a schoolmaster, requiring him to return to his village every two months to teach for a half-day. Mark Twain adds, tongue in cheek, that "to the best of my understanding . . . he must keep this up the rest of his life! I hope so, just for the romantic poeticalness of it." He then engages in some comical statistics to show that, if Szczepanik lives to a ripe age and teaches 396 half-days, he must make 396 round-trips by rail from Vienna to his school, "pay bed and board 396 times in the village, and lose possibly 1,200 days from his laboratory work. . . ." The utter illogic of this *Schlamperei* "solution" is thus exposed and then buttressed with the ironic comment: "I know the inventor very well, and he has my sympathy. This is friendship. But I am throwing my influence with the government. This is politics."[15]

Twain ends "The Austrian Edison" by describing impressionistically (perhaps from newspaper accounts) Szczepanik's first half-day of teaching "under his sentence." He is met by jubilant crowds at the railway station in "his village in Moravia [sic]" and conducted in state "in a fine carriage" to his school. There Twain imagines the inventor leading his charges in "a holiday dance through the enchanted lands of science" after which Szczepanik drives off "under a storm of 'Do widzenia!' (Au revoir!) from the children." Twain then editorializes, "It is out of materials like these that romances are woven; and when the romancer has done his best, he has not improved upon the unpainted facts."

"From the 'London Times' of 1904" is a puzzling, not altogether satisfactory blend of fact and fancy. It narrates events supposedly occurring in Chicago between April 1 and 23, 1904 (some six years after it was written and published), as reported to the *London Times* by "correspondent" Mark Twain involving the inventor Szczepanik as one of its two main characters. The other is a fictional American army officer, Captain Clayton. As exposition, Twain "recollects" their first meeting in Vienna on March 31, 1898, when the two had quarreled about the practicability and usefulness of Szczepanik's telectroscope and had engaged in a scuffle before being separated. He then shifts to Chicago in 1901 whence Szczepanik has supposedly gone following his success at the Paris Exposition with his telectroscope and its subsequent introduction into "the telephonic systems of the whole world" whereby "the daily doings of the globe [are] made visible to everybody, and audibly discussable, too, by witnesses separated by any number of leagues."

Here the inventor again encounters Clayton, and resuming their Vienna quarrel of 1898, the two must again be separated by witnesses on three different occasions. Soon thereafter Szczepanik unaccountably disappears, and two months later the corpse of a murdered man, misidentified as Szczepanik, is found in Clayton's cellar. Clayton is tried and sentenced to death for murdering the inventor despite his continual protestations of innocence. After several reprieves by the governor, whose niece is Clayton's wife, the day of execution finally arrives, but Clayton is saved on the gallows by the telectroscope which reveals Szczepanik alive and well in Peking where he had fled incognito to escape his celebrity.

This happy ending is soon bitterly reversed. Following public clamor for Clayton to be tried again because "*a man was killed,* and Clayton killed him," he is arraigned before the United States Supreme Court, whose fictional chief justice, satirically named "Lemaître," opens the retrial with:

> "It is my opinion that this matter is quite simple. The prisoner at the bar was charged with murdering the man Szczepanik; he was tried for murdering the man Szczepanik; he was fairly tried, and justly convicted and sentenced to death for murdering Szczepanik. It turns out that the man Szczepanik was not murdered at all. By the decision of the French courts in the Dreyfus matter, it is established beyond cavil or question that the decisions of courts are permanent and cannot be revised. . . . The prisoner at the bar has been fairly and righteously condemned to death for the murder of the man Szczepanik, and, in my opinion, there is but one course to pursue in the matter: he must be hanged."

Despite strenuous efforts by others on the bench to counter Lemaître's argument, he prevails. When an opposing justice insists that "Szczepanik is still alive," Lemaître responds: "So is Dreyfus." On this "logic," Clayton is executed despite, this time, a public outcry against the miscarriage of justice. "Correspondent" Twain concludes his report to London, "all America is vocal with scorn of 'French justice,' and of the malignant little soldiers who invented it and inflicted it upon the other Christian lands." [16]

As a work of fiction, "From the 'London Times' of 1904" is decidedly inferior, but as a polemic against "French justice" in the Dreyfus affair, then a matter of great topical interest, it hits the bullseye. Perhaps Clemens's argument about the value of "circumstantial evidence" in his jousts with William Wood over the option on Szczepanik's *Raster* provided Mark Twain the strategy for linking a story about Szczepanik to the "circumstantial" Dreyfus case and with another of Szczepanik's inventions, the *Fernseher*, as the means of obtaining hard prima facie evidence to refute the specious circumstantial. The difficulty with this tale is that Twain allowed his moral indignation to override his artistry. Unlike the masterful "Man That Corrupted Hadleyburg," which he wrote a few weeks later, this parable of injustice can only be understood in the context of events and circumstances in which it was written. Even so, the story is based on a miscalculation about the future of Szczepanik's *Fernseher* which makes the gimmick, intended as rational and realistic, incomprehensible to today's readers except as pure fantasy.

Samuel Clemens's dealings with Kleinberg and Mark Twain's literary uses of Jan Szczepanik and his invention are twin expressions of the writer's constant fascination with technology and gadgetry and the man's capacity for self-delusion concerning his entrepreneurial skills. In both, he was a thoroughly representative American. For instance, he was almost childishly proud of having one of the first three domestic telephones in Hartford, and he boasted proudly, if perhaps inaccurately, that *Adventures of Huckleberry Finn* was the first novel to have its manuscript typewritten. He dabbled with inventions himself and patented a "self-pasting" scrapbook and a history game for children. Moreover, he naively believed he possessed business acumen that, with the right technological investments, could make him at least the equal of Carnegie, Rockefeller, or other tycoons of the age whom he both admired and scorned. More than most Americans, he revered Thomas A. Edison, "the wizard of East Orange," whose laboratory he visited several times. Hence, dubbing Jan Szczepanik an "Edison," whether Austrian or Polish, was the highest compliment he could have paid any inventor.

On the other hand, Mark Twain was blessed with double vision about what most Americans then believed to be the benefits of technological progress. One of his most hilariously satirical characters, for instance, is the jejune Colonel Sellers in *The Gilded Age* and *The American Claimant*, a walking anthology of get-rich-quick schemes involving patent medicines or preposterous machines. And much of his best humor in *A Connecticut Yankee* comes from Hank Morgan's botched attempts to bring progress to Camelot by, among other things, mounting the Knights of the Round Table on bicycles and sending them questing in the countryside in sandwich boards advertising soap and toothbrushes. So when he writes Rogers that "I feel like Col. Sellers" at the onset of negotiations for an option on Szczepanik's designing machine, one senses a redeeming element of self-doubt as Twain, the writer, scoffs at Clemens, the entrepreneur, too.

Moreover, Clemens's costly attraction to James D. Paige's cumbersome, unworkable typesetting machine should not be misconstrued. A natural interest for someone whose first trade had been printing, it was simple bad luck that Ottmar Mergenthaler had patented his more compact, highly successful Linotype at about the same time. In other words, it should be emphasized that, rather than being understood as an easy mark for every Rube Goldberg device that came along, he made it a point to keep abreast of scientific, technological, and industrial developments in newspaper reports and articles in such popular journals as *Scientific American* and *Review of Reviews* and to inform himself as quickly and thoroughly as possible on any new discovery or invention that struck his fancy. One indication of this interest may be seen in the account of Hermann C. Balicer, a young photographic assistant in Szczepanik's Vienna laboratory in 1898, who wrote almost a half-century later: "I well remember the morning that Mark Twain made the first of his many visits to the laboratory. Szczepanik showed him our several inventions, both finished and in preparation; the writer's grasp of the mechanical difficulties was amazingly accurate. He was deeply absorbed in the demonstrations."[17]

Given Clemens's initial enthusiasm and the widespread publicity both the *Raster* and *Fernseher* evoked in 1898, it is perhaps ironic that the "Austrian Edison" lives today almost entirely in the two slight pieces Mark Twain wrote about him in Kaltenleutgeben. In reference books on the history of modern science and electronics, Jan Szczepanik merits no more than passing mention or a footnote. Might he have achieved more had he received recognition and encouragement from the authoritarian state of whose absolute monarch he was then a subject? Edison, Steinmetz, and Westinghouse, then producing electrical marvels in the United States, needed no such stimuli. Austria-Hungary, Twain noted, offered a much less congenial intellectual climate to its *Gelehrten*. Before he had lived two months in Vienna, on November 19, 1897, he wrote Twichell that "the country cannot afford to *allow* great names to grow up . . . can't afford to have geniuses springing up and developing ideas and stirring the public soul." Then he added this revealing anecdote:

> Three days ago the New York World sent and asked a friend of mine (correspondent of a London daily) to get some Christmas greetings from the celebrities of the Empire. She spoke of this.[18] Two or three bright Austrians were present. They said: "There are none who are known all over the world! none who have achieved fame; none who can point to their work and say it is known far and wide in the earth: there are no *names;* Kossuth (known because he had a father) and Lecher, who made the 12-hour speech; two names—nothing more. Every other country in the world, perhaps, has a giant or two whose heads are away up and can be seen, but ours. We've got the *material*—have always had it—but we have to suppress it; we can't afford to let it develop; our political salvation depends upon tranquility—always has." [19]

The Austrians whose conversation Twain capsulized here had, of course, overlooked the septuagenarian Johann Strauss, Jr., who was then certainly world famous, but the Waltz King was perhaps the one exception to their general indictment of a regime that remained to its end officially indifferent to the achievements of its intellectual, scientific, and artistic communities. No doubt his awareness of this situation accounts in part for Mark Twain's hyperbolic treatment of Szczepanik, one of the unsung "poets in steel," as he called inventors.

In any case, it is quite clear his disillusionment with "the infernal machine" (Paige's typesetter) was not a generalized one. It had endured only until his first encounter with Jan Szczepanik. Nor was even this deflated scheme the end of his pursuit of fortune from supposedly sci-

entific sources. During his second winter in Vienna he heard through
Ambassador Tower about a nutritive food supplement, which he at
first refers to as "the Vienna albumen," being made from dried, pow-
dered skim milk which, if properly developed, could end famine in
the world and be a panacea for most human ailments. Or so the Mulberry Sellers within Samuel L. Clemens easily convinced himself. Investments in "Plasmon," which became the trade name of this protein
derivative in various marketing enterprises—the American Plasmon
Company, the Plasmon Products Company, and the British Plasmon
Syndicate—with which Clemens was heavily involved off and on for a
decade thereafter, eventually earned him very little money.[20] No matter. His greed was undeniable, almost of mythic proportions, but it
was really the entrepreneurial game that captivated him again and yet
again. This oft-burnt child seemed to fear no fire. His love affair with
the machine, with the fruits of science and technology, ended only at
the grave.

CHAPTER ELEVEN

Home Thoughts

By the summer of 1898 Samuel Clemens was intensely home-sick. He had not glimpsed his native shores in three years, his longest unbroken stretch abroad, and he had spent altogether barely twelve months since June 1891 at widely separated intervals in visits to Hartford or Elmira or New York. Transatlantic telephone service was still in the distant future, but he had kept in close touch with those back home by letter and, when urgent, by cable. Packet boats and passenger liners then plied the North Atlantic with mail year round, and if one was as alert as Clemens to sailing schedules, one could expect an answer in Vienna to a business letter to New York in only about a week longer than such exchanges usually take by air today. Still, weekly correspondence with Henry Rogers and, less often, with Joseph Twichell, W. D. Howells, and others was a poor substitute for personal visits. What he now called his "Austrian exile" had begun to seem endless.

In early March he told a *New York World* correspondent he was "terribly homesick."[1] His frenetic but vain efforts to capitalize his option on American rights to Szczepanik's inventions then gave him little time to brood upon his homeward yearnings. Nevertheless, his feelings are obvious in his repeated invitations to friends and relations to come over to Vienna or Kaltenleutgeben (as several did) and in his noting poignantly to Rogers that "Jean is deadly homesick, but Clara has to stay here a year yet, to study music, and the rest of us must stay, too, for Mrs. Clemens will not hear of the family ever being divided again.

But I suppose we couldn't go home anyway, for we are not able to live in our house. And I don't suppose we could afford a flat in New York."[2]

In July he contemplated a quick trip alone to New York to settle a disputed book contract with the Harpers, but then he told Rogers, "the family will not allow me to leave them," adding, "if we all go it would end Clara's music in the middle and the past twelvemonth would be wasted." He gave it as "the madam's" decision "that now that we have endured this Austrian exile a year for Clara's sake, she must complete the job, not leave it half finished." He rationalized this with a characteristic self-accusation: "Well, I robbed the family to feed my speculations, and so I am willing to accommodate myself to their preferences."[3] On August 16, as the Clemenses were departing Kaltenleutgeben for a ten-day excursion in the Salzkammergut, he repeated the "exile" theme to Howells: "We are all hoping to end our long exile in the spring & see you then & have a time!"[4]

Not that the Phaeacian pleasures of Vienna had palled. Quite the contrary, he was enjoying himself as he had not since before Susy's death. But he was also hungry for the familiar sights and sounds, tastes and smells of the homeland and almost overcome with nostalgia. His longing for home and the past which colored most of what he wrote in 1898 may have been triggered by the unexpected news of his brother's death on December 11, 1897, another close tie gone, another family funeral like Susy's he had to miss while abroad. However deeply the death of Orion may have grieved him, his notation of it is strangely unemotional, even taciturn: "Cablegram from Keokuk 'Orion died to-day.' He was past 73." Then on December 30, "No letter from Mollie yet; we do not know whether it was sudden or not."[†5] Nothing further except this brief mention to Rogers on December 16: "Clara and I had started into society, and were dining and lunching and going to operas, and getting at times cheerful once more; . . . but we are all once more under a cloud, through the death of my brother, and have resumed our former seclusion."[6] Whatever "seclusion" he may have intended, he simply found it impossible to withdraw from social life at this time, the height of the Vienna season, for more than a fortnight.

Eleven years Samuel Clemens's senior, Orion had once been more like a surrogate father than brother to him, though in later life those roles almost reversed themselves. After their father's death ended young Sam's formal schooling, he followed in Orion's footsteps to learn the printing trade and, as a journeyman, worked for Orion on newspapers in Hannibal and Muscatine, Iowa—jobs that probably determined the future course of his peripatetic life. In July 1861, after deserting his three-week stint in a ragtag Confederate militia unit, Sam had gone west with Orion on the overland stage and had found there his true vocation and nom de plume. Thereafter their careers diverged, but Orion was never far from his brother's thoughts nor, on occasion, from his checkbook because of Orion's often impecunious circumstances in the years when Mark Twain was most successful. Fictionalized in numerous guises, Orion unknowingly repaid his famous brother many times over in story after story, even in Vienna where he turns up one last time as Oliver Hotchkiss in the second ("Schoolhouse Hill") draft version of "The Mysterious Stranger" manuscripts.

Notices of Orion's death, coupled with the reported illness in London of a distant cousin, Dr. James Ross Clemens, prompted one of Mark Twain's most often quoted and misquoted witticisms. A rumor had spread in New York pressrooms during late 1897 that Mark Twain had died in Vienna. When a Viennese correspondent received an urgent request from the *New York World*—"If Mark Twain very ill, 500 words, if dead 1,000"—Twain scribbled a note: "The report of my illness grew out of his illness, the report of my death was an exaggeration." Vienna's newspapers had a jolly time with the story, savoring the version he translated for them: *"Nachrichten über meinen Tod stark übertrieben"* (The report of my death [is] grossly exaggerated).[7]

Even before Orion's death Mark Twain's thoughts were turning homeward in his writing. During the summer in Weggis he had returned imaginatively to Saint Petersburg (his fictional Hannibal) for yet another mining of the rich Tom and Huck vein. He completed four chapters of an excellently plotted, carefully wrought novelette,

Tom Sawyer's Conspiracy, before temporarily setting it aside in Vienna. Although he returned to it sporadically later and tinkered with it for years, he never quite finished what is arguably the best of his Huck Finn sequels, certainly superior to either *Tom Sawyer Abroad* or *Tom Sawyer, Detective.* It was first published in 1969 together with a piece begun in Weggis and continued (but also left unfinished) in Vienna. This sketch, "The Villagers of 1840–43," is a phenomenal feat of memory, cataloguing with disguised names 168 residents of Hannibal in his youth, in many instances giving unflattering, even unsavory details about them. It breaks off abruptly in the middle of his depiction of Orion ("Oscar Carpenter" here), as if he might have been working on it at the moment when news of his brother's death arrived.

On May 20 the Clemenses ended their eight-month residence at the Hotel Metropole to *Sommerfrisch,* as Austrians call moving out to rusticate and mingle with the landscape for the warm months, at the edge of the Wienerwald (Vienna Woods). "We are securing a nice house, satisfactorily furnished, at a little health-resort an hour from Vienna— beautiful woods all about," he wrote Rogers on April 29, adding: "For company there will be a number of old Vienna friends. If a Revolution should happen here we shall pull out and go to Cuba. Or to Spain, or some other health-resort." This last, of course, is a jocular reference to the just-begun war with Spain over Cuba.

They had rented from a Dr. Holzacker a furnished villa with capacious grounds at the western edge of the village, and here they settled for the next five months. The Villa Paulhof, as it was then called (now Sonnenhof), built in 1884, contains eight sizable rooms (200 square meters of floor space in all) plus front and back balconies. Set in a walled half-acre lot with a large back garden beyond which is a hillside grove of firs, the villa and its grounds afforded space to stretch and to breathe in the country air.

Clemens was irked, however, at having to pay the entire five months' rent in advance without provisions for a refund. What if the house burned down the first night? The agent's reply, "I have other houses—

you can have one of those," seemed evasive. "We have examined every house in the place—there is not another that would *begin* to suit," Clemens protested, but that led only to this exasperating colloquy:

> "I should do the best I could for you."
> "The best you could do would be a long way from satisfactory."
> "One can but do one's best."
> "You don't suggest refunding the money."
> "It is not the custom."
> "When a man comes to the cure, he knows its term is 6 weeks & that he must be under the doctor's advice all that time. Does the doctor collect the whole fee in advance?"
> "Oh, no."
> "Why not?"
> "The man m——"
> "Go on. You were going to say the man might die."
> "Yes."
> "Just as the house might burn down."[8]

No use. Custom was custom in Austria, not to be questioned, disobeyed, or changed.

In March, their housekeeper for the past seventeen years, Katy Leary, was called home to Elmira unexpectedly, and she remained away until the last few weeks of their Villa Paulhof sojourn. To keep house nonetheless required servants, so they advertised, only to discover the applicants' glowing references were not trustworthy because Austrian law required employers to give only a good character reference (*Gutachten*) to any discharged servant who wanted one. The truth about an applicant could be learned only by going to a former employer personally to solicit his or her private opinion.[9] Notwithstanding such oddities, by the time they settled in Kaltenleutgeben they had engaged what Mark Twain described as four "good-natured & friendly, & capable & willing" domestics: a cook, two maids, and a general handywoman. On June 4 he wrote, "We have been housekeeping a fortnight, now—long enough to have learned how to pronounce the servants' names, but not to spell them; we shan't ever learn how

Villa Paulhof, Karlsgasse 3, in Kaltenleutgeben (Lower Austria), where
Mark Twain lived from May until October, 1898

to spell them; they were invented in Hungary & Poland, & on paper they look like the alphabet out on a drunk." † 10

One of the maids, whom Twain had nicknamed "Wuthering Heights" because her actual name sounded something like that to him, greatly annoyed "the Executive," as he dubbed Olivia in an aborted sketch about their domestic problems at the Villa Paulhof. "Quick, smart, active, energetic, breezy, good-natured," she also had "a high-keyed voice & a loud one" in which she "talks thirteen to the dozen" and incessantly. What "gravelled the family," especially Olivia, about her was not merely her loquacity but her meddlesome, bossy habits. In the sketch he wrote, Twain pretends not to speak German so she will not bother him, but he eavesdrops on her altercations with "the Executive" because "it spices the monotony." The family's efforts at "always training her, always caulking her" are futile, he says, because "as fast as they stop one leak she will spring another." She blithely shrugs off all criticism with "It's Viennese, gnädige Frau. Custom you see; that's just it. We all do it, it's Viennese." Still, he enjoys the spectacle: "Her talk is my circus, my menagerie, my fireworks, my spiritual refreshment. When she is at it I would rather be there than at a fire."

One reason he may have jettisoned the sketch after seventeen manuscript pages leading nowhere is that his efforts to communicate the humorous incongruity of the situation with appropriate local color and to render Viennese dialect in English were faltering. Despite a few German words sprinkled here and there, "Wuthering Heights" comes out sounding rather Irish, more Katy Leary than Austrian *Stubemädel*. When, for instance, "the Executive" reprimands her for turning away a caller from Vienna for fear of disturbing Mark Twain at his work, asking how the maid knew he was working, "Wuthering Heights" responds: "Know it? Oh, indeed, and well I knew it; for he was that busy that the sweat was leaking through the floor, and I said to the cook, said I ———." † 11 Obviously, his usually keen ear for idiomatic speech had failed him in Kaltenleutgeben.

The resort community, though barely twenty-five kilometers (15.5 miles) from the city center, was still distinctly rural. It did not have

a quarry and cement works at the edge of town and gray stucco suburban apartment houses to mar its prettiness and give it the somewhat
drab industrial look it has since acquired. Not very far from the hunting lodge (now a convent) at Mayerling, where Crown Prince Rudolf
and his mistress were murdered nine years earlier, most of the land
around Kaltenleutgeben in 1898 was still a fiefdom of farms, orchards,
vineyards, and villages belonging to the princely house of Liechtenstein. Unless one owned or hired an equipage, it was accessible from
Vienna only by a train which the impatient Mark Twain pronounced
"the slowest in the world," although the trip took less than an hour.
One boarded at the Sudbahnhof on the main Southern Railway line
and changed at Liesing, on the outskirts of the city, to a branch line as-
cending gradually through Perchtolsdorf 4.5 miles to what Baedeker
described as "a charming village with numerous villas and two hydrotherapics, in the valley of the Dürre Liesing [river]." [12]

The "hydrotherapics" (*Wasserheilanstalt*) belonged to the illustrious
founder of the "Austrian cold water cure," the Bohemian-born Jewish
physician Dr. Wilhelm Winternitz (1834–1917) whose Spartan regimen attracted patients thither from among royalty and nobility, the
rich and the famous of central and eastern Europe. Fürst Otto von
Bismarck came there in 1895; the dying Burgtheater actress Charlotte
Wolters, in 1897; and during the Clemenses' sojourn Queen Elisabeth
of Romania, by birth a German princess who wrote popular novels
and stories in several languages under the pen name Carmen Sylva,
was one of their neighbors as was the Austrian writer Ferdinand von
Saar. If Kaltenleutgeben never acquired the éclat of a Bad Nauheim, a
Marienbad, or an Aix-les-Bains, all of which the Clemenses had visited
earlier, it may have been because one did not patronize a luxury spa
hotel there (it had none!) to drink the mineral waters or take a week's
or fortnight's thermal cure. One had to remain six weeks or more and
rent a cottage or villa.

Dr. Winternitz's treatment facility (*Kuranstalt*) straddled the Dürre
Liesing, a narrow stream (hardly more than a brook at that point)
cascading out of the mountains to join the Reiche Liesing, then the

main river Liesing itself, and eventually the Danube. The water in this stream never exceeds ten degrees Celsius (fifty degrees Fahrenheit), and the good doctor's "cure" was to have his patients plunge into it at seven o'clock every morning, then run up a broad path cleared through the woods on a steep hill, appropriately named "Doktorberg" (Doctor's Mountain), to a meadow where they engaged in some calisthenics and then ran down again to take another cold plunge followed by a hot bath and home to breakfast. The cure lasted a minimum of six weeks during which Dr. Winternitz or an assistant examined each patient every two days, frequently prescribing extra plunges, massages for arthritic joints, and naturopathic medicines such as *Kräutertee* (herbal teas) and elixirs from the roots of various plants. The cure was alleged to be particularly effective for *Kreislauf, Rheuma,* and *Nervenkrankheit* (circulation, rheumatism, and nervous disorders).

Dr. Winternitz had called in person at the Metropole on March 28 to examine the Clemens women "to see if the Kaltenleutgeben baths will suit the complexion of their ailments." †[13] It seemed a foregone conclusion the answer would be affirmative, but it was Olivia and Jean, without Clara, who actually took the cure. A notorious late riser, Clemens would in no way submit himself to a regimen that commenced at 7 A.M. and involved such strenuous, kinesthetically repulsive activity. Moreover, he was skeptical of its efficacy. On July 10, when their course was almost finished, he admitted he was "not happy about this water-cure. I expected it to do great things for Mrs. Clemens, but I think she is not as strong as she was when she began. It may be that the benefit comes *after* the course. I hope so."[14]

For him, Kaltenleutgeben provided an opportunity for one of his favorite pastimes—hiking, in the mountains that ringed the village— and for cycling through the valley with various friends, including Jan Szczepanik, who brought his *Velociped* by train from Vienna on occasional Sundays. On a good day, one could hike in about an hour and a half to the summit of the Höllenstein, some 654 meters (2,120 feet) above the village on the south, where a Roman-built tower (*Julienthurm*) gave a magnificent prospect, in the best weather, of Vienna and its suburbs to the north, the Wienerwald to west and south, and the Danube plains on the east. Unluckily, the weather, at least until late that summer, was seldom the best. It was unseasonably cold and rainy, and Mark Twain is locally quoted (probably apocryphally) as complaining, after his first hike on the Höllenstein, "I viewed the mist and missed the view." Except for an occasional day now and again, it did not become really summer-like until about the time the Clemens family went for an excursion in the Salzkammergut from August 16 to 27.

If ever there was an instance of meteorological conditions influencing literature, this was it. The astonishing amount of writing Mark Twain accomplished in Kaltenleutgeben—unusually large even for someone who habitually did most of his writing during the summer months and despite an active social life at the spa—is directly attributable to the cool, damp weather that often forced him to stay indoors at his desk rather than take some of the long walks he desired. Of course, the weather did not determine what or how he wrote. His subjects and the manner of his dealing with them came from other stimuli within him and in his physical and social environment. Homesickness was one, and it was reinforced by the rural village itself. Perhaps even more than Weggis, and despite its alpine scenery and mild climate, it reminded him of Hannibal, acting upon him in much the same way as Quarry Farm had in the many summers he had spent writing in his octagonal gazebo there. In his walks he traversed fields and farms that, saving a few architectural details, could be transported back to the Missouri of his childhood. These daily reminders inspired one of his most creative descents into the lost antebellum world of his youth. For him, the vineyards of the Wienerwald produced "the reviving wine of the past, the pathetic past, the beautiful past, the dear and lamented past."[15]

"I can call it all back and make it as real as it ever was, and as blessed," he wrote in "Early Days." Along with seven other chapters sketched in Kaltenleutgeben and Vienna, this is irrefutably the best, most enduring part of his autobiography. Unfortunately, it has had many confusing permutations, from the chapters (including these) he published in the *North American Review* in 1906 and 1907, to the voluminous jumble of reminiscences he scribbled and dictated during the next decade from which Paine carved his two-volume posthumous pastiche, to still later compilations by DeVoto and Charles G. Neider.

What Twain originally intended in the memoirs he started at this juncture was not a cohesive autobiography but a series of vignettes to append to such earlier works as *The Gilded Age*, *The Adventures of Tom Sawyer*, *Adventures of Huckleberry Finn*, and others, as glosses on the sources of episodes, the originals of characters, and details from his life experiences. By incorporating such information, he could republish them as "new" works, thus extending their copyright life to benefit his heirs.

"The farm" is the talisman, the mnemonic device that triggers in Mark Twain one of the most eloquent, splendidly orchestrated chains of recollected sense impression in all literature. "The farm" of his nostalgic reverie is that of his Uncle John Quarles where he spent his summer until he was twelve and which he had fictionalized as the Phelps farm in *Huck Finn* and *Tom Sawyer, Detective*. His epiphany begins with a catalogue of gustatory pleasures:

> Fried chicken, roast pig; wild and tame turkeys, ducks, and geese; venison just killed; squirrels, rabbits, pheasants, partridges, prairie-chickens; biscuits, hot batter cakes, hot buckwheat cakes, hot "white bread," hot rolls, hot corn pone; fresh corn boiled on the ear, succotash, butter-beans, string-beans, tomatoes, peas, Irish potatoes, sweet potatoes; buttermilk, sweet milk, "clabber"; watermelons, muskmelons, cantaloupes—all fresh from the garden; apple pie, peach pie, pumpkin pie, apple dumplings, peach cobbler. . . .

This leads directly to remembering how these delicacies were cooked —a paean of praise to southern cuisine—and then the voice of the "wise" old Mark Twain breaks in with a startling modern ring:

> It seems a pity that the world should throw away so many good things merely because they are unwholesome. I doubt if God has given us any re-

freshment which, taken in moderation, is unwholesome, except microbes. Yet there are people who strictly deprive themselves of each and every eatable, drinkable, and smokable which has in any way acquired a shady reputation. They pay this price for health. And health is all they get for it. How strange it is! It is like paying out your whole fortune for a cow that has gone dry.[16]

What follows is a riveting five-page prose poem, one of the most remarkable, perfectly wrought passages of Mark Twain's entire literary output. It begins with "I can call back . . ." to catalogue pell-mell scores of remembered visual, auditory, tactile, olfactory, and gustatory sensations of his childhood. If, instead of being strung together in linear paragraphs (one of them covering more than three pages), the individual sentences, each beginning "I can see," "I can hear," "I can feel," "I know," or "I can remember," were to be ranged as separate verse units in columnar fashion, the result would read amazingly like a poem by Walt Whitman. Indeed, one cannot help recalling "There Was a Child Went Forth" when one reads "I can call back the prairie, and its loneliness and peace, and a vast hawk hanging motionless in the sky, with his wings spread wide and the blue vault showing through the fringe of their end feathers." Or yet again, "I know how a frozen apple looks, in a barrel down cellar in the wintertime, and how hard it is to bite, and how the frost makes the teeth ache, and yet how good it is notwithstanding. I know the disposition of elderly people to select the specked apples for the children, and I once knew ways to beat the game."[17] Everything this child has experienced has become part of him and he of it, and he now renders it retrospectively with such vividness and intensity that his reader experiences it almost viscerally as well. The art of it is that in its seeming "naturalness" this epiphany conceals its art. While the subject and manner are undeniably Whitmanian, the technique is that of European impressionism, almost pointillism, in which the writer skillfully groups highly selected impressions to fabricate a deceptively realistic texture. This is also the technique of a Schnitzler, a Chekhov, a Proust but not one that Mark Twain used before, although he approached it in the opening paragraphs of "A Boy's Ambition" in *Life on the Mississippi* describing the arrival and departure of the daily paddlewheeler in Hannibal.

The other autobiographical sketches composed in Kaltenleutgeben and Vienna are not as captivating as "Early Days" although they surpass all but a few portions he later dictated to Paine and others. The best are a witty vignette of the original of Col. Mulberry Sellers (James Lampton), some humorous reminiscences of his days as a lecturer on Redpath's Lyceum circuit in Boston, and a hilarious anecdote of his acute embarrassment as a lad at having unknowingly been spied upon by girls while cavorting in the nude.

One account in this group of compositions is not a reminiscence of earlier days but a description of a huge, spectacularly colorful Viennese parade that fetched him to the city on June 26. His description of it abounds in such aphoristic observations as, "It is clothes that make a procession; where you have those of the right pattern you can do without length." The spectacle reminds him of the annual Fronleichnam (Corpus Christi) parade he had seen some weeks earlier

> with the Emperor and an archbishop in it, and the archbishop was being carried along under a canopied arrangement and had his skullcap on, and the venerable Emperor was following him on foot and bareheaded. Even if that had been the entire procession, it would have paid. I am old, now, and may never be an emperor at all; at least in this world. I have been disappointed so many times that I am growing more and more doubtful and resigned every year; but if it should ever happen, the procession will have a fresh interest for the archbishop, for he will walk.[18]

Another sketch, written in Vienna two days after his Börsendorfer Saal reading in February, concerns his discovery in a Dresden magazine of yet one more of his favorite (and to him) excruciatingly funny long German compoundings: "*Hottentotenstrottelmutterattentäterlattengitterwetterkotterbeutelratte*" (assassin of a Hottentot mother of stuttering children confined in a kangaroo cage). Good as they are, however, these sketches serve mainly to illustrate by contrast the superiority of "Early Days."

One piece Paine included in this group, though written earlier, is noteworthy for its relevance to his other writings that summer. It is his character sketch of Macfarlane, an eccentric Scotsman he met in 1856 while an itinerant "jour" printer in Cincinnati. An autodidact who nevertheless knew "his dictionary from beginning to end" and was "as familiar with his Bible as he was with his dictionary," Macfarlane was an amateur philosopher whose skepticism and misanthropy had deeply impressed the young Sam Clemens. In Macfarlane's pronouncement "that man's intellect was a brutal addition to him and degraded him to a rank far below the plane of the other animals, and that there never was a man who did not use his intellect daily all his life to advantage himself at other people's expense" one sees the seeds of thought that reached full flower in the "gospel" Mark Twain finished in July and August in Kaltenleutgeben.

Since he asserted in a prefatory note in February 1905 when he was preparing to publish *What Is Man?* anonymously in a private edition of 260 copies that the ideas in it had been gestating some twenty-seven years, one must ask why he finally decided to write it in Austria. The customary explanation that the security Rogers had gained for him in 1898 at last gave him freedom to write for pleasure rather than for money is insufficient. The fact is he was still writing mainly for publication—that is, for money—and making strenuous efforts to sell everything he wrote even though he was not "pot-boiling" as much as he had been during his long struggle out of bankruptcy. A more likely explanation is that in this rural retreat he could reflect upon experiences, intellectually challenging conversations, and his reading during the previous season in Vienna. If financial independence had anything to do with his writing, it was perhaps to make him less timid than he had been, less fearful of alienating those to whom he wished to communicate his cherished convictions. As a result, he began to devise a way to embody ideas he had harbored for many years and to formulate some viable means for elucidating what were now his deepest insights into the wellsprings of human behavior. Thus, it may well be, as he indicated to Howells, that only Olivia's stern veto prevented his trying to publish *What Is Man?* even before they quit Vienna in 1899.[19]

"Selfishness" or "What is the Real Character of Conscience?"—both,

by turns, his early working titles for *What Is Man?*—is less a philosophical treatise, despite its form as a Socratic dialogue, than a study
in social psychology. Much has been made of the influence on Mark
Twain in this and other writings of William E. H. Lecky's *History of
European Morals from Augustine to Charlemagne* (1869), partly because
this influence is easy to document. Twain himself often referred to
Lecky's work as a powerful stimulus, and his well-thumbed, annotated
copy has been a prime exhibit in studies of his intellectual development
and the exegesis of everything labeled "pessimistic" in his later works.

On the other hand, Mark Twain is acknowledged to have been a
voracious reader who compensated for his lack of formal education
by reading almost anything anyone mentioned to him in Europe. Yet
no attention has been given to his reading of Theodor Mommsen's
Römische Geschichte or Schopenhauer's *Die Welt als Wille und Vorstellung*
in Berlin, for instance, or in Vienna of Bjornstjerne Bjornson's *Auf
Gottes Weg* (in German translation), Otto Ludwig's *Aus dem Regen in die
Traufe*, and a curious work, *Die wundersamen Erlebnisse von Freiherr von
Trenck in Spielberg*, all of which were noted by newspaper interviewers among books on his writing table.[20] He maintained that, despite
analogies one critic found in *What Is Man?*, he had not read Nietzsche
or Ibsen because "I didn't need to," thus perhaps tacitly acknowledging that what one encounters in, say, *Beyond Good and Evil* or *The
Genealogy of Morals* had been commonplaces of his European intellectual milieu.[21] It also seems safe to assume he heard discussed and
may even have read in Vienna Max Nordau's *Die konventionellen Lügen
der Kulturmenschheit* (The Conventional Lies of Cultivated Humanity,
1883) and, even more likely, *Entartung* (Degeneration, 1893). All these
writers and their works, as much as Lecky, Darwin, T. H. Huxley and
others referred to in *What Is Man?*, express a weltanschauung that also
pervades this most fin de siècle of Mark Twain's writings.

Despite the religious sound and source of its title (from Psalms 8:4:
"What is man, that thou art mindful of him?"), what Mark Twain
postulates in *his* "bible" is a purely secular, materialistic, mechanistic-
deterministic view of humanity. We are what we are because of our

"make," a combination of our genes ("temperament") and our environment ("training"), and we do what we do for one reason only, to which various names might be given—egoism, selfishness, pride, the desire for self-esteem which translates itself into the need for approval by others. Free will is a chimera. We are creatures of immutable physical laws set in motion at the beginning of time. If God exists—and his existence cannot be proved, only believed—he is totally indifferent if not downright hostile to human beings for the simple reason that they are despicable. Why? Because that which differentiates them from other animals, their vaunted moral sense—the knowledge of good and evil and the ability to choose between them—makes them hypocrites. They will invariably choose evil and try to rationalize it, to justify it, to shirk their responsibility. It is a cosmic joke played on the race. "Whenever I look at the other animals and realize that whatever they do is blameless and they can't do wrong, I envy them the dignity of their estate, its purity and its loftiness, and recognise that the Moral Sense is a thoroughly disastrous thing," Twain concludes.[22]

In his gospel of self-approval, such abstractions as altruism, benevolence, charity, philanthropy, compassion, self-sacrifice, duty, patriotism, heroism, personal merit, and so on, are delusions because human beings are incapable of truly unselfish acts. Whatever we do is motivated solely by our desire for self-esteem through winning the approval of others. To do otherwise is to inflict pain on ourselves, to make ourselves uncomfortable, and we will do anything to avoid that. For instance, a man will leave his weeping wife and children to go off to a senseless war in which he does not believe just to earn the good opinion of his neighbors. Not to go, and thus be branded "unpatriotic" and a "coward," would make him more uncomfortable than seeing his family suffer. So he goes perhaps to his death basking in cowardly self-approval as a "patriot." Mark Twain goes on multiplying examples to show that if "doing one's duty" and "doing good to others" were not socially approved and rewarded, we would never bestir ourselves to such actions.

The form Twain adopts to convey this concept, a dialogue between an old and a young man (abbreviated "O.M." and "Y.M." after the opening exchange), redeems the work from prosaic tediousness and gives it dramatic flavor. The two characters are interesting. The young man is the kind of prig filled with unexamined assumptions, though perhaps not entirely uneducable, who is every university professor's bane almost every term. The old man is a gentle, at times disingenuously humble pedagogue who seems to suffer this fool gladly but who, nevertheless, often attacks with biting wit and sometimes outrageous put-downs. Y.M. plays straight to O.M. who fields the leading questions to which Y.M. brashly, self-confidently, but with diminishing certitude supplies wrong answers that O.M. can then rephrase as questions. To prevent monotony, Twain has O.M. digress into pronouncements and parables which Y.M. then tries to question or shoot down, always unsuccessfully. True to character, Y.M. never discovers he is playing with loaded dice.

Despite its artistry, *What Is Man?* has received the harshest, most negative criticism of any of Mark Twain's works. Since its anonymous private printing in a limited edition in 1906 elicited mostly one-line notices or a mere listing in "books received," it was not until Paine published the first trade edition (*What Is Man? and Other Essays*) in May 1917 under its author's name that the critical vituperation began. The pattern of clichés about the book was set by the *New York Times* reviewer in June 1917:

> It would be difficult to find anything more dreary, cynical, pessimistic than the view of life here revealed. One refuses to believe that it voices the settled, mature convictions held by Mr. CLEMENS—at least one does not wish to believe it. . . . What gain is there in being told that man is merely a machine, and there is practically nothing real in his idealism, no basis for his brave dreams, his aspirations toward a life of spiritual beauty and achievement? There is nothing new in pessimism of this kind.[23]

Even the reviews in 1973 of a splendid definitive text edited from the manuscript sources that included all drafts, cancels, omitted fragments, and working notes continued to denigrate *What Is Man?* as lacking profundity and originality. One of Twain's most recent biographers, for instance, has dismissed it as "of little value as literature, even less as philosophy."[24]

Such criticism ignores the fact that neither profundity nor originality was ever claimed by Mark Twain for his "bible." In his prefatory note of 1905, in fact, he specifically disavows any such intentions: "Every thought in (it) has been thought (and accepted as unassailable truth) by millions upon millions of men—and concealed, kept private."[25] He was merely stating the obvious in terms of the scandalous or, at least, in terms that might scandalize the vast majority of his fellow human beings, whom he judged to be as timorous as he had been most of his life. Lacking formal training in logic and epistemology, he was not attempting to construct an academic argument or a coherent theoretical gestalt to explain all phenomena. His aims and motives were not those of Emerson's *Nature* but the more modest ones (in a different tone) of Franklin's *Way to Wealth*, an attempt by a man of the world to sum up what experience had taught him, to write his testament of "common sense." Avoiding metaphysical theory and sticking strictly to practical questions of ethical-moral conduct ("conscience"), he was in no way a systematic philosopher, nor should he be judged as one. To compare him, for example, to such American contemporaries (or near-contemporaries) as William James, Josiah Royce, or George Santayana is manifestly inappropriate and unfair.

Nor is *What Is Man?* at bottom really pessimistic. In the fourth section ("Training"), the old man admonishes his young interlocutor:

Diligently train your ideals *upward* and *still upward* toward a summit where you will find your chiefest pleasure in conduct which, while contenting you, will be sure to confer benefits upon your neighbor and the community.

Y.M. Is that a new gospel?

O.M. No.

Y.M. It has been taught before?

O.M. For ten thousand years.

Y.M. By whom?

O.M. All the great religions—all the great gospels.

Y.M. Then there is nothing new about it.

O.M. Oh, yes there is. It is candidly stated, this time. That has not been done before.[26]

There is, in other words, a point at which self-interest and the common good converge, or can be made to, and one's goal should be to find that point and dwell there, not because it helps others but because one may enjoy oneself without having to feel guilty about it. This amounts, in effect, to an apology for Phaeacianism, of *leben und leben lassen* (live and let live), and whether it had been gestating twenty-seven years or twenty-seven weeks, it was thoroughly Austrian.

Above all, *What Is Man?* is not a solemn, somber, or even deadly serious work but a joyous one, full of sardonic wit and clever turns of phrase. Its main value is not as a singular essay but, in the fashionable jargon of today's criticism, as a subtext for everything Mark Twain wrote thereafter. In his belletristic writings in Kaltenleutgeben and after, he repeats many of the ideas in his "bible," trying to work out other, more imaginative ways to represent them.

His most brilliant success in this endeavor and, by common consent, one of his most effective, most artistically satisfying works of fiction is his fable of selfishness and greed, "The Man That Corrupted Hadleyburg," on which he worked simultaneously with several other pieces, including his "bible," and "Early Days," and completed in October. His habitual mode of composition was to have several things under way at once and to switch from one piece to another when the going got tough or he became momentarily bored with a subject. "Hadleyburg," which is too well known to need extended comment here, should thus be read as a companion piece to *What Is Man?* and a fictional embodiment of many of its central propositions.

Much energy and print has been wasted in the effort to identify the original of Hadleyburg. Was it a New England village, a small town in upstate New York, or where? Does it matter? The point of the tale is that Hadleyburg is Everytown. It is all the *H* towns in Mark Twain's life—Hannibal, Hartford, Heidelberg—and it could be any other, because, despite the title, it is not the town that is "corrupted" but the "damned" human beings who live in it. Long before the satan figure (another "mysterious stranger") plays his diabolical trick to expose its hypocrisy, the town has been corrupted by pride, self-righteousness, and greed. Like Chaucer's Pardoner, Mark Twain provides yet another parable on the theme *Radix Malorum est Cupiditas* (the root of evil is greed).

None but the town derelict who has nothing, not even his self-respect, and who therefore enjoys scoffing at those who do, is incorruptible. Most corrupt of all is the "honest" couple, Mary and Edward Richards, who are not exposed in their chicanery and lack the courage to expose themselves. Like all hypocrites—to Twain, *all* human beings—they rationalize their plight, refusing to take any responsibility for their actions. Richards exculpates them by saying: "It was ordered. *All* things are ordered." Ironically, he is right, if one accepts the deterministic argument of *What Is Man?*, not because of Divine Providence (which is what Richards means) but because his actions and his wife's are the inevitable result of their "make," like everyone else in this microcosm called Hadleyburg. There is no such creature as an *honest* human being.

This theme in "Hadleyburg" may well have occurred to Mark Twain when he saw himself depicted on the cover of a December 1897 issue of the Viennese humor weekly *Der Floh* clad in a toga, walking streets littered with paving blocks and gas pipes and with members of the Reichsrat scuffling in the background. He is holding aloft a lantern which he is blowing out with the words, "*Pfui! Ich hab'genug gesehen*" (Phooey! I've seen enough). The caption under this four-color "*Mark Twain in Wien*" cartoon is: "*Der amerikanische Diogenes*" (the American Diogenes). The reference, of course, is to the Athenian Cynic philosopher who carried a lantern in daylight, vainly looking for an honest man. The denouement of the story in which the guilt-ridden couple fall into a delirium and confess their duplicity as they are dying is but a slight variation on the same motif he had found in the finale of the Erckmann-Chatrian play *Der polnische Jude* (The Polish Jew), which a Viennese interviewer mentioned as among his reading a year earlier.

The climactic episode of "Hadleyburg," the town meeting at which the hypocrisy of the nineteen community leaders is exposed, uses the same technique as the central section of "Stirring Times in Austria," Mark Twain's report of the *Krawalle* he had witnessed in the Reichsrat the previous November. Depicting the same atmosphere of "delightful pandemonium," the scene is theatrically staged, with the chair attempting to keep order while raucous taunts and insults are exchanged and speaker after speaker is jeered or shouted down by a "storm," a "cyclone," or a "tornado" of voices, the same imagery he had used in "Stirring Times."

Soon after he finished "Hadleyburg," if not before, he began writing what grew into the last book he was to publish in his lifetime: *Christian Science* (1907). Its origins were more modest than a projected book—an article, "Christian Science and the Book of Mrs. Eddy," published in *Cosmopolitan* in October 1899, which eventually became the first four chapters in book 1 of *Christian Science*. Although assumed by every commentator until now to be autobiographical—that is, to be the report of an actual incident in Twain's Kaltenleutgeben (or Weggis?) summer—these chapters are pure fiction and the most entertaining satire Mark Twain wrote while in Austria.

The subject, Christian Science, or more accurately the Church of Christ, Scientist, founded in Boston in 1879 by Mary Baker Glover Eddy (1821–1910), was a hot one for any writer in that era and a still hotter one for Mark Twain. Even though Mrs. Eddy, whose book *Science and Health, with Key to the Scriptures* (1875) was the bible of this new American sect, had retired to live in seclusion in 1889, she had never ceased being the actual leader of her movement which continued to win converts among middle- and upper-class Anglo-Americans and Britons by almost geometric ratios throughout the 1890s. In Mark Twain's somewhat extravagant view, Christian Science was on its way to becoming America's national religion if Roman Catholicism did not get there first. Its rapid growth and the publicity given allegedly avoidable deaths among prominent converts like the novelist Harold

Frederic in 1898, who refused medical aid, had made the cult a subject of curiosity and controversy among readers in the United States.

Moreover, Mark Twain had a personal axe to grind with Mrs. Eddy's religion. His dear, dead Susy had had a mild flirtation with it during and after her years at Bryn Mawr. Although she never converted, her almost obsessive interest in mental healing, which her father shared to a lesser degree, left gnawing doubts about whether she might have been cured had she sought treatment earlier for the symptoms of the meningitis that killed her. Ironically, after her father's death, Clara became a convert to Christian Science, and even before that his Virginia cousin, Nancy Langhorne, who married Viscount Waldorf Astor and became the first woman member of the British Parliament, was a stridently militant convert. He may at times also have feared that brother Orion, who seemed to change "his religion with his shirt," might be a prime candidate for conversion.

More important than any personal motive behind *Christian Science* was his disdain for "the queen of frauds and hypocrites," that "monumental sarcasm of the Ages," as he labeled Mrs. Eddy. "When we contemplate her & what she has achieved," he told Edward Day, "it is blasphemy to longer deny the Supreme Being the possession of a sense of humor."†[27] Even worse than her "anti-medicine show" at the Mother Church in Boston was her partly ghostwritten (with Rev. James Henry Wiggin) textbook, *Science and Health*, which had enjoyed 148 editions between 1875 and 1898 and a sale approaching 500,000 but which Twain reviled as an inept, stylistically botched, perverse interpretation of passages in the New Testament. One must observe, however, that he was almost always jealous of writers (Howells only excepted) whose book sales exceeded his, especially those like Bret Harte, Thomas Bailey Aldrich, and Arthur Conan Doyle, whose popularity made them his rivals.

The opening of what eventually became book 1, chapter 1 of *Christian Science* is vintage Mark Twain, too rich and too little known to the general reader not to be given in full here:

This last summer, when I was on my way back to Vienna from the Appetite-Cure in the mountains, I fell over a cliff in the twilight and broke some arms and legs and one thing and another, and by good luck was found by some peasants who had lost an ass and they carried me to the nearest habitation, which was one of those large, low, thatch-roofed farm-houses, with apartments in the garret for the family, and a cunning little porch under the deep gable decorated with boxes of bright-colored flowers and cats; and on the ground floor a large and light sitting-room, separated from the milch-cattle apartment by a partition; and in the front yard rose stately and fine the wealth and pride of the house, the manure-pile. That sentence is Germanic, and shows that I am acquiring the sort of mastery of the art and spirit of the language which enables a man to travel all day on one sentence without changing cars.[28]

The reference to his "Appetite-Cure" sojourn and his homecoming "accident" are completely fanciful while his realistic description of the typical central European *Bauernhaus* with its "wealth and pride . . . the manure-pile" is comically factual. This and his remark about his "Germanic" sentence set the tone for the purely fictional tale to come.

A woman Christian Science "doctor" (practitioner) from Boston named Mrs. Fuller, "a widow in the third degree," who is summering in a nearby village, is summoned in preference to the only alternative, the village veterinarian ("horse-doctor"). Unable to attend him that night, Mrs. Fuller sends word "she would give me 'absent treatment' now, and come in the morning." When she arrives, she assures him his injuries and pains are unreal, purely a matter of having bad thoughts, and then enunciates the four "fundamental propositions of Christian Science . . . 1. God is All in All. 2. God is good. Good is Mind. 3. God, Spirit, being all, nothing is matter. 4. Life, God, omnipotent Good, deny death, evil, sin, disease."

He is puzzled because "it did not seem to say anything about the difficulty at hand—how non-existent matter can propagate illusions," but she insists that "even if read backward" it will explain his difficulties. She demonstrates this theory, but although it seems clearer when read backwards, he still has doubts. At this point she launches into her "lessons" from *Science and Health*, which Twain burlesques hilariously; then she departs, leaving him her "little book" and promising to continue giving him "absent treatment."

After his bones have "slipped into their sockets with a sound like pulling a distant cork," he sends for the "horse-doctor" to treat his stomachache and head cold. This drastic treatment reminds one of Twain's "Appetite-Cure" burlesque: "He made up a bucket of bran mash, and said a dipperful of it every two hours, alternated with a drench with turpentine and axle-grease in it would either knock my ailments out of me in twenty-four hours or so interest me in other ways as to make me forget they were on the premises." After downing a "dipperful of drench," he settles back to read *Science and Health*, finding that "For of all the strange, and frantic, and incomprehensible, and uninterpretable books which the imagination of man has created, surely this one is the prize sample." One recalls similar judgments he expressed in *Roughing It* (1872) about the Book of Mormon.

The fourth chapter of *Christian Science*, written in Kaltenleutgeben, is an inquiry into the psychology of faith healing. "No one doubts that the mind exercises a powerful influence over the body," he observes; from "the wild medicine-man" to today's "educated physician," healers have ever relied on "the client's *imagination* to help them in their work." Physicians prescribe placebos, knowing their patients' confidence in them will make their "bread pills" effective. Since most ailments are at least partly psychosomatic, the secret of success in all medicine is *der Wille zur Glauben*, the willingness of the patient to believe the cure will indeed work. As proof he cites various examples, from a Missouri farm wife in his childhood who, professing neither religious nor occult powers, cured his mother's toothaches to successful secular "mental healers" he had recently run across in Bavaria and Austria.

Wherein, then, is Christian Science objectionable? Is it not merely another of the immemorial attempts at faith healing, at making spirit prevail over flesh, at asserting the primacy of mind over matter? The attempt at giving persuasive answers to those questions occupies Mark Twain for the remainder of his book. At its conclusion, one wonders if he has not succumbed to rhetorical overkill or if he could not have done it with much less verbiage.

The fact is he reaches the heart of the matter right away, in this fourth chapter. He points out the crucial difference between other forms of "Mind Cure, Faith Cure, Prayer Cure" and Mrs. Eddy's doctrine; the latter arbitrarily forbids use of any medicines or medical procedures whatever, even as a last resort when Christian Science "treatment" fails. This dogmatism he finds excessive, concluding:

> The Christian Scientist was not able to cure my stomach ache and my cold; but the horse-doctor did it. This convinces me that Christian Science claims too much. In my opinion it ought to let diseases alone and confine itself strictly to surgery. There it would have everything its own way.
>
> The horse-doctor charged me thirty Kreutzers, and I paid him; in fact I doubled it and gave him a shilling. Mrs. Fuller brought in an itemized bill for a crate of broken bones mended in 234 places—one dollar per fracture.
>
> "Nothing exists but Mind?"
>
> "Nothing," she answered. "All else is substanceless, all else is imaginary."
>
> I gave her an imaginary check, and now she is suing me for substantial dollars. It looks inconsistent.

By posing the fictional Christian Science "doctor" and "horse-doctor" as foils, he invites us to perceive in them two extremes of incompetence in dealing with human illness. Even more outrageous, the veterinarian is successful whereas the Christian Scientist fails. The thrice-widowed Boston lady, "large and bony, and erect, . . . [with] an austere face and a resolute jaw and a Roman beak" is an obvious caricature that Twain's contemporaries would have had no trouble recognizing as the thrice-married Mrs. Mary Baker Glover Eddy, who was actually from New Hampshire but whose movement was centered in Boston. Although the mother of one of Clara's fellow pupils of Leschetizky (an English lady the Clemenses had met in London) was an ardent Christian Scientist, no one even remotely resembling "Mrs.

Fuller" was in Kaltenleutgeben or Weggis or at any other European summer retreat of Mark Twain's.

Between the Clemenses' return to the city in October 1898 and their departure the following May, Mark Twain wrote four more pieces that became chapters in book 1 of *Christian Science*. These were published (together with the first four) in the English and Tauchnitz editions of *The Man That Corrupted Hadleyburg and Other Stories* (1900) before becoming the first two articles in a four-part series Twain published in the *North American Review*, December 1902–April 1903, and then being incorporated into the completed book in 1907.

These chapters lack the humor and bite of the first four because in them he abandons fiction altogether and takes to the stump. Much of what he writes in these later chapters is his reactions to an article in the *Christian Science Journal* for October 1898 and to newspaper clippings on the subject sent to him by Twichell, and Twain's arguments thereafter become increasingly strident. Still, they are noteworthy for the aphoristic style he had come increasingly to employ in Vienna where it was high fashion. For instance, he begins chapter 5: "Let us consider that we are all partially insane. It will explain us to each other; it will unriddle many riddles; it will make clear and simple many things which are involved in haunting and harassing difficulties and obscurities now."

He then develops this idea in a futile attempt to disarm opposition by conceding, again aphoristically, that our common insanity is an equalizer: "Upon a great religious or political question the opinion of the dullest head in the world is worth the same as the opinion of the brightest head in the world—a brass farthing." He seems unaware, however, that this idea also weakens his argument rather than merely being a clever rhetorical ploy.

The remaining chapters begin his decline into diatribe, elaborating upon his fears about the growth and spread of Christian Science, of the "personality cult" developing around Mrs. Eddy, of her high profits and highly efficient business organization, and of her obfuscating jargon and cant. He returned to the subject in February 1903 when the *North American Review* series was under way, making corrections and revisions to some of what he had written in 1898–99 and writing new chapters dealing mainly with the theological fallacies of her scriptural "keys." This task occupied him off and on until the book finally appeared in February 1907. These later chapters are so tedious, overwrought, and lacking in cohesiveness and cogency that the reader who perseveres to the end must wish Mark Twain had quit the subject with the chapters he wrote in Kaltenleutgeben and Vienna.

Two other pieces written in Kaltenleutgeben deserve mention if only to show the full range and volume of his output during that summer. One is a short story, "Wapping Alice," in which he fictionalized an incident that occurred in the Clemens household in 1877 when he forced a "shotgun" marriage of one of the housemaids and her lover. He shifts the locale from Hartford to London and disguises the characters' names, but more important, in the denouement "Alice," the maid, is revealed to be a transvestite. This is a curious, quite Viennese twist that may indicate Mark Twain's growing interest in problems of sexual identity in a city where transvestitism was widespread. "Wapping Alice," however, was too risqué for his American publishers, and although he first intended patching it up to make it more salable, Twain lost interest in it until April 9, 1907, when he inserted it into an autobiographical dictation. It was not published until 1981 and then only in a private edition.[29]

The other piece, "The Great Republic's Peanut Stand," is a polemical essay written as a dialogue between a "Statesman" and a "Wisdom Seeker" pleading for better American copyright laws. Again, there were no takers for this too-lengthy article on a topic of limited interest to the general reader, and it survives today only in an unpublished fifty-nine-page manuscript.

Two longer works which occupied him sporadically in August and September in Kaltenleutgeben are the fragments of an unfinished novel known by DeVoto's title, "The Great Dark," first published in their entirety in 1968, and "The Chronicle of Young Satan," which he had begun the previous November in Vienna. These will be discussed in detail in the penultimate chapter here.

Leaves were beginning to fall and the nights to turn frosty when the Clemens family moved from the Villa Paulhof to what Twain called the "bran-span new" Hotel Krantz, at Neuer Markt 6, on October 14. Except for their eleven-day August excursion to Ischl and Hallstatt and an occasional day trip to Vienna for events like the parade in June and the empress's funeral in September, the family had been rusticating in Kaltenleutgeben continuously close onto five months. Still, they were sorry to end their summer idyll. The house had been pleasantly quiet and cool even on the few hot days in July and August. "It is a fortunate summer country—Europe," wrote Clemens: "Its foliage and grass remain dense and green and fresh all summer—no parched and brown places. And no flies nor bugs or other insects; and no mosquitoes nor gnats. This house is not afflicted with any of these things; yet its garden is full of trees and thick shrubbery—a good place for them." But the city beckoned, especially since Clara had begun her voice studies with Frau Brandt.

Even before they moved out in May, however, they had resolved not to return to the Metropole if they could find better accommodations at an affordable price. On April 14, Olivia queried George Cole about an apartment he had heard of, which apparently turned out to be undesirable, and throughout the summer she diligently pursued every lead.

By early August they had a good prospect. Clemens told Rogers, "They want us at the new hotel—the Krantz—which is a kind of Splendid Waldorf, but I think they knock off only a third of their regular rates, whereas the Metropole knocks off half." They rejected Herr Krantz's first offer, keeping their fingers crossed that he would respond with a better one. "If they'll come down $125 lower (per month), I think we'll take them up," Clemens wrote, admitting ruefully, "if not, we'll have to go back to the Met—to my dissatisfaction; not that the rooms aren't good enough and the food good enough, but I *do* like lovely furniture." Moreover, Olivia had stopped by to inspect the Krantz "and found on the lobby wall the finest portrait of me she has seen. We don't know who made it or when, but we recognize that it is a hotel that has taste."[30]

It was not until they passed through Vienna on August 27 en route to Kaltenleutgeben from Hallstatt and Bad Ischl that their arrangements with Josef Krantz were settled. Saying with typical Viennese charm that the Clemenses' presence "would be the best advertisement they [the hotel] could have," Herr Krantz offered a capacious eight-room apartment for 2,800 francs per month (then approximately $560) including meals for five people. Since this sum was $120 a month more than they had paid the previous year and $60 more than the Metropole was offering to lure them back, Clemens defended his "extravagance" to Rogers by noting:

> The Metropole is a *long* way short of being as fine a house as the Murry [*sic*] Hill, but the Krantz is a fine building and is completely and richly furnished like the Waldorf—there is nothing approaching it in France, Germany or Austria. We have a dining room, a parlor, a music-parlor, a study, and 4 bedrooms—and there are bathrooms attached to 3 of the bedrooms. . . . I used to be a little ashamed when Ambassadors and dukes and such called on us in that rusty and rather shabby Metropole, but they'll mistake us for millionaires next fall and will probably lend us money.[31]

The pace of Twain's writing slackened after they settled in at the Hotel Krantz and the social season began anew, but his four months in Kaltenleutgeben had been his most productive period in nearly a decade. The experiences and ideas he had absorbed during his previous winter in Vienna had become potent stimuli for his imagination in this rural Austrian setting so powerfully reminiscent of home—of Hannibal and Quarry Farm. It is not merely the amazing quantity of his writing there but the fact that most of what he finished or commenced at the Villa Paulhof was much better than what he had been able to accomplish for a long while. Few of his short stories equal and none surpasses "The Man That Corrupted Hadleyburg," for example, and in his polemical writings he seldom equaled "Concerning the Jews."

Hotel Krantz, 1897. The Clemens family lived here from October 1898 until May 1899. (Picture Archives of the Austrian National Library)

Consider also the excellent moments in the "Early Days" section of the compilation we know as the *Autobiography*, the opening chapters of *Christian Science*, and the grossly undervalued chief work of this summer, *What Is Man?*, and it becomes obvious that the Kaltenleutgeben sojourn brought the last great creative surge in Mark Twain's long career. None of his subsequent summers in Sanna (Sweden); then Dollis Hill; or, after his return to the States, in Saranac Lake, New York; Dublin, Vermont; and York Harbor, Maine, would yield anything like what he had achieved here at the edge of the Vienna Woods. When the family returned to the city that autumn, Olivia wrote glowingly to a friend in Hartford, "I have not known Mr. Clemens for years to write with so much pleasure & energy as he has done during this last Summer."[32] Why have those who see only despondency and "writer's block" in this period of Mark Twain's career not taken Olivia Clemens's comment at face value and examined the evidence that corroborates it?

CHAPTER TWELVE

Diogenes in Vienna

ne day as far as the eye could see," a fin de siècle Viennese journalist recorded in his memoirs, "everything was—red. Vienna has not seen such a day since. What murmuring, spine-tingling! In the streets, on the trams, in the Stadt-park, everyone was reading a red magazine. . . ."[1] The day was April Fool's Day 1899, symbolically chosen by Karl Kraus to launch *Die Fackel* (The Torch), the red-covered magazine of which he was sole propri-etor, editor, and, for all but a few numbers, sole contributor. This was the first of the 922 issues in all that were to appear at irregular intervals until February 1936, five months before Kraus died. Its pre-mier issue was twice reprinted within days, and its second sold 30,000 copies, more than the circulation of all but two of the city's forty-five newspapers, establishing *Die Fackel* as the most eagerly awaited, most widely read, most intently discussed periodical in the Habsburg capi-tal if not, indeed, in the entire Germanic world. For two generations thereafter any Viennese burgher not conversant with the contents of the latest *Fackel* risked being branded an ignoramus or a hopeless reactionary.

At the end of April 1899, when readers opened their third number of Karl Kraus's sensational new journal of belles lettres and opinion, they found a lead article with the tantalizing title "*U.A.*", the German abbreviation for *unter anderen* (among others), which began:

"Anwesend war u.a. Mark Twain"—Wo? Hier und dort. Bei der Eröff-nung einer Kunstausstellung, bei der Soirée eines Staatswürdenträgers,

bei der Auction des Wolter-Nachlasses, beim Concert der russischen
Kirchensänger, bei einer Feuersbrunst, einer Kindstaufe, bei der Bei-
sichtigung eines Zuchthauses und bei einem Bankett der Budapester
Journalisten . . . mit einem Worte: überall.[2]

("Among others present was Mark Twain."—Where? Here and there.
At the opening of an art exhibit, at the soirée of some dignitary, at the
auction of the [Charlotte] Wolter estate, at the concert of the Russian
church singers, at a great fire, a baby's christening, at the inspection of
a new jail, and at a banquet of Budapest journalists . . . in a word: everywhere.)

An innocent enough beginning, to be sure, to what at first seems
a piece of straight reportage. Then in the next sentence one reads:
"I have ascertained that some Viennese papers use this pleasant sign-
off, 'among other present was Mark Twain,' as a sort of comfortable
cliché phrase, while others have concluded that henceforth it is merely
enough to suggest the possibility that the American humorist stayed
away from a particular event." Satirical intent is discernible here, and
in the succeeding paragraph it becomes obvious what Kraus is up to,
thus, "Of course, before now we have been unable to boast a sufficient
number of personalities who, if incapable of contributing anything
else to the age, were constantly prepared to be present among others,
and so to fill this pressing need, Mark Twain hastened to Vienna and
courageously threw himself into the forefront of those who only lead
an existence 'among others.'" At this point Kraus turns his fire on
Neue Freie Presse for its continuous fawning over Mark Twain's every
movement in Vienna, and in the remainder of his article he shifts
his barrage of vitriolic satire back and forth between *NFP* and the
American visitor himself.

Who was Karl Kraus, anyway, and why should he have taunted
Vienna's "illustrious guest" and its most influential newspaper with
such sarcasm? The first part of this question must seem absurd to anyone acquainted with twentieth-century German literature. Among the
writers with whom Mark Twain was associated during his Viennese
sojourn, Karl Kraus was unquestionably the most important and ulti-

mately also the most famous. That he nonetheless remains obscure to English-speaking readers not only reflects upon our neglect of central European literature (Franz Kafka excepted) but also arises because his works defy the best efforts of most translators. In German, this poet-playwright-essayist was a supreme master of verbal subtlety and nuance who occupied a place in Austrian literary history roughly analogous to that of H. L. Mencken in the United States at the same period.

Despite significant political and philosophical differences between the "Sage of Baltimore" and "the Scourge of Vienna," both Mencken and Kraus were household names in their respective lands in the early decades of this century as iconoclastic pundits who relished their special roles as gadflies to the bourgeoisie. Both edited magazines (in Mencken's case, *The Smart Set* and its successor, *The American Mercury*) that became bibles to the rebellious young intellectuals and the heterodox mavericks among the educated middle classes. Both were good for an appropriately acerbic quotation on almost any subject under discussion. Indeed, for four decades *"Karl Kraus hat gesagt . . ."* (Karl Kraus said . . .) followed by an appropriately witty "Kraus-ism" on the day's topic was a standard coffeehouse gambit in Vienna.

What personal contact Mark Twain actually had in Vienna with Karl Kraus cannot now be ascertained. Kraus was then but twenty-five and not the kind of established writer, like Eduard Pötzl, that Twain would have sought out. The Countess Wydenbruck-Esterházy's daughter recalled that both Twain and Kraus were among the choice circle of writers, artists, and musicians her mother cultivated, but whether these two ever visited her salon at the same time is moot.[3] Details in *"U.A."* indicate its author was present at Twain's Concordia speech and at least one of the American humorist's charity benefit readings in Vienna, but if Kraus took either of these occasions to be introduced to Twain, as many of his press colleagues did, he did not record the fact and neither did Twain.

Kraus's satire upon what he implied was Mark Twain's ersatz press-manufactured celebrity in the imperial city was one of the most caustic as well as perhaps most widely read lambastings this American author received at any point in his career. Notoriously thin-skinned and accustomed to receiving only approbation, Twain understandably would have been irked by Kraus's satire, but he kept his own counsel. Neither publicly nor privately did he register any reaction. Were the sarcasms of this brazen upstart beneath his contempt? Was he at a loss for an appropriate response to such seemingly unprovoked criticism? Or did he perhaps recognize more than a kernel of truth in Kraus's indictment of the way Twain and the liberal press in Vienna exploited one another to their mutual advantage?

Whatever the case, it is regrettable that Twain and Kraus probably did not engage in the kinds of informal exchanges Twain had with such other Viennese writers as Eduard Pötzl. Since they were in fundamental agreement about many things, closer acquaintance might have been stimulating to both Kraus and Twain. When one compares their writings one is struck by parallels not only in ideas and viewpoints but also in their means of expression in their respective tongues. Although Kraus eschewed pseudonyms, he was as keen as Clemens in maintaining an idiosyncratic persona, and like Mark Twain he was as skillful in image-making as he was in literary artistry. Both were consummate egoists whose views of humanity and its foibles were paradoxically compounded of moralism and therapeutic nihilism. The apt depiction of Mark Twain on the cover of *Der Floh* as "the American Diogenes," described above, might well have been redrawn a year later to show a brash, young "Austrian Diogenes," Karl Kraus, in the same guise and pose.

The essential similarity of the ideas which informed the lifework of both Twain and Kraus arises from the penchant each had for exposing and demolishing mendacity, sham, pretense, humbug, hypocrisy, and officious pomposity wherever they found it, whether in Gilded Age America or Habsburg Austria. Satire was their common weapon, and the imperial capital was rich in targets for any satirist. It was a city in which almost nothing was what it seemed or pretended to be, in which a double standard of morality fostered a publicly ignored, privately flourishing demimonde for every form of sexual excess and perversion, in which official lying was overlaid with a veneer of bureaucratic *Schlamperei* (sloppiness) coupled with stifling protocol and medieval pomp. Kraus called it "an experimental station for the end of the world."

Illuminating as it may be to compare Karl Kraus to H. L. Mencken or Mark Twain or to such of his contemporary British social satirists as George Bernard Shaw and Max Beerbohm, there is a fundamental difference between Kraus and most of these counterparts. Kraus was born and remained throughout his life an outsider in the society in which he became a celebrity. He was a Jew and, although he renounced his ancestral religion, becoming by turns a Catholic and then a socialist agnostic, was never comfortably at home in any creed or ideology. He was, in fact, a prime example of the uprooted, assimilated, but also alienated artist and intellectual endemic to fin de siècle Vienna of the type one sees in Sigmund Freud, Gustav Mahler, and Ludwig Wittgenstein, among others.

Like his contemporaries Freud and Mahler, Kraus was born to an affluent Bohemian Jewish family who moved to Vienna when he was still very young. Thereafter, he could have said as Mahler did of himself: "I am thrice homeless. As a native of Bohemia in Austria, as an Austrian among Germans, and as a Jew throughout the whole world. Everywhere an intruder, never welcomed."[4] A dilatory student, Kraus quit the University of Vienna without a degree after six sporadic years of study in law, philosophy, and German literature. Stage-struck at an early age, he failed initially in his passionate ambition to be an actor, although later on his solo performances in public readings not unlike Mark Twain's were great hits. He drifted into journalism as a free-lance book reviewer and as Vienna theater correspondent for journals in Berlin, Bremen, Breslau, and Leipzig. When still only a nineteen-year-old student he was included in Eisenberg's *Das geistige Wien* (Intellectual Vienna), a directory of the city's foremost artists and writers.[5]

The tenor of Kraus's career was set in his first major satire, *Die demo-*

lirte Literatur (Demolished Literature), in December 1896. This essay
set Viennese tongues a-wagging because it lampooned the dilettan-
tism of Kraus's own generation and coterie, Jung Wien (the Young
Vienna writers led by Hermann Bahr), whose gathering place, the
Café Griensteidl, had recently been demolished to make way for a
bank. His attack established Kraus's reputation as a literary maverick,
an image he scrupulously cultivated throughout the rest of his life.

The following year, *Eine Krone für Zion* (A Crown for Zion), a pamphlet ridiculing Theodor Herzl's *Der Judenstaat* and the Zionist movement it helped initiate, won Kraus approval from both the anti-Zionist
Jews and the anti-Semites. This tract was already in its third printing
on October 20, 1899, when Kraus formally, though without fanfare,
renounced Judaism, becoming *konfessionslos* (officially without religion)
until after his father's death four years later, when he quietly converted to Catholicism. The extent and nature of Karl Kraus's anti-
Semitism are too large and complex a subject to discuss adequately
here though certainly, as Theodor Lessing said, Kraus was a "shining
example of Jewish self-hatred." On the other hand, Kraus's biographer Harry Zohn may also be correct in observing that Kraus's mas-
ochistic anti-Semitic expressions were motivated by his wish to drive
criticism of Austrian Jewry into more constructive paths, feeling that,
to paraphrase Talleyrand's aphorism about war, "anti-Semitism was
too important a matter to be entrusted to anti-Semites."[6]

Anti-Semitism was also almost certainly a covert factor in Kraus's
Fackel assault on Mark Twain. Like most Austrians, anti-Semites or not,
Kraus would have assumed that anyone whose first name was Samuel
must be Jewish. Few Old Testament names are in the Calendar of the
Saints from which, according to Catholic dogma then observed in Austria, baptismal names had to be taken. One might occasionally meet
an Adam, a Daniel, a David, a Jacob, or more often a Joseph among
Catholic Austrians (then 90 percent of the population) but never a
gentile Aaron, Abraham, Moses, Samuel, Solomon, or another of the
many Hebraic names in common use in nineteenth-century Protes-
tant America. Clemens, which was both a common first name and a

less common surname in Austria, was, like Kraus, indeterminate in its religious signification. Hence any Austrian not cosmopolitan enough to know better might easily have concluded that the pen name "Mark Twain" disguised Jewish identity.

Furthermore, this presumably Jewish-American humorist was a favorite subject for reportage, interviews, and feuilletons mainly in newspapers owned or predominantly staffed by Jews and not politically aligned with either Lueger's Christian Socials or Schönerer's German Nationals. Foremost among these newspapers was *Neue Freie Presse*, whose publisher-editor, Moritz Benedikt, was a baptized Jew and whose feuilleton editor was the Zionist leader Herzl.

Benedikt was actually one of the first to appreciate young Karl Kraus's literary talents and in December 1898 offered Kraus a job as *NFP*'s chief satirical writer, a chair vacant since the death of the esteemed Daniel Spitzer in 1893. Suspecting an attempt to buy him off and irrevocably compromise his radical individualism, Kraus spurned the offer with what became a widely quoted sarcasm: "There are two fine things in this world: to be part of the *Neue Freie Presse*, or to despise it. I did not hesitate for one moment as to what my choice had to be."[7] From then on, *NFP* was Karl Kraus's favorite target, and he missed no chance to fire away at it as the symbol of Viennese journalistic hypocrisy and corrupt commercialism.

Not without justice. A pugnacious young writer was fighting his way up in the immemorial manner by attacking the establishment—the immediate targets being Twain and *NFP*—but he was not tilting at windmills. Although *Neues Wiener Tagblatt* boasted a larger circulation (65,000 compared to *NFP*'s 55,000), Benedikt's daily was the more prestigious and, indeed, one of the most highly respected and influential of all European newspapers, Vienna's counterpart to the *Times* of London or *Le Temps* in Paris. The British historian Wickham Steed, surveying Austrian politics in the early 1900s, said, "The greater part of what does duty for 'Austrian opinion' is dictated or suggested to the public by the editor-proprietor of *Neue Freie Press*."[8]

In large measure, Benedikt had achieved this stature for his newspaper by claiming to be independent while tacitly supporting his government's foreign and domestic policies, covering up the chicaneries of Vienna's leading financiers, and willfully wasting what little freedom of expression he enjoyed rather than rile tempers among officialdom or the dominant haute bourgeoisie. Much of what passed for news in *NFP* and other leading Viennese newspapers was simply disguised advertising. When he founded *Die Presse*, Adolf Zang doubtless spoke for most of his competitors in saying an "ideal newspaper would be a sheet that didn't contain a single line that hadn't been paid for." (*Mein Ideal einer Zeitung wäre ein Blatt, das nicht eine einzige unbezahlte Zeile enthält.*) [9]

For its part, *NFP* not only took no notice of the verbal grenades Karl Kraus hurled its way every chance he had, but it never again mentioned his name or allowed direct references to him or his journal to sully its columns. Other liberal newspapers followed suit with less stringent forms of silent treatment, leaving mainly those on the extreme right, like *Reichspost*, *Vaterland*, and *Wiener Volks-Zeitung*, to cackle loudly over each issue of *Die Fackel* to hit the newsstands.

In effect, Mark Twain served as a handy club for Kraus to bash *NFP* and the "liberal Jewish press" with in this instance. Kraus excoriates the liberal press in "*U.A.*" for reporting with tacit approval "Mark Twain's bad judgment of political conditions in Austria," including the visiting American's "opinion that Austria has produced, up to now, not one single great man." Kraus finds it scandalous that newspapers give "Herr Mark Twain the opportunity to practice his still clumsy German in incessant derision of Viennese culture and customs," and he is incensed by the Concordia members who lined up "with pleasantly smiling faces" to be photographed with a foreigner who had just made disparaging jokes about their language, a language in which the joker himself is guilty of "continually confusing the Dative with the Accusative." Here Kraus adopts a chauvinistic rhetorical stance, unusual for him, in order to imply something politically naive if not disloyal or downright subversive in the favorable treatment accorded Twain's jocular (and occasionally serious) criticisms of Viennese life and Austrian politics in *NFP* and other newspapers.

Still worse, Kraus impugns Twain's motives in seeking publicity in this manner, accusing "this has-been" of coming to Vienna for the sole purpose of using "tasteless jokes" to shore up his fallen reputation as a humorist. It is, Kraus insists, but one more indication of Twain's "long bankrupt ability which, even in this writer's best times, had meant scarcely more than a glib facility in expressing only the grotesque minutiae of life." With heavy irony, Kraus concludes there may be some civic benefit from all the attention Vienna's liberal press has lavished on Mark Twain. It has discomfited those local celebrities whose only raison d'être is their "Among Others-Existence" and who have been upstaged in "the journalistic frog pond" from which "mornings and evenings, the unending melody is lovingly croaked: *u.a., u.a., u.a.* . . ."

From his jibes about Twain's "long bankrupt ability," it seems obvious that up to this point Karl Kraus was not really conversant with Mark Twain's writings. This was not because he was not literate, indeed well read, in English, as his excellent translations of Shakespeare's plays and sonnets clearly indicate, but more likely because he shared the snobbish prejudice of many well-educated, English-speaking Europeans until recent decades that American literature was by definition inferior to that produced in Great Britain, a view English critics did everything they could to foster. It also seems possible from parallels discernible between Twain's writing and what Karl Kraus wrote in succeeding decades that, his curiosity piqued, the waspish editor-publisher of *Die Fackel* thereupon took occasion to familiarize himself with some of Twain's recent works and that they made some impression on him.

Two of Mark Twain's works in particular provide some evidence to justify such speculation. The first is *The Tragedy of Pudd'nhead Wilson*, a short novel published in 1894. The second, published soon after he arrived in Vienna in 1897, is his account of his travels to Australasia, India, and South Africa, *Following the Equator* (or *More Tramps Abroad*, in the edition then available in Vienna). A distinctive feature of both works is a series of cynical epigraphs at the head of each chapter supposedly composed by the first book's title character (David Wilson) for "Pudd'nhead Wilson's Calendar," a name that at once evokes the worldly wise "sayings" of Franklin's *Poor Richard's Almanack*. These aphorisms proved to be the book's most popular feature, making a hit with both the critics and the public and spurring Twain to create more such sententiae for use as chapter epigraphs in *Following the Equator* where they were designated as "Pudd'nhead Wilson's New Calendar." Altogether there are 102 of these "Pudd'nhead Wilson" aphorisms in the two works: 35 in *Pudd'nhead Wilson* and almost twice as many (67) in the second book.

In addition to these published aphorisms, Mark Twain filled page upon page of the two still-unpublished notebooks he kept while in Vienna with about 170 more, including variant versions of some and incomplete sketches for other aphorisms. While two-thirds of these notebook aphorisms remain unpublished, some went into what he was writing at the time, most notably "Concerning the Jews," *What Is Man?*, book 1 of *Christian Science*, and "The Man That Corrupted Hadleyburg." Others turn up in such later works as *Letters from the Earth*.

This use of aphorisms in narrative and descriptive writing characterizes almost everything he wrote during and after his Austrian residence. There was thus a distinct shift in Mark Twain's style in the late 1890s away from the kind of vernacular humor he employed, for example, in *Huckleberry Finn*, and toward more urbane verbal cleverness and subtler wit. It is perhaps ironic that while his earlier works remain his most popular ones, the memorable Mark Twain quotations, those one encounters most often, are his Pudd'nhead Wilson and other aphorisms from this final phase of his career.

In the early years of this century, Karl Kraus emerged as the most prolific, most often quoted of the Viennese aphorists. In the early years of his magazine, Kraus printed his translations of several aphorisms by Oscar Wilde, the Marquis de Sade, and others, but in the March 12, 1906, issue of *Die Fackel* he began a regular feature, called "Abfälle" (rubbish), each containing dozens of his own aphorisms and short aphoristic verses. He continued this until the early 1920s, periodically culling a grand total of some three thousand of these items for republication in three collections: *Sprüche und Widersprüche* (Vienna, 1909), *Pro domo et mundo* (Munich, 1912), and *Nachts* (Leipzig, 1918). Altogether Kraus penned nearly six thousand aphorisms during his career, only a small fraction of which have ever been translated into English.

In turning to the aphoristic style, both Twain and Kraus were drawing upon venerable traditions in their respective literary cultures. Ranging from the pious proverbs of colonial New England that Benjamin Franklin's Poor Richard secularized to the moralistic maxims of Ralph Waldo Emerson and, especially, from such western and southern "crackerbox philosophers" as Artemus Ward (C. F. Browne), Josh Billings (H. W. Shaw), and Bill Nye, there was a well-defined genre of pithy, humorous American "horse sense" aphoristic writing that Mark Twain appropriated for Pudd'nhead Wilson's calendars, for his platform routines, and for the style of his later narratives.

The Austrian literary mode of aphoristic expression of which Karl Kraus became perhaps the foremost exponent belonged mainly to the highbrow culture rather than to vernacular or dialect humorists. Although the *Sprichwort* (folk adage) was used in popular humor by numerous writers as varied as the playwright Johann Nepomuk Nestroy (whom Kraus revered) and the feuilletonist Eduard Pötzl, aphoristic writing as a serious art form, like much else in Austrian (and German) literature, was of French derivation, harking back to La Rochefoucauld and to the Enlightenment *Philosophes*. In late nineteenth-century Vienna this aphoristic style had an unusual flowering in the works, for example, of Marie von Ebner-Eschenbach, Peter Altenberg, Hugo von Hofmannsthal, and Arthur Schnitzler.

Kraus was almost unique among these Viennese contemporaries in coining aphorisms ad hoc and ad libidum to be published independently of any other literary context. Most other Austrian writers embedded their aphorisms in belletristic writing in an effort to make them organic or intrinsic to their style rather than merely decorative.[10] The purpose and effect of this method of writing was to create an impressionistic style with great verbal compression and intensity for the purpose of clarifying (*Klärung*) a perception through a sudden flash of wit (*Einfall*) that, at its most successful, would be a delightful surprise to the reader. The conscious concern Viennese writers gave to this process is reflected in the many aphorisms they wrote to define what an aphorism is or does. For example, Marie von Ebner-Eschenbach wrote, "An aphorism is the final link in a long chain of reflection" (*Ein Aphorismus ist der letzte Ring einer langen Gedankenkette*).[11] And in one of his many aphorisms defining aphorisms, Karl Kraus said: "An aphorism need not be true, but it should surpass the truth. It must go beyond it in one jump." (*Ein Aphorismus braucht nicht wahr zu sein, aber er soll die Wahrheit überflügeln. Er muß mit einem Satz über sie hinauskommen.*)[12]

No aphorist can be unremittingly brilliant. The aphorisms of both Mark Twain and Karl Kraus run a gamut from the pedestrian, banal, and mildly amusing to the brilliant, profoundly disturbing, and unforgettable. Kraus tried to exclude his topically stale and less brilliant "*Abfälle*" aphorisms from his three collections, but he was no more successful than most writers in judging his own achievements. For his part, Mark Twain left some of his best, most tantalizing aphorisms in manuscript while publishing such mundane truisms as "It is easier to stay out than get out." Where their efforts are most congruent, most demanding of comparison, is in their use of the aphorism as a satirical technique and as an expression of their deepest philosophical concerns.

It would be an understatement to say that both writers held a low evaluation of human nature, of what Mark Twain scourged with increasing frequency and ferocity after 1897 as "the damned human race." "The devil is an optimist if he thinks he can make people worse," Kraus wrote, and in another: "Nothing is more narrow-minded than chauvinism or race hatred. To me all men are equal: there are jackasses everywhere, and I have the same contempt for all. No petty prejudices!"[13] In "Concerning the Jews" in 1898 Twain wrote: "I can stand any society. All I care to know is that a man is a human being—that is enough for me; he can't be any worse."[14] One of Pudd'nhead Wilson's most memorable aphorisms is "If you pick up a starving dog and make him prosperous, he will not bite you. This is the principal difference between a dog and a man."[15] And in his Vienna notebooks he wrestled with different versions of "The human race consists of the damned & the ought-to-be damned." Nor does he exempt himself: "When we remember that we are all mad," he mused in a notebook aphorism he repeated in softer form in both *What Is Man?* and *Christian Science*, "the mysteries disappear & life stands explained."†[16]

This shared misanthropy is sometimes expressed with uncanny similarity, as for instance:

> *Twain:* When I reflect upon the number of disagreeable people who I know have gone to a better world, I am moved to lead a different life.[17]

> *Kraus:* If I were sure I would have to share immortality with certain people, I would prefer a separate oblivion. (*Wenn ich sicher wüßte, daß ich mit gewissen Leuten die Unsterblichkeit zu teilen haben werde, so möchte ich eine separierte Vergessenheit vorziehen.*)[18]

Nor are these the only startling parallels evident when one juxtaposes what Mark Twain wrote in the closing phase of his career upon the writings of Karl Kraus.

For example, in a society that then had the highest incidence in the Western world of what Emile Durkheim called in 1897 "anomic suicide," one cannot wonder that suicide and a fascination with death bulk large as symbolic motifs in Kraus's satires. That this theme is also true of Mark Twain during the last fifteen years of his writing career has puzzled some of his most perceptive readers. The standard interpretation that it was the bereavements and misfortunes he suffered during these years that turned his thoughts in this morose direction do not suffice to explain three aphorisms in *Pudd'nhead Wilson*, written well before the death of Susy and other blows of fate supposedly embittered him:

> Whoever has lived long enough to find out what life is, knows how deep a debt of gratitude we owe to Adam, the first great benefactor of our race. He brought death into the world.

Why is it that we rejoice at a birth and grieve at a funeral? It is because we are not the person involved.

All say, "How hard it is that we have to die"—a strange complaint to come from the mouths of people who have had to live.[19]

These musings are intensified and concentrated in an entry for "Pudd'nhead Wilson's New Calendar" in *Following the Equator*: "Pity is for the living, envy is for the dead."

Several of the aphorisms he penned in his notebook in Vienna in 1898 are so dark that he judiciously withheld them from publication:

Favored above Kings and Emperors is the stillborn child.
All people have had ill luck, but Jairus's daughter & Lazarus the worst. *
No real estate is permanently valuable but the grave.
Life.
We laugh & laugh,
    Then cry & cry—
Then feebler laugh—
    Then die.†[20]

None of these, however, quite plumbs the depths of cynical therapeutic nihilism that this unpublished notebook entry evinces: "Of the demonstrably wise there are but two: those who commit suicide, & those who keep their reasoning faculties atrophied with drink."[21] Amid the welter of notes he made (for "The Memorable Assassination") while watching the empress's cortège, one finds: "The suicides seem to be the only sane people."[22] And the protagonist-narrator of "Which Was the Dream?" remarks: "Few of us can see far ahead. Prophecy is not given to us. Hence the paucity of suicides."[23]

Although *Selbstmord*—suicide or self-inflicted euthanasia—was illegal in Austria and a mortal sin for Catholics, an astounding number of Austrian intellectuals committed or attempted suicide during the last decades of the monarchy, and many more contemplated it seriously. The officially condoned version of Crown Prince Rudolf's "suicide" in

---

*Both were resurrected from the dead by Jesus (*Matt.* 9:18–26, *Mark* 5:22–43, *Luke* 8:41–56; *John* 11:1–44, 12:1–2).

a supposed love pact with his mistress in 1889 lent a certain Romantic éclat to an act which was the ultimate expression of therapeutic nihilism. Suicides among leading Austrian writers included Ferdinand Raimund, Adalbert Stifter, and Ferdinand von Saar, while physicist Ludwig Boltzmann, social theorist Ludwig Gumplowicz, and architect Eduard van der Null (who hanged himself when the emperor criticized his design for Vienna's opera house) are among many other prominent figures who took their own lives during this epoch. The most dramatic, perhaps most symbolic suicide was the gifted twenty-three-year-old Jewish writer Otto Weininger, who, after successfully publishing a brilliant, highly controversial antifeminist, anti-Semitic book on sex, race, and character, shot himself in a room he had rented for that purpose in the house where Beethoven died.[24]

There is no evidence that Samuel L. Clemens ever seriously contemplated terminating his own life, especially after he began his successful career as "Mark Twain," but Karl Kraus flirted with the idea and so, too, did Gustav Mahler, Sigmund Freud, and Hugo von Hofmannsthal, among others Twain knew (or knew of) in Vienna. It is hardly surprising, then, that the theme of suicide and of death as a blessed boon appealed to his literary imagination in 1897 and found expression in his aphorisms as well as in his unfinished "Chronicle of Young Satan," where the drowning of two children is demonstrated to have been a fortunate release from what would otherwise have been miserable existences filled with intolerable suffering.

Although Kraus, unlike Twain, did not attempt aphoristic expressions of his preoccupations with suicide and death, they were important as metaphors in his satires, in verses such as "Tod und Tango" about a murder and botched suicide attempt, and especially in his masterpiece, *Die letzten Tage der Menschheit* (The Last Days of Mankind). This mammoth, seven-hundred-page documentary drama with a thirteen-page cast of characters about the First World War in its mythic complexity and experimental techniques with language has sometimes been compared to Joyce's *Ulysses*. Kraus was less concerned with the suicides and deaths of individuals than with the suicide being

committed all around him by the society in which he lived. As Bertolt
Brecht said of him, "When the age came to die by its own hand, he
was that hand."[25]

   To infer direct influences on each other from the similar ways in
which Mark Twain and Karl Kraus expressed similar ideas would
be fatuous. Excepting only the early numbers of *Die Fackel* (April–
May 1899), one cannot assume Twain's familiarity with anything Karl
Kraus wrote, certainly not with the "*Abfälle*" aphorisms that began appearing only after Twain had returned home. Kraus made only one
further direct reference to Mark Twain in his magazine. In a filler
in his eleventh number (mid-July 1899) he reported Twain's remarks
in separate interviews in the *Daily Chronicle* (London) and *New Yorker
Staats-Zeitung* (a German-language newspaper in New York) praising
the city's "enchantments" in the first while condemning its "corrup-
tion" in the second.[26] The balanced, matter-of-fact manner in which
Kraus quotes from these interviews without comment perhaps hints
that since April he had tempered his disdain for the American humorist. If so, might this change have come about from his discovering some
congenial aphorisms in *Pudd'nhead Wilson* and *Following the Equator* in
the interval? One may only speculate. Like so much else about Mark
Twain's Vienna years, his relationship with Karl Kraus remains enigmatic. No doubt common germs both were inhaling from the intellectual atmosphere of Vienna could be scrutinized more closely to help
solve some of the puzzle of these strange affinities. On the other hand,
one may invoke here Karl Kraus's aphorism that "An artist is one who
can make a puzzle out of its solution" (*Künstler ist nur einer, der aus der
Lösung ein Rätsel machen kann*).[27]

CHAPTER THIRTEEN

City of Doctors,
City of Dreams

Throughout his last two decades Clemens was almost daily involved with members of the medical profession in Berlin, London, Vienna, Sanna (Sweden), Florence, and at various European health resorts as well as at home in New York and Connecticut. The chronic ailments besetting his family, especially after Susy's death, seemed intractable and interminable, the most serious being Jean's epilepsy and Livy's neurasthenia and angina. Clemens himself verged on hypochondria, albeit with frequent quite real bouts of neuralgia, rheumatism, lumbago, gout, dysuria, and in his late years, emphysema and the coronary disease that felled him on April 21, 1910. He confided in his Vienna notebook: "We proudly conceal our ailments from the public, but keep the family supplied with information about them. This could be turned around with advantage."†1 It was, one recalls, to "take the cure" at such spas as Aix-les-Bains and Marienbad that the Clemenses went abroad in June 1891 on what turned into a nine-year odyssey.

The Vienna they came to in 1897 was one of the world's foremost centers of medical education, research, and practice. As with its musical hegemony, the city's preeminence in medicine also began in the middle of the eighteenth century when Empress Maria Theresa lured Gerhard van Swieten (1700–1772), a Dutch protégé of the great Boerhaave, to Vienna as her personal physician with the chance to recruit an illustrious medical faculty for Vienna's university. In 1784, her son and successor, Joseph II, gave the faculty its own teaching hospital, the still-functioning Allgemeines Krankenhaus, now Europe's largest hospital, and he established yet another hospital, the Josephinum, to train military surgeons. By the 1850s the Vienna School of Medicine, as it came to be known under the leadership of, among many others, professors Skoda, Rokitansky, Semmelweiss, and Billroth, made Vienna what Berlin's eminent pathologist, Rudolf Virchow, enviously called "the Mecca of Medicine." It remained so until Hitler's minions "purified" the faculty of its Jews in March 1938.[2] For almost a century. Vienna's medical prestige lured American physicians who wanted to hang out shingles back home as specialists in diseases of the rich. At the time of the Clemenses' sojourn, as I have noted earlier, more than two hundred young Americans were studying medicine at the University of Vienna.

From *Augenheilkunde* (ophthalmology) to *Gynaekologie* (gynecology) and every other specialty, Vienna in 1897 had at least one world-renowned pioneering researcher and authority, but in fields such as neurology, brain surgery, psychiatry, and pediatrics it boasted dozens. One of its most eminent medicos was Heinrich Obersteiner (1847–1922), *Ordinarius* for anatomy and pathology in the university, who specialized in pediatric neurology. On October 5, 1897, barely a week after settling his family at the Metropole, Clemens dispatched the following letter to Prof. Dr. Obersteiner:

Dear Sir:

I enclose a letter from Dr. Allen Starr of New York. My wife & I desire to see you regarding the case of our daughter (17 years of age,) who has had six epileptic attacks. She had the first one a year ago last Winter; the second one quite near the first; then followed an interval of more than a year between that one & the third; then an interval of six months between that & the fourth; the fourth was followed within 4 weeks by two more. The sixth & last one occurred in Vienna a week ago to-day.

She does not know what her difficulty is, but thinks herself subject to merely ordinary attacks of fainting, & we prefer to keep her in ignorance regarding their true character.

Can we bring her to see you? & will you kindly tell me at what hour it will be best for us to call?

Very truly yours,

S. L. Clemens

P.S. May I ask you to return Dr. Starr's letter?*3

The New York physician W. Allen Starr, who attended the Clemenses off and on from 1895 until 1906, had studied with Dr. Obersteiner, who drew students to his seminars in Vienna from as far away as Tokyo, San Francisco, and Rio de Janeiro.4 Although the alarming increase in the frequency of Jean's seizures made a consultation urgent, when or even whether Obersteiner saw the Clemenses and what his diagnosis or treatment of Jean's condition might have been remain undisclosed.

In any case, Clemens's notebook bulged with addresses of prominent Viennese medical doctors, and in his search for remedies for his own and his family's ailments, he constantly toured the consulting rooms of leading members of Vienna's medical fraternity. The physicians he consulted were of every theoretical persuasion—allopaths, homeopaths, naturopaths, osteopaths—as well as specialists of nearly every organ and disease. In addition to Obersteiner, his address book lists Dr. Ladislaus (Prince) Batthyany-Strattmann, Dr. Robert Gersuny, Dr. Alexander von Hüttenbrenner, Dr. Ernst (Ritter) von Klarwill, Dr. George Alexander Otis, Dr. Wilhelm Pokorny, and Drs. Alfred and Wilhelm Winternitz.5 The Clemenses' friend Eduard Pötzl, responding on October 15, 1897, to a dinner invitation from Livy, was eager to recommend to them a dentist with gold-plated credentials:

Hochgeehrte gnädige Frau!

empfangen Sie meinen versichertsten Dank für die gestrigen Zeilen. Ich hoffe nächsten Montag wieder besuchsfähig zu sein.

Inzwischen gestatten Sie mir, Ihnen einer Freund Amerikas zu emp-
fehlen, unseren berühmtester Zahnarzt, Dr. E. M. Thomas, Imperiale
Councillor (Kaiserlicher Rath) welcher sein Jugend in Mr. Clemens Vaterland gebracht hat und ein glühender Verehrer von dessen Genie ist. Er
möchte Ihnen eine Aufwartung machen.

Indem ich bitte, mich bei Mr. Clemens und den Fräulein in freund-
licher Erinnerung zu halten, bin ich Ihr ganz ergebener /Ed. Pötzl[6]
(Highly Honored Gracious Lady!
Receive my most assured thanks for your note of yesterday. By next Monday I hope to be fit enough again to be sociable.

Meanwhile, let me recommend a friend of America, our most famous
dentist, Dr. E. M. Thomas, Imperial Councillor, who spent his youth in
Mr. Clemens's fatherland [Missouri?] and is a glowing admirer of his
genius. He would like to pay you a visit. . . .)

The physician they most often saw socially as well as perhaps professionally in Vienna was the expatriate Virginian Dr. George Otis, who
settled in Austria after serving as a Confederate army surgeon in the
Civil War. He subsequently founded the still-active American Medical
Society of Vienna.[7]

Although Clemens's medical address list does not include Dr.
Richard von Krafft-Ebing (1840–1902), certainly the most renowned
Viennese psychiatrist after the death of Freud's teacher, Meynert,
in 1892, Henry Fisher recalls a conversation Krafft-Ebing held with
Mark Twain in the famed psychiatrist's library about the psychology of
lynching and mob violence in general.[8] It seems quite unlikely Twain
could have escaped reading *Psychopathia Sexualis*, Krafft-Ebing's study
of sexual aberrations drawn mainly from court cases, which paved the
way for Freud's theories. By 1897 it was in its ninth enlarged edition
and was a best-seller in seven languages. It was in this encyclopedic study that Krafft-Ebing coined the psychiatric term "masochism"
for the bondage fetishes Leopold von Sacher-Masoch (1836–95) described in his luridly sensational autobiographical novella, *Venus im
Pelze* (Venus in Furs), another sub-rosa best-seller in Vienna at this
period.[9]

Among other prominent names on Twain's list of Viennese physicians are Dr. Alexander von Hüttenbrenner (1842–1905), pediatrician *Primarius* (chief of staff) of Vienna's Children's Hospital, and the pioneering plastic surgeon Dr. Robert Gersuny (1844–1924), an assistant and lifelong friend of the illustrious Dr. Theodor Billroth. In 1882, when Billroth persuaded the medical philanthropist Graf Hans von Wilczek to underwrite the founding of a prestigious private hospital, the Rudolfinerhaus, where girls of good family might train as *Krankenschwestern* (nurses), Dr. Gersuny was appointed its director, a post he filled with distinction until 1910. Gersuny was also founding president of Vienna's *Gesellschaft der Ärzte* (Society of Physicians).[10]

Dr. Wilhelm Winternitz, to whose water cure the Clemens women submitted in the summer of 1898, was one of the few physicians on Twain's list not attached in some way to the University of Vienna. A Bohemian Jew who received his medical education in Prague, Winternitz achieved *Promotion* (the doctorate) at the unusually early age of twenty-three. Soon thereafter he began publishing his theories of hydrotherapy, and he was only thirty-one in 1865 when he established what became a famous and fashionable *Wasserheilanstalt* at Kaltenleutgeben.[11]

At first glance, a puzzling omission in Twain's list might seem to be that of Dozent Dr. Sigmund Freud, a name that leaps to mind today whenever Viennese medicine, especially Viennese psychiatry, at the turn of this century is mentioned. Although one cannot be certain beyond any shadow of doubt, there is sufficient circumstantial evidence to indicate that Samuel Clemens and Dr. Freud probably met more than once in 1898 and that they may even have had a polite social acquaintance. The evidence is mainly from Freud's admiring comments on and allusions to Mark Twain in his own writings, but they also shared a common circle of acquaintances in Vienna, including all but one or two of the doctors mentioned above, and they were indisputably in each other's presence—that is in the same room together—on at least two occasions.

Freud's name would not necessarily have appeared on Clemens's

list of physicians unless the American visitor thought he might need
to consult the then-untenured university lecturer (*Privatdozent*) in
neuropathology who also had a private practice at Berggasse 19.
Although the consultation books in the Freud archives do not contain Clemens's name, Dr. Harald Leupold-Löwenthal, president of the
Sigmund Freud–Gesellschaft, observed that that does *not* necessarily
mean Clemens did not discuss Jean's epilepsy with Freud informally at
some point, only that he did not have an office appointment to do so.
Dr. Obersteiner, Freud's senior colleague in neuropathology, would
have been a more logical choice for such a consultation even if Jean's
father harbored doubts about whether the causes of her disorder were
purely physical. With his seminal work *Traumdeutung* (*The Interpretation of Dreams*), then still *in nubibus*, Freud was still virtually unknown
outside Vienna, not yet the grand guru of psychoanalysis he became
after 1900.

On February 9, 1898, Freud wrote to his close friend Dr. Wilhelm
Fliess in Berlin, in part as follows: "Schweninger's performance, here
at the talking circus, was a real disgrace! I did not attend, of course;
instead I treated myself to listening to our old friend Mark Twain in
person, which was a sheer delight." [12]

Dr. Schweninger, of Berlin, personal physician of the aged architect
of the German Empire, Fürst Otto von Bismarck (who died July 30,
1898), had come to Vienna to expound his theories of medical nihilism, that "the world belongs to the brave, including the brave sick," at
the faculty conference Freud called a "talking circus." [13] Revolted by
such therapeutic nihilism, Freud had chosen instead, at some professional risk, to attend Mark Twain's first public lecture in Vienna, at the
Bösendorfersaal on February 1, 1898.

Twain's performance left such a vivid impression that Freud was able
to conjure it up some thirty-two years later for *Civilization and Its Discontents* (1930) where he wrote that "the field of ethics . . . presents us
with another fact: namely that ill-luck—that is, external frustration—
so greatly enhances the power of the conscience in the super-ego," then
glossed this observation with: "This enhancing of morality as a conse-

Sigmund Freud in his study, Vienna, 1898
(Courtesy Sigmund Freud Copyrights Ltd.)

quence of ill-luck has been illustrated by Mark Twain in a delightful little story, *The First Melon I ever Stole*. This first melon happened to be unripe. I heard Mark Twain tell the story himself in one of his public readings. After he had given out the title, he stopped and asked himself as though he was in doubt: 'Was it the first?' With this, everything had been said. The first melon evidently was not the only one." [14] The story to which Freud refers is part of a lecture Paine titled "Morals and Memory" (in *Mark Twain's Speeches*, 1910), a pastiche of stories Twain worked up in 1895 for his global tour and kept in his repertoire thereafter. It recounts how the eleven-year-old Sam Clemens "extracted" a watermelon from a farmer's wagon and, discovering it was unripe, returned it to the wagon and made the farmer replace the green one he had stolen with a ripe one. The moral of this tale was, Twain said, "Always make sure your melon is ripe before you go to the trouble of stealing it." Freud made perhaps both more and less of this brief anecdote than its author may have intended.

This was neither the first nor last of Freud's allusions to Twain, a writer he found more useful for exemplifying his theories than any other in English save Shakespeare. In *Jokes and Their Relation to the Unconscious* (1905), for instance, Freud draws extensively upon three Twain stories to illustrate his principle that "an economy of pity is one of the most frequent sources of humorous pleasure," multiplying examples of how Mark Twain's humor exploits "economy of pity." His first example is an anecdote Freud recalls from *Roughing It* (chapter 77) about a mining explosion in which a worker (Freud misremembers him as Twain's brother) is blown sky high, "coming down again far away from the place where he had been working." Freud offers this analysis: "We are bound to have feelings of sympathy for the victim of the accident and would like to know whether he was injured by it. But when the story goes on to say that his brother had a half-day's wages deducted for being 'absent from his place of employment' we are entirely distracted from our pity and become almost as hard-hearted as the [employer] and almost as indifferent to the brother's health." [15]

Freud's second example is the genealogical lampoon in "A Burlesque

Biography" (in *The $30,000 Bequest & Other Stories*) in which Twain traces his ancestry to one of Columbus's crew whose "baggage consisted entirely of a number of pieces of washing each of which had a different laundry mark." Freud analyzes the humor in this perceptively, noting that "here we cannot help laughing at the cost of an economy of the feeling of piety into which we are prepared to enter at the beginning of this family history. The mechanism of the humorous pleasure is not interfered with by our knowledge that this pedigree is a fictitious one and that the fiction serves the satirical purpose of exposing the embellishments in similar accounts of other people."

Freud's third example of "economy of pity" is from *The Innocents Abroad* (chapter 27) in which Judge Oliver (also here mistakenly called Twain's brother), after laboriously constructing a lean-to dwelling, is repeatedly harried by a mule and then a cow falling through his makeshift sailcloth roof. Freud observes:

> Repetition makes the story comic, but Mark Twain ends it by reporting on the forty-sixth night, when the cow fell through again, his brother finally remarked: "The thing's beginning to get monotonous." At this our humorous pleasure cannot be kept back, for what we had long expected to hear was that this obstinate set of misfortunes would make his brother *angry*. And indeed the small contributions of humour that we produce ourselves are as a rule made at the cost of anger—instead of getting angry.[16]

In his *Contribution to a Questionnaire on Reading* (1907), Freud listed Mark Twain's *Sketches New and Old* (1875) when he was invited to name "ten good books" of contemporary literature, saying that if the list could be extended to more than ten he would also include *The Adventures of Tom Sawyer* and *Adventures of Huckleberry Finn*.[17] What especially attracted a physician like Freud to Twain's *Sketches*, he admitted, was the inclusion in it of an early medical burlesque, "Curing a Cold" (1864).

Passing references to Twain's writings also occur in Freud's *The Psychopathology of Everyday Life* (1901, rev. 1919) and *The "Uncanny"*

(1919). Finally, it has been clearly demonstrated that Freud's very last essay, "A Comment on Anti-Semitism" (in *Die Zukunft* in Paris, 1938), is basically a reworking of Mark Twain's "Concerning the Jews," although by then the cancer-ridden octogenarian exile psychoanalyst sadly confessed, "I can no longer recall where I read the essay (i.e., 'Concerning the Jews') of which I made a précis nor who it was who was its author." [18]

According to one recent study of Freud's discovery of psychoanalysis, another important source for Freud in Mark Twain's writings, albeit unconscious rather than a deliberate exemplification or direct allusion, was "Stirring Times in Austria," which Freud either read when it appeared in *Harper's* in February 1898 or more likely knew from the detailed laudatory review of it in *Neue Freie Presse* (February 24, 1898). Twain's lengthy description in "Stirring Times" of Dr. Lecher's marathon speech in the Reichsrat apparently figured in Freud's analysis in *Traumdeutung* of the dream he had had about Dr. Lecher and his filibuster shortly after the event. [19]

Did Freud take the opportunity to be introduced to Mark Twain at the Bösendorfersaal reading, as others in attendance did? Would that we knew! They might actually have met some four weeks earlier at the Carltheater where Theodor Herzl's social problem play, *Das Neue Ghetto*, had its premiere on January 5, 1898. Herzl, a neighbor and friend of Freud and an acquaintance of Mark Twain, "papered the house" for his opening, sending both of them tickets. Both attended. Twain, in fact, considered and may even have started an abortive translation of Herzl's play for Broadway, so it is not inconceivable they were introduced to each other in this small theater on such a convivial occasion, hence Freud's reference to Twain as "our old friend" in his letter to Fliess.

The one who could have done Freud this favor was Friedrich Eckstein (1861–1939), his partner in the regular Tuesday night tarok games at the home of their ophthalmologist, Dr. Ludwig Königstein. "The philosopher of the Ringstrasse," as Eckstein was later called, was a charming, affable dilettante who visited Mark Twain in Hartford in

Portrait of Mark Twain by J. Le Owy, autographed to Friedrich
Eckstein, Vienna, 1897 (from Eckstein, *"Alte unnennbare Tage!":*
Erinnerungen aus Siebzig Lehr-und Wanderjahren, 1936)

the early 1880s during a North American *Wanderjahre* upon leaving his studies at the University of Vienna where he and Sigmund Freud had become friends. Son of a prosperous parchment manufacturer in Perchtoldsdorf, Eckstein indulged his fascination with the Eastern cultures by traveling widely in the Middle East and India, eventually becoming a Sanskritist, a vegetarian, and a yoga devotee who mixed mysticism with psychoanalysis, upon which he later wrote some pamphlets. Anna Freud admired his "encyclopedic knowledge."[20]

His interest in the Near East led Eckstein to *In the Levant* (1877), a two-volume account of travels in Lebanon, Syria, and Palestine by Charles Dudley Warner, editor of *The Hartford Courant* and Mark Twain's next-door neighbor as well as his collaborator in *The Gilded Age* (1873). Eckstein traveled to Hartford on his American grand tour expressly to meet Warner, who entertained him royally for several days, introducing him to Harriet Beecher Stowe (another next-door neighbor) and her house guest, Julia Ward Howe (author of "The Battle Hymn of the Republic"), plus, of course, Mark Twain. The Clemens family also offered the young Austrian gracious hospitality, and Eckstein was intrigued and enchanted by the "Hurricane Deck" veranda on the Farmington Avenue mansion Clemens called his "combination Mississippi River steamboat and cuckoo clock."[21]

Noblesse oblige, when the Clemenses landed in Vienna some fifteen years later, one of their first callers at the Metropole was Friedrich Eckstein, by then a successful merchant with a shop in Porzellangasse around the corner from Freud's apartment and office. In memoirs he published four decades later, *"Alte unnennbare Tage!": Erinnerungen aus Siebzig Lehr-und Wanderjahren* (*"Old Ineffable Days!": Memories of Seventy Years of Study and Travel*, 1936), Eckstein recalled finding Mark Twain greatly aged and his family "in deep mourning" because "one of his lovely daughters had shortly before been torn from him in untimely death." Nevertheless, he says, he often visited with Mark Twain during the Clemenses' first Vienna winter and seized every chance to show them *"die Schönheiten der Stadt und ihrer Umgebung"* (the beautiful sights of the city and its environs), even taking Twain on an excursion to the nearby thermal resort of Baden-bei-Wien and the Benedictine abbey at Heiligenkreuz "wherein he found great comfort."[22] Among six illustrations in his book is a cherished memento of Twain: a picture of the humorist taken by the official court photographer, Julius Löwy, autographed atop with a Pudd'nhead Wilson aphorism, "It is one's human environment that makes climate. / Truly Yours Mark Twain," and at bottom "With Kindest Salutations from S. L. Clemens," plus the date "Feb. 1898."

Eckstein does not couple Twain's name with Freud's in his chapter about his friendship with the psychoanalyst, nor does he mention Herzl's premiere, which he no doubt also attended. For his part, Twain makes no mention anywhere of Freud's friend. Nevertheless, Eckstein remains the most plausible candidate for having introduced Twain and Freud to each other, whether at the Carltheater, at the Bösendorfersaal, or at one of Mark Twain's other Vienna readings.

Friedrich Eckstein figures in Freud's analysis of one of his own mnemonic slips in *Psychopathology of Everyday Life*. Freud describes his distress at being unable to recall Eckstein's name even though he had seen this friend with whom he was on a first-name basis (i.e., in Austria, very close) earlier that same day. He says he then "went out into the street to read the names over the shops, and recognized his name the first time I ran across it."[23] Another connection between them was Emma Eckstein (1865–1924), one of Friedrich's six sisters (another was Therese Schlesinger) and the first patient Sigmund Freud treated for hysteria using the techniques of hypnotism and psychoanalysis he learned from J. M. Charcot and Josef Breuer.

At twenty-seven, Emma had stomach cramps and an inability to menstruate that made walking upright painful. In analysis she revealed having been sexually molested when she was eight years old, and after collecting and comparing seventeen more cases of hysteria where there were similar suppressed memories of childhood sexual traumas, Freud enunciated his "seduction theory" of the origin of neuroses in a paper, "*Über die Aetiologie der Hysteria*" (On the Etiology of Hysteria), he presented to the Verein für Psychiatrie und Neurologie in Wien, April 21, 1896. Meanwhile, he consulted his old Berlin friend about Emma's problems, and Fliess, with his own theories (later published) about causal connections between women's menstrual problems and the shape and size of their noses, recommended what is nowadays called a "nose bob." The surgery Fliess performed with Freud's approval on Emma's nose in early February 1895 was botched, as was a second operation by Dr. Gersuny a month later, and the unfortunate lady suffered from both nasal and menstrual problems the rest of her days.[24]

More important for the history of psychoanalysis, Freud's paper postulating the origin of neurosis in "infantile sexual scenes" or "sexual intercourse in childhood" (what is today generalized by the euphemism "child abuse") was greeted by his colleagues in stony silence— no questions, no discussion, no debate. He told Fliess his paper had "an icy reception from the asses," then was peremptorily dismissed by the chairman, Hofrat Dr. Richard von Krafft-Ebing, with a "strange comment": *"Es klingt wie ein wissenschaftliches Märchen"* (It sounds like a scientific fairy tale).[25] After this stinging rebuke, Freud scuttled his seduction theory and took to a line of research and ratiocination which produced the basis of psychoanalysis: that the origin of neuroses lay in infantile sexual fantasies that are revealed by analyzing dreams, the nature of which he defined as the expressions of "a disguised fulfillment of a suppressed or repressed wish."[26] He was apparently more willing to depict children as little ogres, harboring murderous thoughts and perverse sexual desires, than to risk ostracism by suggesting they might be passive victims of incestuous lust or lascivious nannies in respectable Viennese households.

Whether or not, as J. M. Masson, a former director of the Sigmund Freud Archives, persuasively if hyperbolically argued, Freud may have abandoned his seduction theory and suppressed evidence he knew to be valid in order to protect his chances for academic advancement, in Freud's post-1896 obsession with the significance of dreams (his own and others') for understanding the human psyche lies the nexus of his thought with Mark Twain's and with Twain's later writings. It may not entirely be coincidental that Freud was occupied with the formulations that went into *Traumdeutung*, first published in December 1899, at the very time Mark Twain was living in Vienna, exploring the significance of dreams, and toying with ideas of a "dream self" (with dual, even triple identity) in his fiction.

Long before he came to Vienna, Clemens had been fascinated by dreams and their possible significations, and Mark Twain's literary imagination was often fired by the dreams recorded in his notebooks. Sometimes such notations remained dormant a long while before being put to use in his writing as, for example, his "dream of being a knight errant," which surfaced five years later in *A Connecticut Yankee*. He groused about being unable to recall jokes and comical situations in his dreams for later use, but in Weggis he noted an exception: "In a dream I have at last encountered a humorism that actually remained one after waking. The crowned heads were adrift at sea on a raft. They all managed to stay amiable but Victoria. She was constantly cross. 'This was the origin of the V[ictoria] C[ross].' With that sentence the dream ended."[27]

The notebooks he kept in Vienna and Kaltenleutgeben are unusually rich in recorded dreams and his musings upon them. These notations contain ideas that went immediately into the story "My Platonic Sweetheart," as well as into the unfinished novel DeVoto named "The Great Dark" when he edited it for its first publication in *Letters from the Earth* (1962) and two of the three incomplete versions of the novella commonly called *The Mysterious Stranger, A Romance*, the title Paine and Frederick Duneka gave the pastiche of manuscripts they published in 1916. These are "The Chronicle of Young Satan" and the briefer "Schoolhouse Hill." Together with "No. 44, The Mysterious Stranger," into which Twain blended elements from both in 1902 with further additions between then until 1908, and the manuscript cluster containing "The Great Dark," they comprise his most important efforts in sustained narrative during the last fifteen years of his life. For that reason, as well as for the analogues one finds in them to ideas expressed in early writings of Sigmund Freud, these works demand close and extensive attention here.

In these stories—"The Great Dark," "The Chronicle of Young Satan," and "Schoolhouse Hill"—five disparate themes come together. First, there is the long voyage on which Twain embarked in 1891 and which led, with only brief calls at "home port," around the world and into the heart of Europe. By July 1898, when Livy reportedly vetoed returning to New York for at least another year, the voyage had begun to seem truly endless. Anyone who has even vaguely calculated the total nautical miles and months, years even, Mark Twain spent sailing up and down the Mississippi and on the high seas, back and forth across the Atlantic and around the world, cannot wonder that voyaging was a major theme and plot device in his work.

Second is Twain's experience of Austria itself, especially its quaint, antiquated mentality and the "medieval night" in which this supposedly modern state still paradoxically slumbered at the end of the nineteenth century.

Third is his lifelong fascination with the character of Satan, whose biography he wanted to write when he was a schoolboy in Hannibal and whose "rehabilitation" he proposed in "Concerning the Jews." Satan, he complained, had never had a fair shake from Christian apologists, but, as he observed with fine irony, "a person who has for untold centuries maintained the imposing position of spiritual head of four-fifths of the human race, and political head of the whole of it, must be granted executive abilities of the loftiest order."[28] What particularly appealed to his creative imagination was what it might be like to be a totally conscienceless, amoral being with cosmic powers and eternal life, a creature possessing the ultimate freedom.

Hence Twain's Satan is not the Evil One. Only once in working notes does Twain call him "Prince of Darkness," and he bears no resemblance to the arch fiend demon tempter of traditional Christian iconography—the lithe red devil with horns, hooves, forked tail, and pitchfork. In "Conversations with Satan" he is a dapper Viennese boulevardier who could be "mistaken for an Anglican bishop." As the nameless hoaxer in "The Man That Corrupted Hadleyburg," he looks "like an amateur detective gotten up as an impossible English earl." In all three "Mysterious Stranger" manuscripts he is an exceedingly handsome adolescent, nattily attired in the first two, deliberately disguised in rags for his entrance in the third.

An intriguing sidelight to Twain's depictions of the character, perhaps not wholly unrelated to his writing of "The Chronicle of Young Satan," may be seen in a notebook entry in mid-December 1897 when he sat for the Russian sculptress Theresa Fedorowna Ries, who carved an alabaster bust of him she exhibited that season at the Kunstlerhaus.[29] He was enchanted with a statue called "Lucifer" in her atelier, finding it "fine & strong & impressive—majestically so, I think." When he queried her about it "She dropped the fact incidentally, that her grand hellion there in the corner (Lucifer) was *begun as the Virgin, but looked too masculine for the part, so she turned the Mamma of God into Satan* [Twain's italics]!" He thought it "A good change. The Mother & Son have been a little overworked. Jesus died to save men—a small thing for an immortal to do, & didn't save many, anyway; but if he had been damned for the race *that* would have been an act of a size proper to a god, & would have saved the *whole* race. However, why should anybody *want* to save the human race, or damn it, either? Does God want its society? Does Satan?"†[30] Two weeks later he sketched a comic scene which, perhaps fortunately, never left the notebook: "Satan & his little devils at dinner. 'Poppa, poppa, gimme a Christian.'†"[31] And in February he recorded a dream in which he met with "polite objections and evasions" when he tried to sell his soul to Satan. "Certain lines of goods he was overstocked with. Never *had* paid the prices attributed to him by the lying priests."†[32]

Of equal importance with the Satan figures in all these stories is the fourth thematic element, the writer's growing concern with the relations between and juxtaposing of what we call "dreams" versus what we consider "reality" and the implications this dichotomy has for individual identity or selfhood. Do we exist each as separate, single entities, or do we enjoy within our "selves" double, even triple identities? This was a theme much discussed in fin de siècle Vienna, not just quasi-scientifically by Sigmund Freud but also in the literary cafés by Jung Wien belletrists like Bahr and Hofmannsthal and even older writers like Josef Popper-Lynkeus, whose *Träumen als Wachen* (Dreams as Waking, 1899) was widely admired.

While not all these themes can be found in each narrative, a common undercurrent runs through them: namely, the theme of misfortune, disaster, catastrophe so huge and cataclysmic that it cannot be remedied, ameliorated, even assuaged by ordinary means, if at all. No doubt, as critics from DeVoto onward have assumed, this theme reflects the mental anguish and anxiety Clemens experienced, beginning in 1891, from his bankruptcy, sudden bereavement, and family illnesses. By 1898, however, his financial security had been restored by the capable management of Henry Rogers, his intense grief over Susy's death had abated, and Jean's and Livy's health problems, though worrisome, seemed malleable. It is myopic, therefore, not to view the intractable, even insoluble cataclysms in these stories as reflections of the nihilism he was so freely imbibing in Vienna. This may also explain why these narratives were left unfinished, since no credible denouements or resolutions were really imaginable.

In Kaltenleutgeben on August 10, 1898, Twain noted: "Last night dreamed of a whaling cruise in a drop of water. Not by microscope, but *actually*. This would mean a reduction of the participants to a minuteness which would make them nearly invisible to God & he wouldn't be interested in them any longer."†[33] He first thought of using this dream to revise and complete a story he called "Which Was the Dream?," commenced in London on May 23, 1897, and laid aside in Weggis after he had written some ten thousand words. That fragment, first published in 1967, tells of an army general and successful politician, no doubt modeled on Ulysses S. Grant, who falls asleep while writing a story to entertain guests at his daughter's birthday party and, within the span of a few seconds, dreams of experiencing a series of horrendous disasters including the burning of his house, bankruptcy, loss

Mark Twain in the atelier of Theresa Fedorowna Ries, Vienna, 1897
(Photo by Scolik. Picture Archives of the Austrian National Library)

of career and reputation, the disappearance of his family, and finally descent into abject poverty.

Twain became dissatisfied with "Which Was the Dream?" when he began reworking it, and he opted for a fresh start. A week later (August 16) he wrote Howells excitedly about his progress, saying "a new plan" had "suggested itself" and

> straightway the tale began to slide from the pen with ease & confidence. I think I've struck the right one this time. I have already put 12,000 words of it on paper & Mrs. Clemens is pretty outspokenly satisfied with it—a hard critic to content. I feel sure that all of the first half of the story—& I hope three-fourths—will be comedy; but by the former plan the whole of it (except the first 3 chapters) would have been tragedy & unendurable, almost. I think I can carry the reader a long way before he suspects that I am laying a tragedy-trap.[34]

Despite his enthusiasm, work on "The Great Dark" languished while the Clemenses traveled to Bad Ischl and Hallstatt in August, and in early September it was preempted by Twain's reporting on the state funeral of the murdered empress.

By September 21–22, 1898, when he sketched a possible scenario for its finale, he had already written about 35,000 words, but the draft remained unfinished at that point. There is indeed a good deal of arcane humor in its opening chapter, burlesquing a popular nineteenth-century American sea story genre and parodying mariners' jargon. But before long it turns into one of the darkest, most horrific tales Mark Twain ever imagined.

Its frame story is similar to "Which Was the Dream?" While showing his eight-year-old daughter a microscope he bought for her birthday, Henry Edwards puts a drop of polluted water on a slide so he and his daughters may watch with amazement the magnified movements of "tiny animals" (microbes) in the water. Drowsing on his sofa while the children dress for their party, he reflects on what they have just seen: "An ocean in a drop of water—and unknown, uncharted, unexplored by man!"[35] Soon "the Superintendent of Dreams," a cosmic Satan-like figure, appears, and Edwards arranges with him for a ship to take a voyage on this microscopic ocean. "It will be like any other voyage of the sort—not altogether a holiday excursion," the Superintendent says with ironic understatement, adding: "You and your crew will be much diminished as to size, but you need not trouble about that, as you will not be aware of it. Your ship itself, stuck upon the point of a needle, would not be discoverable except through a microscope of very high power." Edwards assents, asking only for "a crew of whalers" and "a naturalist to tell me the names of the creatures we see; and let the ship be a comfortable one and perfectly appointed and provisioned, for I take my family with me."

So begins this nightmare voyage on endless, uncharted seas extending over many years in perpetual night, save for an occasional blinding light when the ship sails into the mirror-reflected illumination. The sea is full of monstrous predatory creatures like a giant squid that surfaces to snatch the captain's young son from the deck and almost succeeds in capsizing the ship. The terrified crew, led by the ship's carpenter, mutinies when word gets around that the navigation instruments don't function and that neither the captain nor first mate has any idea of the ship's location or destination. After vacillating, the captain regains control, but only by terror and violence.

Nor do the Edwardses escape mishap. Although a son is born to them during the voyage, their two daughters get separated from them during a storm and are presumed lost for a long while before being found safe in a remote part of the ship's hold. Yet worse, while Edwards clearly remembers their earlier life, neither his wife nor children can recall anything before the voyage began. Horrified by this loss and beginning to question his own sanity, Edwards prods Alice, his wife, with reminders and reminiscences of past experiences until she begins to acknowledge remembering them, too, although he can never be sure whether she is being truthful or merely trying to mollify him.

The Superintendent of Dreams drops by from time to time, and during one of their colloquies, when Edwards rebuffs him in a fit of pique with, "you can end the dream as soon as you please—right now, if you like," the Superintendent responds:

"The dream? *Are you quite sure it is a dream?*"

It took my breath away.

"What do you mean? *Isn't* it a dream?"

He looked at me in that same way again; and it made my blood chilly, this time. Then he said—

"You have spent your whole life in this ship. And this is *real* life. Your other life was the dream!"

This is the philosophical and psychological, if not the dramatic, climax of the tale, the point of which is that our words "reality" and "dream" are merely arbitrary labels for two different levels of mind: conscious and unconscious, the waking self and the dream self. Twain had employed basically the same theme in different fictional guise a few weeks earlier in his short story "My Platonic Sweetheart."

Throughout the late 1890s Mark Twain followed with deep interest the reports of the Society for Psychical Research. He also informed himself of the work of the great French neurologist Jean-Martin Charcot (1825–93), under whom Sigmund Freud had studied at the Sorbonne in 1885–86, a year that marked the turning point of Freud's thought and career. Twain was keenly interested in the findings of Charcot and his students concerning the use of hypnosis in the treatment of hysteria and in what Twain called "Mental Telegraphy"— his name for thought transference by what is today known as "mental telepathy."[36] He made copious notes on instances of these phenomena while in Vienna and Kaltenleutgeben.

Some of his ideas about the nature of dreams versus reality emanated from his reading of Georg Christoph Lichtenberg, an eighteenth-century professor of mathematics at Göttingen, who was in vogue in fin de siècle Vienna and an acknowledged favorite of and influence upon Karl Kraus, Ernst Mach, Ludwig Wittgenstein, and Sigmund Freud, among others.[37] What he found congenial in Lichtenberg's *A Doctrine of Scattered Occasions*—that one could dream years of experience in a few seconds, that such experiences are real events because they are "also a life and a world," that one "never really knows whether he isn't sitting in a madhouse"—was reinforced by his interest also in Herbartianism, as explained in Sir John Adams's *The Herbartian*

Psychology Applied to Education (London, 1898). Twain, in fact, wrote to Adams (a Scottish pedagogue) in December 1898 expressing his admiration of Herbart and Adams's work.[38]

The writings of Johann Friedrich Herbart (1776–1841), another Göttingen philosopher-psychologist, were also intellectually fashionable in Vienna in 1898 and were taken up as well by those who were attracted to Lichtenberg. Sigmund Freud, for instance, appropriated many of the key terms of his psychoanalytical jargon from Herbart, whose ideas have been succinctly summarized by William Johnston as follows:

> The soul, or self is . . . a reale, tied to a cluster of realia known as the body. Like other realia, each strives to persist against perturbations (*Störungen*) that buffet it. The mind acts like a seismograph to record acts of self-preservation by the self. These self-preserving acts generate presentations (*Vorstellungen*) to resist foreign realia that impinge on the self. Once generated, presentations become indestructible atoms of the soul. They persist beneath what Herbart called the threshold (*Schwelle*) of consciousness, where they vie against one another in an effort to evade consciousness. He coined the term repression (*Verdrängung*) to designate the force that counteracts their drive (*Trieb*) toward the surface.[39]

The Herbartian-Lichtenbergian connections Mark Twain was struggling to absorb and give expression in "The Great Dark" reach their fullest embodiment in an exquisite episode he decided for some unknown reason to cancel from the Kaltenleutgeben draft but which, fortunately, the late John S. Tuckey preserved as an appendix, titled "The Mad Passenger," to his 1967 edition. In it, Edwards befriends an outcast, melancholy fellow passenger (called "mad" by the rest) and learns his pathetic story. A native of another "Empire" (or planet), he had fallen overboard from his yacht in a fierce storm some twenty-two years before and was saved from drowning in the pitch dark only by clinging to the bowsprit of Edwards's ship. Before this sad event, which separated him forever from his wife and infant daughter, he had traveled widely in "Dreamland," as he calls the world, Neptune, Saturn, Uranus, and other planets of our solar system.

Edwards and "M.P.," as he is known to the rest of the ship because "he had a name of a jaw-breaking sort," fall to discussing differences between Dreamland and the foreigner's own country and language wherein it comes out "that in his tongue there were no exact equivalents for our words *modesty, immodesty, decency, indecency, right, wrong, sin.*" Although Edwards finds it puzzling, M.P. argues there is "nothing strange about it, since dreamlands [are] nothing but imitations of real countries created out of the dreamer's own imagination and experience, with some help, perhaps, from the Superintendent of Dreams." The world, he nevertheless asserts, does have a monopoly on a few unpleasant peculiarities, such as "what they term Religions; also curious systems of government, and an interesting but most odd code of morals." [40]

The extensive notes Twain made for concluding "The Great Dark" describe surrealist disasters more bizarre and horrendous than those he had already included. Strange portents occur—a bloody footprint that moves around, a giant blind squid that attacks at intervals, an invisible hand that grabs at crewmen and passengers, mysterious sounds of wings and voices in the dark—and everyone goes mad. Finally, the sea dries up, "the great animals begin to get stranded, & struggle & fight & cry & die & stink." The ship runs aground; the crew and passengers take their meager provisions and set out overland where all save Edwards perish in the intense heat. Just then, he "looks up—is at home—his wife & the children coming to say goodnight. His hair is white." This last detail is significant because Henry Edwards is but thirty-five, and his wife says in her opening statement that "he looks ten years younger." [41]

Fascinating and terrifying as this ending might have been if fleshed out, it seems less satisfying in some respects than the passage with which Twain broke off "The Great Dark" in book 2, chapter 1. Having put down the mutiny and harangued his crew back to their places, the captain makes them a bully speech from the bridge confessing that, although he has no idea where they are, he intends to sail on into the unknown: "Are we rational men, manly men, men who can stand up and face hard luck and a big difficulty that has been brought about by nobody's fault, and say live or die, survive or perish, we are in for it, for good or bad, and we'll stand by this ship if she goes to hell! . . . If it is God's will that we pull through, we pull through—otherwise not. We haven't had an observation for four months, but we are going ahead, and do our best to fetch up somewhere."[42]

One hears in this, as Tuckey pointed out, an echo of Huck Finn's famous "All right, then, I'll go to hell!"[43] One is also strongly reminded of the concluding lines of Tennyson's "Ulysses" and, even more, Walt Whitman's "Passage to India." Despite the fatalistic *que sera, sera* of his penultimate sentence, the captain's speech is a stirring affirmation of a Nietzschean *Wille zur Macht*, not of dour resignation, despair, or pessimism.

The Superintendent of Dreams is the only passive satan character Twain created in Vienna. Like a good travel agent and tour guide, he arranges for the dream voyage and explains things to Edwards from time to time. But he plays no active role in the plot, manipulating events or causing things to happen as the satan figures do in the "Mysterious Stranger" manuscripts. He is an ethereal figure, visible only to Henry, once or twice to Alice (without knowing who he is), and to M.P.

Writing his abortive "Conversations with Satan" soon after settling in at the Metropole set off a train of creative thought that led Twain to commence in late October or early November 1897 a novel he called "The Chronicle of Young Satan" which occupied him off and on until he turned to play writing the following January. He laid it aside then until the summer of 1899, when he was in Sweden, and then again until the following summer at Dollis Hill, near London. By August 1900, two months before the Clemenses returned to the United States, he had completed 423 manuscript pages, breaking off the story at this point and leaving it unfinished midway in chapter 11.

In 1916, Albert Bigelow Paine, as Twain's literary executor, and Frederick Duneka, his erstwhile editor at *Harper's*, chopped off the last part of chapter 10 and all of chapter 11. Then, having cut or bowdlerized passages satirizing Roman Catholic dogma and adding a wholly invented character (an astrologer), they "completed" the work by tack-ing on a conclusion Twain wrote in 1904 for yet another version of the story "No. 44, The Mysterious Stranger." They published this as *The Mysterious Stranger, A Romance* in *Harper's* magazine in October and November 1916 and then for the Christmas trade that year as a children's book, with illustrations by N. C. Wyeth!

Despite the exposure of this editorial fraud by John Tuckey in 1963, despite publication six years later of authoritative texts of all three incomplete manuscript versions of the work, this confection continues to be reprinted and remains the most widely read version. Although at least one eminent Twain scholar claims it is "the closest thing to Mark Twain's intention that we shall ever have," the editorial cutting and pasting by Paine and Duneka is so manifestly indefensible that one must disregard *The Mysterious Stranger, A Romance* as having no textual validity whatever and refer solely to the manuscripts published in 1969.[44]

"The Chronicle of Young Satan" opens: "It was 1702—May. Austria was far away from the world, and asleep; it was still the Middle Ages in Austria, and promised to remain so forever. Some even set it away back centuries upon centuries and said that by the mental and spiritual clock it was still the Age of Faith in Austria. But they meant it as a compliment, not as a slur, and it was so taken, and we were all proud of it."[45]

The specific locale is Eseldorf, German for "donkey town" or "village of asses," which lies "in the middle of that sleep, being in the middle of Austria." The satire on backward, slumbering (hence, dreaming?) Austria is obvious. So too is Twain's withering satire on the established church and the monarchy. Theodor Fischer, the ingenuous adolescent narrator (an Austrian Huck Finn), says:

> Eseldorf was a paradise for us boys. We were not overmuch pestered with schooling. Mainly we were trained to be good Catholics; to revere the Virgin, the Church and the saints above everything; to hold the Monarch in awful reverence, speak of him with bated breath, uncover before his picture, regard him as the gracious provider of our daily bread and of all our earthly blessings, and ourselves as being sent into the world with

the one only mission to labor for him, bleed for him, die for him, when necessary.

Clearly, this country is absolutist Austria-Hungary late in the reign of Kaiser Franz Josef, not the loosely knit Holy Roman Empire of central European states of Leopold I in 1702.

Eseldorf and its environs astonishingly resemble what Twain wrote in his notebook about Salzburg, where the Clemenses spent three days en route to Vienna six weeks earlier: "At its front flowed the tranquil river . . .; behind it rose the woody steeps to the base of a lofty precipice; from the top of the precipice frowned the vast castle, its long stretch of towers and bastions mailed in vines; beyond the river, to the left, was a tumbled expanse of forest-clothed hills cloven by winding gorges where the sun never penetrated; and to the right, lay a far-reaching plain dotted with little homesteads nested among orchards and shade-trees." [46]

In his notebook entry for September 24, 1897, Twain saw Salzburg as a "village . . . made up mainly of churches" supporting "useless priests & monks," adding:

> The fortress is 900 years old, is gray, with long stretches of lofty wall, with square towers & round ones, an imposing mass of masonry perched on a ~~wooded~~ precipitous hill 500 ft above the town.
> The Saltzack flows swiftly through the town, a narrow gray brook.[†47]

If Eseldorf is a fictionalized Salzburg with perhaps some memories of Weggis and even Hannibal tossed in, Twain found his characters' names in Vienna. Theodor Fischer and his two friends—Nikolaus Baumann and Seppi Wohlmeyer—have names of deputies in the Reichsrat, the sessions of which Mark Twain was just then attending. Father Adolf, the villainous priest of the story, was originally Father Lueger, named for Dr. Karl Lueger, the new *Oberbürgermeister* (lord mayor) of Vienna whom Twain disliked, but after changing the priest's name as being perhaps a bit too obvious, he named one of his minor characters Marie Lueger. Father Adolf's "thundering bass" voice and general manner echo what Twain wrote in "Stirring Times" about "bull-voiced" Georg von Schönerer, leader of the German Nationals in the Reichsrat, whom Twain also detested:

> He was a very loud and zealous and strenuous priest, and was always working to get more reputation. . . . And he certainly had talent; he was a most fluent and chirpy speaker, and could say the cuttingest things and the wittiest, though a little coarse, maybe—however it was only his enemies who said that, and it really wasn't any truer of him than of the others; but he belonged to the village council, and lorded it there, and played smart dodges that carried his projects through, and of course that nettled the others; and in their resentment they gave him nicknames privately, and called him the "Town Bull" and "Hell's Delight," and all sorts of things; which was natural, for when you are in politics you are in a wasp's nest with a short shirt-tail, as the saying is.

Other characters have names like Adler, Bart, Brandt, Fuchs, Hein, Hirsch, Klein, Meidling, Müller, Pfeiffer, Siebold, and Sperling. Meidling is the name of one of the city's boroughs, Adler (founder of the Austrian Socialist Party) and Fuchs were Reichsrat deputies, while the rest were names of Gemeinderat (city council) members in Vienna which Twain probably noted while visiting a session in the Rathaus in mid-October 1897. Eseldorf's hostelry and wine tavern is the Golden Stag, English for *Goldener Hirsch,* the hotel where the Clemenses stayed in Salzburg. There are references to the lifting of the second Turkish siege of Vienna in 1683, including a favorite Viennese legend about how coffee was then introduced into the Western world: "among the captured things were bags of coffee, and the Turkish prisoners explained the character of it and how to make a pleasant drink of it." And other such details.

Of greater significance than these direct reflections of the writer's Viennese experiences is the fanciful name assumed by "young Satan" when he visits Eseldorf—Philip Traum. *Traum* is, of course, German for "dream," which is exactly what Philip Traum, this teenage nephew of the devil, is—the "dream self" of the person whose "waking self" is Theodor Fischer. He is the fictional embodiment of what Mark Twain described in a notebook entry on January 7, 1898 (misdated 1897), as "a new 'solution' of a haunting mystery . . . our seeming *duality*—the presence in us of *another person;* not a slave of ours, but ~~wholly~~ free & independent, & with a character distinctly its own."[48] He recalled grappling with this problem in 1876 in his story "The Facts Concerning the Recent Carnival of Crime in Connecticut," but he judged that effort to have been misconceived, feeling that Robert Louis Stevenson had meanwhile come "nearer the thing" in *The Strange Case of Dr. Jekyll and Mr. Hyde* (1886). Stevenson's solution—"the ability of the one person to step into the other person's place *at will*"—was "nearer, yes, but not near enough."

So now, in "The Chronicle of Young Satan," Twain made yet another imaginative thrust at fabulating what Sigmund Freud was at that very moment also formulating psychoanalytically: the coexistence in us of the conscious ("waking") and unconscious ("dream") identities Freud later labeled Ego (*das Ich*) and Id (*das Es*). The plot of the "Chronicle" consists of a sequence of more or less self-contained episodes, rather like fabliaux or cautionary tales, in which little Satan–Philip Traum–*Id* dramatically illustrates for Theodor Fischer–*Ego* the moral cowardice of the human race, misnamed "Moral Sense"—that is, the capacity to know right from wrong and the propensity inevitably to choose and rationalize the latter. A central thread is the effort to exculpate the good priest, Father Peter, from Father Adolf's false charge of having stolen a bag of money Philip Traum, as a deliberate trick, had placed in his path for the old priest to find. When Father Peter's niece, Marget, and her fiancé, Wilhelm Meidling, finally succeed (again, through Traum's tricks) in proving him innocent in a trial scene reminiscent of the denouement of *Pudd'nhead Wilson*, little Satan deprives the old man of his reason, turning him into a fictionalized version of "Emperor Norton," a harmless, deranged San Franciscan Twain knew in the 1860s who had proclaimed himself emperor of the United States.

Traum's object lessons on human nature and "reality" are cosmic and calamitous, though not quite so catastrophic and horrifying as those in "The Great Dark." There are witch-burnings and stonings, religious massacres, and the drowning of Lisa Brandt and Nikolaus

Baumann, cutting short what Satan demonstrates would have been long lives of woeful suffering. In the first episode, Satan–Philip Traum delights the boys by moulding a crowd of tiny people from a handful of dirt and animating them. When they set about building a castle and town, Satan becomes annoyed with them for making too much noise while he is conversing and, taking a board, smashes them all "just as if they had been flies, and went on talking just the same." Theodor then recounts this chilling exchange:

> Our hearts were broken, we could not keep from crying.
> "Don't cry," Satan said, "they were of no value."
> "But they are gone to hell!"
> "Oh, it is no matter, we can make more."

In the same nihilistic vein is Traum's response to the naive faith expressed by a poor woman who has adopted a stray kitten she has no money to feed, that "God will provide for this kitten":

> "What makes you think so?"
> [Her] eyes snapped with anger.
> "Because I know it!" she said. "Not a sparrow falls to the ground without His seeing it."
> "But it falls, just the same. What good is *seeing* it fall?"

Although Satan does a great deal of preaching along with his "showing off" and exemplifying the endless failings and stupidities of the "damned human race" and its disgusting moral sense, a witty satiric tone dominates the entire "Chronicle." The humor is sardonic, often lugubrious and macabre. In one hilarious episode, for instance, Satan turns a bothersome forester to stone. When the coroner's jury disagrees on a technicality about how he has died, his family hauls "the petrifaction" home to hold a wake, funeral feast, and other "due and usual decencies." After some months, however, they begin a public exhibition of him which is

> inordinately successful, children and servants half price, and crowds
> coming from all over the Empire, and even from foreign countries, and

many Italian image-dealers paying a commission for the privilege of making and selling small casts of it. The family quickly grew rich, and in the next generation obtained nobility in Germany at the usual rates. After many, many years it was sold, and passed from hand to hand and country to country, and now for a long time it has been in the Pitti palace in Florence, earning its living as a Roman antique.

The rapacious commercial greed of a race that will milk even tragedies for profit, that will turn a fast buck on disaster T-shirts and such, has seldom been so cogently satirized.

The tone of the second version of the story, the so-called "Schoolhouse Hill" (or Hannibal) draft of six chapters comprising about 16,000 words that Twain wrote in late November and early December 1898, is lighter and more whimsical than that of "The Chronicle of Young Satan." What set his thinking about the story off on a new tack when he returned to it after finishing "The Man That Corrupted Hadleyburg" may be glimpsed in a lengthy notebook entry he made at the Hotel Krantz between November 12 and 19, 1898, beginning: "Story of little Satan, jr., who came to ~~Petersburg (Hannibal)~~ went to school, was popular & greatly liked by ~~Huck & Tom~~ who knew his secret. The others were jealous, & the girls didn't like him because he smelt of brimstone. *This* is the Admirable Chrichton. He was always doing miracles—his pals knew they were miracles, they others thought them mysteries. He is a good little devil, but swears, & breaks the Sabbath."[49] This version turned out to be his final imaginative return to his fictionalized Hannibal (Saint Petersburg), and although it has some deft touches, he could not sustain his interest in it. Since Huck and Tom are two of the boys in it, he may actually have intended to dovetail this new story into "Tom Sawyer's Conspiracy," on which he had tinkered for a year and a half.

Unlike "The Chronicle of Young Satan" and "No. 44, The Mysterious Stranger," which have first-person narration, "Schoolhouse Hill" is narrated in the third person by an anonymous omniscient author. For that reason, it lacks some of the immediacy and interest of the other versions. Its basic conceit is adumbrated in some sly badinage in the "Chronicle" when Marget asks Philip Traum about the "foreign country" his "uncle" (Satan) inhabits:

> "Is he a foreigner himself? Was he born there?"
> "Well, no. No, he was an emigrant. . . ."
> "What nationality?"
> "Mixed. But mainly French."
> "And so that is the language in use?"
> "It is the official language."

Here is yet another of Twain's satiric salvos at the French ("There is nothing lower than the human race except the French" was one of his Vienna notebook aphorisms), and it is extended in "Schoolhouse Hill" by making Satan, Jr., a fifteen-year-old French lad named Quarante-quatre, French for forty-four.[50]

Almost everyone who has written about the Mysterious Stranger manuscripts has speculated about the origin and significance of this strange name which Mark Twain retained in its English form for his "little Satan" in the final version of this story. The sources that have been suggested, some of them quite fanciful, range from the writer's Hannibal schoolmates, the Levin twins who were nicknamed Twenty-Two (twice eleven), to the numerology of Freemasonry (of which he was a member), and to his interest in the occult and even Jewish cabalistic writings. Most recently, Louis J. Budd has made a plausible stab at Twain's borrowing it from a character name in a work by the Polish writer Adam Mickiewicz (1798–1855) that he may have perused in Vienna.[51] Twain's friendships there with numerous Poles—Leschetizky, Szczepanik, the counts De Laszowski and Goluchowski, among them—as well as Jean's studying Polish there lend at least circumstantial credence to this speculation, as does the gratuitous remark Theodor Fischer's mother makes about Traum in the "Chronicle": "His mother was a Pole, probably; I never did think much of those Poles."

Whatever the case, Quarante-quatre is, like Philip Traum, a most beguiling, "surpassingly handsome" lad who, knowing no English when he appears at the school in Saint Petersburg, quickly masters it by skimming a French-English dictionary the schoolmaster hands him. He confounds the village with other such demonstrations of his superior, indeed supernatural, knowledge, but he is more puckishly inclined to save the villagers from disasters and their own follies than to disabuse and enlighten Tom and Huck in the way Philip Traum does Theodor and his pals.

The story does not get very far beyond highjinks, but it does contain, in the characters of Oliver and Hannah Hotchkiss, who lodge Quarante-quatre in their farmhouse, a valedictory portrait of Orion Clemens and his wife, Mollie, that is warmheartedly amusing rather than satirical. Hotchkiss, Twain wrote, changed "his principles with the moon, his politics with the weather, and his religion with his shirt. He was recognized as being limitlessly good-hearted, quite fairly above the village average intellectually, a diligent and enthusiastic seeker after truth, and a sincere believer in his newest belief, but a man who had missed his vocation—he should have been a weather-vane."[52]

Mark Twain was not always so tolerant of his older brother, but Orion had been dead now almost a year, and the glow of memory had obviously begun to mellow Samuel Clemens, whose alter ego could imagine that Oliver's (Orion's) "good Presbyterian wife," Hannah (Mollie)

was fond and proud of her husband, and believed he would have been great if he had had a proper chance. . . . She was patient with his excursions after the truth. She expected him to be saved—thought she knew it would happen, in fact. It could only be as a Presbyterian, of course, but that would come—come of a certainty. All signs indicated it. He had often been a Presbyterian; he was periodically a Presbyterian, and she noted with comfort that his period was astronomically regular. She could take the almanac and calculate its return with nearly as much confidence as other astronomers calculate an eclipse. His Mohammedan period, his Methodist period, his Buddhist period, his Parsi period, his Roman Catholic period, his Atheistic period—these were all similarly regular, but she cared nothing for that. She knew there was a patient and compassionate Providence watching over him that would see to it that he died in his Presbyterian period.

Abandoning his attempt to naturalize the story to America, Twain returned to his Austrian "Chronicle" in the summers of 1899 and 1900, mainly polishing a few passages and inserting topical allusions to the Boer War (1899–1902) and the Boxer Uprising in China (1899–1900) as further examples of man's rapacity and duplicity in so-called "advanced" civilizations. Then, in November 1902, an altogether different plot occurred to him, and he began writing yet another, so-called "Print Shop," version titled "No. 44, The Mysterious Stranger." He worked on this at various widely separated intervals until July 1905 and again near the end of 1908, accumulating altogether 530 manuscript pages. He came closer to completing a cohesive novella with this draft than he had in either of his previous two, so that, if one adds the six pages of ambiguously detached manuscript he wrote early in 1904 and called "Conclusion of the book" as Tuckey did in 1969, one has at last a whole, satisfactorily resolved, structurally unified work. Whether it is more valid to couple this ending with "No. 44, The Mysterious Stranger" than to tack it onto "The Chronicle of Young Satan," as Paine and Duneka did, could be debated, but the fact that Twain wrote these six pages after he had completed thirty-two chapters of "No. 44," as opposed to only ten-and-a-half chapters of the earlier "Chronicle," argues in its favor even if one must juxtapose as the penultimate chapter an episode written later (in 1908) to make it fit smoothly.

Except for substituting "1490—winter" in the opening in place of "1702—May," giving a name (Rosenfeld) to the "vast castle" above Eseldorf, and making a few other minor word changes, he carried the first chapter of the "Chronicle" intact into "No. 44." From then on, however, the two stories differ greatly. August Feldner is the sixteen-year-old who narrates this version. He is an apprentice in the printing shop (hence, "printer's devil") of Heinrich Stein which is quartered in a nearby mouldering castle. The other characters' names—Adam Binks, Gustav Fischer, Maria Vogel, Hans Katzenyammer, and so on—while still recognizably Austrian, are not identifiably Viennese in origin. Most interesting are the comical names of an itinerant compositor (jour printer), Doangivadam, and of the mysterious youth "apparently about sixteen or seventeen years old" who arrives unannounced one day just as Herr Stein's extended family is finishing *Mittagessen* (noonday meal) and gives his name as "Number 44, New Series 864,962," which is thereafter clipped to Forty-Four by the others, though never by himself.

He is not Satan, Jr. (Quarante-quatre), or Satan's nephew (Philip Traum) but, as his "series" name indicates, merely one of hundreds of thousands, even millions of devils or fallen angels expelled from heaven with Satan. His function nevertheless is the same as that of Philip Traum—to educate and enlighten the protagonist-narrator about the nature of reality, man's utter cruelty and depravity, and the indifference of the universe and any conceivable deity in it to human existence. He goes about it in much the same way as Traum does in the "Chronicle," by whisking August Feldner back and forth in time and to remote lands in a twinkling to show him instances in history and in the "future" (i.e., post-1490) of mob violence, murderous dynastic wars, colonial massacres, torture, pillage, and other horrors, mostly committed or justified in the name of religion. There is an important difference in this story from the other two, however, when Forty-Four reveals to August that he can become invisible or disembodied and rematerialize himself at will as another person or duplicate (*Doppelgänger*) with a different name, Emil Schwarz.

The central episode involves Herr Stein's difficulties in filling an order for three hundred Latin Bibles for the University of Prague. His workers grumble when he hires Forty-Four to expedite matters, whereupon Forty-Four prints and binds nearly the whole order overnight. The workers then organize a union and strike to keep the Bibles from being delivered. At this point, Forty-Four clones them and sends in their duplicates as strikebreakers, and a pitched battle ensues between the workers and their scab duplicates.

The point of this cloning is to demonstrate to August/Emil and the reader that, as Forty-Four explains:

> you are not one person, but two. One is your Workaday Self [Ego], and tends to business, the other is your Dream-Self [Id], and has no respon-

sibilities, and cares only for romance and excursions and adventure. It sleeps when your other self is awake; when your other self sleeps, your Dream Self is in full control, and does as it pleases. It has far more imagination than has the Workaday Self, therefore its pains and pleasures are far more real and intense than are those of the other self, and its adventures correspondingly picturesque and extraordinary.

This revelation occurs in chapter 18, evidently written early in 1904, but six chapters later (chapter 24), August/Emil learns from Forty-Four that his dual existence is really triple, that "each human being contains not merely two independent entities, but three—the Waking-Self, the Dream-Self, and the Soul." His soul, which he claims is "immortal" and lives on after the other two selves die with the body— that is, with the brain and nerves by which they are "functioned"—has yet another name: Martin von Giesbach. Yet worse, all three of these selves (August-Emil-Martin) are in love with the same girl in her triad of selves, called Marget Regan–Lisbet Schmidt–Elisabeth von Arnim.

At first glance, this added soul construct would seem to be an equivalent to what Freud called the super-ego (*das über-Ich*) except for the puzzling idea of immortality for this third self. Twain seemed unable to reconcile the apparent contradiction he had raised for himself here about whether we have dual or triple identity, or to resolve the complications of the love plot satisfactorily. In July 1905 he was so dissatisfied with it that he destroyed some 30,000 words of what he had written after chapter 19, a rare step for someone who usually preserved every scrap of manuscript and every laundry list for future scholars. Although he added two new comic chapters, the story became increasingly diffuse and unwieldy.

No doubt it was to extricate himself from the narrative quagmire into which he was falling that he composed the separate "Conclusion of the book," which is its most memorable part and which still has the power to shock, perplex, even to terrify, whether one reads it as the proper ending of "No. 44" or tacked onto the "Chronicle" in *The Mysterious Stranger*. The whole story, Forty-Four announces, has been but a dream:

"Life itself is only a vision, a dream."

It was electrical. By God I had had that very thought a thousand times in my musings!

"Nothing exists; all is a dream. God—man—the world,—the sun, the moon, the wilderness of stars: a dream, all a dream, they have no existence. *Nothing exists save empty space—and you!"*

He elaborates upon this idea in an impassioned speech that comes as close to dramatic poetry as anything Mark Twain ever wrote, then concludes: "He vanished and left me appalled; for I knew, and realized, that all he had said was true."

Several Twain scholars have delineated the many autobiographical as well as varied literary sources of incidents, characters, places, and allusions in the three "Mysterious Stranger" manuscripts. Adolf Wilbrandt's play *Der Meister von Palmyra* (The Master of Palmyra), Goethe's *Faust*, Voltaire's *Zadig*, the apocryphal Gospel of Saint John (which chronicles the boyhood of Jesus Christ), Shakespeare's *The Tempest* and *King Lear*, Milton's *Paradise Lost*, Mather's *Wonders of the Invisible World*, Jonathan Edwards's "Sinners in the Hands of an Angry God," and several works by the Anglo-Irish historian W. E. H. Lecky are among the most easily identifiable literary sources.[53]

Until now, however, no one has paid much attention to the Viennese background and context of the "Mysterious Stranger" manuscripts and "The Great Dark." Yet the marks of Vienna are all over them. Nothing Mark Twain wrote during his twenty months in and near the City of Dreams by the Danube or thereafter is so demonstrably Viennese as these, and in "No. 44, the Mysterious Stranger" one sees the influences of Vienna lingering with the writer years after. It is not just that the "Chronicle" and "No. 44" have Austrian settings, or that he used Viennese names and references in the former. Nor is it the analogues in these works to ideas in the writings of Sigmund Freud, regardless of whether or not, as seems altogether likely, Mr. Clemens and Dr. Freud ever actually shook hands in Vienna.

No, what makes it impossible to imagine any other American at the turn of this century writing narratives like these is a unique combination of elements that distinguishes them from anything Mark Twain himself had previously written. That combination may be generalized quite simply: in style these works are markedly aphoristic, in technique they are impressionistic, in mode and intent they are satiric, and in ideas they are solipsistic and overwhelmingly nihilistic. The ideas one finds in this cluster of fragments and the manner in which these ideas are expressed could only have come from someone who, metaphorically speaking, had been drinking deep from that Pierian Spring in the "Providentia" Fountain (also called *Donnerbrunnen*) that has bubbled since 1739 before the door of the temporary home Mark Twain knew as the Hotel Krantz.

For the nihilist Mark Twain had become in Vienna and would remain the rest of his days, the ultimate weapon and ultimate bulwark of sanity is humor. The "Mysterious Stranger" manuscripts are, despite their depiction of human cruelty, suffering, and degradation, very humorous works. They exemplify what Philip Traum, in a section of "The Chronicle of Young Satan" cut by Paine and Duneka in their bastardized version, declaims aphoristically in a speech charged with Viennese nihilism and Phaeacianism that was also unmistakably Mark Twain's lifelong credo:

> No religion exists which is not littered with engaging and delightful comicalities, but the race never perceives them. Nothing can be more deliciously comical than hereditary royalties and aristocracies, but none except royal families and aristocrats are aware of it.
> . . . All forms of government—including republican and democratic—are rich in funny shams and absurdities, but their supporters do not see it. . . . Will a day come when the race will detect the funniness of these juvenilities and laugh at them—and by laughing at them destroy them? For your race, in its poverty, has unquestionably one really effective weapon—laughter. . . . Against the assault of Laughter nothing can stand.[54]

CHAPTER FOURTEEN

Auf Wiedersehen!

hen their day of departure, their 606th in Vienna, finally came, Clemens was surprised to find himself a bit wistful. A year earlier he had chafed to pack up and book passage on the next liner for New York. Now he felt almost at home as the illustrious *Stammgast* (favored guest) at the Krantzes' comfortable new hotel in Neuer Markt. Soon after settling there the Clemenses had been guests at Josef and Marianne Krantz's *Silberhochzeit* (twenty-fifth wedding anniversary festivities) and, a few months later, at the christening of their twin granddaughters in the Capuchin church across the square.[1] Even though the Emperor's Jubilee, the "great show" Clemens eagerly looked forward to, had dissolved in official tears for the murdered Elisabeth, it had been a good winter and an eventful spring. Their trip to Budapest had been festive, Rogers continued to send encouraging financial reports, and Mark Twain was successfully placing most of what he had finished in Kaltenleutgeben and during the autumn. A new volume (*The Man That Corrupted Hadleyburg and Other Stories and Sketches*) plus collected editions of his complete works were under way both at Harper and Brothers and at Bliss's American Publishing Company.

Anticipating a second Austrian summer, Clemens arranged in April to take a cottage for the season in Reichenau, not a health resort this time but a picturesque mountain village in the Raxalpe, some forty miles southwest of the city, where Sigmund Freud and his family sum-

mered in the 1890s. Noted for climate and good air, Reichenau was
more secluded, hence likely to be less socially active than Kaltenleutgeben had been the summer before. Clemens told Pötzl the family
would move to Reichenau at the end of May and return to the city in
late summer since the Raxalpe are higher in elevation and frost comes
earlier there than in the little valley where Kaltenleutgeben nestles.
Then they would head back to the States in October.[2]

Jean's epilepsy, however, had not yielded to treatments in Vienna.
In fact, her seizures were becoming more frequent. Her longest interval without an incident had shortened to six weeks, and in April and
early May they sometimes came on as often as twice a day.[3] Clemens
had some information about an osteopath named Jonas Henrik Kellgren with a fashionable practice in Belgravia (in London) and an
even more flourishing sanatorium in his native Sweden. Kellgren's
kneadings, pommelings, and aerobics, called the "Swedish Movements
Cure," were reported to be efficacious in cases of "non-hereditary"
epilepsy. Why not give Kellgren a try?

If the idea of skeletal manipulations to treat epilepsy seems preposterous today, it is because of advances in medical knowledge about this
disease since 1899. Moreover, the Clemenses were desperate, ready for
anything, be it ever so bizarre, that gave the slightest promise of success with Jean's malady. The decision was almost foregone. On May 19,
Neues Wiener Tagblatt announced that the Reichenau arrangements had
suddenly been scratched and "Wien wird in den nächsten Tage einen seiner
interessantesten Gäste verlieren . . ." (In coming days Vienna will lose one
of its most interesting guests . . .). Mark Twain and his family, the
report continued, would depart on the twenty-fourth for London with
stopovers en route, probably in Dresden and Berlin. This "last minute
change in disposition," NWT said, was necessitated by "Mark Twain's
presence being required in London." No reason was specified, nor, of
course, was the well-guarded secret of Jean's illness hinted at.[4]

There were other reasons why Clemens might have gone to London
instead of New York anyway, though not so urgent. Through Ambas-

sador Tower he became privy early in 1899 to a health food derived from skim milk, first called "Vienna albumen" and later given the trade name Plasmon. A Berlin-based company headed by A. H. Goerz, brother-in-law of Georg Siemens, the electrical tycoon, was then forming a British syndicate to market Plasmon world-wide. Having tried it himself, Clemens became convinced it was a panacea for all manner of ailments and, because it was inexpensive to produce, could instantly solve the problem of famine in places like India. He saw yet another chance at a fortune if he could get to London to grab a share of the American rights to Plasmon, which he soon did. The American Plasmon Company lost money, but he did realize some profit when the British Plasmon Syndicate, in which he had invested five thousand pounds, was eventually sold to Bovril.[5]

Meanwhile, capricious Clara had yet another yearning for further musical training. Blanche Marchesi had opened a studio in London to continue the instructional methods her famous mother, Mathilde Graumann Marchesi (1821–1913), had used to coach the stellar voices of Emma Calvé, Nellie Melba, Mary Garden, and many another Golden Age diva. Clara began her studies with Mlle Marchesi soon after her family reached London. A diva, of course, she never became.

Notwithstanding the urgent need to get Jean into Dr. Kellgren's care in London, there was unfinished business to attend to in Vienna. During his twenty-month sojourn Mark Twain had met almost everybody who was anybody in the literary, musical, artistic, theatrical, medical, intellectual, and public life of Austria-Hungary with one glaring exception: the emperor himself. Why the monarch had not received him earlier can only be guessed. But at last there came an eleventh-hour invitation to meet His Majesty that could not be refused, even if it meant postponing departure.

How this came about is an interesting question. The Viennese newspapers are unanimous in reporting it as the emperor's idea: "*Seine Majestät der Kaiser hatte den Wünsch geäussert, Mark Twain kennen zu lernen*" (His Majesty the emperor had expressed the wish to make Mark

Twain's acquaintance) was the way the *Fremden-Blatt* put it.[6] The request for an audience, however, came from the American ambassador on behalf of his famous countryman in the following very formal way:

United States Legation
Vienna, 17th May, 1899

His Excellency
  Count Goluchowski,
    I. and R. Minister
      of Foreign Affairs
  Your Excellency:

Mr. Samuel L. Clemens, (Mark Twain), the distinguished American author and humorist, who has been residing in Vienna and enjoying the hospitality of Austria-Hungary for more than a year and a half, is about to return to America.

Before leaving, Mr. Clemens would like, if possible, the honor of an audience of His Majesty the Emperor and King for the purpose of expressing his profound regard.

In view of Mr. Clemens's distinguished position in the world of letters and in view of his high standing as a citizen of the American Republic, I have the honor to request that Your Excellency will kindly use your good offices toward the end desired by Mr. Clemens—if consistent with usage and if agreeable to His Majesty.

I avail myself at the same time of this opportunity to renew to Your Excellency the assurances of my highest consideration and personal esteem.

/s/ Addison Harris /
United States Minister[7]

This request might actually signify something other than mere protocol. Notwithstanding his pose as a professional democrat, with such repeated scoffings at royalty and nobility as his claiming the only difference between a prince and a pauper to be their clothes, Mark Twain sought introductions to princes and potentates every chance he had. In Berlin during the winter of 1891–92, for instance, he was delighted to be asked to dine with Wilhelm II; at Bad Nauheim in July 1892, he was overjoyed by the chance to meet His Royal Highness, the Prince of Wales (later Edward VII); and soon after his arrival in

Vienna, he was pleased to be invited to tea at the Metropole by a fellow guest, the German princess royal (Wilhelm's sister), to whom he later sent specially bound, ornately inscribed copies of *Personal Recollections of Joan of Arc* and *More Tramps Abroad*.[8] His constant introductions to the high and mighty of Europe prompted Jean's quip that "soon Papa won't have anybody left to meet but God."

Nevertheless, Austrian censors would not have permitted newspapers to report baldly that the emperor "had expressed the wish to make Mark Twain's acquaintance" unless it were undeniably true. Perhaps His Majesty was tactfully advised by his foreign minister that it would be a faux pas, even an unintended insult to the United States, to let someone of so "distinguished [a] position in the world of letters" who had "high standing as a citizen of the American Republic" leave the country after a long residence without receiving him. Mark Twain had, after all, been received by Frau Schratt, the emperor's mistress, and he had attended several public events where the emperor put in an appearance. So not to acknowledge Vienna's "famous guest" in this way could be construed as a deliberate snub.

That the name of the esteemed Polish statesman Count Agenor Goluchowski von Goluchowo (1849–1921), *k.u.k. Aussenminister* (imperial and royal minister of foreign affairs) from 1895 until 1906, is among those listed socially in Mark Twain's Vienna address book supports this supposition. Twain had undoubtedly met the foreign minister at diplomatic receptions in the American or British embassy, and Goluchowski was alert enough to the American humorist's celebrity in Vienna to have made such a suggestion to his imperial boss. The fact is, furthermore, that the man who insisted on always being addressed *Seine Apostolische Majestät, unser allergnädigster Kaiser und Herr* (His apostolic Majesty, our most gracious emperor and lord) could never, whatever he might privately wish, publicly or officially *ask* to meet anyone of lesser rank, be he or she the monarch's subject or a distinguished foreign citizen. When His Majesty felt such a desire, one of his ministers saw to it that a request for an audience was forthcoming from the other party through proper administrative channels. Ambassador Harris's letter was thus more than likely one Count Goluchowski had requested of the American legation in keeping with this elaborate court protocol.

In his sixty-ninth year, five years Clemens's senior, Franz Josef von Habsburg-Lothringen was already something of a relic. Next to Victoria, whose longevity he would eventually surpass, he was then the longest-reigning monarch in Europe. By 1899, he had worn the dual crowns of Austria-Hungary for over a half century, having been manipulated onto the throne by his scheming mother and old Prince Metternich in the upheavals of 1848. Never really beloved as a ruler and only briefly popular following an unsuccessful attempt on his life by a Hungarian tailor in 1853 and the young monarch's arranged marriage a year later to his beautiful cousin, Elisabeth of Bavaria, "old mutton chops" was nevertheless loyally venerated in late life as a kind of grandfather figure. *Der Alte* in German, *Proháska* in Czech, *Nagyapa* in Magyar (all synonyms for the Old Man) were names his subjects used for *Der Kaiser* whose death, many rightly feared and some hoped, would doom the Danube empire that outlasted him by only two years. The sorrows he had suffered from the murder (called "suicide") of his neurotic son and heir in a drunken brawl in 1889 and the assassination nine years later of his estranged wife by a witless anarchist earned the lonely old man sympathy from those who otherwise detested everything he symbolized.

Neither stupid nor uneducated, Franz Josef was nevertheless an unimaginative, humorless superbureaucrat who led an almost Spartan life, spending most of his waking hours at his desk or holding audiences, and sleeping in an iron army cot. His ideals in life may be seen from the facts that he always wore the uniform of a *Feldmarschall* in public and that his favorite music was that provided each afternoon at teatime beneath his office window by the *Burgkapelle* (his palace guards' band). Treating state banquets like an officers' mess, he ate rapidly without conversing. Since no one dared eat after the emperor had finished, dinner guests at Schönbrunn often went home hungry. He read only army manuals and government documents, attended the theater,

Emperor Franz Josef I

Empress Elisabeth, portrait painted
by F. X. Winterhalter

concerts, or exhibits only when obliged to, and seemed really to enjoy only hunting trips in the mountains around Bad Ischl. Consumed by remorse when the despondent architect of his new Imperial-Royal Court Opera committed suicide in 1869 after the emperor offhand-edly criticized the design of the stairs, Franz Josef thereafter strictly limited his comments about all public, social, or cultural events to "*Es war sehr schön. Wir haben uns sehr gefreut*" (It was very lovely. We enjoyed it very much). Why on earth he wanted to meet Mark Twain, unless Count Goluchowski advised it, is difficult to imagine.

Why Mark Twain found *Der Alte* congenial and "a real monarch" in contrast to Wilhelm II whom he put down as an insufferable martinet and a "cock-a-hoop sovereign" is even more puzzling. Perhaps it was because the audience was short and Franz Josef a polite listener as opposed to the lengthy dinner party in the Berlin home of Clemens's cousin, Mollie von Versen (wife of a Prussian general), where the Ger-man emperor monopolized conversation, usurping Twain's customary role as chief raconteur. As a ruler, Franz Josef was rigid and taciturn, hating change and innovation—for example, he would not permit typewriters or telephones in the Hofburg, though he finally acqui-esced to electric lighting—and he constantly scuttled ministries, such as Badeni's, rather than let them effect compromises that could have saved his realm. In the end, his policies or those he approved were utterly disastrous.

One can scarcely believe that, despite what he said for public con-sumption, Mark Twain did not have a more realistic and accurate as-sessment of the man he went to meet at the Hofburg promptly at one o'clock on the afternoon of Thursday, May 25, 1899. Mark Twain ar-rived in correct court dress—swallow-tailed coat, pin-striped trousers, silk hat, white gloves, and all—in an *Equipage* (horse-drawn carriage) provided him for the occasion by Ambassador Harris. Twain entered the Hofburg from Heldenplatz where he was met by two footmen who conducted him to the portal. There the *Pfortner* (porter) handed him over to another pair of footmen who conducted him up two flights of stairs and through several rooms to an anteroom where he was met by the *Obersthofmeister* (grand master of the court), Prince Alfred Montenuovo, who accompanied him into the emperor's study and formally presented the American guest to His Majesty.

At the conclusion of the audience, the elaborate ceremonial was repeated in reverse, with Mark Twain and Prince Montenuovo bowing, then stepping backward a few paces through the room's double doors (since no one was permitted to turn his back on the emperor) which a servant closed after them. Mark Twain was conveyed to Mr. Harris's waiting carriage in which he returned to the Hotel Krantz. Reporters from most of Vienna's leading newspapers had gathered there to query him about the audience at a kind of impromptu news conference.

Both *Fremden-Blatt* and *Neues Wiener Tagblatt* gave lengthy coverage to Twain's comments the next day, and *NWT* added more the following day. There is more than a little self-promotion in the false humility of Mark Twain's statements as reported in *NWT*: "It is a great distinction that has been granted me, and one I value greatly, that the Emperor of Austria had the special kindness to receive me in audience. The distinction is even greater because the monarch received me in his study, not together with other audience-seekers."[9]

He had originally understood, he said, that he would be part of a group on a "normal audience day" with only a moment face to face (*Augesicht zu Augesicht sehen*) with the emperor before the whole thing would be over and done with.

> How astonished I was, therefore, when I was informed the monarch would receive me in a private audience. I perceived a special kind of courtesy in this not for my humble self [*Wenigkeit*] but much more for the country I belong to and a goodwill gesture toward the literary circles of my nation. This honor springs from the same spirit that prompted the message from Emperor Wilhelm to my ailing colleague, Rudyard Kipling, the spirit of pure courtesy that really values the realm of letters [*Schriftstellerthums*] which both allies in such high measure contain.

Realizing the emperor's time was precious, he had composed a short speech in German which he committed to memory with great difficulty. Alas, when the time came he couldn't get out a word; he had simply forgotten the whole speech! True or not, this failure smacks a bit of his story about his introduction to President Grant in the White House in 1869 when he was struck speechless in the great general's presence. On this occasion, however, the emperor "pressed my hand warmly and drew me into conversation. At this I recovered myself and explained my misfortune. He was amused that I couldn't now recall what had taken me so many hours to memorize, and he assured me such a speech was quite unnecessary."

The emperor asked the inevitable question: how had he liked his twenty-month sojourn in Vienna? Twain's response went far beyond mere politeness with, "I can truthfully say that in all my travels I have never felt so well as in this wonderful *gemütlichen* Vienna, a city from whose splendid yet graceful proportions I have derived so much inspiration that I could put to good use."* Here his German faltered, he said, and when he sometimes lapsed into English for a word he needed, the emperor would immediately provide its German equivalent. His Majesty then praised the way Americans had behaved in their recent war (with Spain), at which Twain professed himself "very flattered" on behalf of all his countrymen. He concluded: "The audience had lasted rather a long while, so the Emperor then released me with special grace. This audience will be numbered among my finest memories."

Fremden-Blatt was synoptic, depending less on direct quotation but in some ways more revealing in its coverage. It emphasized the emperor's pleasure at "becoming acquainted with the famous American guest about whom he had so often heard" and, perhaps hyperbolically, noted His Majesty was well-enough informed about Mark Twain's writings to ask "what Mark Twain had worked on in Vienna, how he liked the city, and much more." Mark Twain responded glowingly

---

* There is simply no adequate English equivalent for gemütlich. The dictionary definitions of "comfortable, cosy, snug" in this context (that is, in reference to a place) are too pallid.

in German, which "he has not completely mastered," but when he begged pardon for his clumsy pronunciation and halting speech, "the Emperor smilingly replied 'Oh, I understand quite well. Please continue.'" Recalling Twain's having recently spent a week in the other Habsburg capital, Budapest, Franz Josef asked his impressions of that city, and so on. This description of Twain's audience concluded by noting, "it lasted more than a quarter of an hour"—perhaps somewhat less than indicated in *NWT*—and that Mark Twain had afterward pronounced himself *"sehr begeistert"* (quite taken) with the monarch, awed by his energetic activity and ability to keep well informed about so many different things and abreast of current events and overjoyed with the magnanimity of his reception. "Now I grasp why Austrians attach so much love to their Emperor," Mark Twain tendentiously concluded.[10]

The reporters then turned to questions about his immediate travel plans and whether or not he might someday return to Vienna. About returning, he demurred: "It hasn't been ruled out, but first I must make a long visit to my homeland, which I haven't seen for many years." Aside to Pötzl, however, he confided: *"Ich glaube kaum"* (I hardly think so). His presence in London, he explained, was "urgently necessary" (no reason given), but thereafter he planned to spend the "high summer in the Scottish mountains and partly on the coast and then in the autumn return to America." Curiously, the Viennese press customarily referred to Mark Twain's "homeland" (*Heimatland*) as "Florida," no doubt because newspaper files correctly showed his birthplace as Florida, Missouri.[11]

His audience with the emperor had, in short, been a quarter hour or so of polite, self-conscious chitchat and pleasantries between two world-renowned elderly gentlemen, albeit of unequal station. How could it have been otherwise? Twain quickly dispelled any notion it might have been more, cabling the New York newspapers, "It was only a pleasant and informal conversation about things that had nothing to do with world politics." Nevertheless, his description of it as being "one of the finest moments of my life," "always to be numbered among my finest memories," and the like is no sentimental exaggeration. Socially and politically, it was the high point and grand climax of his entire Viennese sojourn. How theatrical to have saved it for the end, for his last full day in the city!

But the old hoaxer couldn't resist a parting joke, so he told Eduard Pötzl he concluded his cable by revealing that he had wanted to tell the emperor about a plan he had sent the secretary of state, in Washington, for securing world peace but had been afraid "His Majesty might laugh at it or find it too radical." At this news, he said, all the American newspapers had rushed to telegraph the secretary of state to learn what his plan was and had thereby found out he had "discovered a method for suddenly withdrawing all the oxygen from the atmosphere and thus destroying the entire human race in four minutes." [12] In other versions of this hoax, he claimed to have recommended to the emperor that he commission Jan Szczepanik to invent such a device for withdrawing the oxygen from the air and then, as its sole proprietor, His Majesty could compel world peace by threatening to use it. The idea of an ultimate weapon recalls his letter to Nikola Tesla some six months earlier, and he trotted it out again because his meeting with Franz Josef happened to coincide with the opening of the peace conference at The Hague.

Another jest during his last weeks in Vienna backfired. On his arrival in September 1897, he had told interviewers his reason for coming was to gather fresh material for novels, stories, and essays. So, on leaving, why not tell another lie—say he had gathered material for a book that would contain sketches (Charakterköpfe) of personalities he had come to know in Vienna? Among them, he told the press (not only the locals but the London Times and Spectator as well), would be

> monarchs and princes . . . tailors, cobblers, coachmen—oh, they can be very interesting!—then poets lawyers, novelists and humorists—thieves, desperados, forgers, printers and pastors, pirates, Negroes, Indians, cooks and waiters—historians and swindlers—high society, low society— Chinese, English, Irish, the Viennese—in short, all nationalities. I have hundreds of names on my list. During these last years in my Vienna sojourn I have finished a volume. Vienna has been a bonanza for me. [13]

One may only wish he had been serious and had indeed written such a book. The announcement was evidently intended to foster interest in what he really had written in Vienna that would soon be published, and it would probably have achieved that end save for one added detail: he announced he would not permit this book to be published for a hundred years after his death! Why? Because he wanted to speak his mind frankly in it without fear of offending. "This book gives me the freedom that I can't obtain in any other way. . . . One can't draw someone in an unprejudiced way as he has known that person unless he need have no fear of hurting the feelings of a son or grandchild."[14]

At this his Viennese friends and foes alike recoiled. Had he not been rather candid and sometimes unflattering already? What might he then say about them a century hence without any constraints at all to be polite? Moreover, he coupled this announcement with some stinging words about Austria's lack of an independent judiciary system. After praising Vienna as a "wonderful city" full of interesting people, where one could not "throw a stone without crippling an interesting person," he then concluded by picking up a newspaper and, pointing to a report of a parliamentary debate over some recent court verdicts, observing sarcastically: "I will return to Vienna only when such things are impossible. I've heard people talk about brutality (*Verrohung*) in America. But there is no political party or any party faction in America that would challenge the sanctity of the rule of law or undermine the authority of the judge's bench."[15]

No doubt he was smarting from the snide remarks he had suffered about what he himself denounced in a posthumously published essay as "The United States of Lyncherdom"—the propensity of Americans, especially in the South, to take the law into their own hands. No doubt also there were many in Vienna who would have found his criticism quite just. But to couch it in the context of an announcement of his "Vienna gallery," as *Fremden-Blatt* called it, was to invite an uneasy, even negative press reaction, and in the anti-Semitic newspapers, like *Reichspost*, the reaction was downright vitriolic. He thus felt obliged to have Pötzl report the whole thing had been a joke, a *schnurrige Lüge* (droll lie), and that no such book had been written or was contemplated.[16] Still, it was an insensitive blunder that put his valedictory under an unnecessary cloud. Once again he had inaccurately gauged the sensibilities of his Viennese audience. Their fear of his candor reflected their knowledge, which he should have understood after two years, of the duplicitous nature of Viennese society. Nothing was really what it pretended to be, and most of them—Karl Kraus and a few others excepted—were quite content that it should stay like that, come what may.

Prince Montenuovo having docketed the imperial audience on May 25, the Clemenses had perforce to postpone their departure for two days. It was rescheduled for three o'clock on the afternoon of Friday, May 26, 1899. The agent from Thomas Cook and Sons arrived with a van at the Hotel Krantz at ten that morning to take away the trunks and hampers that were to be sent directly to London. At 2 P.M. he returned with two cabs to convey the four Clemenses plus Katy Leary with their traveling luggage to the railway station—the Franz-Josefs-Bahnhof in Alsergrund, Vienna's *IX.Bezirk* (ninth district). By the time they reached the station a crowd had already gathered, their farewell bouquets filling the family's compartment, and "the station seemed full of our beloved friends, among them distinguished men and women," Clara, who probably experienced even more of Vienna than her father had, remembered indelibly. "Was life to be one long series of farewells?" she wondered, confessing that she and Jean "wept frankly with all the tragedy of youthful suffering in our hearts. While the inexorable revolution of the wheels started our journey we knew we were gazing on those dear faces for the last time."[17]

Their first destination, after a journey of seven-and-a-half hours by express train, was Prague, where they spent four days as guests of Prince Thurn und Taxis at his country estate just outside the city. They broke the trip again for a day's rest in Nuremberg and two days in Cologne before pushing on to London, where they arrived June 3. By the end of that month they were persuaded to spend the summer at Dr. Kellgren's sanatorium in the Swedish village of Sanna, where they all "took the cure" for their various ailments, swatted flies day and night, and enjoyed "brilliantly colored sunsets." [18] Then they returned to London, but it was actually more than a year before they sailed at last for New York aboard the S.S. *Minnehaha*, October 6, 1900.

Ultimately, Dr. Kellgren's treatments were no more efficacious for Jean than any of the others had been, and she spent the next eight years in and out of sanatoriums and "rest homes" as her seizures came and went, sometimes with long periods of abatement alternating with periods of severe depression that drove her very near to homicidal violence. At nine o'clock on the morning of Christmas Eve 1909, Katy Leary found her dead in her bathtub, evidently drowned in a final epileptic seizure.

Clemens himself never again saw Vienna. Only Clara came back in 1909 when her old teacher, Leschetizky, prematurely summoned her and some of his other pupils to his deathbed, then recovered to live six more hale and hearty years. In October of that year she suddenly married Ossip Gabrilowitsch, another of old Leschy's darlings whom she had first met at a dinner party her parents gave at the Hotel Metropole in April 1898.

The whole family with their faithful Katy Leary trekked back to Europe yet once more, however, to Florence in October 1903, because the gravely ill Livy hoped she might somehow find a cure for her worsening neurasthenia in the last place where, a decade earlier, they had all lived together in something like harmony and happiness. She died there seven months later. For her tombstone in Elmira, her husband composed a very Viennese epitaph: *"Gott sei dir gnaden, O meine Wonne"* (God be gracious to you, O my heart's delight).

Eduard Pötzl, their old friend at *Neues Wiener Tagblatt*, writing her obituary in Vienna, sent condolences. In response he received a printed, black-letter *Dankbrief* that Clemens mailed to literally hundreds all over the globe who had sent similar messages of sympathy.[19] It contained an apology for its impersonal formality, but at the bottom of this one he scrawled "Goodbye, dear Pötzl, if we meet no more. SLC." This seems a poignant sequel to Clara's "we knew we were gazing on those dear faces for the last time," and it foreshadows her father's last unfinished sentence to Clara at his bedside before he lapsed into unconsciousness on the afternoon of April 21, 1910, and died a few hours later: "Goodbye dear, if we meet ———." [20]

Its "famous guest," Samuel L. Clemens, had indeed left Vienna forever, but Vienna never left Mark Twain.

Mark Twain's Concordia Speech

Translated from "Mark Twain bei der 'Concordia,'" *Neue Freie Presse*, Morgen-blatt, Nr. 11924, Wien, Dienstag, den 2.November 1897, S.1, alle untere Spal-ten, S. 2, Spalt 1, as compared with other newspapers and corrected with *Rechenschaftsbericht der "Concordia" für 1897* (official record).

am deeply touched, gentlemen, to be received so hospitably here by my own professional colleagues in this land so distant from my own. My heart is full of gratitude but my poverty in German words compels me to a great economy of expression. Pardon me if I read what I want to say.[1] I don't speak German well but several experts have assured me that I write it like an angel. Maybe so, maybe so—I don't know. I've not yet made any acquaintances among the angels. That comes later,[2] whenever it pleases the Deity. I'm not in any hurry.

For a long time, gentlemen, I have nursed an ardent desire to give a speech in German but no one has ever permitted me to do so. People who have no appreciation of the art have always put obstacles in my way and thwarted my desire, sometimes violently. Those people have always said to me: "Be still, sir! For God's sake, be quiet! Find another way to make yourself tiresome."

1. Here the Concordia secretary wrote: "Er las aber nicht" (But he did not read).
2. Several other newspaper accounts in addition to *NFP* noted parenthetically here: "nach oben zeigend" (pointing upward).

In the present instance, as usual, it was difficult for me to obtain permission. The committee greatly regretted that it could not grant permission because of the Concordia's rule that it must protect the German language. Dear me! How could anyone have dared say such a thing to me? I am certainly the truest friend of the German language—not just now, but for a long time—yes, even for twenty years past. And I have never wanted to injure the noble language; on the contrary, I have wished only to improve it; I just want to reform it. It has been my life's dream. I have already visited various German-speaking governments and pleaded for contracts. Now I have come to Austria on the same mission. I would effect only a few changes. I just want to compress the method of speech—the luxurious, elaborate construction; to suppress, abolish, eradicate the eternal parentheses; to forbid the introducing of more than thirteen subjects in one sentence; to pull the verb so far forward that one may discover it without a telescope. In a word, gentlemen, I want to simplify your beloved language so that when you need it for prayer it can be understood Up Yonder.

I implore you, take my advice and effect these reforms I have mentioned. Then you will possess a magnificent language and, what's more, when you want to say something you'll at least understand what you've said. But often nowadays after you've given out a mile-long sentence and rested up from it, you must feel a stirring curiosity to determine for yourself what you've actually said. Several days ago a correspondent in one of the local papers constructed a sentence containing 112 words with seven parentheses inserted therein and the subject changed seven times. Just think, gentlemen, that in the course of the trip through one single sentence the poor, persecuted, tired subject had to make seven transfers.

Now, when the reforms I have mentioned are executed, things won't be so bad any more. One more thing. I would very much also like to reform the separable verb a bit. I don't want to let anyone do what Schiller did: he stuffed the whole history of the Thirty Years' War between the two parts of a separable verb. That aroused even Germany itself and Schiller was—thank God!—refused permission to write the history of the Hundred Years' War. After all these reforms have been effected, the German language will be the noblest and most beautiful in the world.

Now that the character of my mission is known, I ask you to be so kind as to give me some valuable help. In a humorous feuilleton about me, Herr Pötzl wanted to make the public believe that I came to Vienna to clog up the bridges and obstruct traffic while I collect observations and make drawings. But don't let yourselves be misled by him. My frequent presence on the bridges is for a completely innocent reason. There is the necessary space. There one can string out a noble, long German sentence along the bridge railing and view its entire contents at one glance. At one end of the railing I can attach the first part of a separable verb and the final part I can fasten to the other end—then spread the body of the sentence in-between. Usually the city's bridges[3] are long enough for my purpose, but when I want to study Pötzl's writings, I travel out to use the splendid, endless Reichsbrücke.[4] But that's a calumny. Pötzl writes the most beautiful German. Perhaps not as pliant as mine, but in many little details much better. Pardon these flatteries. They are well-deserved.

Now I am killing my speech—nay—I want to say, I am bringing it to a close. I am a foreigner, but here among you in Vienna's hospitable atmosphere I have completely forgotten it. And so again and yet again—I offer you my heartiest thanks!

3. "City's bridges" refers to those on the Danube Canal.
4. "Reichsbrücke" was the major bridge over the Danube River at Vienna, hence several times longer than the canal bridges.

APPENDIX B

"American Representation in Austria"

1899.

[*by "Mark Twain"*]

Mr. Addison Harris, of Indianapolis, is the new U.S. Minister here (Vienna). This is retrogression—a return to old and bad methods. An American Minister has nothing to do in Vienna but swing around in the diplomatic circle and cause the Republic to be respected in that society. The requirements of the post are society requirements, not political. The proper equipment is substantially this:

1. A private income of $40,000.
2. Experience of swell society life in the European capitals.

The title "American Representation in Austria" is not Mark Twain's but was added to this untitled piece by Albert Bigelow Paine when he made a typescript copy of the original. Paine's editorial emendations here are bracketed. Twain misspells the name of the Secretary of Legation, Charles Hrdlicka.

This previously unpublished work by Mark Twain is © 1992 by Manufacturers Hanover Trust Company as Trustee of the Mark Twain Foundation, which reserves all reproduction or dramatization rights in every medium. It is published with the permission of the University of California Press and Robert H. Hirst, General Editor, Mark Twain Project.

3. Easy adaptability to unfamiliar customs, and common-sense enough to respect them.

4. The gift of reserve—upon occasion.

5. The gift of talk, and the tact to know when to exercise it.

6. Personal dignity, native courtesy, trained good manners.

7. The hospitable instinct, and the disposition to give it liberal scope.

8. Familiarity with the French and German languages.

9. The genius to know and keep in mind that the Minister is the United States of America on exhibition and under criticism—not his private self.

Mr. Tower, who was lately translated from this post to the higher one at St. Petersburg fulfilled all of these conditions. Mr. Addison Harris fulfills not a single one of them. He has a poor income. He has but little pride. If he had any considerable degree of it he would not have accepted a post whose mean salary required him to live like a pauper and revel in sumptuous hospitalities which he must return with ham and lemonade.

He has evidently had no experience of European society—nor of well-bred society anywhere.

He *has* the gift of reserve—and must exercise it upon all occasions, for he has no facility with his tongue and nothing to talk about.

He lacks personal dignity, address, graciousness; and his manners, while not always poor [are] noticeably so sometimes.

The hospitable instinct is not a part of his composition.

He speaks his own language only. He will have to do his society rounds with an interpreter. He had to take one with him when he had his audience with the Emperor.

He has a parlor and bedroom in this hotel where we live (the Krantz). After three weeks' occupancy they are stark naked of books, pictures, flowers, bric-a-brac and the other trifles which entertain the eye, rest the spirit and furnish the comfort which the home-look gives, and distinguishes the habitation of a civilized person from the barrack of a semi-civilized one.

On the floor above lives a very, *very* minor representative of Britain—a commerce-agent, not even so much as a consul. Inside of two days' occupancy his quarters were become a pleasure to the eye and a satisfaction to the spirit. It is because the man is an educated gentleman, and civilized surroundings are a necessity of his training. When you enter the place he comes cordially to meet you and seat you and offer you wine, cigars, cigarettes, a pipe—anything you can be persuaded to have; and straightway the talk begins, and flows easily and brightly on. When you enter that American cavern the Minister receives you well-meaningly but without heartiness—a reception which is not intended to be ungracious but which through absence of tact and training gets that complexion and hence is uninspiring. He gets the ladies seated at one side of the room, and you and himself at the other side of it, which is an uncosy arrangement and makes two conversations necessary where one would be more comfortable, at least as a beginning. He is meditative; therefore, to prevent a chill from falling, you open the talk yourself. There being some more meditation and no response, you tug out another remark; this time on the all-absorbing topic, the stirring topic, the topic which is inflaming two worlds—the Dreyfus case. There is a halting, disjointed, uninterested, ignorant reply, and you realize that the Envoy Extraordinary and Minister Plenipotentiary of the United States of America knows nothing about the matter. What to do next? God knows. He is not smoking, he does not ask you to smoke; the materials are not present. He is not taking a glass of anything, he does not ask you to take a glass; the materials are not present.

By this time his attitude is unambassadorial; it is the United States of America at its unofficial ease, oblivious of the ladies; it is lying on its back in its arm-chair, with its neck resting upon the chairback and its legs sprawled abroad—the Great Republic scorning the artificial conventions of an effete civilization.

It being Mr. Harris's turn now to furnish something, and I being out of subjects, I wait. Then he lazily says—

"I wish there was a good history of Austria to be had. Here I am,

Minister to the Country, and I don't know anything more about it than a Choctaw does."

"A dead one, you mean." But that was only a thought; I did not say it, for I long ago learned that we must not say everything that comes into our minds.

The subject changed again; for it was one of those unsettled conversations, you know. It was one of those fires which keep going out every time you stop blowing on it. Mr. Harris produced a small primer and said he had borrowed it and it was a useful thing to have; he was going to look around and buy a copy; the price was ten Kreutzers. It gave the details of the construction of the State, county and municipal governments, with the salaries of the officials. He thought the pay of the army officers was astonish[ingly] slender. I was able to agree to that. He thought the pay of the judges was also very poor. I combatted that—not because he wasn't in the right but because agreeing with things is paralyzing to conversation. I said that three thousand Gulden here was better than eight thousand dollars in America. This was a kind of ragged poor lie, and really a thing to be ashamed of for a person of my attainments, but it was better than nothing, and I stuck to it, supporting it with arguments and statistics which were remarkably thin and ignorant—but talk resulted, and that was the main thing.

Then there was another change: the Minister had hired a teacher and was going to learn German. There were three possible replies:

1. It is the custom. Our representatives usually take infant-class courses in the rudiments of their trade after they have assumed its responsibilities.

2. Why in Halifax didn't you learn it before you came?

3. God bless you, sir, it is a noble idea and does you infinite credit.

I used a chastened form of Reply No. 3.

Next morning was the great annual parade—a review of 30,000 or 40,000 troops by the Emperor—a fine and brilliant spectacle. America had three representatives present in the assemblage of swell spectators: The Minister, the Secretary of Legation (Herdliski), the Naval Attaché (Beehler), and General Ruger, who held great commands in the Civil War and gained high distinction. The Minister and Beehler were unshaven. I did not examine their shirts.

Herdliski (born and reared in Cincinnati) is a diligent, good-natured, well-meaning, meddling, tactless, chattering, vulgar ass. In his rightful place, behind the counter of a cheap grocery, selling candles and soap and compelling the customer's good will, he would be a very useful man and not criticisable by any fair-minded person; also in a barber shop, either as head of it or in the line of promotion, his brisk, obliging, and chatty and sociable ways would make him a favorite and insure prosperity. But as a Secretary of Legation he is wasted.

Beehler—but Beehler is impossible. A good enough man, I think there is no doubt of that; but just an ass, just a lubberly, slovenly, common-place, unlicked, kind-hearted, self-complacent ass, and in no way qualified as an ornament; and that—among other things—is what a Naval Attaché ought to be. I wonder where our Government fishes for its average foreign-service officials.

Notes

In addition to the standard MLA abbreviations, names of people and sources repeatedly cited in these notes are abbreviated as follows:

AM   William M. Johnston, *The Austrian Mind, An Intellectual and Social History, 1848–1938*. Berkeley: U of California P, 1972.

AZ   *Arbeiter-Zeitung*.

CC   Clara Clemens.

DRT   *The Devil's Race-Track: Mark Twain's Great Dark Writings*, ed. John S. Tuckey. Berkeley: U of California P, 1980.

DVB   *Deutsches Volksblatt*.

DZ   *Deutsche Zeitung*.

EE   Mark Twain, *Europe and Elsewhere*, ed. Albert Bigelow Paine. New York: Harper, 1923.

EP   *Extrapost*.

F   *Die Fackel*.

FB   *Fremden-Blatt*.

Fl   *Der Floh*.

FM   *Mark Twain's Fables of Man*, ed. John S. Tuckey. Berkeley: U of California P, 1972.

FW   *The Standard Edition of the Complete Works of Sigmund Freud*, 24 vols., trans. and ed. James Strachey, Anna Freud, et al. London: The Hogarth Press and the Institute of Psychoanalysis, 1953–74.

F/WL   *Figaro* (with *Wiener Luft* supplement).

IWEB   *Illustrirtes Wiener Extrablatt*.

K   *Kikeriki!*

KL   Mary Lawton, *A Life With Mark Twain (The Memoirs of Katy Leary, for Thirty Years His Faithful and Devoted Servant)*. New York: Harcourt, 1925.

Levetus   "Mark Twain in Vienna: Personal Recollections of Amelia S. Leve-
             tus, 1912," ts., Original in the Rare Book Collection, Detroit Pub-
             lic Library.

MFMT   Clara Clemens, *My Father, Mark Twain*. New York: Harper, 1931.

MSM   *Mark Twain's Mysterious Stranger Manuscripts*, ed. William M. Gib-
             son. Berkeley: U of California P, 1969.

MT   Mark Twain

MTA   *Mark Twain's Autobiography*, ed. Albert Bigelow Paine. New York:
             Harper, 1924.

MTB   Albert Bigelow Paine, *Mark Twain: A Biography*, 3 vols. New York:
             Harper, 1912.

MTHHR   *Mark Twain's Correspondence with Henry Huttleston Rogers*, ed. Lewis
             Leary. Berkeley: U of California P, 1969.

MTHL   *Mark Twain–Howells Letters*, 2 vols., ed. Henry Nash Smith and
             William M. Gibson. Cambridge: Harvard UP, 1960.

MTJ   *Mark Twain Journal*.

MTL   *Mark Twain's Letters*, 2 vols., ed. Albert Bigelow Paine. New York:
             Harper, 1917.

MTN   *Mark Twain's Notebook*, ed. Albert Bigelow Paine. New York:
             Harper, 1935.

MTOA   *Mark Twain's Own Autobiography: The Chapters from the North Ameri-
             can Review*, ed. Michael J. Kiskis. Madison: U of Wisconsin P,
             1990.

MTP   Mark Twain Papers, Bancroft Library, University of California,
             Berkeley.

MTS   *Mark Twain's Speeches*, ed. Albert Bigelow Paine. New York:
             Harper, 1923.

N&J   *Mark Twain's Notebooks and Journals*, vol. 1 (1855–73), ed. Frederick
             Anderson, Michael B. Frank, and Kenneth M. Sanderson; vol. 2
             (1877–83), ed. Frederick Anderson, Lin Salamo, and Bernard L.
             Stein; vol. 3 (1883–91), ed. Robert Pack Browning, Michael B.
             Frank, and Lin Salamo. Berkeley: U of California P, 1975, 1975,
             1979.

NB 40, 42   MT. Notebook 40 (January 1897–July 1900), ts.; Notebook 42
             (June 1897–March 1900), ts., MTP.

NFP   *Neue Freie Presse*.

NWB   *Neuigkeits-Weltblatt*.

NWJ	*Neues Wiener Journal.*
NWT	*Neues Wiener Tagblatt.*
OLC	Olivia Langdon Clemens.
OVZ	*Oesterreichische Volkszeitung.*
RP	*Reichspost.*
S&B	*Mark Twain's Satires and Burlesques,* ed. Franklin R. Rogers. Berkeley: U of California P, 1967.
SLC	Samuel Langhorne Clemens.
VL	*Das Vaterland.*
VS	*Volkstimme.*
VT	*Volkstribüne.*
WB	*Wiener Bilder.*
WIM	*What Is Man? and Other Philosophical Essays,* ed. Paul Baender. Berkeley: U of California P, 1973.
WIM(P)	*What Is Man? and Other Essays,* ed. Albert Bigelow Paine. New York: Harper, 1917.
WMT	*Works of Mark Twain,* 25 vols., Harper & Brothers Edition. New York: Collier, 1922.
WSB	*Wiener Salonblatt*
WT	*Wiener Tagblatt*
WWD	*Mark Twain's Which Was the Dream? and Other Symbolic Writings of the Later Years,* ed. John S. Tuckey. Berkeley: U of California P, 1967.

CHAPTER ONE
Mark Twain and Vienna

1. Levetus, 1–2.

2. *WMT* 8: 185.

3. This view of the relationship of person and persona is the underlying thesis of Justin Kaplan, *Mr. Clemens and Mark Twain* (New York: Simon, 1966).

4. Everett Emerson, *The Authentic Mark Twain, A Literary Biography of Samuel L. Clemens* (Philadelphia: U of Pennsylvania P, 1984) 20. See also Sara de Saussure Davis and Philip D. Beidler, eds., *The Mythologizing of Mark Twain* (Tuscaloosa: U of Alabama P, 1984) throughout.

5. For an overview of Viennese life at this period, see Allan Janik and Stephen Toulmin, *Wittgenstein's Vienna* (New York: Simon, 1973), as well as Carl

Schorske, *Fin-de-Siècle Vienna: Politics and Culture* (New York: Knopf, 1980) and the memoirs of Hilde Spiel and Stefan Zweig cited later herein.

6. Clemens M. Gruber, *Die Schicksalstage von Mayerling* (Judenburg: Erich Mlakar, 1989) exposes the romantic legend of a lovers' suicide pact in the death of Crown Prince Rudolf as a fiction concocted by the emperor's advisors and sanctioned by him. Gruber then documents the actual circumstances in which Rudolf and his mistress, Baroness Mary Vetsera, were accidentally slain in a drunken brawl. Henry Fisher, *Abroad with Mark Twain and Eugene Field* (New York: Nicholas L. Brown, 1922) indicates Mark Twain knew the facts of this case when he was in Vienna. (See chap. 4, below.)

7. *MTB*, 1048–83.

8. Compare accounts of this in *MFMT* and *KL*, throughout.

9. Max Lederer, "Mark Twain in Vienna," *Mark Twain Quarterly* 7 (Summer-Fall 1945): 1–12, and Karl Stiehl, "Mark Twain in der Wiener Presse zur Zeit seines Aufenthaltes in Wien, 1897–1899," diss., U of Vienna, 1953, throughout.

10. Emerson, 276.

11. *WMT* 4: 150.

12. *AM*, 115–27, and throughout.

13. Quoted by Karl Kraus in *F* 11 (July 1899): 30.

14. Ibid.

CHAPTER TWO

Wanderjahre

1. *MTHL* 2: 645.

2. *WIM*, 493.

3. *MTHL* 2: 698.

4. *MTHHR*, 299.

5. NB 42, 18–20.

6. *MTL*, 646.

7. NB 42, 37–38.

8. NB 42, 39.

9. SLC, letter to Robert Barr, 29 September 1897, MTP photocopy, courtesy Charles W. Sachs, Scriptorium, Beverly Hills, Calif.

10. *MFMT*, 190.

11. NB 42, 39; see also *MTHHR*, 302.

12. SLC, letter to Mrs. Laura Rothmann, 30 September 1897, MTP photocopy from a Paul C. Richards catalogue.

13. *MTHHR*, 302; SLC, letter to Consul-General Bailey Hurst, 8 October 1897, Mark Twain Memorial, Hartford, Conn.

14. *MTHHR*, 302.

15. *MTHHR*, 360.

16. MT, "Conversations with Satan," Ms., Paine 255, MTP (italics added).

CHAPTER THREE

Zeitungskrieg!

1. Stiehl, 6.

2. *WMT* 24: 200–202.

3. *AM*, 48–50.

4. *MTHHR*, 302.

5. *F/WL*, 8 Oct. 1897: 8.

6. Levetus, 2–3.

7. Levetus, 2–3.

8. *NWT*, 2 Oct. 1897: 1–2; see also Eduard Pötzl, "Der Stille Beobachter," *Gesammelte Skizzen*, 18 vols. (Wien: Robert von Mohr, 1910) 11: 5–7.

9. Dr. Johannes Pötzl, personal interview with the author, Vienna, 2 June 1988.

10. Hans Tietze, *Die Juden Wiens: Geschichte, Wirtschaft, Kultur* (1933. Wien: Edition Atelier, 1987) 216.

11. SLC, letter to J. Henry Harper, 13 Oct. 1897. Photocopy in MTP, courtesy John Feldman.

12. SLC, letter to Ferdinand Gross, 10 Oct. 1897. Photocopy in MTP, courtesy Victor Jacobs.

13. For the fullest of the dozen or more Viennese newspaper reports of MT's Concordia appearance compare *EP*, 1 Nov. 1897: 2; *FB*, 2 Nov. 1897: 4; *IWEB*, 2 Nov. 1897: 5; *NFP*, 2 Nov. 1897: 1–2; *NWJ*, 2 Nov. 1897: 3; *NWT*, 2 Nov. 1897: 4; *WT*, 2 Nov. 1897: 3. See also Levetus, 27–29 and *Rechenschaftsbericht der "Concordia" fuer 1897* (Minutes of the "Concordia" for 1897). Stadt-und Landesbibliothek, Vienna.

14. Peter Eppel, *"Concordia soll ihr Name sein . . ."* (Wien: Boehlau Nachfolger, 1984) 120–34 and throughout.

15. This is inscribed on an unpublished photograph owned by Dr. Johannes Pötzl, Vienna.

16. NB 42: 49, 44.

17. For some typical examples of such stories, see *IWEB*, 13 Oct. 1897: 4; 17 Oct. 1897: 3; 30 Oct. 1897: 4; and *NFP*, 2 Oct. 1897: 1.

18. *AM*, 351.

19. Eppel, 103; Anna Katona, "Mark Twain's Reception in Hungary," *American Literary Realism* 16 (Spring 1983): 113.

20. Katona, *ALR*, 108–9.

21. Katona, *ALR*, 111.

22. Anna Katona, "An Interview with Mark Twain," *Hungarian Studies Review* 9 (Spring 1982): 74–81.

23. Katona, *ALR*, 111.

24. *MTHL*, 2: 690.

25. *MTS*, 176–77.

26. Katona, *ALR*, 112.

27. NB 40: 55.

28. Katona, *ALR*, 111–12.

29. *MTHL*, 2: 690–91.

30. *AM*, 342–43.

31. *MTHL*, 2: 691.

32. Clementina Katona Abranyi, "Mark Twain a nökérdésröl" (Mark Twain on the Women's Issue) in *Négy Lirikus és Egyebek* (Four Poets and a Miscellany) (Budapest, 1909), quoted in Katona, *ALR*, 114.

CHAPTER FOUR
Witness to History

1. Typical of the coverage given in the Viennese press to MT's visit to the city council meeting are the reports in *NFP*, 16 Oct. 1897: 6; *OVZ*, 16 Oct. 1897: 5–6; and RP, 17 Oct. 1897: 5, among many others.

2. Special attention to MT's comments was given by the reporter in RP, 17 Oct. 1897: 5.

3. For a detailed assessment of Lueger's achievements and his importance in fin de siècle Vienna, see especially Richard S. Geehr's biography *Karl Lueger*,

Mayor of Fin de Siècle Vienna (Detroit: Wayne SUP, 1990), as well as earlier discussions in *AM*, 63–66; Janik and Toulmin, 52–58; and Schorske, 133–48.

4. Quoted in Richard S. Geehr, ed., *"I Decide Who Is a Jew!": The Papers of Dr. Karl Lueger* (Washington, D.C.: UP of America, 1982) 3.

5. *NFP*, 17 Oct. 1897: 6.

6. Emerson, 14.

7. *F/WL*, 23 Oct. 1897: 171.

8. *EE*, 229–33.

9. *EE*, 230–31.

10. Hilde Spiel, *Vienna's Golden Autumn, 1866–1938* (London: Weidenfeld and Nicolson, 1987) 91–99, 126–30, and elsewhere.

11. *AM*, 47, 267.

12. William J. McGrath, *Freud's Discovery of Psychoanalysis: The Politics of Hysteria* (Ithaca: Cornell UP, 1986) 219–29.

13. Joseph Redlich, *Emperor Francis Joseph of Austria* (London, 1929), qtd. in John W. Mason, *The Dissolution of the Austro-Hungarian Empire, 1867–1918* (London: Longmans, 1985) 9.

14. Compare the accounts given by MT in NB 42: 42–48 with those in such Viennese newspapers, for example, as *NFP*, 5 Nov. 1897: 2; *WT*, 6 Nov. 1897: 4; and *OVZ*, 27 Nov. 1897.

15. The fullest considerations of "Stirring Times in Austria" to date are in William R. Macnaughton, *Mark Twain's Last Years as a Writer* (Columbia: U of Missouri P, 1979) 65–71, and Walter Grünzweig, "Comanches in the Austrian Parliament: Austria as a Metaphor for Mark Twain's Disillusionment with Democracy," *MTJ* 23 (Fall 1985) 3–9.

16. *WMT* 24: 197–243.

17. NB 42: 48.

18. *WMT* 24: 242.

19. *OVZ*, 27 Nov. 1897: 3.

20. *MTL*, 2: 652.

21. *WMT* 24: 243.

22. *NFP*, 27 Feb. 1898: 6.

23. MT, "The 'Austrian Parliamentary System'? Government by Article 14," *Lords and Commons*, 25 Feb. 1899, 59–61, as corrected against Ms. Paine 58, MTP.

24. Instances of SLC's privately repeated expressions of unease about the

political stability in Austria-Hungary and the possibility of revolution or civil war while he was in Vienna may be seen in: *MTHHR*, 358; *MTL*, 2: 650–51; and NB 40: 26.

25. *DRT*, 57.

26. NB 40: 33.

27. *MTL*, 2: 666–67.

28. *MTHHR*, 363.

29. *WIM(P)*, 167–81.

30. *WIM(P)*, 170.

31. NB 40: 38.

32. NB 40: 38.

33. *WIM(P)*, 175.

34. NB 40: 37, 38–39.

35. *MTL*, 2: 668.

36. *WIM(P)*, 175.

37. *WIM(P)*, 170–71.

38. NB 40: 38.

39. *WIM(P)*, 177.

40. *WIM(P)*, 177–81.

41. NB 40: 36.

42. Stefan Zweig, *The World of Yesterday* (1943. Lincoln: U of Nebraska P, 1964) 18.

43. *WIM(P)*, 172–73.

44. *AM*, 34.

45. Fisher, 66. "Count Something" (Fisher evidently forgot the name) in this anecdote was Count Hoyos, whose address is in MT's Vienna notebook, lending credence to MT's references here to Rudolf as "murdered" and "killed in a low debauch." Hoyos may have told MT the truth about the death of the crown prince (as he did others), debunking the romantic story of suicide officially countenanced and now almost universally accepted.

CHAPTER FIVE
"Leschy"

1. Ethel Newcomb, *Leschetizky As I Knew Him* (1921. New York: Da Capo, 1967) 309–11.

2. *MFMT*, 189–90.

3. *KL*, 165.

4. Newcomb, xv–xvi.

5. *MFMT*, 191–92.

6. Hamlin Hill, *Mark Twain: God's Fool* (New York: Harper, 1973) xxv–xxvi, 20–21, and elsewhere.

7. NB 42: 1–2.

8. *MFMT*, 188.

9. *WMT* 4: 137.

10. *S&B*, 17–25. See also *N&J* 1: 167–72.

11. *WMT* 13: 63–80; *N&J* 2: 262.

12. *MFMT*, 191; NB 40: 45.

13. *NFP*, 30 Nov. 1897: 8.

14. SLC, letter to Johann Strauss, Jr., 25 May 1899, qtd. in full in Otto Hietsch, "Mark Twain and Johann Strauss," *Jahrbuch für Amerikastudien*, 210–11. Original in the Strauss-Meyssner Collection, Stadt-und Landesbibliothek, Vienna.

15. SLC, letter to Frau Adele Strauss, 6 June 1899, qtd. in full in Hietsch, 210–11. Original in the Strauss-Meyssner Collection, Stadt-und Landesbibliothek, Vienna.

16. *NFP*, 19 Nov. 1897: 6.

17. WT, 2 Feb. 1898: 5.

18. *NWT*, 25 Feb. 1898: 6.

19. John G. Waterhouse, "Perosi," *The New Grove Dictionary of Music and Musicians* 14: 539–40.

20. *NFP*, 9 April 1899: 6.

21. Carl Dolmetsch, "Mark Twain Abroad," *Musical America* 110 (Mar. 1990), 53. (Corrected against the original.)

22. Dolmetsch, 55.

23. Dolmetsch, 54. (Corrected against the original.)

24. *MFMT*, 189–90.

25. *KL*, 165–66.

26. Newcomb, 187–88.

27. Dolmetsch, 55. (Corrected against the original.)

28. NB 40: 31.

29. *MTHHR*, 357–58.

30. NB 40: 31–32.

31. NB 40: 32.

32. OLC, letter to Mary B. Cheney, 7 Oct. 1898. Mark Twain Memorial, Hartford, Conn.

33. Newcomb, 280.

34. K. J. Kutsch and Leo Riemens, *A Concise Biographical Dictionary of Singers* (New York: Chilton, 1969) 54–55.

35. *KL*, 162.

36. *New York World* 11 June 1899: 4.

37. NB 42: 68.

38. NB 42: 49.

39. *MSM*, 93.

40. Dolmetsch, 56. (Corrected against the original.)

CHAPTER SIX

"The Most Beautiful Theater in the World"

1. Thomas Schirer, *Mark Twain and the Theatre* (Nürnberg: Carl Hans, 1984), provides the only comprehensive account of MT's dramatic efforts. For MT's theatrical efforts in Vienna see Schirer, 94–100, 127–28.

2. *NWT*, 2 Oct. 1897: 2.

3. Zweig, 24.

4. Zweig, 15.

5. *NFP*, 20 Oct. 1897: 1.

6. *MTHL*, 2: 685.

7. *WMT* 10: 212–25.

8. *AM*, 165.

9. [W. A. Mozart], *The Letters of Mozart and His Family*, ed. Emily Anderson (London: Macmillan, 1938) 3: 1351.

10. Hermann Bahr, *Neue Rundschau* 23 (1912): 1303, qtd. in AM, 166.

11. *MTHHR*, 305.

12. *WMT* 10: 213–14.

13. *WMT* 10: 222–25.

14. *FB*, 9 March 1899: 5.

15. NB 40: 54–55.

16. SLC, letter to Auguste Wilbrandt-Baudius, 10 March 1899. MTP. Photocopy courtesy Charles W. Sachs, Scriptorium, Beverly Hills, Calif.

17. Edgar H. Hemminghaus, "Mark Twain's German Provenience," *Modern Language Quarterly* 6 (1945): 476–78.

18. NB 42: 52–54.

19. NB 42: 53.

20. MT. "Is He Dead?" ms., Paine 126. MTP. This ms. in a hand other than MT's bears in his own hand the notation "Vienna, Feb. 21, 1898," presumably the date on which it was received from his copyist. A letter from SLC to Henry Rogers (*MTHHR*, 318) indicates the play was completed 5 February 1898.

21. *MTHHR*, 316.

22. NB 40: 12; *MTHHR*, 323–24.

23. *MTHHR*, 358.

24. *MTHHR*, 316.

25. *MTHHR*, 318.

26. SLC, postcard to Siegmund Schlesinger, 1 Feb. 1898. Mark Twain Memorial, Hartford, Conn.

27. Contract of SLC and Siegmund Schlesinger, 24 Feb. 1898. Lockwood Memorial Library, State U of New York, Buffalo.

28. *MTB*, 1075.

29. Fisher, 57–58.

30. SLC, letter to Siegmund Schlesinger, 20 May 1898. Department of Rare Books and Special Collections, University of Rochester Library, Rochester, N.Y.

31. SLC, letter to Siegmund Schlesinger, 30 May 1898. Special Collections, Case Library, Colgate University, Hamilton, N.Y.

32. SLC, letter to Siegmund Schlesinger, 28 July 1898. Department of Rare Books and Special Collections, University of Rochester Library, Rochester, N.Y.

33. SLC, postcard to Siegmund Schlesinger, 20 Oct. 1898. Original in the Rare Books Collection Detroit Public Library, Detroit, Mich.

34. NB 40: 52–53.

35. Tietze, 216–17.

36. *MTB*, 1075.

37. *MTHHR*, 316.

38. *NFP*, 11 March 1898: 6.

39. *MTHHR*, 345.

40. *MTHHR*, 353.

41. SLC, letter to Bettina Wirth, 19 June 1898. Mark Twain Memorial, Hartford, Conn.

42. Alf Hayman, letter to Dr. Clarence C. Rice, 27 Feb. 1899, Barrett Collection, Alderman Library, U of Virginia.

43. *NFP*, 15 March 1898: 5–6.

CHAPTER SEVEN
"Choice People"

1. NB 42: 49.

2. Nora Wydenbruck, *My Two Worlds, an Autobiography* (London: Longmans, 1956) 65.

3. Wydenbruck, 65.

4. Clementine Wydenbruck von Ruzičič, personal interview with Sholom J. Kahn, 23 and 28 September 1967. Transcript courtesy Prof. Sholom J. Kahn, Hebrew U of Jerusalem.

5. *MTHHR*, 318.

6. NB 40: 8.

7. *NFP*, 2 Feb. 1898: 7.

8. Sigmund Freud, letter to Wilhelm Fliess, 9 Feb. 1898. *The Complete Letters of Sigmund Freud to Wilhelm Fliess, 1887–1904*, trans. and ed. J. M. Masson (Cambridge: The Belknap P of Harvard UP, 1985) 298–99.

9. *MTHHR*, 318.

10. *NFP*, 2 Feb. 1898: 7.

11. *MTHHR*, 318.

12. Qtd. in Louis J. Budd, *Our Mark Twain, the Making of His Public Personality* (Philadelphia: U of Pennsylvania P, 1983) 136.

13. NB 42: 4–6.

14. *MTL*, 2: 657–60.

15. NB 42: 8–11.

16. *AM*, 39.

17. *NFP*, 9 Jan. 1898: 5; see also Eppel, 122.

18. *NWT*, 9 March 1898: 6.

19. CC, letter to George Cole, 30 March 1898. Department of Special Collections, University Research Library, U of California, Los Angeles.

20. *KL*, 163–64.

21. *New York World*, 11 June 1899: 4.

22. NB 40: 8–11.

23. *NFP*, 15 March 1898: 6.

24. See, for example: WT, 23 March 1898: 5; *NFP*, 26 March 1898: 1; and *NWT*, 28 March 1898: 4.

25. NB 40: 18.

26. CC, letters to George Cole, 12 and 14 April 1898. Department of Special Collections, University Research Library, U of California, Los Angeles.

27. NB 40: 20.

28. *NFP*, 10 May 1898: 1.

29. E. Gerard [Emily De Laszowska], *The Extermination of Love: A Fragmentary Study in Erotics*, 2 vols. (Leipzig: Tauchnitz, 1901) 1: "Dedication."

30. NB 40: 27.

31. MT, "My Platonic Sweetheart," Ms., box 16, no. 3a MTP, 8, 9, 23, and *Harper's Monthly Magazine* 126 (Dec. 1912), 14–20 (hereafter: MPS).

32. MPS, *Harper's*, 15. (Corrected against the manuscript.)

33. MPS, *Harper's*, 18. (Corrected against the manuscript.)

34. MPS, *Harper's*, 20. (Corrected against the manuscript.)

35. Emerson, 220.

36. *WMT* 24: 352.

37. *WMT* 24: 346–47.

38. NB 40: 21.

39. Typical of the misunderstanding of this piece is that in Emerson, 223.

40. NB 40: 20.

41. See appendix B for the full context of this passage.

42. *National Cyclopedia of American Biography* 27: 191–92 and *Dictionary of American Diplomatic History*, 476–77.

43. OLC, letter to Charlemagne Tower, 24 Dec. 1897. Alderman Library, U of Virginia, Charlottesville. See also *NFP*, 25 Nov. 1898: 7; *WSB*, 26 Nov. 1898: 6; and *NFP*, 28 Nov. 1898: 1.

44. NB 40: 12.

45. *NFP*, 3 May 1899: 5.

46. *National Cyclopedia of American Biography* 26: 124–25.

47. *WMT* 24: 226–40.

48. *Dictionary of American Diplomatic History*, 476–77.

CHAPTER EIGHT
Concerning the "Jew" Mark Twain

1. Adolf Hitler, *Mein Kampf* (1926. London: Hutchinson, 1974) 114.

2. *WMT* 24: 263–87.

3. For detailed parallel discussions of this subject, see *MTJ* 23 (Fall 1985): 10–27.

4. Marsha L. Rozenblitt, *The Jews of Vienna, 1867–1914: Assimilation and Identity* (Albany: SU of New York P, 1983) 13–45 and throughout.

5. Zweig (*The World of Yesterday*) sheds much light on the way affluent assimilated Jews in Vienna were able to ignore or shrug off the rise of anti-Semitism in their midst.

6. Geehr, *"I Decide Who Is a Jew!"* 3.

7. *MTL* 2: 647.

8. *FM*, 279–89.

9. *FM*, 445–48.

10. Tietze, 235.

11. Zweig, 22.

12. Eppel, 354–57.

13. *F/WL*, 14 Oct. 1897: 171.

14. *K*, 10 Oct. 1897: 2.

15. *K*, 20 Oct. 1897: 2.

16. *NFP*, 17 Oct. 1897: 6.

17. *NWJ*, 10 Oct. 1897: 5.

18. Erckmann-Chatrian, *The Polish Jew* (1869. New York: Ward, Lock, 1911) throughout.

19. *NWJ*, 10 Oct. 1897: 5.

20. *RP*, 12 Oct. 1897: 3.

21. NB 40: 7–8.

22. NB 42: 54.

23. For examples of this press coverage, see IWEB, 23 Feb. 1898: 53; *NWT*, 23 Feb. 1898: 7; *RP*, 24 Feb. 1898: 44; *WT*, 23 Feb. 1898: 2, and 1 Mar. 1898: 7.

24. *NFP*, 24 Feb. 1898: 2–3 and 27 Feb. 1898: 6.

25. *K*, 20 Feb. 1898: 2.

26. NB 42: 57–58.

27. *WMT* 24: 263–87. Subsequent references to and quotations from "Concerning the Jews" are to this edition. This essay continues to be reprinted and

anthologized with increasing frequency. For example, see also MT, *Concerning the Jews* (Philadelphia: Running Press, 1985).

28. *MTHHR*, 353–54.

29. M. S. Levy, "A Rabbi's Reply to Mark Twain," *Overland Monthly* 24 (October 1899): 364–67. See also *MTJ* 23 (Fall 1985): 26–27.

30. Marion Richmond, "The Last Source in Freud's Comment on Anti-Semitism," *Journal of the American Psychoanalytic Association* 28 (1980): 563–74.

31. *RP*, 6 May 1899: 9.

32. *VL*, 21 May 1899: 6.

33. *RP*, 26 May 1899: 9.

34. NB 42: 69.

35. NB 40: 48.

CHAPTER NINE

"Lay Down Your Arms!"

1. Hal Holbrook, *Highlights from the CBS Television Network Special "Mark Twain Tonight!"* Columbia Masterworks, OS 3080, 1968.

2. *WIM*, 84–85.

3. NB 40: 11.

4. MT, "A Defence of Royalty & Nobility," Ms., DeVoto 313a, MTP: 9.

5. Count Coudenhove's address is listed in NB 42: 6, and he is mentioned several times throughout NB 40 and 42 as among other guests at social functions attended by SLC in Vienna.

6. SLC, letter to Bertha von Suttner, 17 Feb. 1898. Missouri State Historical Society, Columbia, Mo.

7. For examples of press coverage, see: IWEB, 23 Feb. 1898: 4; *NFP*, 23 Feb. 1898: 4; *NWT*, 23 Feb. 1898: 2; *WT*, 23 Feb. 1898: 4.

8. Bertha [Kinsky] von Suttner, *Memoirs of Bertha von Suttner: The Records of an Eventful Life*, 2 vols. (Boston: Ginn, 1910): throughout.

9. MT, "The New War Scare," ts., Paine 46, MTP.

10. SLC, letter to Bettina Wirth, 19 June 1898. Mark Twain Memorial, Hartford, Conn.

11. *MTHL*, 2: 673.

12. *Humoristische Blätter* (Vienna), 17 April 1898: 5.

13. *NFP*, 19 Oct. 1898: 2.

14. Suttner 2: 212.

15. *OVZ*, 19 Oct. 1898: 8.

16. *NFP*, 19 Oct. 1898: 2; see also Suttner 2: 213.

17. *NFP*, 19 Oct. 1898: 2.

18. Suttner 2: 212; see also William T. Stead, "Character Sketch [of] Mark Twain," *Review of Reviews*, 16 Aug. 1897, 123–33.

19. Stead, 123.

20. Qtd. in Margaret Cheney, *Tesla: Man out of Time* (New York: Dorset, 1981): 125. (Corrected against the original in the Library of Congress.)

21. Cheney, 170, 264–65.

22. *MTL* 2: 672–74.

23. *NFP*, 27 Jan. 1899: 1.

24. SLC, letter to Bertha von Suttner, 27 March 1899. Missouri State Historical Society, Columbia, Mo.

25. SLC, letter to Bertha von Suttner, 10 May 1899. Stadtsbibliothek, Vienna.

26. *NWT*, 27 May 1899: 4.

27. SLC, letter to Bertha von Suttner, 7 May 1899 [1900]. Yale Collection of American Literature, Beinecke Rare Book and Manuscript Library, Yale University.

28. *MSM*, 155–56.

CHAPTER TEN

The Austrian Edison

1. Levetus, 20.

2. SLC, letter to Amelia S. Levetus, 15 March 1898, qtd. in Charles Hamilton Catalogue, 11 Mar. 1966, item 278.

3. NB 40: 13.

4. NB 40: 14.

5. *MTHHR*, 335.

6. *MTHHR*, 335–36.

7. *MTHHR*, 336–37.

8. *MTHHR*, 327–49.

9. NB 40: 15–16.

10. *MTHHR*, 332n.

11. NB 40: 16.

12. NB 40: 17–18.

13. Levetus, 20.

14. *New York World*, 11 June 1899: 4, cols. 2–3.

15. *WMT* 10: 263–67.

16. *WMT* 24: 313–28.

17. H. C. Balicer, "Szczepanik's 'Portrait' of Mark Twain," *Publisher's Weekly* 131 (20 Feb. 1937): 968. Qtd. in Thomas Burnham, "Mark Twain and the Austrian Edison," *American Quarterly* 6 (1954): 364–72.

18. This "friend of mine" was either Bettina Wirth, Bavarian-born wife of the financial editor of *Neue Freie Presse* and a long-time correspondent for the London *Daily News*, or Amelia S. Levetus, of the London *Daily Graphic*.

19. *MTL* 2: 651.

20. Hill, xix, 10–12, 37–38, and elsewhere.

CHAPTER ELEVEN
Home Thoughts

1. *New York World*, 13 March 1898: 7.

2. *MTHHR*, 324.

3. *MTHHR*, 351–52.

4. *MTHL* 2: 677.

5. NB 42: 51.

6. *MTHHR*, 307–8.

7. For examples, compare: *AZ*, 22 Jan. 1898: 5; *NFP*, 21 Jan. 1898: 1; and *WT*, 21 Jan. 1898: 3.

8. NB 40: 20–21.

9. NB 40: 21.

10. MT, "Kaltenleutgeben," ms., DeVoto 236, MTP, 1, 2, 4–6, 16.

11. "Kaltenleutgeben," 15.

12. Karl Baedeker, *Southern Germany and Austria, including Hungary, Dalmatia and Bosnia*, 7th ed. (Leipzig: Baedeker, 1891): 241.

13. NB 40: 18.

14. *MTHHR*, 352.

15. Compare the version edited by Paine in 1924 (*MTA*) with that published by MT himself in the *North American Review* in 1906–7 (*MTOA*) thus: *MTA* 1: 129–30 and *MTOA*, 120–21.

16. Compare also *MTA* 1: 98 and *MTOA*, 114.

17. Compare also *MTA* 1: 110–15; *MTOA*, 120–23.

18. *MTA* 1: 167–68.

19. *MTHL* 2: 689.

20. See, for example: *NFP*, 1 Oct. 1897: 1; *NWT*, 2 Oct. 1897: 1.

21. MT, "Autobiographical dictation, 4 Sept. 1907," ts., MTP.

22. *WIM*, 475.

23. *New York Times Review of Books*, 3 June 1917: 216, qtd. in *WIM*, 19.

24. Emerson, 219.

25. *WIM*, 124.

26. *WIM*, 169–70.

27. SLC, letter to Edward Day, 21 March 1903. West Virginia and Regional History Collection, West Virginia University Libraries, Morgantown.

28. This and subsequent quotations from and references to *Christian Science* are to the definitive text in *WIM*, 215–58. See also *WMT*, 25.

29. MT, "Wapping Alice," ms., DeVoto 344a, MTP. See also Mark Twain, *Wapping Alice* (Berkeley: Friends of Bancroft Library, 1981).

30. *MTHHR*, 325–26.

31. *MTHHR*, 360.

32. OLC, letter to Mary B. Cheney, 7 Oct. 1898. Mark Twain Memorial, Hartford.

CHAPTER TWELVE

Diogenes in Vienna

1. Joseph Redlich, qtd. in Harry Zohn, *Karl Kraus* (New York: Twayne, 1971) 14.

2. This and subsequent quotations from *U.A.* are from *F* 3, April 1899: 1–11.

3. Clementine Wydenbruck von Ruzičič, personal interview with Sholom J. Kahn, 23 and 28 September 1967.

4. Qtd. in *AM*, 138.

5. Ludwig Eisenberg, *Das Geistige Wien: Kuenstler-und Schriftsteller-Lexikon*, 2 vols. (Wien: C. Daberkow, 1893) 1: 286.

6. Zohn, 26.

7. Edward Timms, *Karl Kraus, Apocalyptic Satirist: Culture and Catastrophe in Habsburg Vienna* (New Haven: Yale UP, 1986) 34.

8. Qtd. in Timms, 32.

9. Tietze, 210.

10. Marie von Ebner-Eschenbach, "Aphorismen," *Gesammelte Werke*, 9 vols. (Vienna: Boehlau Nachfolger, 1961) 1: 865.

11. Franz Mautner, "Der Aphorismus als Literatur," *Wort und Wesen* (Frankfurt/Main: Insel, 1974) 285–87.

12. Karl Kraus, *Aphorismen*, ed. Christian Wagenknecht (Frankfurt/Main: Suhrkamp, 1986) 117.

13. Karl Kraus, *No Compromise: Selected Writings of Karl Kraus*, trans. and ed. Frederick Ungar (New York: Ungar, 1977) 227; and *Half-Truths and One-and-a Half Truths: Selected Aphorisms*, trans. and ed. Harry Zohn (Montreal: Egendra, 1976) 41.

14. *WMT* 24: 264.

15. *WMT* 5: 142.

16. NB 42: 67.

17. *WMT* 5: 108.

18. Kraus, *Aphorismen*, 68.

19. *WMT* 5: 69, 76.

20. NB 42: 67–68.

21. NB 42: 13.

22. NB 40: 38.

23. *WWD*, 176.

24. *AM*, 158–62.

25. Qtd. in Timms, 18.

26. *F* 11 (July 1899) 30.

27. Kraus, *Aphorismen*, 338.

CHAPTER THIRTEEN
City of Doctors, City of Dreams

1. NB 42: 68.

2. Erna Lesky's *Die Wiener Medizinische Schule im 19. Jahrhundert* (Graz-Koeln: Boehlau Nachfolger, 1965) offers the most comprehensive history of Vienna's development as a "Mecca of Medicine."

3. MTP photocopy, courtesy Robin Craven.

4. Lesky, 386–88.

5. NB 40 and 42: throughout.

6. Eduard Pötzl, letter to OLC, 15 Oct. 1897. MTP photocopy, Original in Clifton Waller Barrett Collection, Alderman Library, U of Virginia, Charlottesville.

7. Lesky, 488.

8. Fisher, 59–61.

9. *AM*, 232–37.

10. Lesky, 358, 364, 443, 445, 550.

11. Lesky, 336–39.

12. Sigmund Freud, letter to Wilhelm Fliess, 9 Feb. 1898, *Freud-Fliess*, 298–99.

13. *Freud-Fliess*, 300.

14. *FW*, 21: 64–145, 126n.

15. *FW*, 8: 230–31.

16. *FW*, 8: 230–31.

17. *FW*, 9: 245–47.

18. Richmond, 563–74.

19. McGrath, 219–225.

20. Jeffrey Moussaieff Masson, *The Assault on Truth: Freud's Suppression of the Seduction Theory* (New York: Farrar, 1984) 241–45.

21. Friedrich Eckstein, *"Alte unnenbare Tage!" Erinnerungen aus Siebzig Lehr- und Wanderjahren* (Wien: Herbert Reichner, 1936) 274–77.

22. Eckstein, 279.

23. *FW*, 4: 236.

24. Masson, 55–107, and throughout.

25. Masson, 3–13. For a defense of Freud's scientific motives in revising his theory after being rebuked by his colleagues, see Peter Gay, *Freud: A Life for Our Time* (New York: Norton, 1988) 751. Despite Gay's argument, the weight of evidence still seems to be on Masson's side.

26. *FW*, 5: 244.

27. MTN, 386.

28. *WMT* 24: 265.

29. Theresa Feodorowna Ries, *Die Sprache des Steines* (Wien: Krystall, 1928): 26–27.

30. NB 42: 51.

31. NB 42: 53.

32. NB 40: 12–13.

33. NB 40: 29.

34. *MTHL* 2: 675–76.

35. *WWD*, 104. Subsequent references to or quotations from "The Great Dark" and "The Mad Passenger" are from this edition.

36. *MSM*, 27.

37. Janik and Toulmin, 134, 176; *WWD*, 17.

38. SLC, letter to Sir John Adams, 5 Dec. 1898. Clark Library, U of California, Los Angeles.

39. *AM*, 281–82.

40. *DRT*, 135.

41. NB 40: 43–46.

42. *DRT*, 128.

43. *WWD*, 43.

44. James M. Cox, *Mark Twain: The Fate of Humor* (Princeton: Princeton UP, 1966) 272.

45. *MSM*, 25.

46. *MSM*, 35–36.

47. NB 42: 38.

48. MTN, 357–58.

49. MTN, 370.

50. NB 42: 57.

51. Louis J. Budd, "Another Stab at No. 4," *Mark Twain Circular* 3 (July–August 1989) 1–3.

52. *MSM*, 190.

53. *MSM*, 32.

54. *MSM*, 165.

CHAPTER FOURTEEN

Auf Wiedersehen!

1. *NFP*, 15 Nov. 1898: 6.

2. *NWT*, 19 May 1899: 7.

3. Hill, 7.

4. *NWT*, 19 May 1899: 7.

5. Hill, 10–12, 37–38.

6. *FB*, 21 May 1899: 4.

7. Oesterreichische Staatsarchiv Nr. 28373, pr. 18.V. 1899, Stadt-und Landesbibliothek, Vienna.

8. *MTN*, 340.

9. *NWT*, 26 May 1899: 3; 27 May 1899: 4. The official record of the audience, lacking any decipherable comment, is contained in the *Vormerk-Journal fuer die Audienzen und Beeidigungen bei seiner kaiserlich und koeniglich Apostolische Maejestiaet* (Mai 1899) Band 1899. Oesterreichische Staatsarchiv. Stadt-und Landesbibliothek, Vienna.

10. *FB*, 26 May 1899, 3–4.

11. Compare *NWT*, 26 May 1899: 4 and *FB*, 26 May 1899: 3–4.

12. Compare *NWT*, 27 May 1899: 4 and *New York Journal*, 28 May 1899: 30, cols. 1–3.

13. Compare *NWT*, 19 May 1899: 7; *The Times* (London), 23 May 1899: 4; and *Spectator* (London), 27 May 1899: 744–45.

14. *FB*, 25 May 1899: 5.

15. *NWT*, 19 May 1899: 7.

16. *NWT*, 27 May 1899: 4.

17. *MFMT*, 214.

18. *MFMT*, 214.

19. SLC, printed letter "To whom this shall come," Florence, June 1904, with added handwritten note at bottom. Original owned by Dr. Johannes Pötzl, Vienna.

20. Hill, 266.

Bibliography

[Alden, Henry M.]. "This Busy World." *Harper's Weekly* 42 (9 July 1898): 662.

"An American Defender of the Faith." *The Jewish Chronicle* 1.588 (8 Sept. 1899): 11.

Auernheimer, Raoul. "Mark Twain and the Gestapo." *Christian Science Monitor* 10 Oct. 1941, mag. sec.: 6.

Baedeker, Karl. *Southern Germany and Austria, including Hungary, Dalmatia and Bosnia*. 7th ed. Leipzig: Baedeker, 1891.

Baetzhold, Howard G. *Mark Twain and John Bull*. Bloomington: Indiana UP, 1970.

Blair, Walter, ed. *Mark Twain's Hannibal, Huck and Tom*. Berkeley: U of California P, 1969.

Bridgman, Richard. *Travelling in Mark Twain*. Berkeley: U of California P, 1987.

Brooks, Van Wyck. *The Ordeal of Mark Twain*. Rev. ed. New York: Dutton, 1933.

Budd, Louis J. *Mark Twain, Social Philosopher*. Bloomington: Indiana UP, 1962.

———. *Our Mark Twain: The Making of His Public Personality*. Philadelphia: U of Pennsylvania P, 1983.

———, ed. *Interviews with Samuel L. Clemens, 1874–1910*. Arlington, Tex.: American Literary Realism, 1977.

Burnham, Thomas. "Mark Twain and the Austrian Edison." *American Quarterly* 6 (1954): 364–72.

Cardwell, Guy. *The Man Who Was Mark Twain: Images and Ideologies*. New Haven: Yale UP, 1991.

Carpenter, C. E. "Mark Twain, 1898." *Mark Twain Quarterly* (Fall 1936), 4–5.

Cheney, Margaret. *Tesla: Man out of Time*. New York: Dorset, 1981.

Clare, George. *Last Waltz in Vienna*. London: Macmillan, 1981.

Cox, James M. *Mark Twain: The Fate of Humor*. Princeton: Princeton UP, 1966.

Cummings, Sherwood. *Mark Twain and Science*. Baton Rouge: Louisiana SUP, 1987.

Davis, Sara de Saussure, and Philip D. Beidler, eds. *The Mythologizing of Mark Twain*. Tuscaloosa: U of Alabama P, 1984.

DeVoto, Bernard. "Mark Twain About the Jews." *Jewish Frontier* 6 (May 1939): 7–9.

———. *Mark Twain's America*. Boston: Little, 1932.

———, ed. *Mark Twain in Eruption*. New York: Harper, 1940.

———, ed. *Mark Twain. Letters from the Earth*. New York: Harper, 1962.

Dolmetsch, Carl. "Mark Twain Abroad." *Musical America* 110.2 (March 1990): 53–56.

———. "Mark Twain and Sigmund Freud: Vienna's Odd Couple?" *The William and Mary Gazette* 15 (Summer 1986): 8–12.

———. "Mark Twain and the Viennese Anti-Semites: New Light on 'Concerning the Jews.'" *Mark Twain Journal* 23 (Fall 1985): 10–17.

———. "'Vom Mississippi zur Donau': A New Mark Twain Memorial in Lower Austria." *Mark Twain Journal* 24 (Spring 1986): 43–44.

Eble, Kenneth E. *Old Clemens and W.D.H., the Story of a Remarkable Friendship*. Baton Rouge: Louisiana SUP, 1985.

Eckstein, Friedrich. *"Alte unnennbare Tage!" Erinnerungen aus Siebzig Lehr-und Wanderjahren*. Wien: Herbert Reichner, 1936.

Ehrlich, Sigmund, and Julius Stern. *Journalisten-und Schriftsteller Verein "Concordia," 1859–1909. Eine Festschrift*. Wien: Verlag der Concordia, 1909.

Eisenberg, Ludwig. *Das Geistige Wien: Kuenstler-und Schriftsteller-Lexikon*. 2 vols. Wien: C. Daberkow, 1893.

Ellis, Helen E. "Mark Twain: The Influence of Europe." *Mark Twain Journal* 14 (Winter 1968–69): 12–16.

Emerson, Everett. *The Authentic Mark Twain, A Literary Biography of Samuel L. Clemens*. Philadelphia: U of Pennsylvania P, 1984.

Enkvist, Nils Erik. *British and American Literary Letters in Scandinavian Public Collections*. Oslo: Abo Akademi, 1964.

Eppel, Peter. *"Concordia soll ihr Name sein. . . ."* Wien: Boehlau Nachfolger, 1984.

Erckmann-Chatrian [Émile Erckmann and Louis Gratien Charles Alexandre Chatrian]. *The Polish Jew*. 1869. New York: Ward, Lock, 1911.

Fatout, Paul, ed. *Mark Twain Speaking*. Iowa City: U of Iowa P, 1976.

————. *Mark Twain Speaks for Himself.* West Lafayette, Ind.: Purdue UP, 1979.

Feigl, Suzanne, ed. *Wiener Humor um 1900.* Wien: Verlag der Oesterreichischen Staatsdruckerei, 1986.

Fisher, Henry W. *Abroad with Mark Twain and Eugene Field: Tales They Told to a Fellow Correspondent.* New York: Nicholas L. Brown, 1922.

Foner, Philip S. *Mark Twain: Social Critic.* New York: International, 1958.

Fraenkel, Josef, ed. *The Jews of Austria, Essays on Their Life, History and Destruction.* London: Valentine, Mitchell, 1967.

[Freud, Sigmund]. *The Complete Letters of Sigmund Freud to Wilhelm Fliess, 1887–1904.* Trans. and ed. J. M. Masson. Cambridge: Belknap P of Harvard UP, 1985.

"A Friendly Critic. Mark Twain on the Jews." *The Jewish World* 43 (September 29, 1899): 12.

Gay, Peter. *Freud: A Life for Our Time.* New York: Norton, 1988.

Geehr, Richard S. *Karl Lueger, Mayor of Fin de Siècle Vienna.* Detroit: Wayne SUP, 1990.

————, ed. *"I Decide Who is a Jew!": The Papers of Dr. Karl Lueger.* Washington, D.C.: UP of America, 1982.

Geismar, Maxwell. *Mark Twain, an American Prophet.* New York: Simon, 1968.

Gerard, E. [Emily De Laszowska]. *The Extermination of Love: A Fragmentary Study in Erotics.* 2 vols. Leipzig: Tauchnitz, 1901.

Gettke, Ernst, and Alexander Engel. *Im Fegefeuer (Der Brautstand) Schwank in drei Akten.* Wien: Druckerei "Reichswehr" G. David & U. Reiss, 1898.

Gillman, Susan Kay. *Dark Twins: Imposture and Identity in Mark Twain's America.* Chicago: U of Chicago P, 1989.

Gribben, Alan. *Mark Twain's Library: A Reconstruction.* 2 vols. Boston: Hall, 1980.

Gruber, Clemens M. *Die Schicksalstage von Mayerling.* Judenburg: Erich Mlakar, 1989.

Gruenzweig, Walter. "Comanches in the Austrian Parliament: Austria as a Metaphor for Mark Twain's Disillusionment with Democracy." *The Mark Twain Journal* 23 (Fall 1985): 3–9.

Grunwald, Max. *History of the Jews in Vienna.* Philadelphia: Jewish Publication Society, 1936.

Gstrein, Heinz. *Juedisches Wien.* Wien-Muenchen: Herold, 1984.

Haeussermann, Ernst. *Das Wiener Burgtheater.* Wien: Molden, 1975.

Harnsberger, Caroline. *Mark Twain's Clara*. Evanston, Ill.: Ward Schori, 1982.

Hemminghaus, Edgar H. *Mark Twain and Germany*. New York: AMS Press, 1966.

———. "Mark Twain's German Provenience." *Modern Language Quarterly* 6 (December 1945): 459–78.

Herzl, Theodor. *Das neue Ghetto*. Wien-Berlin: R. Loewit, 1920.

———. "Mark Twain in Paris." Trans. Alexander Behr. *Mark Twain Quarterly* 9 (Winter 1951): 16–20.

von Hibler, Leo. "Mark Twain und die deutsche Sprache." *Anglia* 65 (1940): 206–13.

Hietsch, Otto. "Mark Twain und Johann Strauss." *Jahrbuch fuer Amerikastudien* 8 (1963): 210–11.

Hill, Hamlin. *Mark Twain: God's Fool*. New York: Harper, 1973.

Hitler, Adolf. *Mein Kampf*. 1926. London: William Hutchinson, 1974. [English edition]

Janik, Allan, and Stephen Toulmin. *Wittgenstein's Vienna*. New York: Simon, 1973.

Kahn, Sholom J. *Mark Twain's "Mysterious Stranger": A Study of the Manuscript Texts*. Columbia: U of Missouri P, 1978.

———. "Mark Twain's Philosemitism: 'Concerning the Jews.'" *Mark Twain Journal* 23 (Fall 1985): 18–26.

Kaplan, Justin. *Mr. Clemens and Mark Twain*. New York: Simon, 1966.

Katona, Anna. "An Interview with Mark Twain." *Hungarian Studies Review* 9 (Spring 1982): 74–81.

———. "Mark Twain's Reception in Hungary." *American Literary Realism* 16 (Spring 1983): 107–20.

Kinch, J. C. B., comp. and ed. *Mark Twain's German Critical Reception, 1875–1986: An Annotated Bibliography*. Bibliographies and Indexes in World Literature No. 22. Westport: Greenwood, 1989.

Klett, Ada M. "Meisterschaft, or the True State of Mark Twain's German." *The American-German Review* 7 (December 1940): 10–11.

Koehler, Gerhard. "Adolf Wilbrandt in Dramen am Burgtheater." Diss. University of Vienna, 1970.

Kraus, Karl. *Aphorismen*. Ed. Christian Wagenknecht. Frankfurt/Main: Suhrkamp, 1986.

———. *Half-Truths and One-and-a-Half Truths, Selected Aphorisms*. Trans. and ed. Harry Zohn. Montreal: Egendra, 1976.

————. *In These Great Times*. Trans. and ed. Harry Zohn. Montreal: Engendra, 1976.

————. *No Compromise: Selected Writings of Karl Kraus*. Trans. and ed. Frederick Ungar. New York: Ungar, 1977.

Krumpelmann, John T. *Mark Twain and the German Language*. Baton Rouge: Louisiana SUP, 1953.

Langmann, Philipp. *Bartel Turaser, Drama in Drei Akten*. Leipzig: Robert Friese, 1897.

Lederer, Max. "Einige Bemerkungen zu Adolf Wilbrandts *Der Meister von Palmyra*." *Modern Language Notes* 56 (1946): 551–55.

————. "Mark Twain in Vienna." *Mark Twain Quarterly* 7 (Summer-Fall 1945): 1–12.

Lesky, Erna. *Die Wiener Medizinische Schule im 19. Jahrhundert*. Graz-Koeln: Boehlau Nachfolger, 1965.

Levy, M. S. "A Rabbi's Reply to Mark Twain." *Overland Monthly* 24 (October 1899): 364–67.

Lorch, Fred W. *The Trouble Begins at Eight, Mark Twain's Lecture Tours*. Ames: Iowa SUP, 1968.

Ludwig, Otto. *Aus dem Regen in die Traufe*. Frankfurt/Main: Meidinger, 1857.

Machlis, Paul, ed. *Union Catalog of Clemens Letters*. Berkeley, Los Angeles: U of California P, 1986.

Macnaughton, William R. *Mark Twain's Last Years as a Writer*. Columbia: U of Missouri P, 1979.

"Mark Twain in Budapest." *Chicago Record* 24 March 1899: 3.

"Mark Twain in London." *New York Tribune* 10 June 1899: 8 (reprinted from *The Chronicle* [London] 3 June 1899: 3).

"Mark Twain in Vienna." *Daily Graphic* [London] 17 Nov. 1897: 18.

"Mark Twain in Vienna." *New York World* 13 Dec. 1897: 6.

"Mark Twain Proud and Happy." *New York World* 13 Mar. 1898: 7.

"Mark Twain's Bequest." *The Times* [London] 23 May 1899: 4.

"Mark Twain's 'Best' Picture." *New York World* 11 June 1899: 4.

"Mark Twain's Promised Biographies." *Spectator* [London] 82 (27 May 1899): 744–45.

Mason, John W. *The Dissolution of the Austro-Hungarian Empire, 1867–1918*. London: Longmans, 1985.

Masson, Jeffrey Moussaieff. *The Assault on Truth: Freud's Suppression of the Seduction Theory*. New York: Farrar, 1984.

McGrath, William J. *Freud's Discovery of Psychoanalysis: The Politics of Hysteria.* Ithaca: Cornell UP, 1986.

Michel, Robert. "The Popularity of Mark Twain in Austria." *Mark Twain Quarterly* 8 (Winter 1950): 5–6, 19.

Morton, Frederick. *A Nervous Splendor, Vienna, 1888/89.* London: Weidenfeld and Nicolson, 1979.

Newcomb, Ethel. *Leschetizky As I Knew Him.* 1921. New York: Da Capo, 1967.

Parsons, Coleman O. "The Background of *The Mysterious Stranger.*" *American Literature* 30 (March 1960): 55–74.

Phillips, Catherine Coffin. *Cornelius Cole, California Pioneer and United States Senator.* San Francisco: Nash, 1929.

Pötzl, Eduard. *Gesammelte Skizzen.* 18 vols. Wien: Robert von Mohr, 1910.

Richmond, Marion B. "The Lost Source in Freud's 'Comment on Anti-Semitism': Mark Twain." *Journal of the American Psychoanalytic Association* 28 (1980): 563–74.

Ries, Theresa Fedorowna. *Die Sprache des Steines.* Wien: Krystall, 1928.

Rodney, Robert M., comp. and ed. *Mark Twain International: a Bibliography and Interpretation of His Worldwide Popularity.* Westport: Greenwood, 1982.

Rozenblitt, Marsha L. *The Jews of Vienna, 1867–1914: Assimilation and Identity.* Albany: SU of New York P, 1983.

Schillingsburg, Miriam Jones. *At Home Abroad: Mark Twain in Australasia.* Jackson: U of Mississippi P, 1988.

Schirer, Thomas. *Mark Twain and the Theatre.* Erlanger Beitraege zur Sprache- und Kulturwissenschaft, Band 71. Nuernberg: Carl Hans, 1984.

Schoenemann, Friedrich. "Mark Twain and Adolf Wilbrandt." *Modern Language Notes* 34 (1919): 372–74.

Schorske, Carl E. *Fin-de-Siècle Vienna, Politics and Culture.* New York: Knopf, 1980.

Scott, Arthur L. *Mark Twain at Large.* Chicago: Regnery, 1969.

Smith, Henry Nash. "How True Are Dreams? The Theme of Fantasy in Mark Twain's Later Work." *Quarry Farm Papers No. 1.* Elmira College Center for Mark Twain Studies at Quarry Farm, 1989.

————. *Mark Twain: The Development of a Writer.* Cambridge: Harvard UP, 1962.

Smith, Janet, ed. *Mark Twain on "The Damned Human Race."* New York: Hill and Wang, 1962.

Spiel, Hilde. *Vienna's Golden Autumn, 1866–1938*. London: Weidenfeld and Nicolson, 1987.

Stewart, Herbert L. "Mark Twain on the Jewish Problem." *Dalhousie Review* 14 (January 1935): 455–58.

Stiehl, Karl. "Mark Twain in der Wiener Presse zu Zeit seines Aufenthaltes in Wien, 1897–1899." Diss. U of Vienna, 1953.

von Suttner, Bertha. *Memoirs of Bertha von Suttner: The Records of an Eventful Life*. 2 vols. Boston: Ginn, 1910.

Szczepanik, Jan. *Herstellung von Jacquard-Patronen auf photographischen Weg (System Jan Szczepanik)*. Wien: Société des inventions Jan Szczepanik & Cie., 1899.

Tietze, Hans. *Die Juden Wiens: Geschichte, Wirtschaft, Kultur*. 1933. Wien: Edition Atelier, 1987.

Timms, Edward. *Karl Kraus, Apocalyptic Satirist: Culture and Catastrophe in Habsburg Vienna*. New Haven: Yale UP, 1986.

Tuckey, John S. *Mark Twain and Little Satan: The Writing of "The Mysterious Stranger."* West Lafayette, Ind.: Purdue UP, 1963.

———. "Mark Twain's Later Dialogue: The 'Me' and the Machine." *American Literature* 41 (1969–70): 532–42.

"Twain to Franz Josef 'Gesprochen.'" *New York Journal* 28 May 1899: 30, cols. 1–6.

Vagts, Alfred. "Mark Twain at the Courts of the Emperors." *Jahrbuch fuer Amerikastudien* 9 (1964): 149–51.

Wagenknecht, Edward. *Mark Twain: The Man and His Work*. Rev. ed. Norman: U of Oklahoma P, 1961.

Waissenberger, Robert, ed. *Vienna, 1890–1920*. Wien-Heidelberg: Carl Ueberreuther, 1984.

Wassilko, Theophila. *Fuerstin Pauline Metternich*. Wien: Verlag fuer Geschichte und Politik, 1959.

Wector, Dixon. "Mark Twain as Translator from the German." *American Literature* 13 (1941): 257–63.

Weishart, John J. "Once Again: Mark Twain and German." *Mark Twain Journal* 12.4 (1955): 16.

Wiehner, Joseph. "Mark Twain." *Volks-Bildung Blaetter* [Krems] 193 (November 1898): 161–64.

Wilbrandt, Adolf. *Der Meister von Palmyra, dramatische Dichtung in Fuenf Akten*. Stuttgart: Cotta, 1889.

Wilbrandt-Baudius, Auguste. *"Aus Kunst und Leben," Erinnerungen einer alten Burgschauspielerin.* Wien: Amalthea, 1919.

Wydenbruck, Nora. *My Two Worlds, An Autobiography.* London: Longmans, 1956.

Zohn, Harry. *Karl Kraus.* Twayne World Authors Series 116. New York: Twayne, 1971.

Zweig, Stefan. *The World of Yesterday.* 1943. Bison Books repr. Intro. by Harry Zohn. Lincoln: U of Nebraska P, 1964.

Index

References to illustrations are printed in italic type.

"Abfälle." *See* Kraus, Karl
Abrányi, Clementina Katona, 59
Adams, Sir John, 282–83
Adler, Max, 171
Adler, Victor, 171, 288
Admirable Chrichton, 291
A Hét, 54, 57
Alden, Henry, 82
Allgemeiner Oesterreichischer
   Frauenverein (General Austrian
   Women's Association), 122
Altenberg, Peter, 165, 255
American Hebrew, The, 178
American Publishing Co., 299
Anders, Wilhelm, 130
Anti-Semitism, 51, 63, 129, 130, 160–80,
   250. *See also* Jews
Artists' Benevolent Guild, 144
Ausgleich, 69, 78
Austrian Friends of Peace
   (Oesterreichische Friedensfreunde),
   173, 182. *See also* Suttner, Baroness von
Austrian Press Club, 41–46, 165

Badeni, Count (Graf) Kasimir, 67,
   69–72, 122, 133
Bad Ischl, 104, 105, 280, 306
Bahr, Hermann, 16, 43, 180, 278
Barbi, Alice, 106
Bardi, Countess Adelgonde (do Bourbon
   y do Braganca) von, 135, 141–42

Bartel Turaser, 127–28
Batthyany-Strattmann, Prince Ladislaus,
   184, 263
Bauer, Julius, 46
Baumann, Nicholas, 287, 288
Beehler (naval attaché), 321–22
Beerbohm, Max, 249
Beer-Hoffmann, Richard, 43, 165
Beethoven, Ludwig van, 91, 92
Benedikt, Moritz, 43, 165, 171, 180,
   251–52
Benislava, Donnimirska (Mme.
   Leschetizka), 103, 104, 133
Berger, Baron (Freiherr) Alfred von:
   Habsburg, 87, 119
Billings, Josh, 255
Billroth, Theodor, 184, 262, 265
Bismarck, Prince (Fürst) Otto von, 221,
   266
Bjornstjerne, Bjornson: *Auf Gottes Weg*,
   228
Blumen Mary (Mary's Flower Shop), 99
Bok, Edward, 82
Bösendorfer Saal, 136, 141
Brandt, Marianne (Marie Bischoff), 106,
   241
Brecht, Bertolt (quoted) 260
Breuer, Josef, 165, 273
Bristol hotel (Vienna), 24, 155
Buchbinder, Bernhard, 130
Budapest, 51, 54–59

Budapesti Hirlap, 55
Burckhardt, Max, 113, 124
Burgtheater, 112–14
de Busirei, Count (Graf), 140

Café Central, 152
Café Griensteidl, 152
Carl-Theater, 111, 129, 270
"Carmen Sylva," 135, 221
Century The, (magazine), 82, 207
Chamberlain, Houston Stewart, 163
Charcot, Jean-Martin, 273, 282
Chatto & Windus (publisher), 54, 98
Chiavacci, Vincenz, 43
Christian Social Party (Austria), 63, 163, 251
Church of Christ, Scientist (Christian Science), 234–40
City council (Vienna), 62–65, 288
City hall (Vienna), 9, 62–63
Clemens, Clara Langdon, 12, 21, 23, 24, 25, 26, 85, 90, 95, 97, 101, 102, 105–7, 132–33, 144, 145, 214, 215, 222, 241, 312–14
Clemens, James Ross, 216
Clemens, Jane Lampton (Jean), 21, 23, 85, 135–36, 143, 144, 214, 222, 261, 278, 300, 312, 313
Clemens, John Marshall, 61
Clemens, Mollie, 215, 293
Clemens, Olivia Langdon (Livy), 21, 26, 84, 94, 96, 122, 138, 141, 143, 214, 222, 241, 244, 261, 278, 313
Clemens, Olivia Susan (Susy), 21, 87, 215, 261
Clemens, Orion, 143, 215–17, 293
Clemens, Samuel Langhorne (Mark Twain): world lecture tour, 2; foreign language fluency, 4, 11, 40, 47–50; myopic views about, 14–15; political interests, 60–61; on music, 97, 107; as aphorist, 253–56; health problems, 261
—WORKS: "About Play-Acting," 117–18,
119; "Adam's Diary," 146; *Adventures of Huckleberry Finn*, 2, 54, 115, 210, 224, 269, 285; *The Adventures of Tom Sawyer*, 2, 54, 96, 152, 224, 269; *Ah Sin* (play, with Bret Harte), 110; "American Representation in Austria," 156, 315–22; "At the Appetite Cure," 153; "At the Shrine of St. Wagner," 96; "The Austrian Edison Keeping School Again," 207–8; "The 'Austrian Parliamentary System'? Government by Article 14," 78–79; "The Awful German Language" (appendix to *A Tramp Abroad*), 45; *Bartel Turaser* (trans. play), 127–28; "Beauties of the German Language" (*Autobiography*), 48; "A Burlesque Biography," 268–69; "Candidatenfreuden" (trans. of "Running for Governor"), 61; "The Californian's Tale," 146; "Cannibalism in the Cars," 39; "The Celebrated Jumping Frog of Calaveras County," 2, 48; *Christian Science*, 12, 234–40, 244, 254, 257; "Concerning the Jews," 11, 131, 161, 164, 173, 174–78, 243, 254, 256, 270; *A Connecticut Yankee in King Arthur's Court*, 2, 13, 15, 20, 48, 61–62, 96, 211, 275; "Conversations with Satan," 27–28, 30, 285; "Curing a Cold," 269; "The Czar's Soliloquy," 195; "A Defence of Royalty & Nobility," 184; "Diplomatic Pay and Clothes," 158–59; "Dueling," 67–69, 131; "Early Days" (*Autobiography*), 11, 223–26, 244; "Encounter with an Interviewer," 39, 57; "Facts Concerning the Recent Carnival of Crime in Connecticut," 289; "The Five Boons of Life," 117; *Following the Equator (More Tramps Abroad)*, 2, 21, 54, 253–54, 258, 260, 303; "From the 'London Times' of 1904," 173, 207, 209–10; *Der Gegenkandidat*, 121–23,

126; "The Genuine Mexican Plug," 57, 146; "German for Hungarians," 56; *The Gilded Age*, 39, 110; "The Golden Arm," 138; *Die Goldgraberin*, 124–26; "The Great Dark," 240, 275, 276, 278–82. "The Great Republic's Peanut Stand," 240; "Il Trovatore" (burlesque), 96; *The Innocents Abroad*, 2, 14, 269; *In Purgatory* (trans. play, *Im Fegefeuer*), 128; *Is He Dead?* (play), 119–21; "Is He Living or Is He Dead?" (story), 120; "Kaltenleutgeben," 219–20; *Letters from the Earth*, 13, 254; *Life on the Mississippi*, 4, 226; "The Lucerne Girl," 57; "The Mad Passenger," 283–84; "Man's Place in the Animal World," 181–82; "The Man That Corrupted Hadleyburg," 11, 96, 131, 232–34, 242, 254, 277; "Meisterschaft," 48; "The Memorable Assassination," 82–87, 258; "Mental Telegraphy," 282; "Morals and Memory," 57, 136, 268; "My Platonic Sweetheart," 149–52, 275, 282; *The Mysterious Stranger* group (incl. "The Chronicle of Young Satan," "No. 44, The Mysterious Stranger," "Schoolhouse Hill," and *The Mysterious Stranger, A Romance*), 28, 107–8, 116–17, 131, 196, 240, 275–77, 285–98; "Newhouse's Jew Story," 164; "The New War Scare," 187; "Niagara," 46; "Ornithorhyncus," 136; *Personal Recollections of Joan of Arc*, 303; *The Prince and the Pauper*, 2, 54; "Randall's Jew Story," 164; *Roughing It*, 4, 60, 268; "Die Schrecken der deutschen Sprache" (Concordia Speech), 44–46, 252–53, 315–17; *Simon Wheeler* (play), 110, 120; *Sketches New and Old*, 269; "Stirring Times in Austria," 11, 72–78, 82, 174, 234, 270; "The Stolen Watermelon" (*see* "Morals and Memory"); "The Stolen White Elephant," 39; "The Story of Grandfather's Old Ram," 138; "Those Extraordinary Twins," 39; *Tom Sawyer Abroad*, 217; *Tom Sawyer, Detective*, 217, 224; "Tom Sawyer's Conspiracy," 217, 291; "To the Editor of *The American Hebrew*," 164; "To the Person Sitting in Darkness," 181; *The Tragedy of Pudd'nhead Wilson*, 13, 60, 96, 253–54, 257; *A Tramp Abroad*, 4, 21, 48; "The United States of Lyncherdom," 311; "The Villagers of 1840–43," 217; "Wapping Alice," 240; "The War Prayer," 181; "Washoe Joke" (Petrified Man), 65; *What Is Man?*, 12, 19, 227–32, 242, 254, 257; "Which Was the Dream?," 278–80; "A Word to Our Blushing Exiles," 189

Cole, Cornelius, 145
Cole, George, 145, 147, 241
Concordia, 41–46, 165
Cook, Thomas & Sons, 23, 24, 312
Cooper, James Fenimore, 15, 20
Cosmopolitan (magazine), 120
Coudenhove, Count (Graf) Richard, 135, 184
Crane, Stephen, 138, 140
Czapka, Stefan, 107
Czerny, Carl, 91, 92, 94

Danube Canal (Donaukanal), 10, 27, 28
Danube River (Donau, Duna), 27, 55, 58
Die demoliirte Literatur. See Kraus, Karl
Deutsches Volkstheater, 38, 111, 127
DeVoto, Bernard, 13, 14, 178, 224, 278
Diefenbach, Herr, 190
Doangivadam, 294
Döbling ("Cottageviertel"), 7, 26, 100
Dreyfus, Alfred, 172–74, 175, 185, 209, 210, 320
Duneka, Frederick, 275, 285, 286
Duplicates (Doppelgänger), 295–96
Dutschka, Mme. von, 101

Dutschka, Ritter von, 133
Dyck, Ernest van, 42

Ebner-Eschenbach, Marie von, 165, 184
Eckstein, Emma, 273–74
Eckstein, Friedrich, 270–73
Eddy, Mary Baker Glover, 234, 235, 238, 239
Edmondson, Robert Edward, 178
Edwards, Jonathan: *Sinners in the Hands of an Angry God*, 297
Egidy, Manfred von, 189–91
Elisabeth, Austrian empress (Kaiserin), queen of Hungary, 62, 81–88, 304
Elisabeth, queen of Romania, 135, 221
Emerson, Ralph Waldo, 15, 231, 255
Emmerich, Robert, 114
Engel, Alexander, 128
English-French Conversation Club, 146
Erckmann-Chatrian: *Le Juif polonais* (Der polnische Jude; The Polish Jew), 112, 130, 167–68, 189
Eseldorf, 286–87, 288, 294. *See also* Salzburg
Esterházy. *See* Wydenbruck-Esterházy, Countess
Établissement Ronacher (vaudeville theater), 112, 130–31, 189
Eulenberg, Count (Graf) von, 133, 155

Die Fackel (magazine). *See* Kraus, Karl
Falkenhayn, Count (Graf) Franz, 71
Feldner, August, 294–96
Fernseher. *See* Szczepanik, Jan
Ferstel, Heinrich von, 9
Figaro (incl. *Wiener Luft*), 66–67, 166
Fischer, Theodor, 287–95
Fisher, Henry W., 88, 124–25, 264
Fliess, Wilhelm, 266, 274
Forty-Four (No. 44, New Series 864, 962), 28, 295–97
Francis Joseph (Franz Josepf) I von Habsburg-Lothringen, Austrian

emperor (Kaiser), king of Hungary, 8–9, 302–9, *305*
Franklin, Benjamin, 153, 158, 231, 254–55
Franz Ferdinand, Archduke (Erzherzog), 99, 141
Franz Josefs-Bahnhof (Vienna), 312
Freud, Sigmund, 8, 136, 165, 172, 249, 259, 264–75, 267, 278, 282–83, 289, 296–97, 299
—WORKS: *Civilization and Its Discontents*, 136, 266, 268; "A Comment on Anti-Semitism," 161, 178–79, 270; *Contribution to a Questionnaire on Reading*, 269; *The Interpretation of Dreams (Traumdeutung)*, 71, 266, 275; *Jokes and Their Relation to the Unconscious*, 268–69; *The Psychopathology of Everyday Life* 269, 273; "Uber die Aetiologie der Hysteria," 273–74; *The "Uncanny"* 269–70
Fried, Alfred Hermann, 187
Frohman, Charles, 128, 130

Gabrilowitsch, Ossip, 92, 106, 107, 147, 313
Gartner, Eduard, 99, 137
Gelber, Adolf, 166, 167, 170
Gemeinderat, 62–65, 288
Gerard, E. *See* De Laszowska, Countess Emily
German-Austrian Writers' Association (Deutschösterreichische Schriftseller-Genossenschaft), 41
German National Party (Austria), 36, 63, 64, 70, 251, 288
Gersuny, Robert, 263, 265
Gettke, Ernst, 128
Ghika (Romanian minister), 155
Gilder, Richard Watson, 82
Girardi, Alexander, 42, 46
Gniewicz, Herr von, 190

De Gobineau, Count Arthur, 163
Goethe, Johann Wolfgang von, 2, 154, 297
Goluchowski von Goluchowo, Count (Graf) Agenor, 292, 302, 303, 304
Gospel of Saint John (Apocrypha), 297
Grant, Ulysses S., 61, 138, 278, 308
"Griechenbeisl" (Reichenberger's), 153
Griesbach, Martin. See Feldner, August
Gross, Ferdinand, 39–41, 42, 44, 166
Grünfeld, Alfred, 42, 46, 47, 99
Grünfeld, Sigmund, 137
Györy, Ilona, 57

Habsburg, Otto von, 80
Hague Peace Conference, The, (1899), 189, 193–95
Hallstatt, 104–5, 280
Hansen, Theophil von, 9
Hanslick, Eduard, 43, 100
Harper, Henry, 40
Harper and Brothers, 299
Harper's Monthly, 23, 149
Harris, Addison Clay, 156, 158, 302, 304, 306, 307, 318–21
Harris, William K., 130
Hasenauer, Carl, 112
Hawthorne, Nathaniel, 15
Hay, John, 155
Herbart, Johann Friedrich, 283. See also Adams, Sir John
Hertzka, Theodor, 43
Herzl, Theodor, 42, 129–30, 250, 270
Hitler, Adolf, 27, 63–64, 160–61, 163
Hofburg, 7, 306
Hofburgtheater (Burgtheater), 112–14
Hoffmann, Josef, 9
Hofkapelle, 111
Hofmannsthal, Hugo von, 16, 259, 278
Hofoper, 8, 111
Hohenfels, Stella, 114
Hohenlohe, Princess, 146, 151
Holbrook, Hal, 181

Howells, William Dean, 12, 15, 19, 20, 56, 57, 62, 109, 188, 214
Hoyos, Marquis (Count), 155, 330 (n. 45)
Hrdlicka, Charles, 318n, 321, 322
Hungária hotel (Budapest), 55
Hurst, Bailey (consul-general), 26, 42, 44
Hüttenbrenner, Alexander von, 263, 265

Im Fegefeuer (farce, Gettke and Engel), 128, 131
Impressionism, 16, 225–26
Irving, Washington, 15

James, Henry, 6, 109
Jewish World, The (London), 178
Jews: in Budapest, 58; targets in riots, 72; importance in Vienna, 164–66; responses to anti-Semitism, 170–72. See also Clemens, Samuel Langhorne: "Concerning the Jews"
Joan of Arc, 87
Jokai, Mór, 54
Joseph II, Austrian emperor (Kaiser), 262
Jubilee Singers, 22
Jugendstil, 9
Julienthurm (Höllenstein), 222–23
"Jung Wien" (Young Vienna), 16, 250, 278

Kaiserin Elisabeth Westbahnhof (Vienna), 24
Kant, Immanuel, 163
Karl I von Habsburg-Lothringen, Austrian emperor (Kaiser), king of Hungary, 88, 99
Katona, Anna, 55, 57, 59
Keleti (eastern) Station (Budapest), 59
Kellgren, Jonas Henrik, 300, 312–13
Khevenhüller, Princess, 135, 140
Kikeriki!: Antisemitische Humorblatt, 166–67, 169, 174
Klaw and Erlanger Managers' Exchange, 130

Kleinberg, Ludwig, 199, 200, 205–6, 210
Klimt, Ernst, 112
Klimt, Gustav, 8, 112, 132, 150
Kossuth, Ferenc, 58–59
Krafft-Ebing, Hofrat Richard von, 264, 274
Kralik, Emil ("Habakuk"), 43
Krantz, Josef, 82, 241, 242
Krantz, Marianne, 299
Krantz hotel, 27, 82, 84, 89, 241–42, *243*, 299, 307, 312
Kraus, Karl, 2, 16, 43, 50, 165, 171, 179, 245–60, 282, 312
Kreisler, Fritz, 99, 137
Eine Krone für Zion. See Kraus, Karl
Kürnberger, Ferdinand (quoted), 80

Ladies Home Journal, 82
Lanckoronski, Count (Graf), 140
Landesberg, Alexander, 99
Langdon, Charles, 129, 147
Langdon, Jervis, 129, 147
Langhorne, Nancy (Lady Astor), 235
Langmann, Philipp, 127
Lanz, Adolf Josef, 163
La Rochefoucauld, François (Duc de), 255
De Laszowska, Countess Emily (Gerard), 141, 147–49, 151
De Laszowski, Count (Graf), 147, 292
Lavino, William S., 42, 76
Leary, Katy, 12, 101, 102, 143, 144, 145, 218, 312, 313
Lecher, Otto, 71, 73–74, 270
Lecky, W. E. H., 228, 297
Lehner, Gilbert, 42
Léon, Victor, 43
Leschetizky, Theodor, 23, 90–95, 101–5, 108, 133, 147, 292, 313
Lessing, Theodor (quoted) 250
Die letzten Tage der Menschheit (The Last Days of Mankind). *See* Kraus, Karl
Leupold-Loewenthal, Harald, 266

Levetus, Amelia S., 33, 46, 198–99, 206
Levin twins, 292
Lewinsky, Joseph, 42, 46
Lex Falkenhayn, 71
Lichtenberg, Georg Christoph, 282–83
Liechtenstein, Prince Alois, 136
Lipótvárosi Kaszino, 56, 57, 58
Locke, D. R., 49
Longfellow, Henry Wadsworth, 15
Loos, Adolf, 9
Löwenhaupt (Swedish minister), 155
Luccheni, Luigi, 81, 82, 87
Lucifer, 28, 277
Ludwig, Otto: *Aus dem Regan in die Traufe*, 228
Lueger, Karl, 9, 63–65, 163, 251, 287
Lueger, Marie, 287
Lutz, Robert (publisher), 4

McClure's Syndicate, 19
Mach, Ernst, 8, 282
McKinley, William, 154, 187
Magyar Hirlap, 54, 55
Mahler, Gustav, 8, 97, 100, 108, 134, 165, 171, 249, 259
Marchesi, Blanche, 106, 301
Marchesi, Mathilde (Graumann), 301
Maria Theresa, Archduchess (Erzherzogin), 141–42
Maria Theresa, Austrian empress (Kaiserin), 261
Matsch, Franz, 112
Mayreder, Rosa, 122
Meidling, Wilhelm, 289
Meidling (Vienna district), 288
Der Meister von Palmyra (play), 114–18. *See also* Wilbrandt, Adolf von
Melville, Herman, 15
Mencken, H. L., 247, 249
Mephistopheles (Mephisto), 28
Merchants' Association (Kaufmännische Verein) Hall, 41, 46, 118

Metropole hotel (Vienna), 26, 27, *28*, 33, 146, 166, 217, 241, 242
Metternich, Princess (Fürstin) Pauline, 134, 136, 140, 147, 165, 184
Mickiewicz, Adam, 292
The Mikado (Gilbert and Sullivan), 96
Millet, Jean François, 119–20
Miss Baillie's Home for English Governesses, 146
Milton, John: *Paradise Lost*, 297
Mommsen, Theodor: *Romische Geschichte*, 228
Montenuovo, Prince Alfred, 307, 312
Müller hotel (Vienna), 24
Musikvereinsaal (Gesellschaft der Musikfreunde in Wien), 17, 97

Nansen, Fridtjof, 147
Nasby, Petroleum V., 49
Nestroy, Johann Nepomuk, 50
Neue Freie Presse, 251–52
Das neue Ghetto (play, Herzl), 129, 170, 270
Neues Wiener Tagblatt, 35, 36
New York *Sun*, 19
New York Tribune, 60
New York World, 107, 214
Nicholas II, Russian emperor (Czar), 83, 189, 193, 195
Nietzsche, Friedrich, 163, 228, 285
Nigra (Italian minister), 155
Nordau, Max, 51, 228
Nordbahnhof (Vienna), 54
Nüll, Ernst van der, 9, 259
Nye, Bill, 255
Nyugati (northern) Station, Budapest, 55

Obersteiner, Heinrich, 262–63, 266
Odyssey, The, (books 5, 6), 16
Oesterreichische Journalisten und Schriftsteller Verband, 41–46, 165
Olbrich, Joseph, 9
Otis, George Alexander, 264

Otthon (Hungarian Journalists' Association), 54, 56
Otto, Archduke (Erzherzog), 99

Paige, James W.: typesetting machine, 14, 20, 201, 211, 212
Paine, Albert Bigelow, 12, 127, 224, 275, 285, 286, 294
Paraty (Portugese minister), 155
Peace Apostle, The. See Stead, William T.
Perosi, Lorenzo, 100–101
Pester Lloyd, 51
Pesti Hirlap, 57
Pesti Napló, 55, 57
Phaeacianism, 16, 44, 149, 232, 298
Plasmon, 213, 301
Poe, Edgar Allan, 28
Der polnische Jude, 112, 130, 167–68, 189
Popper-Lynkeus, Josef: *Träumen als Wachen* (Dreaming as Waking), 278
Potter, Alice, 146
Pötzl, Eduard, 17, 35–38 (photo, 37), 43, 57, 131, 152, 247, 248, 255, 263–64, 309, 311, 313
Prater, the, 13, 24, 58

Quarante-Quatre, 28, 292–93, 295

Raimund-Theater, 128–29, 131
Rákosi, Jenö, 56
Raster, *202–3. See also* Szczepanik, Jan
Rathaus, 9, 62–63
Rauchinger, Heinrich, 206
Reichenau (Raxalpe), 299, 300
Reichsrat (Austrian parliament), 69–80, 77, 287, 288. *See also* Clemens, Samuel Langhorne: "The 'Austrian Parliamentary System'? Government by Article 14"; "Stirring Times in Austria"
Review of Reviews. See Stead, William T.
Rice, Clarence, 130
Richter, Hans, 8, 99–100, 108

Ries, Theresa Fedorowna, 150, 277, 279
La risurrezione di Cristo (Perosi), 100
La risurrezione di Lazzaro (Perosi), 100
Rogers, Henry Huttleston, 12, 20, 21, 26,
    120, 121, 127, 130, 138, 214, 215, 241,
    242, 278, 299
Roosevelt, Theodore, 61
Rooy, Anton van, 107
Rudolf, Crown Prince, 87, 88, 182,
    258–59, 326 (n. 6), 330 (n. 45)
Ruger, General, 321–22
Rumbold, Sir Horace, 145, 158
Ruzičič, Clementine
    (Wydenbruck-Esterházy) von, 135–36

Saar, Ferdinand von, 16, 221, 259
Sacher's Hotel de l'Opera (Vienna), 24,
    190
Sacher-Masoch, Leopold von: *Venus im
    Pelze* (Venus in Furs), 264
Sade, Marquis de, 254
Salzburg, 23–24; fictional Eseldorf,
    287–88
Salzkammergut, 104–5
Sanna (Sweden), 244, 312–13
Satan (Little Satan, Satan, Jr.), 27–28, 30,
    175, 277, 288–91, 292, 295
Saville, Frances, 99, 137
Schildkraut, Josef, 130–31
Schiller, Friedrich, 16, 44
Schirach, Baldur von, 161
Schlenther, Paul, 124
Schlesinger, Ferdinand, 38
Schlesinger, Josef, 38
Schlesinger, Marie, 122
Schlesinger, Max, 38, 166
Schlesinger, Samuel, 38, 39
Schlesinger, Siegmund, 17, 109–10,
    121–27, 130, 166
Schlesinger, Therese (Eckstein), 273
Schmidt, Friedrich von, 9, 63
Schnabel, Arthur, 99, 103, 136–37
Schnitzler, Arthur, 8, 69, 114, 129, 165,
    172

Schönerer, Georg (Ritter von), 36,
    73–74, 163, 288
Schopenhauer, Arthur: *Die Welt als Wille
    und Vorstellung*, 228
Schratt, Katharina von, 104, 124, 303
Schwarz, Emil. *See* Feldner, August
Schweininger, Dr., 266
Semmering, 103
Semper, Gottfried, 9, 112
Shakespeare, William: *King Lear* and *The
    Tempest*, 297
Shaw, H. W., 255
Siccardsburg, August von, 9
Sieveking, Martinus, 164–65
Singer, Wilhelm, 43
Sobieski, Jan, 16
Socialist Party (Austria), 76, 171
Society for Psychical Research, 282
Sonnenthal, Adolf (Ritter) von, 42, 114,
    116
Spanish-American War, 81, 129, 155,
    174, 185, 187–89, 190
Spiegl, Edgar von, 42, 180
Starr, W. Allen, 262–63
Stead, William T., 191, 193
Steed, Wickham (quoted) 251
Stein, Herr, 294, 295
Stein, Leo, 99
Stevenson, R. L.: *The Strange Case of
    Dr. Jekyll and Mr. Hyde*, 289
Stewart, William, 60
Stoker, Bram, 120, 130
Strauss, Adele, 98
Strauss, Eduard, 17, 144; "Für Alle
    Welt," 97
Strauss, Johann, Jr., 8, 17, 97, 98, 104,
    108, 184, 212: *Die Fledermaus*, 10; *Der
    Zigeunerbaron*, 54; "An der Elbe," 97
Sudbahnhof (Vienna), 84, 221
Sulzberger, Cyrus L., 178
Superintendent of Dreams. *See* Clemens,
    Samuel Langhorne: "The Great Dark"
Suttner, Baron (Freiherr) Arthur von,
    186–87

Suttner, Baroness (Freifrau) Bertha Kinsky von, 173, 182, *183*, 185, 186–87, 189, 190, 194–95, 197
Swieten, Gerhard van, 261
Switzerland, 4, 11, 81, 88; Lake Lucerne (Vierwaldstättersee), 21; Pilatus, 21; Rigi, 21; Vitznau, 22; Weggis, 21, 22, 23, 27, 223; Lucerne (Luzern), 21, 23; Geneva, 87
Szczepanik, Jan, 194, 198–212, 222, 292, 310
Szeps, Moritz, 43, 165

Tauchniitz, Bernhard (publisher), 4
Tennyson, Alfred Lord: "Ulysses," 285
Territorial Enterprise, The, 6, 60, 65
Tesla, Nikolá, 191–92
Theater an der Wien, 98, 111
Theater in der Josefstadt, 111
Therapeutic nihilism, 16, 266, 290, 298
Thompson, Denman: *The Old Homestead*, 119
Thurn und Taxis, Prince, 312
Tirolerhof hotel (Innsbruck), 23
Tóth, Béla, 57
Tower, Charlemagne, 42, 44, 75, 133, 154–56, 159, 213, 300
Traum, Philip, 28, 107, 288–93, 298
Trenck, Friedrich von: *Die wundersamen Erlebnisse des Freiherrn v. Trenck in Spielberg*, 168–70
Twain, Mark. *See* Clemens, Samuel Langhorne
Twichell, Rev. Joseph H. (Joe), 12, 22, 83, 164, 214

Uhl, Friedrich, 165
Union for Defense Against Anti-Semitism (Verein zu Abwehr des Antisemitismus). *See* Jews

Die Velodramatische Revue des Jahres 1897, 130–31

Venedig in Wien" (Venice in Vienna), 10, 24
Versen, Mollie (Clemens) von, 138
Victoria, queen of England, 21, 81, 275, 304
Vienna, University of: medical faculty, 261–62
Vienna Philharmonic, 97, 99–100
Vienna Woods. *See* Wienerwald
Villa Bühlegg, 21, 22
Villa Paulhof (Sonnenhof), 81, 125, 135, 207, 217, 218, *219*, 220
Villa Silling, 26
Villa Tannen, 22
Virchow, Rudolf, 262
Vogelsang, Baron (Freiherr) Karl von, 163
Volksoper, 112
Die Volksstimme, 61
Voltaire (François-Marie Arouet): *Zadig*, 297
Vororte-Correspondenz, 38

Die Waffen Nieder! (novel, magazine). *See* Suttner, Baroness
Wagner, Otto, 9
Wagner, Richard, 96, 97, 163
—WORKS: *Lohengrin*, 96; *Die Meistersinger von Nürnberg*, 43, 97; *Parsifal*, 107, 108; *Der Ring des Nibelungen* (Ring Tetralogy), 97, 100, 106, 107; *Tannhäuser*, 62, 96
Walker, Edyth, 99, 137
Ward, Artemus (pseud. C. F. Browne), 49, 255
Warner, Charles Dudley, 272
Webster, Charles L., and Co., 20
Weggis, Switzerland, 21, 22, 23, 27, 223
Weinberger, Charles, 99
Weininger, Otto, 171, 259
Weiss, Karl ("C. Karlweis"), 43
Whitman, Walt: "There Was a Child Went Forth," 225; "Passage to India," 285

Wiener Luft, 66–67, 166
Wiener Volkstheater (Prater), 111
Wiener Volkszeitung, 67
Wienerwald (Vienna Woods), 8, 217, 223, 244
Wilbrandt, Adolf von, 114–18, 297
Wilbrandt-Baudius, Auguste, 118
Wilczek, Count (Graf) Hans von, 265
Wilde, Oscar, 16, 39, 254
Wilhelm II, German emperor (Kaiser), 62, 83–84, 302, 306, 307
Winternitz, Alfred, 199, 263
Winternitz, Jakob von, 43
Winternitz, Wilhelm, 134, 221–22, 263, 265
Wirth, Bettina, 46, 72, 188
Wittgenstein, Karl, 172
Wittgenstein, Ludwig, 165, 282
Wittgenstein, Paul, 92
Wlaschim, Dagobert, 107, 206

Wohlmeyer, Seppi, 287
Wolf, Karl Hermann, 67
Wolter, Charlotte, 113, 221, 246
Wood, William M., 200–201, 209
Wright, Laura, 152
Wydenbruck-Esterházy, Countess (Grafin) Misa, 81, 132, 133–35, 136, 140, 147, 151, 184, 247
Wyeth, N. C., 286

Young Czechs (parliamentary faction), 69

Zang, Adolf (quoted), 252
Zasche, Theodor (Theo), 3, 42, 166
Zionism, 129, 170, 177, 250
Zita, Austrian empress (Kaiserin), queen of Hungary, 80
Zola, Émile, 173–74, 185